*f*P

BULL BY THE HORNS

FIGHTING TO SAVE MAIN STREET
FROM WALL STREET AND
WALL STREET FROM ITSELF

SHEILA BAIR

FREE PRESS

New York   London   Toronto   Sydney   New Delhi

FREE PRESS
A Division of Simon & Schuster, Inc.
1230 Avenue of the Americas
New York, NY 10020

First Free Press hardcover edition September 2012

FREE PRESS and colophon are trademarks of Simon & Schuster, Inc.

For information about special discounts for bulk purchases,
please contact Simon & Schuster Special Sales at
1-866-506-1949 or business@simonandschuster.com.

The Simon & Schuster Speakers Bureau can bring authors to your live event.
For more information or to book an event, contact the Simon & Schuster Speakers
Bureau at 1-866-248-3049 or visit our website at www.simonspeakers.com.

Manufactured in the United States of America

3   5   7   9   10   8   6   4   2

ISBN 978-1-4516-7248-0
ISBN 978-1-4516-7250-3 (ebook)

To my beloved children,
Preston and Colleen,
and my husband, Scott,
a true saint.

Contents

BULL BY THE HORNS

Prologue

Monday, October 12, 2008

I took a deep breath and walked into the large conference room at the Treasury Department. I was apprehensive and exhausted, having spent the entire weekend in marathon meetings with Treasury and the Fed. I felt myself start to tremble, and I hugged my thick briefing binder tightly to my chest in an effort to camouflage my nervousness. Nine men stood milling around in the room, peremptorily summoned there by Treasury Secretary Henry Paulson. Collectively, they headed financial institutions representing about $9 trillion in assets, or 70 percent of the U.S. financial system. I would be damned if I would let them see me shaking.

I nodded briefly in their direction and started to make my way to the opposite side of the large polished mahogany table, where I and the rest of the government's representatives would take our seats, facing off against the nine financial executives once the meeting began. My effort to slide around the group and escape the need for hand shaking and chitchat was foiled as Wells Fargo Chairman Richard Kovacevich quickly moved toward me. He was eager to give me an update on his bank's acquisition of Wachovia, which, as chairman of the Federal Deposit Insurance Corporation (FDIC), I had helped facilitate. He said it was going well. The bank was ready to go to market with a big capital raise. I told him I was glad. Kovacevich could be rude and abrupt, but he and his bank were very good at managing their business and executing on deals. I had no doubt that their acquisition of Wachovia would be completed smoothly and without disruption in banking services to Wachovia's customers, including the millions of depositors whom the FDIC insured.

As we talked, out of the corner of my eye I caught Vikram Pandit looking our way. Pandit was the CEO of Citigroup, which had earlier bollixed its own attempt to buy Wachovia. There was bitterness in his eyes. He and his primary regulator, Timothy Geithner, the head of the New York Federal Reserve Bank, were angry with me for refusing to object to the Wells acquisition of Wachovia, which had derailed Pandit's and Geithner's plans to let Citi buy it with financial assistance from the FDIC. I had little choice. Wells was a much stronger, better-managed bank and could buy Wachovia without help from us. Wachovia was failing and certainly needed a merger partner to stabilize it, but Citi had its own problems—as I was becoming increasingly aware. The last thing the FDIC needed was two mismanaged banks merging. Paulson and Bernanke did not fault my decision to acquiesce in the Wells acquisition. They understood that I was doing my job—protecting the FDIC and the millions of depositors we insured. But Geithner just couldn't see things from my point of view. He never could.

Pandit looked nervous, and no wonder. More than any other institution represented in that room, his bank was in trouble. Frankly, I doubted that he was up to the job. He had been brought in to clean up the mess at Citi. He had gotten the job with the support of Robert Rubin, the former secretary of the Treasury who now served as Citi's titular head. I thought Pandit had been a poor choice. He was a hedge fund manager by occupation and one with a mixed record at that. He had no experience as a commercial banker; yet now he was heading one of the biggest commercial banks in the country.

Still half listening to Kovacevich, I let my gaze drift toward Kenneth Lewis, who stood awkwardly at the end of the big conference table, away from the rest of the group. Lewis, the head of the North Carolina–based Bank of America (BofA)—had never really fit in with this crowd. He was viewed somewhat as a country bumpkin by the CEOs of the big New York banks, and not completely without justification. He was a decent traditional banker, but as a deal maker, his skills were clearly wanting, as demonstrated by his recent, overpriced bids to buy Countrywide Financial, a leading originator of toxic mortgages, and Merrill Lynch, a leading packager of securities based on toxic mortgages originated by Countrywide and its ilk. His bank had been healthy going into the crisis but would now be burdened by those ill-timed, overly generous acquisitions of two of the sickest financial institutions in the country.

Other CEOs were smarter. The smartest was Jamie Dimon, the CEO of JPMorgan Chase, who stood at the center of the table, talking with Lloyd Blankfein, the head of Goldman Sachs, and John Mack, the CEO of Morgan Stanley. Dimon was a towering figure in height as well as leadership ability, a point underscored by his proximity to the diminutive Blankfein. Dimon had forewarned of deteriorating conditions in the subprime market in 2006 and had taken preemptive measures to protect his bank before the crisis hit. As a consequence, while other institutions were reeling, mighty JPMorgan Chase had scooped up weaker institutions at bargain prices. Several months earlier, at the request of the New York Fed, and with its financial assistance, he had purchased Bear Stearns, a failing investment bank. Just a few weeks ago, he had purchased Washington Mutual (WaMu), a failed West Coast mortgage lender, from us in a competitive process that had required no financial assistance from the government. (Three years later, Dimon would stumble badly on derivatives bets gone wrong, generating billions in losses for his bank. But on that day, he was undeniably the king of the roost.)

Blankfein and Mack listened attentively to whatever it was Dimon was saying. They headed the country's two leading investment firms, both of which were teetering on the edge. Blankfein's Goldman Sachs was in better shape than Mack's Morgan Stanley. Both suffered from high levels of leverage, giving them little room to maneuver as losses on their mortgage-related securities mounted. Blankfein, whose puckish charm and quick wit belied a reputation for tough, if not ruthless, business acumen, had recently secured additional capital from the legendary investor Warren Buffett. Buffett's investment had not only brought Goldman $5 billion of much-needed capital, it had also created market confidence in the firm: if Buffett thought Goldman was a good buy, the place must be okay. Similarly, Mack, the patrician head of Morgan, had secured commitments of new capital from Mitsubishi Bank. The ability to tap into the deep pockets of this Japanese giant would probably by itself be enough to get Morgan through.

Not so Merrill Lynch, which was most certainly insolvent. Even as clear warning signs had emerged, Merrill had kept taking on more leverage while loading up on toxic mortgage investments. Merrill's new CEO, John Thain, stood outside the perimeter of the Dimon-Blankfein-Mack group, trying to listen in on their conversation. Frankly, I was surprised that he had even been invited. He was younger and less seasoned than the rest of the group. He had been Merrill's CEO for less than a year. His main accomplishment had been to engineer its overpriced sale to BofA. Once the BofA acquisition was complete, he would no longer be CEO, if he survived at all. (He didn't. He was subsequently ousted over his payment of excessive bonuses and lavish office renovations.)

At the other end of the table stood Robert Kelly, the CEO of Bank of New York (BoNY) and Ronald Logue, the CEO of State Street Corporation. I had never met Logue. Kelly I knew primarily by reputation. He was known as a conservative banker (the best kind in my book) with Canadian roots—highly competent but perhaps a bit full of himself. The institutions he and Logue headed were not nearly as large as the others—having only a few hundred billion dollars in assets—though as trust banks, they handled trillions of dollars of customers' money.

Which is why I assumed they were there, not that anyone had bothered to consult me about who should be invited. All of the invitees had been hand-picked by Tim Geithner. And, as I had just learned at a prep meeting with Paulson, Ben Bernanke, the chairman of the Federal Reserve, and Geithner, the game plan for the meeting was for Hank to tell all those CEOs that they would have to accept government capital investments in their institutions, at least temporarily. Yes, it had come to that: the government of the United States, the bastion of free enterprise and private markets, was going to forc-ibly inject $125 billion of taxpayer money into those behemoths to make sure they all stayed afloat. Not only that, but my agency, the FDIC, had been asked to start temporarily guaranteeing their debt to make sure they had enough cash to operate, and the Fed was going to be opening up trillions of dollars' worth of special lending programs. All that, yet we still didn't have an effective plan to fix the unaffordable mortgages that were at the root of the crisis.

The room became quiet as Hank entered, with Bernanke and Geithner in tow. We all took our seats, the bank CEOs ordered alphabetically by insti-tution. That put Pandit and Kovacevich at the opposite ends of the table. It also put the investment bank CEOs into the "power" positions, directly across from Hank, who himself had once run Goldman Sachs. Hank began speaking. He was articulate and forceful, in stark contrast to the way he could stammer and speak in half sentences when holding a press conference or talking to Congress. I was pleasantly surprised and seeing him in his true element, I thought.

He got right to the point. We were in a crisis and decisive action was needed, he said. Treasury was going to use the Troubled Asset Relief Pro-gram (TARP) to make capital investments in banks, and he wanted all of them to participate. He also alluded to the FDIC debt guarantee program, saying I would describe it later, but his main focus was the Treasury capital program. My stomach tightened. He needed to make clear that they all had to participate in both the Treasury and FDIC programs. My worst fear was that the weak banks such as Citi would use our program and the strong ones wouldn't. In insurance parlance, this is called "adverse selection": only the high risks pay for coverage; the strong ones that don't need it stay out. My mind was racing: could we back out if we didn't get 100 percent participation?

Ben spoke after Hank, reinforcing his points. Then Hank turned to me to describe the FDIC program. I could hear myself speaking, walking through the mechanics of the program. We would guarantee all of their newly issued debt up to a certain limit, I said, for which we would charge a fee. The purpose of the program was to make sure that they could renew their maturing debt without paying exorbitant interest rates that would constrain their ability to lend. The whole purpose of the program was to maintain their capacity to lend to the economy. We were also going to temporarily guarantee business checking accounts without limit. Businesses had been withdrawing their large, uninsured checking accounts from small banks and putting the money into so-called too-big-to-fail institutions. That was causing problems in otherwise healthy banks that were small enough to fail. It was essential that all the big banks participate in both programs, otherwise the economics wouldn't work. I said it again: we were expecting all the banks to participate in the FDIC programs. I looked around the table. Were they listening?

Hank asked Tim to tell each bank how much capital it would accept from Treasury. He eagerly ticked down the list: $25 billion for Citigroup, Wells Fargo, and JPMorgan Chase; $15 billion for Bank of America; $10 billion for Merrill Lynch, Goldman Sachs, and Morgan Stanley; $3 billion for Bank of New York; $2 billion for State Street.

Then the questions began.

Thain, whose bank was desperate for capital, was worried about restrictions on executive compensation. I couldn't believe it. Where were the guy's priorities? Lewis said BofA would participate and that he didn't think the group should be discussing compensation. But then he complained that the business checking account guarantee would hurt his bank, since it had been picking up most of those accounts as they had left the smaller banks. I was surprised to hear someone ask if they could use the FDIC program without the Treasury capital program. I thought Tim was going to levitate out of his chair. "No!" he said emphatically. I watched Vikram Pandit scribbling numbers on the back of an envelope. "This is cheap capital," he announced. I wondered what kind of calculations he needed to make to figure that out. Treasury was asking for only a 5% dividend. For Citi, of course, that was cheap; no private investor was likely to invest in Pandit's bank.

Kovacevich complained, rightfully, that his bank didn't need $25 billion in capital. I was astonished when Hank shot back that his regulator might have something to say about whether Wells' capital was adequate if he didn't take the money. Dimon, always the grown-up in the room, said that he didn't need the money but understood it was important for system stability. Blankfein and Mack echoed his sentiments.

A Treasury aide distributed a terms sheet, and Paulson asked each of the CEOs to sign it, committing their institutions to accept the TARP capital. My stomach tightened again when I saw that the terms sheet referenced only the Treasury program, not the FDIC's. (We would have to separately follow up with all of the banks to make sure they subscribed to the FDIC's programs, which they did.) John Mack signed on the spot; the others wanted to check with their boards, but by the end of the day, they had all agreed to accept the government's money.

We publicly announced the stabilization measures on Tuesday morning. The stock market initially reacted badly, but later rebounded. "Credit spreads"—a measure of how expensive it is for financial institutions to borrow money—narrowed significantly. All the banks survived; indeed, the following year, their executives were paying themselves fat bonuses again. In retrospect, the mammoth assistance to those big institutions seemed like overkill. I never saw a good analysis to back it up. But that was a big part of the problem: lack of information. When you are in a crisis, you err on the side of doing more, because if you come up short, the consequences can be disastrous.

The fact remained that with the exception of Citi, the commercial banks' capital levels seemed to be adequate. The investment banks were in trouble, but Merrill had arranged to sell itself to BofA, and Goldman and Morgan had been able to raise new capital from private sources, with the capacity, I believed, to raise more if necessary. Without government aid, some of them might have had to forego bonuses and take losses for several quarters, but still, it seemed to me that they were strong enough to bumble through. Citi probably did need that kind of massive government assistance (indeed, it would need two more bailouts later on), but there was the rub. How much of the decision making was being driven through the prism of the special needs of that one, politically connected institution? Were we throwing trillions of dollars at all of the banks to camouflage its problems? Were the others really in danger of failing? Or were we just softening the damage to their bottom lines through cheap capital and debt guarantees? Granted, in late 2008, we were dealing with a crisis and lacked complete information. But throughout 2009, even after the financial system stabilized, we continued generous bailout policies instead of imposing discipline on profligate financial institutions by firing their managers and boards and forcing them to sell their bad assets.

The system did not fall apart, so at least we were successful in that, but at what cost? We used up resources and political capital that could have been spent on other programs to help more Main Street Americans. And then there was the horrible reputational damage to the financial industry itself. It worked, but could it have been handled differently? That is the question that plagues me to this day.

In the following pages, I have tried to describe for you the financial crisis and its aftermath as I saw it during my time as chairman of the Federal Deposit Insurance Corporation from June 2006 to July 2011. I have tried to explain in very basic terms the key drivers of the crisis, the flaws in our response, and the half measures we have undertaken since then to correct the problems that took our economy to the brink. I describe in detail the battles we encountered—both with our fellow regulators and with industry lobbyists—to undertake such obviously needed measures as tighter mortgage-lending standards, stronger capital requirements for financial institutions, and systematic restructuring of unaffordable mortgages before the foreclosure tsunami washed upon our shores. Many of those battles were personally painful to me, but I take some comfort that I won as many as I lost. I was the subject of accolades from many in the media and among public interest groups. I was also subject to malicious press leaks and personal attacks, and my family finances were investigated. I even received threats to my personal safety from people who took losses when we closed banks, warranting a security detail through much of my tenure at the FDIC. But I am taking the reader through it all because I want the general public to understand how difficult it is when a financial regulator tries to challenge the conventional wisdom and make decisions in defiance of industry pressure.

I grew up on "Main Street" in rural Kansas. I understand—and share—the almost universal outrage over the financial mess we're in and how we got into it. People intuitively *know* that bailouts are wrong and that our banking system was mismanaged and badly regulated. However, that outrage is indiscriminate and undirected. People feel disempowered—overcome with a defeatist attitude that the game is rigged in favor of the big financial institutions and that government lacks the will or the ability to do anything about it.

The truth is that many people saw the crisis coming and tried to stop or curtail the excessive risk taking that was fueling the housing bubble and transforming our financial markets into gambling parlors for making out-sized speculative bets through credit derivatives and so-called structured finance. But the political process, which was and continues to be heavily influenced by monied financial interests, stopped meaningful reform efforts in their tracks. Our financial system is still fragile and vulnerable to the same type of destructive behavior that led to the Great Recession. People need to understand that we are at risk of another financial crisis unless the general public more actively engages in countering the undue influence of the financial services lobby.

Responsible members of the financial services industry also need to speak up in support of financial regulatory reform. All too often, the bad actors drive the regulatory process to the lowest common denominator while the good actors sit on the sidelines. That was certainly true as we struggled to tighten lending standards and raise capital requirements prior to the crisis. There were many financial institutions that did not engage in the excessive risk taking that took our financial system to the brink. Yet all members of the financial services industry were tainted by the crisis and the bailouts that followed.

As I explain at the end of this book, there are concrete, commonsense steps that could be undertaken now to rein in the financial sector and impose greater accountability on those who would gamble away our economic future for the sake of a quick buck. We need to reclaim our government and demand that public officials—be they in Congress, the administration, or the regulatory community—act in the public interest, even if reforms mean lost profits for financial players who write big campaign checks. Our government is already deeply in debt because of the lost revenues and stimulus measures resulting from the Great Recession. Financially, morally, and politically, we cannot afford to let the financial sector drive us into the ditch again.

I am a lifelong Republican who has spent the bulk of her career in public service. I believe I have built a reputation for common sense, independence, doing the right thing for the general public, and ignoring the special interests. Many of my positions have received editorial endorsements ranging from *The Wall Street Journal* to *The New York Times*, from the *Financial Times* to *The Guardian* to *Mother Jones*. My most cherished accolade during the crisis came from *Time*, which, in naming me to its 2008 "100 Most Influential People" list, called me "the little guy's protector in chief." I've always tried to play it down the middle and do what I think is right.

I want to explain why we are where we are in this country and how we can find ways to make it better. Our current problems are as bad as anything we have faced since the Great Depression. The public is cynical and confused about what it has been told concerning the financial crisis. In this book, I have tried to help clear away the myths and half-truths about how we ran our economic engine into the ditch and how we can get our financial and regulatory system back on track. We need to reclaim control of our economic future. That is why I wrote this book.

Sheila Bair, April 2012

CHAPTER 1

The Golden Age of Banking

I woke at 5 A.M. to the sound of a beeping garbage truck working its way down the street, noisily emptying rows of metal trash cans. I had fallen asleep four insufficient hours earlier. My eyes opened at the sound of the commotion; my mind was slow to follow. The room was pitch black, save for tiny rectangles of light that framed the bedroom windows where the thick shades didn't quite line up with the window frames.

I was disoriented. This was not my home. My own image came into focus, staring back at me from a full-length mirror that stood just a few feet from my bed. My mind cleared. I was in my good friend Denise's basement apartment on Capitol Hill, the one she used four times a year to show a line of women's designer clothing that she sold to her friends and colleagues. The rest of the time the apartment stood empty, and she had offered me its use.

Full-length mirrors were everywhere, used by her customers to view themselves when they tried on the colorful array of suits, dresses, and casual wear. For the month I would stay in this apartment, I found it somewhat disquieting to constantly be confronting my own image. At least the mirrors were slenderizing, the silver backings molded no doubt for that purpose to help sell the clothes.

I carefully navigated out of bed and gingerly shuffled across the parquet wood floor of this foreign room until I found the light switch on the wall. As I flipped it on, the room jarringly transformed from near blackness to glaring fluorescent light. I found a coffeemaker on the counter of the apartment's tiny efficiency kitchen, as well as a pound of Starbucks, helpfully left by Denise. I made a full pot of coffee and contemplated a long walk on the Mall to fill the time. I still had two hours to kill before driving to my first day of work as chairman of the Federal Deposit Insurance Corporation.

What a strange turn of events had brought me here. Four years ago, after nearly two decades in mostly high-pressure government jobs, I had left Washington with my family in search of a career that would provide a better work-life balance. I had worked as legal counsel to Senator Robert Dole (R–Kans.). I had served as a commissioner and acting chairman of the Commodity Futures Trading Commission (CFTC) and then headed government relations for the New York Stock Exchange (NYSE).

In 2000, I decided, "enough." I resigned my well-paying position with the NYSE and opted for a part-time consulting arrangement that gave me plenty of time to spend with my eight-year-old son, Preston, and one-year-old daughter, Colleen, whom my husband, Scott, and I had just adopted from China. But in early 2001, I was contacted by the new Bush administration, which convinced me to go back into the government as the assistant secretary of financial institutions of the U.S. Treasury Department. At the time, the financial system was in a relative state of calm, and the Bush folks assured me that I would have a nine-to-five existence at Treasury with no travel and plenty of time in the evenings and weekends for the family. The job had an interesting portfolio of issues but nothing of crisis proportions— issues such as improving consumer privacy rights in financial services and deciding whether banks should be able to have real estate brokerage arms.

Then came the 9/11 terrorist assault, followed by the collapse of Enron. What had started out being a nine-to-five job became a pressure cooker as I was tasked with heading a coordinated effort to improve the security of our financial infrastructure, strengthen protections against the illicit use of banks for terrorist financing, and help reform corporate governance and pension abuses to address the outrageous conduct of the Enron management. Nine to five became 24/7.

I completed my major projects and in the summer of 2002 said farewell to Washington. My husband and I moved to Amherst, Massachusetts, a serene and idyllic New England college town. He commuted back and forth from D.C.; I took a teaching post at the University of Massachusetts. The arrangement worked perfectly for four years, with adequate income, great public schools, and most important, a flexible work schedule with plenty of time for the family.

Then, in the early part of 2006, came a second call from the Bush administration: would I be interested in the chairmanship of the FDIC?

The FDIC was created in 1933 to stabilize the banking system after runs by depositors during the Great Depression forced thousands of banks to close. By providing a rock-solid guarantee against bank deposit losses up to the insurance limits ($100,000 when I assumed office in 2006; now $250,000), the agency had successfully prevented runs on the banking system for more than seven decades. I had worked with the agency during my

Treasury days and had also served on an advisory committee it had set up on banking policy.

In addition to its insurance function, the FDIC has significant regulatory authorities. For historical reasons, we have multiple federal banking regulators in the United States, depending on whether the banks are chartered at the federal or state level. In 2006, we had four bank regulators: two for federally chartered banks and two for state-chartered institutions. The Office of the Comptroller of the Currency (OCC) chartered and supervised national banks, which includes all of the biggest banks. The Office of Thrift Supervision (OTS), which was abolished in 2011, chartered and regulated thrifts, which specialize in mortgage lending. The FDIC and Fed worked jointly with the state banking regulators in overseeing the banks that the states chartered. If the state-chartered bank was also a member of the Federal Reserve System, it was regulated by the Fed. Those that were not members of the Federal Reserve System—about five thousand of them, the majority—were regulated by the FDIC.

The FDIC was also a backup regulator to the Federal Reserve Board, the OCC, and OTS, which meant that it had authority to examine and take action against any bank it insured if it felt it posed a threat to the FDIC. Importantly, in times of stress, the agency had sole power to seize failing insured banks to protect depositors and sell those banks and their assets to recoup costs associated with protecting insured deposits.

The Bush administration had vetted Diana Taylor, the well-regarded banking superintendent of the state of New York, to replace Donald Powell, a community banker from Texas who had been chairman since 2001. Don had left the FDIC some months earlier, leaving Vice Chairman Martin Gruenberg to be the acting chairman. It was an awkward situation. By statute, the FDIC's board had to be bipartisan, and by tradition the opposing party's Senate leadership had a strong hand in picking the vice chairman and one other board member. Marty was popular and well regarded but was essentially a Democratic appointee, having worked for Senate Banking Committee Chairman Paul Sarbanes (D–Md.) for most of his career. Understandably, the Bush administration was anxious to install one of its own as the chairman.

For whatever reason Diana's nomination did not proceed, and the Bush people were looking for a known quantity who could be confirmed easily and quickly. They viewed me as both. I had worked for Bush 43 at the Treasury Department and Bush 41 as one of his appointees on the Commodity Futures Trading Commission. In fact, I had been promptly and unanimously confirmed three times by the Senate (President Bill Clinton had reappointed me to the CFTC). That was due, in no small measure, to my early career with Senator Bob Dole, who was much loved in the Senate. Certainly, I had built my own relationships and record with senators, but Dole's afterglow had always helped ensure that I was well treated during the Senate confirmation process.

It was a difficult decision to make. We were happy in Amherst, and the family was reluctant to move. It was an ideal existence in many ways. We lived in a 150-year-old house across the street from the house where Emily Dickinson had lived and scribbled her poems on scraps of paper at a desk that overlooked our home. As I was a bit of an amateur poet myself, her house served as my inspiration when I wrote a rhyming children's book about the virtues of saving money. Our home stood two blocks from the village green. The kids and I walked everywhere—to school, to work, to shop. We hardly even needed a car. The people were friendly. The schools were good. Why should we move?

On the other hand, I was a government policy person at heart, and I thought—as I had when I took the Treasury Department job—that the FDIC position had an interesting portfolio of issues. For instance, Walmart had filed a controversial application for a specialized bank charter, exploiting a loophole in long-standing federal restrictions on commercial entities owning banks. In addition, Congress had recently authorized the FDIC to come up with a new system for assessing deposit insurance premiums on all banks based on their risk profile. Those were not exactly issues that would make the evening news, but as a financial policy wonk, I found them enticing.

So I agreed to accept, and, as expected, the confirmation process went quickly. The Bush people were eager for me to assume office, which didn't leave my husband and me enough time to find a new house and move the family. So here I was, living in a friend's borrowed apartment, while Scott, Preston, and Colleen stayed behind in Amherst until I could find us a place to live.

After downing my first cup of coffee, I thought better of the Mall walk—it was starting to rain. Instead, I made a mad dash to the drugstore to buy papers. I was drenched by the time I got back to the apartment. I plopped down on the living room couch, my wet skin sticking unpleasantly to the black leather upholstery. I dug into the papers in accordance with my usual ritual: *The Wall Street Journal* first, followed by *The New York Times*, then *The Washington Post*, finished off with the *Post*'s crossword puzzle. With my sleep-deprived brain, I didn't make it far on the puzzle. I regretted that I would be exhausted for my first day at the office.

It was really pouring rain by the time I left the apartment. I ran a half block to where I had parked our beat-up white Volvo sedan the night before, ruining my leather pumps in the process. I turned on the ignition and pressed "play" on the CD player, which held a Celtic Woman disc given to me by my kids for the trip. The soothing sounds of "Orinoco Flow" filled the car—a fitting song as I navigated flooded streets to reach the FDIC's offices at 550 17th Street N.W., a stone's throw from the White House. (Perhaps as an omen of things to come, the rains that day reached torrential levels, forcing the unprecedented closing of the Smithsonian museums and other government buildings.) The guard at the entry to the FDIC's parking garage raised a halting hand to signal that I should stop for the customary trunk search but then waved me on when he recognized my face from the photo that he—and all of the other security guards—had been given of the new FDIC chief.

I parked the car and headed for the small executive elevator that the FDIC reserved for its board members and their guests. I was already familiar with the FDIC building from my service on its advisory committee, so I was able to find my sixth-floor office with no difficulty. As I walked in the door, I was greeted by Alice Goodman, the longtime head of the FDIC's legislative affairs office. I had not yet had a chance to fill key staff positions, such as chief of staff, so I had asked Alice to serve temporarily as my acting deputy, to help me start learning and mastering the FDIC's organization, sift through the meeting requests, and organize the office. Alice had quite ably worked on my Senate confirmation and was willing to take a temporary detail to the Office of the Chairman. Soon I would hire Jesse Villarreal, who had worked for me at the Treasury Department, to serve as my permanent chief of staff.

Also helping out was Theresa West, a cheery, conscientious woman who was on detail from another division to serve as an administrative assistant. I was amazed that there was no secretary permanently assigned to the chairman's office. At the Treasury Department, the secretaries were the backbone of the organization, providing continuity and institutional memory to the political appointees, who came and went. Later, Brenda Hardnett and Benita Swann would join my office to provide crucial administrative support through most of my FDIC tenure.

The morning was spent on administrative necessities, such as filling out tax and benefit forms and other paperwork. Midway through the morning, Theresa suggested that we go to the security office so I could be photographed for my ID badge. We took the elevator to the basement and entered a small office staffed by a single young woman who was intently talking on the phone. As Theresa announced that the chairman was there for her ID photo, I was astonished to see the young woman hold up an index finger and continue talking on the phone. I was even more amazed to have to stand there for some time longer as the young woman finished what was clearly a personal call. Embarrassed and stammering, Theresa tried vainly to take charge of the situation through throat clearing and stern looks, but the woman just kept talking. I weighed my options. I could escalate by ordering the woman to terminate her phone call—reports of which would no doubt spread like wildfire throughout the agency—or I could let it go. I chose the latter.

What I didn't realize at the time—but was soon to discover—was that this employee's disaffection was only the tip of the iceberg for much wider issues of employee cynicism and anger caused by years of brutal downsizing. In the summer of 2006, FDIC employee morale problems ran deep through the agency. They would become a major preoccupation and challenge for me during my first several months at the FDIC.

In June 2006, the agency employed about 4,500 people with a billion-dollar operating budget. Since the 1990s, the agency's staff had been shrinking as the workload from the savings and loan crisis subsided. In 1995, the number of FDIC staff stood at 12,000. By 2001, that number had shrunk to 6,300. By the time I arrived, it had shrunk by another 1,800. There was no doubt that some of the downsizing had been necessary. However, in hindsight, the staff and budget reductions had gone too far. And it soon became clear to me that the layoffs—or "reductions in force," as the government calls them—had been carried out in a way that, rightly or wrongly, had given rise to a widespread impression among employees that decisions were based on favoritism and connections with senior officials, not on merit or relevance to core functions.

But the extreme downsizing was really just one symptom of a much more serious disease. That disease was the deregulatory dogma that had infected Washington for a decade, championed by Democrat and Republican alike, advocated by such luminaries as Clinton Treasury Secretary Robert Rubin and Federal Reserve Board Chairman Alan Greenspan. Regulation had fallen out of fashion, and both government and the private sector had become deluded by the notion that markets and institutions could regulate themselves. Government and its regulatory function were held in disdain.

That pervasive attitude had taken its toll at the FDIC, which had built a reputation as one of the toughest and most independent of regulators during the savings and loan crisis of the 1980s.

With more than $4 trillion in insured deposits, a robust regulatory presence was essential to protect the FDIC against imprudent risk taking by the institutions it insured. But the staff had been beaten down by the political consensus that now things were different. Quarter after quarter, banks were experiencing record profitability, and bank failures were at historic lows. The groupthink was that technological innovation, coupled with the Fed's seeming mastery of maintaining an easy monetary policy without inflation, meant an end to the economic cycles of good times and bad that had characterized our financial system in the past. The golden age of banking was here and would last forever. We didn't need regulation anymore. That kind of thinking had not only led to significant downsizing but had also severely damaged FDIC employees' morale, and—as I would later discover—led to the adoption of hands-off regulatory philosophies at all of the financial regulatory agencies that would prove to be difficult to change once the subprime crisis started to unfold.

The FDIC's flirtation with lighter touch regulation had also exacerbated tensions with our Office of the Inspector General (OIG). Virtually all major federal agencies have an OIG. These are independent units generally headed by presidential appointees whose job is to detect and prevent fraud, waste, abuse, and violations of law. War was raging between our senior management team and the FDIC's OIG when I arrived at the FDIC. I must have spent at least twenty hours during my first week in office refereeing disputes between the OIG's office and our senior career staff. I was amazed to learn that the FDIC OIG totaled some 140 people, which was many times the size of OIGs at other federal agencies.

Fortunately, in sorting out and resolving the raging disputes between FDIC management and OIG staff, I had an ally in Jon Rymer, a bank auditor by background, who had been confirmed as the new FDIC IG at the same time I was confirmed as chairman. So we were both entering our respective jobs with fresh perspectives and no axes to grind. Jon was intelligent, soft-spoken, and highly professional. His bespectacled, mild-mannered appearance and demeanor belied a steely toughness, cultivated no doubt by his twenty-five years in active and reserve duty with the army.

Jon and I were able to develop a good working relationship, and over time, we achieved better mutual respect and understanding between FDIC executive managers and the OIG. There was still tension, as was appropriate. But I actually came to enjoy the fact that we had this huge OIG that was constantly looking over our shoulders. It helped keep us on our toes and was one reason why when the financial crisis hit and we were forced to quickly put stabilization measures into place, we received clean audits and widespread recognition for our effective quality controls. In giving speeches, I would brag about the size and robust efforts of our OIG. And its investigation division would later play a lead role in ferreting out and punishing the rampant mortgage broker fraud that had contributed to scores of bank failures.

The agency's focus on downsizing and deregulation had also created major problems with its union, the National Treasury Employees Union (NTEU). Predictably, the NTEU had fought the downsizing tooth and nail, but it had other major grievances as well. One was a recently instituted pay-for-performance system, which forced managers to make wide differentiations among employees in making pay increase and bonus decisions. This was arguably an improvement over the old system, which had been akin to Lake Wobegon, where "everybody is above average," and basic competence would routinely result in a salary increase and year-end bonus. But the new system required managers to force employees into three buckets. The top rated 25 percent received sizable salary and bonus packages. The middle 50 percent received a more modest amount, and the bottom 25 percent received nothing. In essence, the system assumed that each division and office had 25 percent stars and 25 percent flunkies, with everyone else in the middle. Managers hated it. Employees hated it. The only people who liked it were the management consultants the agency had paid a pretty penny to create it.

The union was also outraged at a deregulatory initiative called Maximum Efficiency, Risk-Focused, Institution Targeted (MERIT) examinations, which severely limited our supervisory staff's ability to conduct thorough examinations at thousands of banks. By law, most banks must undergo a safety and soundness exam every year. These exams traditionally entail bank examiners visiting the banks on site and doing detailed reviews of loan files to determine whether the loans were properly underwritten and performing. In addition to reviewing loans, the examiners also look at a bank's investments and interview staff and senior executives to make sure policies and procedures are being followed. As any good examiner will tell you, it is not enough to simply examine a bank's policies to know whether it is being operated prudently; individual loan files must also be examined to make sure that the bank is following its procedures.

With MERIT, however, the FDIC had instituted a new program that essentially said that if a bank's previous examination showed that it was healthy, at the next exam, the examiners would not pull and review loan files, but instead would simply review policies and procedures. Prior to MERIT, examiners had been encouraged and rewarded for conducting thorough, detailed reviews, but under the MERIT procedures, they were rewarded for completing them quickly, with minimal staff hours involved. Career FDIC examiners derisively called MERIT exams "drive-by" exams. Their protests escalated as they became more and more concerned about the increasing number of real estate loans on banks' balance sheets. They knew, even in the summer of 2006, that real estate prices wouldn't rise forever and that once the market turned, a good number of those loans could go bad.

As it turned out, though I took the FDIC job because of my love for financial policy issues, I found that a substantial part of my time was spent dealing with management problems. In grappling with those issues, I worked closely with our chief operating officer, John Bovenzi, a ruddy faced, unflappable FDIC career staffer who had worked his way up to the top FDIC staff job. I also relied on Arleas Upton Kea, the head of our Division of Administration. A lawyer by training, Arleas was a savvy, impeccably dressed professional, toughened by the fact that she was the first black woman to have clawed her way up the FDIC's management ladder. Finally, I relied heavily on Steven App. Steve had recently joined the FDIC from the Treasury Department, where he had worked in a senior financial management position. I had known Steve when I was at Treasury and had tremendous respect for him. He would later play a key role in ramping up our hiring and contractor resources quickly, as well as working with me to manage the considerable financial demands that were placed on the agency as a result of the financial crisis.

At Arleas's suggestion, we hired a consultant and conducted detailed employee surveys to try to get at the root causes of the low staff morale. The surveys showed that employees felt that they were disempowered, that their work wasn't valued, and that they were cut off from any meaningful input in decision making. To counter their feeling of disempowerment, I created a Culture Change Council whose primary duty was to improve communication up and down the chain of command. I instituted quarterly call-ins for employees. We opened the phone lines and invited all employees to ask me any question they wanted. The first few calls were somewhat awkward. Most FDIC employees had never had a chance to interact directly with the chairman, and they weren't quite sure what to ask. So I found myself fielding questions on how to get a handicap parking space at one of our regional offices or how to sign up for our dental plan. Eventually the employees started focusing on broader, agencywide matters, and I found the calls tremendously helpful in learning what was on the minds of the rank and file. When I took office, the FDIC was ranked near the bottom of best places to work in the government, a ranking based on employee satisfaction surveys conducted by the Office of Personnel Management each year. Based on a survey completed before I left office, it was ranked number one. It took a lot of time to restore employee morale and trust at that disheartened agency. But we did it, and that best-place-to-work ranking is one of my proudest achievements.

Ultimately, we would revamp the pay-for-performance system, scrap MERIT exams, and begin hiring more examiners to enforce both safety and soundness requirements and consumer protection laws. We also started increasing the staff of our Division of Resolutions and Receiverships—the division that handles bank failures—which had been cut to the bone. These rebuilding efforts took time, and within a year I would find myself still struggling to revitalize an agency at the cusp of a housing downturn that would escalate into a financial cataclysm. It takes time to hire and train examiners and bank-closing specialists. We had to replenish our ranks just as the financial system started to deteriorate. In retrospect, those "golden age of banking" years, 2001–2006, should have been spent planning and preparing for the next crisis. That was one of the many hard lessons learned.

CHAPTER 2

Turning the *Titanic*

A s demanding as the FDIC management issues were, there were also important policy decisions to be made. Regulation had become too lax, and I found myself fighting to change course on a number of fronts.

Most of our major policy decisions had to be approved by the FDIC board of directors. Virtually all of the FDIC staff reported to me, and I had the power to set the board agenda and control staff recommendations that came to it for approval. But board approval was required for all rule makings. I soon learned I had a deeply divided board, one that ran the full gamut of regulatory and economic philosophies.

The FDIC board is made up of five individuals, no more than three of whom can be of the same political party. In addition, by statute, the Office of the Comptroller of the Currency, which regulates the largest national commercial banks, and the director of the Office of Thrift Supervision, which regulates the major national mortgage lenders, sit on the FDIC board.

The board also has a vice chairman and one internal director, who must have a background in state banking regulation. Because the president usually appoints members of his own party to head the OCC and OTS as well as the FDIC chairman, the vice chairman and internal director are generally members of the other party. That was the case with the FDIC board in 2006. John Dugan, the comptroller of the currency, and John Reich, the director of the OTS, were both staunch Republicans with long industry experience, Dugan as a banking lawyer and Reich as a community banker. Our vice chairman, Marty Gruenberg, on the other hand, was a lifelong Democratic Hill aide, having spent most of his career with Senator Paul Sarbanes. Our internal director, Thomas Curry, was a former Massachusetts banking supervisor. Though a registered independent, Tom had close ties to the Senate Democratic leadership and Sarbanes's office.

On the policy front, my first major challenge was to issue for public comment rules that would require all banks to start paying premiums for their deposit insurance. The FDIC has never been funded by taxpayers. Even though the FDIC's guarantee is backed by the full faith and credit of the U.S. government, it has always charged a premium from banks to cover its costs. However, in 1996, banking industry trade groups convinced the Congress to prohibit the FDIC from charging any premiums of banks that bank examiners viewed as healthy, so long as the FDIC's reserves exceeded 1.25 percent of insured deposits. This essentially eliminated premiums for more than 90 percent of all banks, which in turn created three problems.

First, because of those limits, the FDIC was unable to build substantial reserves when the banking system was strong and profitable so that it would have a cushion to draw from when a downturn occurred without having to assess large premiums.

Second, it created a "free rider" problem. There were nearly a thousand banks chartered since 2006 that had derived substantial benefits from deposit insurance without having had to pay a cent for this benefit. That was grossly unfair to older banks, which had paid substantial premiums to cover the costs of the S&L crisis.

Finally, it did not allow us to differentiate risk adequately among banks. Like any insurance company, we thought that banks that posed a higher risk of failure should pay a higher premium, in much the same way that a life insurance company charges higher premiums of smokers or an auto insurer charges higher premiums of drivers with a history of traffic violations. Based on historical experience, we knew that even banks with high supervisory ratings (known as "CAMELS") can pose significantly different risks to the FDIC. For instance, a bank may appear to be well run and profitable, thus warranting a good supervisory rating. However, we know that new banks that have grown rapidly are statistically more likely to get into trouble. In addition, the way banks get their funding can impact risks to the FDIC. For instance, brick-and-mortar banks with "core" deposit franchises—that is, those with established customers who have multiple loan and deposit relationships with it—are more stable and pose fewer risks to the FDIC than those that rely on a broker to bring them deposits and thus lack a personal relationship with their depositors.

In early 2006, after years of pushing by the FDIC, Congress finally passed legislation permitting us to charge all banks a premium based on their risk profiles. The legislation also gave us flexibility to build the fund above 1.25 percent to 1.50 percent, at which point the agency would have to pay dividends from its reserves back to the industry. It was now time to propose rules to implement those new authorities, and we were already getting serious pushback from the industry.

The FDIC staff had already been working on a new system that would require all banks to pay a premium for their deposit insurance. The effort was led by our highly competent head of the Division of Insurance and Research (DIR), Arthur Murton; his deputy, Diane Ellis; and Matthew Green, a DIR associate director who had once worked for me at the Treasury Department. They had crafted a rule that relied on a combination of CAMELS scores, financial ratios, and, in the case of large banks, credit ratings. Their proposal also gave FDIC examiners the ability to adjust a bank's CAMELS score if we disagreed with the score assigned to the bank by its primary regulator. That was consistent with our statutory authority to serve as backup regulator for banks we insured. The base annual rate for most banks would be 5 to 7 basis points, or 5 to 7 cents on each $100 of insured deposits. That would bring in an estimated $2 billion to $3 billion in assessment income per year. At the time, our reserves stood at around $50 billion, or 1.22 percent of the $4 trillion in deposits we insured.

To the board's credit, all of the members recognized the imperative of moving ahead with rules to implement the premium increases, notwithstanding industry opposition. The industry was still experiencing record profits (indeed, by the end of 2006, annual banking profits had reached an unprecedented $150 billion). The clear mandate of the legislation—at the behest of the FDIC—was to build up reserves while the industry was profitable, so that we could have a surplus to draw upon if and when a downturn occurred.

However, directors Reich and Dugan were opposed to the staff proposal because they did not want FDIC examiners to be second-guessing the CAMELS scores their own examiners assigned to OTS- and OCC-regulated banks. The board had been at a stalemate for months on this issue, with Vice Chairman Gruenberg and Director Curry supporting the staff. The staff was hoping that the new chairman would support them as well.

I was sympathetic to the staff position, but I also did not want my first board meeting to be a split vote. I had worked in Washington for many years and knew that closely divided votes lacked the authority of consensus positions and invited scrutiny and second-guessing by the private sector and in Congress. That would set a very bad precedent. I went ahead and scheduled a meeting so that the board knew I was serious about moving ahead, but at the eleventh hour, I was able to broker a compromise. I agreed that the FDIC would not alter another regulator's assigned CAMELS score, but we would preserve the right to adjust the premium up or down if we didn't think the CAMELS score accurately reflected the risk of the institution. In my view, that was a distinction without a difference, but it did the trick. Within two weeks of my assuming office, on July 12, 2006, we proposed the new rule on a 5–0 vote.

The attack from the industry was severe. Steve Bartlett, the president and CEO of the Financial Services Roundtable, which represents the largest financial firms, argued for the status quo, claiming that "given the insignificant risks that such institutions present in the modern regulatory scheme, it is unnecessary to impose any new assessment on the safest, best-performing members of the FDIC system." James Chessen, the chief economist of the American Bankers Association, was even more vehement: "The banking industry is in exceptional health, and there is no indication that large amounts of revenue are needed by the FDIC. Additional money sitting idly in Washington adds little to the financial strength of the FDIC, but has real consequences for the communities that banks serve. That money would be better used supporting loans in the local community."

It was not the first time I would hear that our regulatory initiatives would hurt lending. Throughout my tenure at the FDIC, that was the standard refrain from industry lobbyists virtually anytime we tried to rein in risky practices or ask the industry to pay for the costs of bank failures. Of course, later, as the crisis hit and the Deposit Insurance Fund (DIF) became depleted, industry lobbyists argued that banks were too stressed to pay premiums. So there you had it: in good times, we shouldn't collect because we didn't need the money, and in bad times, we shouldn't collect because the industry was stressed.

I also learned from that early experience that trade group lobbyists frequently did not reflect the views of better-managed banks. A number of older, more established banks contacted me in support of what we were doing. Under the statutory scheme set up by Congress, the newer, "free-rider" banks would pay the lion's share of the initial assessments, as older banks were given credit for premiums they had paid to clean up the S&L mess. That made sense from the standpoint of fairness. (However, the existence of those large credits also impeded our ability to replenish the fund quickly.)

Notwithstanding lobbying pressure, we stuck to our guns. We finalized the rule in November 2006, again on a unanimous vote, and started collecting premiums in the first quarter of 2007. But it was too late to build up the fund sufficiently before the crisis hit. Later, we would be forced to increase assessments and require banks to prepay their premiums to maintain sufficient industry-funded reserves. But our financial condition would have been even worse if we had succumbed to industry pressure and shelved the rule.

Another major issue that divided the board was the question of whether Walmart should be approved for a bank charter and deposit insurance. The general rule—somewhat unique to the United States—is that nonfinancial commercial entities such as Walmart cannot own banks. However, there was an arcane exception to this overarching separation of banking and commerce for banks chartered in Utah. Specialty banks, known as "industrial loan charters" (ILCs), had been used in the past primarily by car manufacturers and other companies that wanted to create banks to make loans for their customers to buy their products. Now Walmart wanted to use it to set up its own bank.

Community banks feared that Walmart would use its bank charter to open up full-service banking branches in its thousands of stores, undercutting small local banks that do not have the same deep pockets and economies of scale. Walmart insisted that it wanted the charter only to perform narrow services such as processing credit card payments. My internal directors were uncomfortable with the Walmart application, as was John Reich, who had deep ties to the community banks. John Dugan, on the other hand, was somewhat sympathetic, not surprising given the fact that he had once worked for Senator Jake Garn, the Utah Republican who had championed the ILC exception.

I wasn't sure where I came out on the policy issues associated with Walmart having a bank. On the one hand, with Walmart's huge imprint, I could see that its entry into the banking business could theoretically expand banking services into lower-income communities. On the other hand, the impact on community banks could be severe. I agreed with John Dugan on the legal analysis: the law seemed to say clearly that commercial entities such as Walmart were entitled to own an ILC. But our approval of the Walmart application could dramatically change the face of banking in the United States. Was that really what Congress had intended by approving what was supposed to be a limited number of commercially owned specialty banks?

Like Hamlet, I couldn't make a decision. So I punted. I asked and got approval from the board to place a moratorium on all ILC applications to give Congress some time and incentive to think about whether it wanted to put some limits on who could have an ILC charter. We had already received several strongly worded letters protesting the Walmart application from influential members of Congress, such as Barney Frank, the chairman of the House Financial Services Committee. I basically threw the hot potato back to them. Here, Congress, you created this ILC exception; we will give you more time to consider whether you really want it to be this broad. I'm not usually one to dodge issues; in fact, I pride myself as the type of person who tackles problems head-on. But I didn't see any downside to delaying a decision on the ILC issue, particularly given the fact that the controversy surrounding it had been a major distraction for the agency.

The moratorium gave us time to focus on what I considered to be more important matters. According to data analysis presented by our economics staff, the housing market was starting to turn dramatically and a down cycle in housing could pose significant risks to banks insured by the FDIC.

In the second quarter of 2006, there were more than $4 trillion in real estate–related assets sitting on bank balance sheets, representing more than 36 percent of total assets. A precipitous decline in housing prices would create real problems for insured banks. I wanted that looming risk to be our primary focus. Safety and soundness regulation had become too lax. It was imperative that the deregulatory trend that had overtaken Washington be reversed. Our first priority had to be to make sure that banks had enough capital to withstand losses from a housing downturn. Capital was the key to keeping banks solvent as storm clouds gathered on the economic horizon. Yet, instead of moving to increase capital levels, I would find myself in a lonely battle against the other bank regulators—indeed, against the entire global financial regulatory community—to prevent the banks we insured from reducing their capital levels. That fight centered on something called the Basel II advanced approaches, and it was one of the most brutal fights of my public career.

CHAPTER 3

The Fight over Basel II

Managing my diverse board on FDIC-specific issues was hard enough. But some of the most important decisions to be made on bank regulatory policy had to be done on an interagency basis to ensure consistency in how banks were supervised. That meant that we also needed to reach agreement with the Federal Reserve Board. Prior to Ben Bernanke's arrival in 2006, the Fed had been led by Alan Greenspan for nearly two decades, and during that time, the institution had acquired a strong antipathy to regulation.

Early in my tenure, the other bank regulators were still moving in the direction of less regulation, at least for larger institutions. Adding fuel to their fire was the fact that some of our foreign competitors, particularly in Europe, were taking industry self-regulation to new extremes. In particular, a number of European regulators had embraced "principles-based" regulation, which, in my view, meant articulating high-level standards but then leaving it to the banks themselves to interpret and enforce those standards.

Most problematic was Europe's implementation of a new framework for setting capital requirements for large banks, known as the "Basel II advanced approaches." They had been developed by a group called the Basel Committee on Banking Supervision. The Basel Committee was established in 1974 to promote international cooperation in bank supervision and in particular, to set global standards for bank capital requirements. The group met four times a year, usually in Basel, Switzerland, and was made up of bank regulators from the major developed nations.

Of all the things that a bank regulator does, setting and enforcing capital requirements are probably the most important. Why? Because banks have certain government benefits that other for-profit commercial entities do not enjoy, which also means that they pose big risks to the government if they fail. For one thing, they have deposit insurance. That allows them to readily obtain funds for their operations from bank depositors, who do not have

strong incentives to ask about the safety of the bank because they know the
FDIC will protect them from loss if they stay below our insured deposit
limits. Banks also have what is called "discount window" access, which is
the ability to borrow money from the Federal Reserve System to make sure
they always have enough cash on hand to meet their deposit withdrawal and
other obligations.

There are good reasons for deposit insurance and Federal Reserve discount window lending. They give the public confidence that the money they
have in banks is safe and readily accessible. And by strengthening banks'
ability to attract bank deposits, the banks have more money to lend out to
households and businesses to support economic growth. However, because
the people who own and run banks don't have to work very hard to attract
deposits and because they know the FDIC will have to cover the losses on
insured deposits if the bank gets into trouble, they have incentives to take
a lot of risks. That is what is known as "moral hazard." The moral hazard
problem is worse for very large institutions that the market perceives as
being too big to fail. With the very largest financial institutions, the markets
assume that the government will protect everyone, not just insured depositors, if they get into trouble. And as we saw with the bailouts of 2008, those
assumptions proved to be mostly right. (But more about that later.)

The FDIC has a number of ways it can try to protect itself against banks
taking imprudent risks with insured deposits. First, we think it is important
to charge banks a premium to cover the costs of bank failures. By requiring the banking system to cover those losses, we give well-managed banks
an incentive to look out for the weaker ones. Second, we look to safety and
soundness regulation, which is why we think it is so important for examiners to conduct vigorous analysis of a bank's books and operations. Finally,
and most important, we can set capital requirements.

A bank's capital is, in essence, its "skin in the game." It is the amount of
their own money that the bank's owners have to stake to support the bank's
lending and other investments. The most basic form of capital—also called
"common equity"—is raised by a bank selling stock to shareholders or by
retaining its earnings (instead of paying those earnings out in dividends or
big employees bonuses). Raising money through common equity is different from raising money through debt issuance. Common-equity owners
have no right to have their investments paid back. If the bank is profitable,
they share in the profits through dividend payments and appreciation in the
value of their shares. If the bank does poorly, however, they have no right
to dividends and may suffer a drop in the value of their shares. That is why

bank regulators say that common-equity capital is "loss-absorbing." In contrast, when a bank issues debt to fund itself, it is legally obliged to pay the loan back, along with the agreed-upon interest. If it is unable to fulfill that commitment, it is in default—in bank regulatory parlance, it fails.

Insured deposits are a form of bank borrowing. When you put money on deposit at a bank, you are in essence lending the bank your money, which the bank in turn can use to make loans or other investments. The bank is legally obligated to give that money, plus any promised interest, back to you, in accordance with your deposit agreement. If it fails to do so, it is in default, and if the amount of money you have deposited is under the insured deposit limits, the FDIC will step in, take control of the bank, and make you whole.

Left to their own devices, banks will not want to risk much of their own money. Why should they if they can get funding through insured deposits or, if they are a large institution, by issuing debt that bondholders believe is implicitly backed by the government? That is why, even with capital regulation, most banks have much lower capital levels than nonfinancial, commercial entities that do not have access to government-supported funding.

Here are two highly simplified examples that demonstrate why banks cannot be relied upon to set their own capital requirements.

Let's say we have two banks that have made loans totaling $100 million. Bank A's owners have funded their loans by putting up $5 million of their own money—capital—and the remaining $95 million they have attracted with insured deposits. Bank B's owners have put up $20 million of their own capital, and the remaining $80 million they have attracted with insured deposits.

If both banks make a $1 million profit, Bank A's shareholders' return on their investment is 20%. However, Bank B's shareholders' return is only 5%. As you can see, the rate of return on shareholders' equity investment goes up quite a bit the less of their own money they invest. That larger return provides more money for dividend payments for them and bonuses for the executives at Bank A. Such "leveraged" returns, that is, investing with borrowed money, can be quite profitable when times are good. In these examples, the borrowing is done through insured deposits.

On the other hand, let's say those banks made a lot of bad loans and have lost $10 million. Bank A becomes insolvent; that is, it fails. Its shareholders are wiped out to the tune of $5 million, with the FDIC paying out $5 million to fully protect the $95 million in deposits. (The other $90 million would be recouped by the FDIC through selling Bank A's good loans.) In contrast, Bank B's shareholders would lose half of their investment. But with $10 million remaining in equity capital, the bank is still solvent. It has not failed. The FDIC suffers no losses, and the bank survives to make further (and hopefully better) loans.

In both scenarios, Bank A's shareholders come out better. Their return on equity is higher in the first scenario, and their losses are less in the second scenario because they can push half of the losses onto the FDIC.

Now let's say that Bank A has $2 trillion in loans and other assets, as opposed to $100 million, and that its shareholders therefore think it is too big to fail. Their assumption is that the government will bail the bank out, even if it makes stupid loans and other investments and ends up with losses that exceed its capital. In that case, the shareholders will be completely focused on maximizing returns regardless of risk, because they assume the government will step in and protect their equity investment, if necessary.

These examples illustrate precisely why regulators cannot leave it to banks themselves to set their own capital levels, and that is particularly true of large institutions.

The Basel Committee finalized its first agreement on bank capital standards, Basel I, in 1988. Basel I provided for a fairly simple method of determining bank capital, assigning specific capital requirements to four different categories of bank assets. For instance, for a mortgage (which used to be viewed as low risk), Basel I required the bank to put up capital equity to 4 percent of the loan amount. For other types of loans—for instance, a loan to a business—the requirement was 8 percent. However, as banking activities became more complex, Basel Committee members began work on a new framework that they believed would do a better job of setting capital levels based on risk. Unfortunately, the main idea behind the Basel II effort was to let a bank's management heavily influence how much capital to hold.

Basel II was controversial from the start. Work on it began in 1998, but the accord was not approved and published until 2004. Studies of how the accord would impact capital consistently showed that it would lead to dramatic declines in the amount of capital held by large U.S. banks. For that reason, the FDIC fought and delayed U.S. implementation, and we were even more determined to stop it as we watched capital levels decline among big European banks as they moved forward with Basel II adoption.

It makes sense to consider the riskiness of a bank's assets as one factor in setting capital levels. Certainly, a prudently underwritten mortgage with a 20 percent down payment is going to be less risky than an unsecured credit card line. Trying to "risk weight" assets for capital purposes is something bank regulators have done for a long time. However, instead of regulators setting clear, enforceable parameters for determining the riskiness of bank assets, Basel II essentially allowed bank managers to use their own judgment. That not only opened the door to lower capital levels, it also inserted a great deal of subjectivity and variation among similarly situated banks in how much capital they would actually hold. That was proving to be the case in Europe. As we discovered during the crisis, the Basel II advanced approaches grossly underestimated the risk of most assets, particularly home loans and derivatives, and also produced wide variations in capital levels among the European banks using it.

Another major concern we had with the Basel II advanced approaches was that their methodology relied heavily on how loans had performed historically. Historically, mortgages had performed well, but that didn't mean their good performance would continue in the future (as we soon found out). We were also concerned that in good economic times, when loan delinquency and default rates are low, bank managers could say that they didn't need much capital. But as delinquency and default rates went up in an economic downturn, the Basel II methodology would say that capital needed to be higher, causing banks to try to raise capital during periods of market distress. (As it turned out, that concern was only theoretical, but for all of the wrong reasons. Even as Europe later plunged into recession and delinquency and default rates spiked, most European banks using Basel II said that their assets were becoming less risky and lowered their capital levels even more!)

Our Basel II staff expert at the FDIC was an intense, soft-spoken career government servant by the name of George French. George was battle-scarred from his years of effort in fighting the Fed and OCC over Basel II. The idea for the advanced approaches had originally come from one of the Fed's regional banks, the New York Federal Reserve Bank (NY Fed). It was a source of embarrassment to the Fed that Europe was implementing the framework ahead of the United States. George's first lieutenant in the war was Jason Cave, an affable but equally ferocious (when needed) advocate of stringent bank capital standards. They had received strong support in this years-old battle from former FDIC Chairman Don Powell, as well as from Vice Chairman Gruenberg when he had served as the acting chairman. But enticed by the prospect of lower capital standards, the biggest banks with all of their lobbying muscle were closing in, and the FDIC was becoming more and more isolated.

Lobbying of the new chairman started early. Both John Dugan and Federal Reserve Board Governor Susan Bies reached out to me during my first

few weeks in office, hoping that I would show more flexibility than my predecessors in letting Basel II move forward. As an academic at U.Mass. and
member of the FDIC's Advisory Committee on Banking Policy, I had been
supportive of the FDIC's views on Basel II. It made no sense to me to have a
capital framework that let big banks essentially set their own capital requirements while the smaller banks were subject to tougher, more prescriptive
standards. Big banks posed much greater risks to the financial system if they
failed, so if anything their capital requirements should have been stronger,
not weaker. On the other hand, I did not want to appear insensitive to the
views of my regulatory colleagues and felt obliged to hear out their arguments.

Sue Bies was a former banker and had been the Fed's point person on
Basel II for several years. Of all the regulators, she was clearly the most
determined. But John Dugan was also pushing hard. Both argued that
Basel II was more sophisticated than the current rules, relying, as it did,
on the complex models banks used to predict the probability and severity of future losses. I think they truly believed that the capital reductions
under Basel II were justified based on their confidence in the ability of the
large banks to manage risk adequately. That confidence, of course, later
proved to be woefully misplaced. Their other main argument was that we
needed to move forward to maintain the competitiveness of the U.S. financial system. In other words, Europe was letting its banks operate with lower
capital, and we needed to let ours do so as well.

Both Dugan and Bies said that they wanted all four bank regulatory agencies to adopt the same set of bank capital rules. (In the summer and fall of
2006, OTS Director John Reich was still on the fence about Basel. Later, he
would join the Fed and OCC.) But they also intimated that the OCC and
Fed would be willing to proceed independently of the FDIC if there was no
interagency agreement. That was a serious threat to the FDIC position. As
the primary regulators of the major financial institutions, the Fed and OCC
had the raw legal authority to ignore our concerns and implement Basel II
for their banks on their own. If they did so, they would not be obliged to
include any of the safeguards the FDIC wanted against capital reductions.

Given the FDIC's waning leverage, I reluctantly agreed to issue a proposed
rule for comment implementing the advanced approaches but insisted that
certain conditions previously negotiated by the FDIC and Vice Chairman
Gruenberg be included. One was a three-year transition period that capped
the amount of capital reduction for any individual bank at 5 percent per
year, though the caps would come off after the third year. Another was a

permanent 10 percent cap on the amount of total capital that could decline among all banks using the advanced approaches.

Even with those safeguards, our staff analysis showed that the big U.S. banks would be able to lower their capital levels significantly. Citigroup's capital release would have been $2.5 billion. Bank of America could have released $14.6 billion. Washington Mutual, a major West Coast mortgage lender and the OTS's biggest charter, could have released $2.3 billion. All of those institutions would later fail or run into serious trouble. Without the FDIC safeguards, those capital reductions would have been even higher. Indeed, our studies showed that the total capital held by big banks would decline by 22 percent, with a median decline of 31 percent among individual institutions.

We were on the ropes but still swinging, so I decided that there was no defense like an offense. I was scheduled to go to my first meeting of the Basel Committee in Mérida, Mexico, in October 2006. The chairman of the Basel Committee, Nout Wellink, who headed the central bank of the Netherlands, had paid a courtesy call on me in Washington that summer. During the meeting, he had said he would be open to considering an international leverage ratio to address declining capital levels in Europe under Basel II. Nout was a gentlemanly career central banker who (quietly) shared many of my concerns about Basel II, and I was flattered that he had made a point of visiting me to encourage discussion of an international leverage ratio. The Basel II accord—and the capital reductions it entailed—were particularly worrisome for smaller countries such as the Netherlands, which was home to very large banking institutions whose assets far exceeded their country's GDP. The failure of one of those behemoths could bring the whole country down. On the other hand, politically, Nout could not break from other EU nations, and the larger countries—Germany and France in particular— had no problem in letting their big banks take on a lot of leverage. To his credit, Nout saw even then the problems that were developing in Europe over Basel II implementation, and he wanted to try to head them off.

How would a leverage ratio have helped the situation?

Basel II set capital standards based on the perceived riskiness of a bank's assets. The leverage ratio, on the other hand, is a simple measure of bank capital to the value of total assets. So if a bank has $1 trillion in assets—be they mortgages, credit card debt, derivatives, or government securities— and the required ratio is 5 percent, capital has to equal $50 billion. That $50 billion is a floor below which the amount of capital cannot fall, even if the bank says its assets are very low risk. It prevents banks from gaming the risk weighting of assets and also helps prevent wide fluctuations in bank capital through economic cycles. The United States has had a leverage ratio for insured banks for decades, and it has proven to be a good tool against excess leverage. (It saved our bacon during the crisis.) Canada and Australia also use leverage ratios.

I thought an international leverage ratio was a "capital" idea and enthusiastically embraced Nout's overture. We notified the other U.S. regulators that I would be bringing it up in Mérida. They were not pleased. I told them I thought that an international leverage ratio was the best way to stem capital declines in Europe. If we were worried about international competitiveness, we should be trying to increase capital in Europe, not decrease it here. I thought we at least had an understanding that they wouldn't try to undermine me, particularly since Nout was sympathetic.

However, shortly before the Mérida meeting, I had a conference call with Nout. He warned me that the Germans, French, and EU were up in arms about my proposing an international leverage ratio and that he wouldn't be able to support me. He also told me that he suspected the other U.S. regulators were encouraging the opposition. He specifically mentioned that John Dugan was letting Basel Committee members know that the other U.S. regulators did not support my initiative. That was amazing to me. After putting a gun to my head to implement a capital accord that they knew would lead to significant capital reductions at U.S. banks, the Fed and OCC weren't even willing to stand aside and let us take a shot at getting something going with an international leverage ratio. Undeterred, I told Nout that I still wanted to bring it up.

I will never forget walking into the large, brightly lit conference room at the Mérida hotel where we were staying on October 4, 2006. With me I had Jason Cave, who had armed me with compelling arguments surrounding the problem of declining capital and variations among nations implementing Basel II. It was roasting hot in Mérida, and I wore a sleeveless linen dress. I had underestimated the Mexicans' penchant for air-conditioning. It was freezing in the room, and of course everyone else was dressed in long-sleeved business suits. With every ounce of physical control I had, I kept my body from shivering, terrified that my international colleagues would view the slightest tremor not as a reaction to the sixty-degree temperature but as fear and nervousness in confronting them. I knew I was going to be alone, but what I had to say needed to be said. If they were going to continue to forge ahead with the lunacy that was Basel II, I was going to at least make it uncomfortable for them.

So I laid it all out. I talked about the importance of capital to financial stability, I talked about the risks of leaving capital adequacy too much to banks' discretion, I talked about the risks of low capital in periods of economic distress, I talked about the dangers of a "race to the bottom" in capital standards and all of the studies that had been conducted showing that the advanced approaches under Basel II would lead to jaw-dropping capital reductions.

Nout was right. They didn't take it well. Danièle Nouy, the head banking regulator from France, led the assault, basically asking who did I think I was, trying to undermine an international agreement that had been years in the making? (Looking back, I think a major obstacle to international regulators' acknowledging the problems with Basel II was that they had spent so much time on it that they did not want to admit they had made a mistake and all those years of effort had been a waste.) But Danièle's remarks were tame compared to those of Patrick Pearson, the representative from the European Union, who used the meeting as a platform to launch into an anti-U.S. diatribe. Germany also weighed in (though I think strategically they had wanted Danièle to take the lead so the assault would not appear to be gender-biased). I was disappointed that Daniel Zuberbühler of Switzerland also piled on, suggesting that the leverage ratio was a "stone age" measure. (Daniel later recanted and became a supporter of an international leverage ratio. He showed a lot of courage in changing his position, and his support was pivotal when the Basel Committee finally approved a leverage ratio in 2010.) My fellow U.S. regulators remained stone silent.

I returned to my hotel room that evening, saddened and frustrated by how the meeting had gone and deeply disappointed that my U.S. colleagues were undermining my efforts. I had clearly made myself unpopular at that first meeting and wasn't sure what I had achieved in return. But I took solace in the fact that I did what I thought was right. Fortunately, my son, Preston, who had accompanied me on the trip, greeted me back at the hotel with enthusiastic stories about a tour he had taken of the rain forest that day. Listening to his vivid descriptions of the exotic birds and plants he had seen on the tour helped me put the unpleasant meeting out of my mind for a few hours. Even though it was expensive for our family to cover their travel costs, I tried to take one of my kids with me whenever I traveled, and Preston, already a seasoned traveler at thirteen, was always up for a trip.

As bad as the Mérida meeting was, I did get one thing out of it. Nout was able to engineer agreement on a "stock-taking" exercise to review how Basel II was being implemented, its impact on capital levels, variations among banks in the capital treatment of the same or similar assets, and whether "supplemental capital measures" (a euphemism for the leverage ratio) were warranted. The study at least kept the issue alive, albeit on the back burner. Nout and I had breakfast the next morning with Klaas Knot, Nout's successor as the president of the Dutch central bank, where we hammered out the language describing this review. Later that day, I mentioned the agreement in a speech I gave to an international regulatory group on the need for a global leverage ratio. Nout told me later that a number of Basel Committee members had reacted very angrily to my speech.

A few days after the Mérida meeting, there was a scathing article in *The Economist* that I suspected had been leaked by the Germans. The article essentially said that I was trying to derail "a seven-year mission to make the world's banks more efficient," suggested that I was a "Luddite," and called the Mérida meeting a "frank exchange of views." That was my first experience with press leaks coming out of the Basel Committee. It was a complete blindside. We called *The Economist* and complained vigorously about its failure to contact us and get our perspective. Later, *The Economist* would come our way in understanding the folly of Basel II. As the media would eventually turn against them, Basel II proponents would accuse us of leaking to the press, though we never did. Our policy was not to initiate any discussion of the Basel meetings. We would respond to leaks by others only to make sure our perspective was heard. Ironically, I think that helped us with the media. Reporters live for leaks, but I don't think they respect those who try to manipulate them with selective divulgence of sensitive information. We never played that game but would respond with only corrections when reporters called with misinformation leaked by others. That policy served us well throughout the crisis.

Meanwhile, in the United States, political pressure was mounting to let the major commercial banks and thrifts start implementing Basel II. In June 2004, the Securities and Exchange Commission (SEC) had given investment banks the authority to start using Basel II as an alternative to the traditional net capital rules that had imposed hard-and-fast capital requirements on those institutions. Predictably, the Basel II rules were permitting the investment banks to take on significantly more leverage, prompting outcries from the commercial banks and thrifts that that too was putting them at a competitive disadvantage. That action by the SEC was later widely credited as leading investment banks to take on excess leverage, which in turn contributed to the downfall of the investment houses Bear Stearns, Lehman

Brothers, and Merrill Lynch. SEC Commissioner Harvey Goldschmid prophetically stated at the time, "If anything goes wrong, it's going to be an awfully big mess."

In addition, New York Senator Charles Schumer and New York City Mayor Michael Bloomberg commissioned a high-profile study by McKinsey & Company, a major New York–based consulting firm, on financial regulation and the competitiveness of the U.S. financial system. The study consisted primarily of a survey of big-bank CEOs. Not surprisingly, their report, issued in January 2007, gave a ringing endorsement to full implementation of the Basel II capital accord as well as transitioning to European-style principles-based regulation. (Not so prominent in the report was the fact that McKinsey & Company provided the models and consulting services that big banks could use to implement the Basel II advanced approaches.)

The McKinsey report was followed by a letter from Senators Schumer and Mike Crapo (R–Idaho) in mid-March to the four banking regulators, calling upon us to write a "harmonized, balanced" rule to implement Basel II that would put U.S. banks onto a "more equal footing" with international competitors. Amazingly, the letter criticized the safeguards the FDIC had insisted upon, including the 10 percent cap on capital reductions, as "redundant" and argued that limitations on capital reductions should be imposed only during the transition period. We also started receiving subtle inquiries from the Treasury Department about where things stood on Basel II implementation. Treasury officials did not weigh in on the substance of the debate but made clear that they wanted an agreement to move forward.

Undeterred, I continued to speak out against Basel II and on June 25, 2007, delivered a major speech to a conference of bank risk managers in Paris. By that point, delinquencies and defaults on subprime mortgages were rising significantly. I pointed out that the Basel II approach assumed low mortgage default rates because historically that had been the case. Indeed, studies that the FDIC and other regulators had conducted of Basel II's impact showed that the amount of capital banks would hold against mortgages would decrease by a whopping 64 percent, with some banks seeing a 90 percent reduction. Did we really want to see such precipitous drops in capital just as the housing market was turning and delinquencies and defaults were spiking up?

The speech drew a sharp rebuke from Senator Schumer. On June 28, he sent a letter to me, stating "I believe your determination to keep complex, financial institutions tethered to the outdated Basel I standards actually jeopardizes the safety, soundness, efficiency, and competitiveness of our markets" and further that "I do not agree that more capital is always better, particularly where banks create strong systems to internalize their risks." The letter concluded with an open invitation to call him, which I did. We ended up having a short meeting; in a bit of irony, his office asked that I meet him at the headquarters of the Democratic Senatorial Campaign Committee, the fund-raising arm of Senate Democrats, which he then chaired. Accompanied by Eric Spitler, my senior legislative aide, I met Schumer in the lobby of the campaign committee and walked to the Capitol as he was late for another meeting. I had to walk fast to keep up with him, while breathlessly explaining that we needed to maintain caps on capital reductions until we had a better understanding of how the accord could impact financial stability. He waved us off at the bottom of the Capitol steps. Eric and I dejectedly walked back to our car. I knew I might be making an enemy of Schumer, a powerful member of the Senate Banking Committee, and that worried me. But I couldn't back down. If I did, the big banks we insured would seize the opportunity to take on more leverage, further destabilizing a financial system that was already showing signs of stress.

Negotiations among the four banking regulators continued. Though John Reich initially had been in the middle and sympathetic to some of the FDIC's positions, he began to ally with the other regulators once the head of the largest thrift that he regulated, Washington Mutual, started weighing in. (WaMu, a major player in high-risk mortgage lending, later failed.) Even with the safeguards we had built into the rule, WaMu would have experienced a capital reduction of $2.4 billion under Basel II. Without the caps, its capital reductions would have been even higher. WaMu CEO Kerry Killinger was actively lobbying us on the issue.

Fortunately, the cavalry arrived in the form of Senate Banking Committee Chairman Christopher Dodd (D–Conn.) and ranking Republican member Richard Shelby (R–Ala.). During a July 19, 2007, oversight hearing with Federal Reserve Board Chairman Ben Bernanke, both of those senators asked highly pointed questions regarding the Basel II accord and its likely impact on capital levels. Dodd repeatedly emphasized that he felt it was important for all the regulators to agree on the same standard, which was of tremendous help given Fed and OCC threats to go their own way if we kept holding out. Shelby pressed hard on the prospect of capital reductions and how that would impact financial stability. He reminded Chairman Bernanke of all the poorly capitalized savings and loans that had failed during the S&L crisis and cautioned that he didn't want problems landing in the lap of Congress in the future.

That helped.

Shortly after the hearing, I received a call from Ben suggesting that he come to my office to see if the two of us could hammer out an agreement.

At 4:30 on the afternoon of July 19, I sat down at my computer with Ben standing at my side, and we hammered out a compromise. It was my first experience working directly with Ben, and it portended positive future dealings. Unlike others in the regulatory community—whose first tactic was always to try to strong-arm us—Ben would listen to our concerns and try to find ways to address them.

Under our agreement, the FDIC would agree to give up the 10 percent aggregate cap, but in return, the 15 percent cap on individual banks' capital reductions would remain in place unless and until all four banking regulators issued a public report finding that there were no "material deficiencies" in the framework. My hope was that if Basel II had the outcomes we had predicted (and that were already becoming apparent with their implementation by European banks and U.S. investment banks), there was no way that the bank regulators would issue such a report. They would likely err on the side of caution and just leave the caps in place. The important point was that the caps would not automatically come off. If the bank regulators wanted to entertain capital reductions beyond 15 percent, they would have to get all of the agencies to issue a public report defending that step before it occurred.

Ben asked me to circulate the agreement to the other regulators, which I did. Since we were removing the 10 percent aggregate cap, I assumed that the other regulators would be pleased. Instead, the agreement was met with anger by both John Dugan and Randy Kroszner, who had replaced Sue Bies as the Fed's point person on Basel. Dugan insisted on language that would let the OCC move ahead with capital reductions even if the other regulators thought the accord was flawed. Since the OCC already had the legal authority to do so—the other bank regulators could not bind it—we agreed so long as the OCC agreed to publicly explain its reasons for letting bank capital drop more than 15 percent. I think the real problem with both Dugan and Kroszner was that Ben and I had worked out an agreement without them. Dugan had always viewed the FDIC as "third tier" behind the Fed and OCC, and I don't think he liked the precedent of the FDIC chairman working directly with the chairman of the Fed. Similarly, I think that Kroszner felt I had gone around him, which I had, but at the behest of his own chairman.

In any event, the agreement broke the impasse, and we moved ahead with a final rule. But I did not let up in my public criticism of Basel II as we continued to watch capital levels at European banks and U.S. investment banks decline. In the end, we were victorious. By December 2007, the weight of market opinion had swung our way, as the subprime crisis was renewing concern about the adequacy of the banking system's capital base. Given heightened scrutiny by both the media and financial analysts of U.S. investment banks and European banks' increasing leverage under Basel II, the Fed and OCC decided to take it slow. To this day, not a single commercial bank or thrift has ever used Basel II to set its capital requirements, and the Dodd-Frank financial reform law essentially killed Basel II as a means of reducing big bank capital. Randy Kroszner's term at the Fed expired in a short time, and he was eventually replaced by Daniel Tarullo, who as a professor at Georgetown Law School had been an outspoken critic of Basel II. I was not happy with the fact that it had taken an impending crisis to put the final brakes on the Basel II experiment. But the fact that the FDIC had delayed for so long meant that going into the crisis, FDIC-insured banking organizations' capital levels stayed at about 8 percent, while investment banks and European banks implementing Basel II approached levels as low as 2 percent.

CHAPTER 4

The Skunk at the Garden Party

In the interagency discussions that occurred early in my tenure, I frequently found myself isolated in advocating for stronger regulatory standards. I never viewed myself as "regulatory." I thought my advocacy for things such as stronger capital and better lending standards was just common sense. However, the deeper I got into interagency discussions, the more convinced I became that the OTS and OCC generally took whatever positions were most advantageous to their larger institutions. That meant that sometimes they would support stronger standards if they thought the impact would be to hurt institutions regulated by other regulators. With the Fed, it was more ideological. Though Ben Bernanke would ultimately steer the Fed toward more balanced regulatory policies, in 2006 and 2007, that agency still had a strong love affair with relying on market forces to "self-regulate."

When I arrived at the FDIC, the banking regulators had already proposed for public comment two pieces of "regulatory guidance" designed to address increasing risks in commercial real estate (CRE) lending and so-called nontraditional mortgages (NTMs). By far the most important fights would be waged over tightening mortgage-lending standards. However, because the commercial real estate lending guidance provides insights into bank regulators' decision making, I include a brief discussion of it here.

John Dugan had spearheaded both pieces of guidance and had come in for his share of criticism from many in the industry who were content with the status quo. I respected John for trying to tighten regulatory standards in those two key areas and was offended by the heat he was taking both in the media and on Capitol Hill. However, as I became more deeply involved in interagency negotiations to finalize both documents, I came to realize that both documents had been drafted in a way that would not have much of an impact on the big national banks the OCC regulated. Rather, the primary impact of the CRE guidance would fall on small community banks, while large West Coast thrifts regulated by the OTS were the primary target of the NTM guidance. So the OCC was pushing tougher regulatory standards, but the standards did little to address risk taking by the biggest national banks.

To be sure, the OCC was correct in focusing on CRE lending. Commercial real estate was overheating in tandem with the overheated housing market. Far too many banks, large and small, were funding speculative residential housing developments, as well as strip malls and office buildings tied to those developments. CRE loan balances had grown from about 7 percent of bank assets in 2002 to nearly 15 percent of bank assets in 2006. The quality of that type of lending had deteriorated markedly, with lending decisions being based too often on inflated land values rather than a developer's documented ability to pay.

However, the CRE guidance that had been proposed for comment before I arrived focused primarily on CRE lending concentrations, as opposed to underwriting quality. That is, it discouraged banks from making commercial real estate loans that exceeded 300 percent of a bank's capital. It had a tougher requirement for construction and development (C&D) loans: 100 percent of capital. The lower threshold on C&D loans made sense to me. They were typically made on high-risk, speculative land developments where the bank had to wait until the project was built and sold or leased out before it knew whether the loan would be repaid. However, loans on income-producing commercial real estate—hotels, office buildings, shopping malls, multifamily apartment buildings, and so on—were far less speculative and generally performed well.

Bank examiners do not like concentrations for the same reason that you do not put all of your retirement savings into a single stock or a single sector. For instance, you wouldn't invest your entire 401(k) in Google, nor would you put it all into technology stocks (at least I hope you wouldn't). If Google or the technology sector gets into trouble, you could lose most or all of your savings. In contrast, if you have your retirement money spread among a diversified group of investments, your risk of taking a big loss on a single investment goes down. That is why index funds and well-diversified stock mutual funds are so popular with retirement investors.

For similar reasons, bank regulators put fairly strict limits on a bank making a lot of loans to a single borrower. That makes sense. However, it gets trickier when regulators try to limit concentrations in a category of assets such as CRE loans. There are many different types of developments that count as commercial real estate, and just because one sector might get into trouble, e.g., housing developments, that doesn't mean that another sector, e.g., hotels, will also suffer problems. Moreover, because thousands of community banks tend to specialize in commercial real estate lending, any limits based on the size of their portfolios relative to their capital will impact them disproportionately. A large bank may be making the same number of commercial real estate loans, and in fact its loans might be higher risk. But if the regulatory approach is to focus more on concentrations than loan quality, the large bank will escape scrutiny. That is because it has huge portfolios of other loans—credit cards, home mortgages, and commercial and industrial loans, to name just a few—so that the proportion of its commercial real estate loans in relation to its capital will be relatively small.

In retrospect, I wish we had focused less on concentration and more on loan quality. Once the crisis hit, the myth that large banks were less risky because they had diversified loan portfolios proved to be just that: a myth. All of their portfolios suffered losses. And as it turned out, the quality and performance of the commercial real estate loans made by the smallest community banks were better than those originated by larger institutions.

That was a prime example of how regulatory policy can have a disproportionate competitive impact on the industry. As examiners began enforcing the guidance, smaller banks were required to either reduce their CRE concentrations or put in better risk management controls. Meanwhile, the larger banks with which they had to compete for CRE loans did not come under the same scrutiny because they did not have CRE concentrations. The guidance did at least focus examiners on weaknesses in commercial real estate and probably averted some CRE-driven failures among smaller, weaker institutions. But we could have accomplished a better result with a heavier focus on loan quality for all banks, large and small.

We finalized the CRE guidance in December 2006, but the bigger battles on mortgage-lending standards were still to be fought. The guidance on nontraditional mortgages did focus on underwriting and risk management standards, but it had a different problem. Specifically, it applied only to loans that had what is called "negative amortization" features, that is, loans where the monthly payment was not sufficient to reduce the principal. Those types of loans, also known as "option ARMs" or "pick a pay," were popular with the major West Coast thrift institutions, including WaMu, Countrywide, and Golden West, all regulated by the OTS. The big national banks, for the most part, did not originate them. The mortgages were typically structured to provide borrowers with the option of making extremely low payments during the first five years of the mortgage term, during which time the principal balances would actually increase. At the end of the five years, they would have to start paying a higher interest rate and also have to start paying down the entire accumulated principal, so the "payment shock" of the loans was substantial.

Traditionally, NTM loans were made to borrowers with higher net worth or good credit scores; however, with the housing craze, their availability had become widespread. At the heart of the guidance was a requirement that before making that type of loan, the bank or thrift had to qualify the borrower at the fully indexed rate. That essentially meant that the lender had to determine whether the borrower's income would be sufficient to cover the mortgage payment when the loan reset and the borrower had to start both paying a higher interest rate and paying down the accumulated principal. It was not sufficient to simply determine whether the borrower could manage the smaller payment during the introductory period.

I strongly supported this as a basic principle of good underwriting, the process of determining whether a borrower qualifies for a loan. But I questioned why we were limiting the guidance only to loans that had negative amortization. That essentially excluded the entire subprime market, which was characterized by the notorious hybrid ARMs also known as 2/28s and 3/27s. And it was with the subprime loans, not NTMs, where we were seeing the biggest problems. By the end of 2006, subprime loan delinquencies were over 13 percent, while NTM delinquencies stood at only 4 percent. Subprime loans did not have negative amortization, but they did have steep payment resets. It seemed obvious to me that we should also require originators of those products to qualify borrowers at the fully indexed rate.

Subprime hybrid ARMs were a noxious product. They were typically marketed in lower-income communities to more vulnerable borrowers. Even the "starter rates" were set significantly above market during the first two to three years, with huge interest rate resets after the starter period. In 2006 and early 2007, our data showed that the typical starter rate was 7% to 9%, with an interest rate jump of 4 to 6 percentage points after two to three years. That meant that the borrower was paying a rate of 11% to 15% on his mortgage, representing a payment increase of one-third. Our data also showed that even at the lower starter rate, borrowers could barely make the payments. The monthly payments (excluding taxes and insurance) on those loans commonly made up 40 to 50 percent of gross income, so borrowers had very little chance of making the higher payment once the interest rate reset. But that was the whole idea. Unable to afford the higher payment, the subprime borrowers would refinance over and over into another 2/28 or

3/27, generating successive rounds of high fees for the originators. It was the mortgage equivalent of churning.

Those fees included not only the usual costs associated with refinancing. In about 80 percent of hybrid ARM contracts, the fine print also imposed prepayment penalties. Those payments could be severe, typically 1 to 3 percent of the loan balance. Some of the more abusive lenders required borrowers to pay prepayment penalties even after the interest rate reset. More commonly, the prepayment penalties expired at the end of the starter period. However, if the borrower was not careful in timing the refinancing, he or she could get still get whacked with a prepayment penalty. The option ARMs addressed in the NTM guidance were bad products, but subprime hybrid ARMs were worse, and that is where we were seeing the biggest problems. But the OCC, supported by the Fed, flatly refused to amend the NTM guidance to apply to subprime mortgages. One of the reasons, I suspected at the time, was that some of the biggest national banking organizations generated a substantial number of subprime loans, though national banks typically did not originate NTMs.

Helped by public pressure from consumer groups and key members of Congress, the FDIC was finally able to convince the other bank regulators to move forward with guidance strengthening subprime lending standards, but the OCC and Fed wanted it done separately from the NTM guidance. So we finalized the NTM guidance in September 2006, and it was not until June 2007 that we were able to finalize stronger standards for subprime lending. We wrangled with the other regulators for months on the strength of the standards. Curiously, though the OCC had insisted on a very specific standard for the NTM guidance, requiring lenders to make sure that the borrower could make the mortgage payment at the fully indexed rate, they wanted a more vague "ability to repay" standard for subprime loans. Steven Fritts, our lead negotiator, advised me in an email in January 2007 that the OCC had said it would be a deal killer if that weren't included. In addition, the Fed was fighting us on restricting prepayment penalties. It was not uncommon for the OCC and Fed to team up against the FDIC, dividing the issues among them. So, as if fighting a hydra-headed monster, we would get agreement with one on one issue, and then the other would come out of the woodwork with a completely different concern and so on.

Also slowing down the process was heavy lobbying from nonbank mortgage lenders, which did the bulk of the subprime lending. Though they were not FDIC-insured institutions, they feared—rightly so—that once federal bank regulators tightened standards for insured banks, the state regulators that regulated them would follow course and do the same. On January 25, 2006, a whole army of them came to see me to try to convince me that we shouldn't issue subprime guidance. Calling themselves the Coalition for Fair and Affordable Housing, they argued that the increasing delinquency rates among subprime mortgages were simply a reflection of economic conditions, not poor underwriting. They also engaged in a good deal of borrower bashing. I remember one lobbyist quite seriously saying that borrowers didn't care as much as they used to about paying their mortgage. "If they need to buy a new washing machine, they will do that instead of paying their mortgage," he said. I was incredulous. If borrowers were having to make such trade-offs, it might be because the lenders were giving them mortgages they could barely afford.

The lobbyists were right in one sense. Economic conditions were causing borrowers to default on their mortgages. But that was because they had been given loans that were unaffordable at reset and, with declining home values, refinancing was no longer an option. That was exactly why we wanted lenders to qualify borrowers based on their ability to pay at the fully indexed rate so that we could be sure the borrower could continue making payments on the loan without having to resort to refinancing.

While on the one hand bashing subprime borrowers, the lobbyists also complained that by tightening standards on hybrid ARMs, we would be constricting credit to lower-income borrowers. They argued that the lower interest rate subprime borrowers received during the two- to three-year introductory period qualified more low-income borrowers to buy homes. I had heard the same argument from the Fed and OCC, and it really sent me through the roof. We had closely analyzed the terms sheets of several of the mortgage bankers and found that the thirty-year fixed rate they offered subprime borrowers was typically lower than or about the same as the so-called teaser rate they offered on hybrid ARMs. Hybrid ARMs were not being offered to expand credit through lower introductory payments; they were purposefully designed to be unaffordable, to force borrowers into a series of refinancings and the fat fees that went along with them.

In February 2007, after months of discussions, I sent an email to Dugan, Kroszner, and Reich pleading urgency in issuing the subprime guidance and stating flatly that we would not agree to a standard that was weaker than that applied to NTMs. Driven primarily by soaring delinquency rates among subprime hybrid ARMs, late mortgage payments had reached a

three-and-a-half-year high, and the foreclosure rate had more than doubled, from 2.2 percent to 4.8 percent. Twenty nonbank subprime lenders—
still the smaller players at that point—had gone under. I felt that we were
already falling well behind the curve. I took a page out of the playbook
the OCC and Fed had used during the Basel discussions: I threatened that
the FDIC would go its own way and issue separate, stronger guidance if
we could not get interagency agreement to move forward. It worked. On
March 2, all the regulators agreed to publish the guidance for comment, and
we finalized it on June 29. That might seem like a long time, but for bank
regulators, it was lightning speed.

We were able to get the OCC to agree to apply the same "fully indexed
rate" standard we had used in the NTM guidance. I argued, successfully,
that it made no sense and would be confusing to banks as well as consumers
to have differing standards, depending on whether the bank was originating a nontraditional mortgage or a subprime loan. But we had a particularly
hard fight with Randy Kroszner at the Fed over prepayment penalties. I felt
that the penalties were anticompetitive and arguably discriminatory, as they
were not used with prime borrowers. From a safety and soundness perspective, we did not want hybrid ARM borrowers locked out of refinancing as
home prices continued to decline. In the end, we compromised on language
providing that prepayment penalties should expire no later than sixty days
before the interest rate reset.

Unfortunately, it was too late for the guidance to have a major impact.
For one thing, much of the damage had already been done. By the second quarter of 2007, subprime loans outstanding totaled $1.3 trillion. For
another, both the subprime and NTM guidance documents were enforced
unevenly by the regulators, particularly the OTS and state regulators that
had authority over nonbank lenders. The FDIC was the primary regulator
for only one major subprime lender, Fremont Investment & Loan, which we
chased out of the subprime business in February 2007, well before the guidance was finalized. By doing so, we averted what would have been a costly
failure. But instead of cracking down on thrifts doing high-cost mortgage
lending, the OTS let a number of them grow their portfolios of subprime
and NTM loans. By the summer of 2007, the major nonbank mortgage
lenders such as New Century and Ameriquest were starting to fail. Unbelievably, OTS was allowing its major thrifts to pick up a lot of their business.
Insured thrifts actually grew their mortgage loan balances from $727 billion
at the end of 2006 to $795 billion by the third quarter of 2007. All of the

high-risk mortgage lenders regulated by the OTS eventually failed or were acquired. Their losses were massive. None survived, and the OTS itself was abolished by Congress.

The subprime lending abuses could have been avoided if the Federal Reserve Board had simply used the authority it had since 1994 under the Home Ownership Equity Protection Act (HOEPA) to promulgate mortgage-lending standards across the board. The Fed was the only government agency with the authority to prescribe mortgage-lending standards for banks and nonbanks. As the Financial Crisis Inquiry Commission (FCIC) concluded in its 2011 report:

> There was an explosion in risky subprime lending and securitization, an unsustainable rise in housing prices, widespread reports of egregious and predatory lending practices, dramatic increases in household mortgage debt. . . . Yet there was pervasive permissiveness; little meaningful action was taken to quell the threats in a timely manner.
>
> The prime example is the Federal Reserve's pivotal failure to stem the flow of toxic mortgages, which it could have done by setting prudent mortgage-lending standards. The Federal Reserve was the one entity empowered to do so and it did not.

In March 2007, I testified strongly in favor of the Fed issuing an anti-predatory lending regulation under HOEPA; it was a step that consumer advocates such as Martin Eakes had been pushing for years. I could barely contain my anger when the Fed's witness countered with a go-slow approach. Disregarding the pronounced deterioration of the subprime market, she argued that the Fed needed to do a "careful review" and it was concerned about "constraining responsible credit." In July 2008, Chairman Bernanke would finally direct the reluctant Fed staff to promulgate HOEPA regulations, which would take effect at the beginning of 2009. By that time, though, the damage was done. Ben publicly acknowledged that their failure to act earlier had been a key shortcoming in the Fed's handling of the crisis. Why did the Fed delay? As Fed General Counsel Scott Alvarez put it, "The mind-set was that there should be no regulation; the market should take care of policing, unless there already is an identified problem. . . . We were in the reactive mode because that's what the mind-set was of the '90s and the early 2000s."

CHAPTER 5

Subprime Is "Contained"

The resistance we encountered from other regulators in tightening up subprime lending standards was symptomatic of their early tendency to discount the severity of the potential problems. Even into 2008, both the Fed and Treasury (of which the OCC and OTS were a part) downplayed potential systemic risks from the subprime debacle.

At the FDIC, we were not so sanguine. Richard Brown, our chief economist, and Christopher Newbury, the head of our risk analysis research unit, had been monitoring the performance of housing generally and subprime loans in particular. At a briefing for me in October 2006, they presented troubling data. The performance of subprime mortgages was deteriorating markedly. At the same time, insured banks' purchase of securities backed by these loans was increasing.

Unfortunately, their analysis was hampered by a lack of data: our information systems were limited to loans FDIC-insured banks held on their balance sheets. Since most of the subprime and other high-risk loans were being sold into Wall Street securitizations by both bank and nonbank mortgage originators, it was necessary to purchase information about those loans from private vendors. I authorized purchase of a private database, and once we had the data, our analysis of it confirmed the staff's worst fears. The loans were a true parade of horribles: lack of documented income, little if any down payments, steep interest rate adjustments, abusive prepayment penalties, and mortgage payments that frequently exceeded 50 percent of the borrower's gross income.

I couldn't believe it. When I had served at the Treasury Department in 2001–2002, I had worked with the late Ned Gramlich on predatory lending practices in lower-income neighborhoods. At the time, Ned was a governor with the Federal Reserve Board and had responsibility for consumer issues. Consumer groups were reporting increasing instances of unregulated, nonbank mortgage brokers entering lower-income neighborhoods and "push marketing" mortgages with steep payment resets, negative amortization, and exorbitant prepayment penalties. Those were not "affordability" loans. Rather, the brokers frequently targeted existing home owners who had built equity in their homes, convincing them to pull cash out of their houses by refinancing their safe thirty-year fixed mortgages into complex subprime mortgages. The brokers were not banks and thus fell outside the lending standards applicable to insured institutions. Some were affiliated with banks, but the Fed had not used its authority over bank affiliates to examine the brokers for abusive practices, even though Ned had pushed Chairman Greenspan to do so.

In 2000, the Treasury Department and the Department of Housing and Urban Development (HUD) had issued a report recommending stronger lending standards for both bank and nonbank mortgage originators. The report suggested that either Congress enact a law to address mortgage-lending abuses for both banks and nonbanks or the Fed use the authority it had under HOEPA to establish marketwide lending standards. Notwithstanding Ned's concerns, the Fed was disinclined to use its rule-making authority, and the industry had successfully stopped antipredatory lending proposals on Capitol Hill. In 2005, Congressmen Barney Frank and Spencer Bachus (R–Ala.) tried to put together a bipartisan effort to establish national lending standards. However, the effort met stiff opposition from the industry, which complained to the Republican leadership. Bachus was forced to stop negotiating with Frank under pressure from the House GOP leadership. Similarly, Senator Paul Sarbanes's efforts to pass a national antipredatory lending law were stymied by industry lobbying efforts.

In the face of federal inaction, a number of state legislatures had enacted antipredatory lending laws that were helping somewhat. However, the OTS gave the thrifts that it regulated "field preemption," meaning that its regulation of mortgage lending prevailed over state laws and those laws, for the most part, could be ignored by the national thrifts. When I served at Treasury, the OCC was considering giving the national banks it regulated the same broad preemption. I received briefings from Julie Williams, the OCC's general counsel, on its plans, as well as from the comptroller, Jerry Hawke. As I was assistant secretary for financial institutions, they were obliged to consult me on banking policy issues. (By contrast, there were strict firewalls between the OCC and the Treasury Department regarding supervisory matters for particular institutions, as was appropriate.)

I had no authority other than to give the OCC my views, but that I did, and I didn't mince words. I thought that preempting state consumer mortgage-lending laws was a singularly bad idea, particularly since the OCC had failed to promulgate any rules of its own to address the abuses we were seeing. The states were trying to protect their citizenry against a growing array of harmful lending practices. Unless the OCC was going to promulgate standards providing the same level of protection, I didn't think it should be getting in the states' way. In taking that position, I was given strong support by two of my career staff Treasury advisers, Edward DeMarco and Mario Ugoletti. We were highly skeptical of the OCC's objectives and suspected that by expanding the scope of state preemption, the OCC hoped that large, state-regulated banks such as JPMorgan Chase would "flip" their charters and become national banks. The OCC backed off its proposal while I was in office, but in 2003, after I left the Treasury, it moved ahead. Sure enough, soon thereafter, JPMorgan Chase switched from being chartered by New York State to being OCC-regulated.

Ned and I worked together to convince the major mortgage lenders to agree to a set of best practices that would address the steep payment resets and lack of affordability. But the agreement was voluntary, and it did not hold. By 2006, practices that Ned and I had viewed as predatory in 2001 had become mainstream among most major mortgage lenders. How could things have deteriorated so quickly in five years?

In a word, securitization.

In its most basic form, the securitization process involves an issuer—typically a major financial institution—that accumulates a large volume of residential mortgages. The issuer might originate the mortgages itself, or it might obtain them from other lenders or independent mortgage brokers. Working with a Wall Street investment bank, the issuer packages the mortgages together into "pools" and divides the right to the cash flows of those mortgages into securities that are sold to investors, typically institutional investors such as pension funds, mutual funds, hedge funds, and insurance companies, as well as Fannie Mae and Freddie Mac (more about them later). The securities are sold from different "tranches." That simply means that the securities are grouped into different priorities for payment of the cash received from the mortgage payments. The top, or more senior, securities must be paid in full before the lower, or more junior, securities receive any payments. As a result, if some of the mortgages in the pool default, investors holding the junior tranches will suffer losses first, protecting investors holding the senior tranches.

Here is a highly simplified example. Issuer X pools $1 billion worth of mortgages into a securitization and divides the pool into three tranches. To keep the math simple, let's say that if all the mortgages perform, they will produce $100 million a year in mortgage payments. Investors in the top tranche of the securitization buy securities that promise $80 million of the cash flows each year, and under the terms of the securitization, they must be paid before any other investors. Investors in the second tranche, commonly called the "mezzanine" tranche, buy securities promising $10 million of the annual cash flows. They are paid only after the top tranche has received all of their expected proceeds. Investors in the bottom, or "equity," tranche hold an interest in the remaining $10 million in cash flows. However, they are paid last. Investors in the mezzanine and equity tranches will pay less for their shares, as they have more risk than the top tranche. If any of the loans in the pool starts to default, the cash flows to the equity- and mezzanine-tranche investors are reduced before the upper-tranche investors are impacted. So it would seem that the upper tranche has substantial protection: loans representing more than 20 percent of the cash flows would have to default before their payments would be reduced. And prior to 2006, mortgage loans had historically very low default rates, less than 2 percent.

That extra level of protection for the top or senior tranches, known as "overcollateralization," was the primary reason the ratings agencies routinely gave them triple-A ratings. Unfortunately, neither the investors nor the ratings agencies looked down into the pools to adequately analyze the quality of the individual loans in them. (And in fairness, the SEC did not require detailed loan-level disclosure and enough time for investors to analyze the disclosures before they invested, a problem it is now trying to correct.) If they had, they would have seen what we saw when we bought our data: little income documentation, high debt-to-income ratios, and steep, unaffordable payment resets. The "affordability" of the loans was determined based on borrowers' ability to refinance or flip the property, not on a documented income capacity to pay. Thus, as the housing market turned and home prices started to decline, massive defaults could be expected.

The ratings agencies and investors did not do their homework. But what about the financial institutions originating the loans? Why didn't they do a better job? Well, ask yourself: if you ran a business where you could sell a product and be paid up front, while suffering no losses regardless of how defective the product might be, how would that impact your behavior? From a purely economic standpoint, you would generate as much volume as possible to maximize your income. And that is exactly what happened.

Prior to securitization, mortgage lending was dominated by banks and thrifts, which would use customers' deposits to make and hold mortgages to their customers. They were careful about loan quality because if a mortgage went bad, the loss was theirs. But with the advent of securitization, the funding came from investors, not depositors, so a bank—or a balance sheet—wasn't required to make a mortgage loan. Stand-alone, nonbank mortgage lenders, such as the defunct Option One and New Century, churned out mortgages funded by immediate sale of the loans into securitizations. The lenders were virtually unregulated. Poorly trained and equally unsupervised mortgage brokers popped up all over the country, particularly in "hot" housing areas such as Florida, Nevada, and California. The brokers would originate the mortgages and sell them to a nonbank lender. The lender would get a short-term loan—frequently from a large national bank or thrift—to fund the mortgage for the home owner. The lender would then pay the loan back once the mortgage was sold to a securitization set up by a Wall Street investment bank and immediately pocket the rest of the securitization proceeds as profits.

The short-term loans made by commercial banks and thrifts were called "warehouse" loans, and they were permitted by banking regulators because the institutions held risk for a very short time period before the loans were repaid from securitization proceeds. In that indirect way, a number of large national banks and thrifts helped fuel the subprime crisis, even though they did not originate the loans. The FDIC pushed to have the subprime and NTM guidance apply to loans that banks and thrifts funded through warehouse loans, but the idea was strongly opposed by the industry and resisted by the other regulators.

Some FDIC-insured banks and thrifts also originated their own subprime and NTM loans, which were of somewhat higher quality than those purchased from independent mortgage brokers. But there again, economic incentives to assure good-quality underwriting were weak because the banks were selling the loans and passing on the risk of future default to investors through securitizations. Regulators and accountants also gave banks incentives to securitize loans. If they kept the loans in their own portfolios, they would have to hold capital and reserves against them to protect against potential losses. If, on the other hand, they sold them into securitizations, the regulators and accountants assumed that the risk had been transferred, so there were no capital and reserve requirements.

However, at the FDIC, we were concerned that this risk transfer was illusory. When large banks and thrifts sold loans into securitization pools, the contracts typically included "reps and warranties," which obliged them to buy back a defaulting loan if it did not meet the lending standards specified in the contract. As competitive pressures to relax lending standards inten-sified, we had no confidence that the quality of bank and thrift securitized loans would be sufficient to withstand demands by investors to "put back" bad loans. In addition, even if the loans met the contractually specified stan-dards, we suspected that the major banks and thrifts would feel obliged to buy back defaulting loans to maintain their reputations with investors. Our fears were on target. So far, the major banks have bought back billions of securitized loans and, by their own estimates, face another $72 billion in litigation exposure.

Our staff was also concerned about insured banks' risk in holding the equity tranches, also known as "residuals" of the securitizations that they sponsored. Remember the 10 percent equity tranche in the above example? Frequently, a sponsoring bank would keep that tranche of securities and sell it into another securitization-type structure called a collateralized debt obli-gation (CDO). This is how it would work: a Wall Street firm would buy the equity tranches and pool them into a securitization similar to the structure it used for mortgages. That is, it would "retranche" the securities using the same technique of overcollateralization. It would then slice up the pool of those tranches, creating a new top tranche that had a priority claim on the expected cash flows, with the lower tranches having the right to any cash flows that were left after the top tranche was paid. There again, the ratings agencies would hand out triple-A ratings to the top tranche, believing that there was a very low probability that all of the equity tranches would go bad at the same time. Of course, that was a fallacious assumption—the equity tranches were the most toxic pieces of larger pools of very toxic mortgages, and they almost all did go bad.

Adding to this witch's brew of poisonous assets was the credit default swap (CDS) market. Credit default swaps are a form of protection that investors and others can buy against the risk of default on a security they own. Investors in CDOs would "wrap" them in CDS protection provided by an insurance company or derivatives dealer. (American International Group—AIG—sold a lot of that kind of protection, eventually leading to its failure and need for a bailout.)

The CDO market has been all but wiped out. Some big banks or their affiliates—Citigroup being a prime example—had a large exposure to the CDO market. And there again, the regulatory and accounting treatment of those products provided all the wrong incentives. If banks kept the equity tranches on their balance sheets, they had to hold a substantial amount of capital and reserves against them. If they sold them to a Wall Street firm to be put into a CDO and then bought back the triple-A-rated portion, the capital requirement was quite low.

Magnifying the losses was the fact that Wall Street firms created "synthetic" CDOs, which allowed big financial institutions and their trading partners to make speculative bets on how certain CDOs would perform without actually owning them. Similarly, hedge funds and other speculators could buy CDS protection against the default of mortgage-backed investments, without actually owning them. It was like a game of fantasy football, with speculators tracking and wagering money on the performance of synthetic—that is, pretend—mortgage investments. That created trillions of dollars in speculative trading, many multiples of the size of the underlying subprime mortgage market. That is why hundreds of billions of dollars' worth of mortgage losses translated into trillions of dollars of trading losses—losses that brought our financial system to its knees and caused the worst recession since the Great Depression. The accounting rules allowed many of the speculative investments to be held off balance sheet, making their risks invisible to regulators and market analysts until they started producing losses. I believe that speculative use of CDSs should be banned, given the damage they caused to our economy.

Another source of indirect exposure to the subprime mortgage market was reflected in FDIC-insured banks' and thrifts' huge holdings of securities issued or guaranteed by Fannie Mae and Freddie Mac. Fannie and Freddie, known as government-sponsored enterprises (GSEs), were created by Congress decades ago to provide support for housing finance. Fannie, like the FDIC, was a Depression-era New Deal agency. As envisioned by Congress, Fannie and Freddie were supposed to buy good-quality mortgages from mortgage lenders, package them into pools, and sell them to investors. To entice investment to support housing finance, Fannie and Freddie would guarantee continued principal and interest payments on those securities, even if the mortgages backing them went sour. Since Fannie and Freddie retained the risk that the mortgages might default, they would charge a guarantee fee from the banks and other lenders that originated and sold them the loans. Congress also required that in carrying out their mission, Fannie and Freddie support affordable housing for low- and moderate-income borrowers.

In the late 1990s and early 2000s, some people at Fannie and Freddie got the idea that they could make a lot of money by issuing bonds at very cheap interest rates (because investors assumed, given their government charter, that they were implicitly backed by the government) and using that money to invest in subprime mortgage-backed securities (MBSs) from Wall Street firms. The securities had very high rates of return (remember those 7% to 9% interest rates on 2/28s and 3/27s). By using that strategy, Fannie and Freddie operated like giant hedge funds, raising money cheaply from the debt markets (because bond investors assumed that they were backed by taxpayers) and using that cheap money to buy high-yielding mortgage-backed securities from Wall Street. For a while, Fannie and Freddie made money like crazy, paying their executives and shareholders huge bonuses and dividends. Indeed, in 2005, they gobbled up a full one-third of such securities from Wall Street. The Department of Housing and Urban Development actually encouraged them to do this by counting their investments in these toxic securities as credit in meeting "affordable housing" goals.

Insured banks and thrifts happily bought the debt the GSEs issued that supported the investment strategy, again with encouragement from the regulatory structure. That is because for decades, bank regulations viewed GSE debt as being nearly as safe as Treasury debt and thus required that banks hold very little capital against those securities. By giving banks favorable capital treatment on GSE debt, bank regulations encouraged insured institutions to fund them and reinforced the notion that the GSEs had an implicit backstop from the federal government. Of course, their investments in subprime securitizations eventually went sour, generating huge losses and forcing the GSEs into government conservatorship, where they still operate.

To sum up, between 2001 and 2006, the securitization market had exploded. Without adequate regulatory oversight, all of the economic incentives were to generate loan volume regardless of loan quality. There were no effective regulatory requirements that those who originated and securitized these loans hold any of the risk that the loans might default later on. Investors were holding the ultimate risk, but they did not do their own due diligence, nor did the ratings agencies, on which investors relied. The majority of the toxic subprime and NTM loans was originated by nonbank originators, though large banks and thrifts played a significant role. Some of the large banking organizations, most notably Citigroup, had substantial subprime operations. In addition, many large banks and thrifts provided short-term "warehouse" financing to nonbank mortgage originators making toxic subprime loans. Finally, the GSEs played a major role not by directly buying and guaranteeing subprime mortgages but after the fact, by gobbling up the senior-tranche subprime securities packaged and sold by Wall Street investment houses. Though greed was the primary motivation for the subprime craze, the government played a role by giving favorable capital and accounting treatment to banks that securitized their loans and also by giving the GSEs credit toward their affordable housing goals.

In the second quarter of 2006, when I assumed the chairmanship of the FDIC, the direct exposure of insured banks to privately issued securitization interests was not substantial: $252 billion, or about 2.2 percent of total assets. There was a temptation to take comfort from that relatively low number. Fortunately, the FDIC had had extensive experience with securitization; indeed, it had pioneered using securitization as a way to dispose of toxic assets inherited from failed banks and thrifts in the 1980s. Our staff knew all too well about put-back risk, as well as the larger dangers of steep home price declines when the housing bubble popped and the unsustainable mortgages started going bad. I think other regulators kept believing that the subprime problem was going to hit primarily the nonbank lenders that had originated most of the toxic loans; hence their public comments that the problem would be "contained." Certainly, the specialty subprime lenders were the first to go; not a one has survived on a stand-alone basis—they have either been purchased by another financial institution or have gone bankrupt. But even if their direct exposure to subprime loans was limited, insured banks had huge exposure to residential real estate in general. They held more than $4 trillion in residential real estate–backed loans, representing more than 36 percent of bank assets. Our economists understood that substantial declines in the collateral backing those loans could have severe ramifications for the banks we insured.

So we had very good reasons for aggressively pushing stronger lending standards, even though I know the other regulators resented our advocacy. They, not the FDIC, were the primary regulators of the big players in the mortgage market, and they felt we were meddling in their business. Tensions became even more pronounced when we started advocating for banks and thrifts to restructure subprime mortgages. The truth is, by the time we finalized the guidance strengthening subprime lending standards, most of the damage had been done already. By mid-2007, there were $1.8 trillion of mortgages securitized by Wall Street outstanding. More than 7.5 million U.S. households held subprime loans. Strengthening lending standards would help only prospectively. What about all the bad loans that had already been made?

There again, the FDIC staff were on top of the analysis. Having long used securitization to dispose of failed bank assets, the FDIC had some of the top experts in the field. They included James Wigand, who ran most of our failed-bank resolutions, and one of his deputies, George Alexander. Also on the team was Michael Krimminger, who served as my top legal adviser throughout the crisis. A senior FDIC attorney, Mike was one of the foremost legal experts in the area of securitizations and bank resolutions. Working with data provided by Rich Brown and his team, we decided that the toxic loans need to be restructured in scale to avoid a foreclosure crisis that would put severe downward pressure on home values and throw millions of American families out of their homes.

CHAPTER 6

Stepping over a Dollar to Pick Up a Nickel: Helping Home Owners, Round One

Loan restructuring, also known as "modification," is a time-tested tool used in the banking industry to minimize losses when a borrower runs into trouble. It is almost always the case that foreclosing on a distressed borrower—be it a business or a consumer—and seizing and liquidating the collateral will generate heavy losses for the lender. Therefore, if the terms of the loan can be changed, or modified, to make it affordable so that the borrower can resume making payments, the lender will usually mitigate its losses and realize substantially greater recoveries. Think about it. Losses on foreclosed property sales can typically approach 40 to 50 percent of unpaid principal balances. (The losses can be much higher if the distressed borrower owes significantly more than the property is worth, as is now the case with more than 10 million home owners.) That means the lender has a lot of leeway to make a significant payment reduction before it will become more profitable for it to foreclose on the loan. Why not try modification first? After all, if the borrower defaults again on the loan even after the payment has been reduced, the lender still has the option to foreclose. If collateral values are stable or increasing, the lender has nothing to lose. On the other hand, if collateral values are going down, the delay caused by a modification could mean that the lender will have lower recovery possibilities once the property is finally sold in foreclosure.

However, even with this "redefault" risk, it generally makes economic sense for a lender to try a modification first. If the lender is successful in rehabilitating the loan, the payoff will usually be much greater than any incremental losses in recoveries caused by several months of delay in the foreclosure sale. That is the reason that when banks hold loans in their own portfolios, they will aggressively work with distressed borrowers to restructure their obligations. A good example of this is the commercial real estate loans held in portfolios by community banks. The commercial real estate market has had its share of problems, but the fiasco being predicted by pundits in 2008 and 2009 has not materialized. One of the reasons is that so many of the loans are held in portfolio by community banks that have worked with their commercial borrowers to restructure loans, under guidelines issued by the regulators. In fact, if there has been a problem with commercial loan restructuring, it is that some banks have been too willing to accommodate borrowers, even when it is clear that the borrower's finances are hopeless and the loan needs to be charged off. Contrast this to the spectacle we have seen in the residential housing market, where foreclosures, not modifications, have been the norm, and more than 6 million people have already lost their homes. Why the difference? A major culprit, again, is securitization.

What FDIC staff understood early on—frankly, before anyone else—was that the usual forces of economic self-interest would not result in the kind of wide-scale restructuring that was needed to avoid a massive wave of foreclosures. That was because through the securitization process, those who owned the mortgages were different from those who would be responsible for restructuring them and the legal contracts governing the modification process created economic incentives skewed in favor of foreclosure.

It has been in community banks' economic self-interest to restructure their commercial real estate loans, because they own those loans. They have strong incentives to avoid incurring the steep losses associated with foreclosures. However, securitized loans are owned by a diverse group of investors with differing economic incentives. The investors do not service their own loans; that is, they do not collect the mortgage payments each month and take action against borrowers who become delinquent. Rather, they hire a financial institution to do the servicing. Loan servicing has become an increasingly concentrated business that is now performed principally by our largest banks or their affiliates.

Prior to the crisis, the job of a residential mortgage servicer consisted primarily of collecting mortgage payments and passing them on to investors. When a loan would occasionally default, the servicer would simply refer the loan to a foreclosure attorney. Servicers were not set up to deal with mortgage default because it happened so infrequently. Similarly, the agreements under which they operated compensated them based on a flat fee; they were not paid more for dealing with a delinquent loan, so their economic incentive was to do as little as possible with a troubled borrower.

Indeed, during the go-go years leading up to the crisis, competition among servicers for the fees generated by the burgeoning securitization market intensified, driving fees down further and making the business one purely of volume, not of effective servicing. Not surprisingly, under that flat fee structure and in the face of intense competition, servicers never invested sufficient resources to deal with significant delinquencies. There are minimal costs associated with collecting mortgage payments from performing borrowers and passing them on to investors. However, when a loan becomes delinquent, working with a troubled borrower to restructure a loan can be a time-consuming, labor-intensive process, particularly if each modification is individually negotiated. Servicers were not compensated for making the extra effort, so why bother?

Actually, as we would soon discover, if anything, servicers had affirmative economic incentives to go to foreclosure quickly. That was because when a loan they serviced became delinquent, they were required to continue to advance the mortgage payments to the investors out of their own pockets. If they modified the loan instead of foreclosing, they would be reimbursed by the borrower slowly, over a period of years, by taking out a small part of the borrower's new monthly payment. On the other hand, if they went to foreclosure, they were paid immediately, off the top, from foreclosure sale proceeds. If you were they, which would you do?

Why wouldn't investors tell the servicers to modify loans? After all, if a foreclosure cost more money than a modification, it was the investors, not the servicers, who took the loss. But in point of fact, just the opposite happened, with some investors threatening to sue servicers over modifying loans. Why would investors want to sue servicers for trying to rehabilitate delinquent loans? After all, that would usually save them money over the cost of foreclosure. The answer to that question goes to the heart of what I believe was probably the single biggest impediment to getting the toxic loans restructured: the conflicting economic incentives of investors themselves.

Remember the tranches we discussed? As you will recall, most mortgage securitizations were set up to provide the senior tranche—the triple-A portion of the securitization—with substantial overcollateralization. What that meant was that if a mortgage defaulted, it had no impact whatsoever on the senior tranche—unless the defaulting mortgages exceeded 20 to 30 percent of the mortgage pool. However, here is the catch: because of the way in which many securitization documents were written, if, instead of a foreclosure sale, the loan was modified, the reduced mortgage payments flowed through to all investors in the securitization pool, meaning that everyone's income was reduced, including that of the triple-A investors.

So again, what would you do if you were a triple-A investor? If a loan becomes delinquent and the servicer modifies it with a 30 percent payment reduction, your portion of the payment flows from that mortgage will be reduced along with all the other bond holders. If, however, the servicer simply forecloses on the loan, even if the losses on foreclosure amount to 50 percent, you will still prefer the foreclosure because that entire loss will be absorbed by the lower tranches. From the standpoint of investors as a whole, it obviously makes more sense for the loan to be modified with a 30 percent loss instead of a 50 percent loss on foreclosure. However, from the standpoint of the triple-A bondholders, it makes more sense to foreclose. And the triple-A bondholders were more numerous and more powerful than investors holding the subordinate tranches.

Working with Jim Wigand, Mike Krimminger, and George Alexander, I decided that the best thing to do would be to get all stakeholders in a room together and try to hash out some type of agreement to start modifying subprime hybrid ARMs. Delinquencies on subprime hybrid ARMs were increasing quickly, and nearly half a trillion dollars' worth of such loans were scheduled to reset in 2007 and 2008. The answer seemed obvious: eliminate the reset and simply extend the starter rate. In other words, convert the loan into a thirty-year fixed-rate mortgage, keeping the monthly payment the same as it had been during the starter period. We thought that investors—even Triple-A investors—should support such a step. We weren't really proposing that their payments be reduced, just that they give up a payment increase that they had never had a realistic expectation of receiving. As previously discussed, hybrid ARMs were designed to force refinancings after two to three years, not to be paid at the higher rate for the life of the loan. Our data confirmed that the debt-to-income ratios on these loans were extremely high. Indeed, more than 90 percent of hybrid ARMs were refinanced at the end of the starter period. The number of borrowers who continued paying after reset was minuscule. Without some relief, subprime borrowers would default on a large scale, generating heavy losses for all bondholders, as well as the broader housing market.

So we organized three roundtables with servicers, investors, accountants, lawyers, ratings agencies, consumer advocates, and other regulators to see if we could build consensus around the idea. The roundtables were held on April 16, May 29, and July 20, 2007. The good news was that there was general consensus that servicers had the legal authority to do wide-scale interest rate reductions of the type we suggested without compromising the favorable accounting and tax treatment of the securitization trusts. What's more, servicers were generally supportive of our proposal to freeze the starter rate (though looking back now, I wonder if they were just telling us what we wanted to hear).

However, we received strong pushback from some in the investment community, most notably Mark Adelson of Nomura Securities, who went public with vigorous opposition. In a scathing research note, "Modify This!," Adelson disingenuously characterized modification efforts as geared solely toward helping borrowers at the expense of MBS investors. "The fact that a loan modification allows a defaulted borrower to keep his home is irrelevant—it should not be a consideration," he railed. "The only consideration should be the lender's/investor's economic interest." (Throughout our struggles to achieve wide-scale loan restructurings, our industry opponents would usually fail to acknowledge the business justification and broader economic arguments in favor of loan mods. That was a smart tactic. Focusing on assistance to borrowers, of course, inflamed popular resentment against subprime borrower bailouts.)

In his public comments, Adelson would conveniently omit the fact that foreclosures would benefit triple-A bondholders over the interests of borrowers and investors in subordinate tranches, while modifications would cost them money. However, in a May 2007 Nomura Securities research note recounting an industry forum on subprime mortgage loss mitigation strategies, he acknowledged the "conflicts between different classes of investors" and that "modifications favor the interests of subordinate and residual classes." And in a not-so-veiled threat, he suggested that that was one area "likely to spawn litigation, both between investors and servicers and among competing classes of investors." Using assumptions that seem laughable now, he referenced research predicting a housing slump with 8 percent price declines over three to four years, with estimated losses on subprime loans originated in 2006 at 8 to 10 percent—well below the thick levels of protection then enjoyed by triple-A investors. Of course, if that had been a realistic assumption, it would have made economic sense for the triple-As to push for foreclosures over modification, as they would never have been touched by loss rates of 8 to 10 percent. But that was greed-induced la-la land. Home prices declined more than 30 percent, and bond investors took a beating, hitting a trough of around 30 cents on the dollar in early 2009.

We invited dozens of participants to the roundtables, and only Adelson vocally opposed our proposal to modify subprime loans on a large scale. Everyone else in the room was pretty much nodding in agreement on the need to extend the starter rate when the borrower couldn't refinance. Some attendees were extremely helpful. For instance, Marty Rosenblatt, a senior partner at Deloitte & Touche, was invaluable in helping the group navigate the accounting issues associated with modifying loans inside securitization pools. Many of the industry representatives also made positive contributions, including Lewis Ranieri of the Hyperion Group, Mike Heid of Wells Fargo, Larry Litton of Litton Loan Servicing, and George Miller of the American Securitization Forum. We were able to establish definitively that the servicers did have the flexibility under both the tax laws and accounting rules to modify the loans. The lawyers also confirmed that the securitizations imposed a contractual obligation on servicers to maximize value for the investment pool as a whole, to address concerns that senior MBS investors might try to halt loan mods. I was delighted that there seemed to be so much support.

Loan modifications made sense for investors as a whole, home owners, and the economy. How could we not move forward with such an obviously needed initiative? Yet, looking back, I see that I was naive. As annoyed as I was with Adelson at the time, in retrospect, with him I at least knew my enemy and the true agenda.

As for the rest, some were probably disingenuous. Others were sincere about supporting systematic modifications, though their commitment was weak and they failed to execute with the staff training and resources necessary to make systematic modifications work. But there was another factor motivating their happy talk: at the time that we held our roundtables, efforts were gaining steam to pass legislation forcing restructuring through the bankruptcy process. The servicing industry, as well as MBS investors, were eager to create the impression in Washington that they were on top of things and government action was unnecessary. At least I wasn't the only one who was duped. Following our efforts, Senate Banking Committee Chairman Chris Dodd and ranking Republican member Richard Shelby held their own roundtable in May. At the end of that meeting, Dodd was able to get all the participants to commit publicly to what they had all told us privately: that they would work to restructure the loans of subprime borrowers and pursue foreclosure only as a last resort.

We had established that the private sector had the legal tools to restructure loans, and we were told by securitization industry leaders that they would be doing so. Working with the other bank regulators, we reinforced the roundtables by issuing guidance on April 17, 2007, that encouraged banks and bank affiliates to work with mortgage borrowers to restructure unaffordable loans. At the FDIC, we followed that up with special training programs for our examiners to make sure a review of loan restructuring was part of the examination process. I even made a personal video for our examiners emphasizing what I viewed as the crucial importance of the effort. But we were not the primary regulator of any of the major servicers. And I do not think that the other regulators shared our sense of urgency in making sure banks were staffed up and ready to deal with the wave of distressed mortgages coming their way. So we received a lot of happy talk from the securitization industry, but by the fall of 2007, it was clear that the major servicers were still pursuing foreclosure as the default option. Indeed, according to a survey conducted by Mark Zandi, the chief economist of Moody's Analytics, less than 1 percent of subprime mortgages were being restructured. The vast majority of troubled loans were going into foreclosure. The few loans that were being modified were not being done systematically but individually and laboriously negotiated with the borrowers, one by one.

I convened our staff experts and asked them to try to explain to me what was going on. Had our roundtables accomplished nothing? How could the industry be so clueless? Couldn't it see what was coming and the need to get ahead of it with proactive, systematic modifications? There were many factors, said our staff experts: inertia, ineptitude, skewed economic incentives, tranche warfare, they were all playing a part. But perhaps the biggest problem was a culture that frankly worked against providing relief for borrowers. The Wall Street–dominated securitization industry never left money on the table. Systematic modifications, which would give everyone an extension of the starter rate, might mean that some borrowers who could afford to pay the higher rate might get a payment lower than they could really afford. The industry clearly didn't want to give up its chance at having those 11% to 13% rates of return from subprime home owners, notwithstanding the strong evidence presented by Rich Brown and others on our economic team that there was no way the vast majority of subprime borrowers could make the higher payments. The culture was for the servicers and the investors they worked for to squeeze every penny they could out of borrowers, and that meant that they would negotiate loan by loan. "These guys will step over a dollar to pick up a nickel," said George Alexander, our most seasoned securitization expert. No truer words were ever spoken.

I was scheduled to speak to a securitization group in New York on

October 4, 2007, so I decided to engage it directly on why more borrowers weren't being helped. I tried to take a constructive approach, noting with approval a public statement that its trade group, the American Securitization Forum, had issued in June. It reaffirmed the conclusions we had reached in our roundtable that servicers had both the legal authority and the contractual obligation to modify loans when restructuring would maximize value for investors as a whole. But then I went on to say, "Frankly, I'm frustrated that the servicing restructuring has not reached the level that I had hoped it would. . . . We have a huge problem on our hands. We can't just sit here doing this kind of case-by-case, laborious restructuring process with all these millions of subprime hybrid ARMs. . . . [S]ome categorical approaches are needed, and needed urgently."

I finished my speech, and the lackluster applause spoke volumes. I looked over the crowd of predominantly thirty-something white male Wall Street deal makers, and those who weren't glaring at me were casting sideways glances at each other or rolling their eyes. I thought they were going to throw rotten eggs and tomatoes at me. Then the question-and-answer session began. A hand shot up in the back of the room. The gentleman started lecturing me about how it wasn't possible to help "these people," referring to subprime borrowers. "You give them a break," he said, "and they will just go out and buy a flat-screen TV."

So why, I asked, if he felt that way about "these people," did he extend mortgage loans to them to begin with? I will never forget his answer: "Bad regulation."

So there you had it, straight from the heart of U.S. capitalism. It had been okay for the masters of the universe who filled that conference room to shovel out millions of mortgages to people who clearly couldn't afford them because no one in the regulatory community had told them to stop. And if there was a problem now, it was because regulators hadn't protected these securitization whiz kids from their own greed and corruption.

So much for the self-regulating market.

At that same conference, I felt I was seeing the true face of the industry for the first time. Those were the folks on the ground who were driving what was really going on in the housing market, not the polished lawyers and trade association heads whom we were hearing from in D.C. I was angry, and I decided to go on the offensive. I did not have any regulatory power over them, but I could at least try to engage the other regulators, who did have direct authority, as well as ratchet up public pressure and cast a media spotlight on what was going on. On October 8, I sent an email to Dugan, Kroszner, and Reich, asking for support for our proposal to extend the starter rate on hybrid ARMs. I also directly engaged Chairman Bernanke, who was the most sympathetic among my regulatory colleagues. A few weeks later, I ran an op-ed in *The New York Times* calling for systematic wide-scale conversion. "The mortgage crisis is growing," I said, "and the mortgage industry has the ability to solve much of the problem on its own." Much to my surprise, I received editorial endorsements from both *The New York Times* and *The Wall Street Journal*.

Not everyone was complimentary, however. The op-ed led to an onslaught of negative blogs accusing me of trying to help "deadbeats" and questioning why subprime borrowers should get a break on their mortgages when others would not. Many of the bloggers obviously viewed subprime borrowers as flippers and speculators, not families trying to hold on to their homes. That was an erroneous perception. Indeed, our data showed that more than 93 percent of subprime loans had been made to individuals or families occupying their homes. Professional investors and speculators generally opted for the NTM loans—option ARMs—that provided extremely low payments for five years. Real estate professionals were too smart to take out the abusive 2/28s or 3/27s. Those, for the most part, were marketed to lower- and moderate-income people who lacked financial sophistication.

Notwithstanding the public misunderstanding, I understood the popular resentment. My husband and I have never had anything but fixed-rate mortgages and have always made our payments on time. But the larger point was this: if all of those loans went into foreclosure, it would create a tremendous downward pressure on the housing market, hurting home values for all of us. That, of course, was exactly what happened.

But the political backlash was real, and it hampered our efforts to convince the Bush Treasury Department to support our position. As usual, there were differences in views among the bank regulators. I had reached out to Ben Bernanke, and the Fed was the most supportive of our position. Surprisingly, the OCC appeared to be coming our way; in a November interview with *American Banker,* John Dugan was quoted as saying that "there's been a realization that maybe the best way to do [loan restructuring] is some kind of systematic approach."

Up until that point, I had had very few dealings with Treasury Secretary Hank Paulson. My early requests for a courtesy meeting with him after I became FDIC chairman had been unsuccessful. It had taken months before he finally agreed to a meeting and then, when I had arrived at his office, I had been redirected to Robert Steel's office down the hall. Hank had stopped by for about five minutes to say hello. Clearly, the former CEO of Goldman Sachs didn't think the head of an agency that insured $100,000 bank deposits was worth his time. That would later change, but in 2007, he still had better things to do.

Bob, Hank's undersecretary for domestic finance, was, however, highly accessible as well as interested in what we had to say on loan mods. Bob had worked with Hank for years at Goldman Sachs. He was friendly and personable, a good counterpoint to Hank's abrupt, no-nonsense way of doing business. I found him easy to work with, funny, and disarmingly charming (in contrast to his somewhat cutthroat reputation on Wall Street). David Nason, who held my old job as the assistant secretary for financial institutions and reported to Bob, was also extremely helpful. Bob had participated in our roundtables, and we had been conversing regularly on the need for a government program for systematic loan modifications.

Our efforts to convince Treasury to launch such a program were given a tremendous boost when, in November 2007, California Governor Arnold Schwarzenegger picked up on our proposal and convinced all of the major servicers in California to commit to extending the starter rate on subprime hybrid ARMs for a "sustainable period" of five to seven years. We had been pushing for a permanent extension of the starter rate, but the five years did give borrowers significant payment relief. At Governor Schwarzenegger's request, I had sent Mike Krimminger to California to provide technical assistance to the governor's staff, and the governor had asked Mike to speak at the press conference he held announcing the program. My chief of staff, Jesse Villarreal, and I watched the press conference on TV and had a good laugh when Schwarzenegger introduced Chairman Bair's representative, Michael Kreeeeemeenger.

That agreement was a major step forward, given California's large and hard-hit subprime mortgage market. With California leading the way, we were sure that other states would start following suit with systematic loan modifications. Bob Steel seized on the opportunity and convinced Hank and the White House that the Treasury should get ahead of piecemeal state efforts by coming up with a national agreement to restructure subprime loans. By the end of November, other regulators were also giving our ideas public support. To his credit, Hank got on the phone with the heads of all the major banks and told them he wanted their participation. Once the secretary of the Treasury became personally involved, things started to happen. By December, we had a national agreement. Dubbed the Hope Now alliance, the program would qualify up to 1.8 million home owners for a streamlined loan modification process.

But the agreement—like almost all of our reform efforts—was a watered-down compromise among the various bank regulators and industry. John Reich, the head of the Office of Thrift Supervision, was a particularly vocal critic of our proposal, arguing for a loan-by-loan approach and starter rate extensions of only three years. We ended up with five years. I also felt that the criteria to qualify borrowers were far too complicated (a nod to the industry), and, most troubling, they required servicers to determine whether individual borrowers could afford the steep reset before they could be given the modification. My fear was that that particular provision would be used as a ruse to engage in borrower-by-borrower negotiations, instead of the faster, more efficient systematic approach. But perhaps the biggest defect was the lack of detailed reporting on loan modification activity. Without detailed public reports, there would be no way to hold servicers accountable for complying with the agreement, which was crucial, given that the agreement was voluntary. I wanted the FDIC to have operational oversight of the program, but the other regulators would never agree to that, so program administration rested with the Treasury, which—as experience has shown—was ill-equipped to run a program of this nature.

For those reasons, Hope Now never lived up to expectations. Hundreds of thousands of subprime borrowers did receive modifications under it, and I take pride in that, though many more went into foreclosure. I will never forget participating in a foreclosure-prevention town meeting in southern Los Angeles at Exposition Park a few months after Hope Now was announced, at Governor Schwarzenegger's invitation. We arrived a little before 9 A.M. and saw thousands of people lined up outside the building, notwithstanding the stifling heat and humidity, waiting to talk with a servicer. I provided brief remarks to a standing-room-only crowd, explaining the Treasury program to them and how we expected it to work. In stark contrast to the arrogance and disdain I confronted on Wall Street, there I saw families with young children, elderly people, working people in their denims or uniforms. No Armani suits in that room. I saw fear, confusion, and exhaustion in their faces. They were caught in mortgages they could not afford, dealing with a complex loan-servicing process they could not understand. There were no flippers or speculators in that room, just people terrified about losing their homes.

The intensity of emotions emanating from the faces of those frightened people was overwhelming. I've always had protective instincts. (Staff at the FDIC jokingly called me "she-bear," in reference to my fierce defense of the staff when I thought they were being mistreated or unfairly criticized.) Their vulnerability and their obvious need for help from the powers that be touched me deeply. Up to that point, I had approached loan modifications in the abstract, from a macroeconomic standpoint: we needed to get the loans restructured to minimize losses and prevent unnecessary foreclosures that would hurt the housing market. Here I was confronted with the human tragedy of the subprime debacle. I tried to be calm and reassuring, but the desperation in the faces looking up at me made me want to break down and cry.

After my remarks, I visited the individual servicers' booths, where people were lined up to apply for loan modifications. I wanted to see for myself whether servicers were following up on their commitments. I unobtrusively approached a booth being manned by Litton Loan Servicing. Seated at the table was a nurse with a 2/28, who had never been late on her mortgage, but her loan was scheduled to reset. She explained that she supported her elderly father, who was with her. She was already working double shifts just to make ends meet, and she could not make the higher payment. After verifying all the information she gave him, the Litton representative agreed to give her a two-year extension. I challenged him on the spot, asking why she wasn't getting the five-year extension, per the Treasury agreement. He was operating under instructions from his superiors, he replied. I couldn't believe it. After all that time and effort fighting for a minimum five-year extension, the servicers were still pretty much doing what they wanted.

When I returned to my office in Washington, I called Larry Litton, the head of the firm, to complain. He told me that the nurse's mortgage was held in a pool where the investors would not agree to an extension longer than two years. The irony was that Litton Loan Servicing actually had one of the highest rates for loan modifications at that time, but its efforts, like those of the others, were falling far short. And one of the many obstacles—as it was with the nurse in California—was resistance from triple-A investors. Fannie Mae and Freddie Mac, which owned nearly a third of the triple-A mortgage-backed securities packaged by Wall Street, could have exercised leadership in supporting systematic loan modifications, but they didn't. They just didn't want to give up the prospect of those resetting higher rates.

As was the case with most of the government's response to the subprime crisis, Hope Now was too little, too late. Subprime foreclosures were already starting to spin out of control, and the spillover into the prime market was becoming evident by the end of 2007.

In early 2008, we took another run at Treasury with a more aggressive program called Home Ownership Preservation (HOP) loans. Under the proposal, the government would provide low-interest loans to borrowers with unaffordable mortgages, which we defined as loans where the payment exceeded 40 percent of the borrower's gross income. They could use the loan to pay down up to 20 percent of their principal balances. The borrowers would also be given a five-year grace period before they had to start paying the government back. In return for paying down 20 percent of the principal, however, the investors who held the loans in their securitization pools had to agree to permanently modify the loan to keep the payment below a 35 percent debt-to-income (DTI) ratio. If the borrower defaulted, the government would have first claim on proceeds from liquidating the house. Since the government's loan covered only 20 percent of the mortgage, there was little chance that it would have to take a loss. The program was designed to entice mortgage-backed investors to agree to meaningful restructuring of those unaffordable mortgages in return for getting immediate cash to pay down 20 percent of the principal.

But there again, investors balked because they didn't want to give up their priority claim to foreclosure proceeds, and the Treasury Department had no stomach at that point for any program that used government money, even one where it would be virtually impossible for the government to lose money. So we watched helplessly as the mortgage market continued to deteriorate and subprime foreclosures escalated, ravaging low- and middle-income neighborhoods. Industry recalcitrance, regulatory squabbling, and Treasury's indifference had impeded the bold steps that were necessary to get ahead of the curve.

The year 2008 would bring with it economic Armageddon, trillions of dollars' worth of investor losses, the largest bank failures in history, and a choke hold on credit flows to the real economy that would end up costing more than 8 million people their jobs. It didn't have to be that way.

CHAPTER 7

The Audacity of That Woman

Though our regulatory colleagues viewed us as being alarmist over the growing subprime crisis, in fact, even I did not fully appreciate at the end of 2007 how deeply some large financial institutions were exposed to mortgage-related losses, how badly some of them had been managed, and how cataclysmic the consequences would be.

My first clue was the structured investment vehicle (SIV) fiasco, which occurred in August 2007. That was when the canary in the coal mine started gasping for breath. A number of large financial institutions, led by Citigroup, started having trouble accessing enough funding to support their mortgages and MBS investments. Citi and a few other large banks had set up something called "structured investment vehicles" as a way to invest in mortgages and mortgage-backed securities. For reasons that still today remain a mystery to me, they were allowed by their regulators—the Fed and the OCC—to keep the investments off balance sheet, meaning that they were not included in the financial reports insured banks filed with us, and, most important, they were not required to hold capital or reserves against those assets to absorb losses. Indeed, our examiners did not know anything about SIVs until the Federal Reserve Board alerted us to Citi's difficulties.

Here was the problem: Citi's SIVs issued "commercial paper"—extremely short term bonds of usually thirty days or less—to finance the acquisition of mortgages and mortgage-backed securities. It was nothing short of idiotic for Citi and others to be funding such long-term assets with very short term bonds, but they did so because the rate they had to pay investors on short-term commercial paper was much lower than what they would have paid on bonds of multiyear duration. So that maximized their "spread," the difference between the interest rate they paid on the commercial paper and the amount they received on the long-dated mortgage assets. The problem was that extremely risk-averse investors, such as money market mutual funds, bought that commercial paper, and as mortgage delinquencies started to rise, those investors became concerned that the assets held by the SIVs would suffer big losses. So they decided to start putting their money elsewhere.

That was a very bad result for the FDIC, because as funding for those assets started to dry up, Citi and others were forced to consolidate SIV mortgage assets onto their balance sheets, where they could be backed by more stable insured deposits. Consolidation exposed the banks and bank holding companies to losses on those assets, even though they had not held capital and reserves against this risk because the assets were held off balance sheet. The use of the SIV funding structure was one of many instances of unbelievable Citi mismanagement we were only beginning to understand and that would later lead to the need for three bailouts of that bank.

The next clue came on Friday, March 14, 2008, when I received an early-morning call from one of our senior examiners advising me that Bear Stearns would be declaring bankruptcy that day. "Investment banks fail," I told him and went back to sleep for another precious thirty minutes before getting up to go to work.

But when I got to the office, I was given a different narrative. Now I was hearing that JPMorgan Chase was going to buy Bear Stearns for about $2 a share in a government-assisted transaction. The New York Federal Reserve Bank, led by Tim Geithner, would assume the risk of loss on about $30 billion in high-risk mortgage securities held by Bear. I was getting most of my information from CNBC. No one from the Fed or Treasury was talking to me. However, at the time, I did not think that was remarkable, given the fact that Bear Stearns was an investment bank, which we did not insure and for which we had no responsibility.

What I did think was remarkable was why the NY Fed was even getting involved. Among the five major securities firms, Bear was the smallest. It was one of the weaker firms that had fed on the subprime mortgage craze in the extreme. Why didn't the NY Fed just let it go down? I was also incredulous that the NY Fed was claiming that it had legal authority to step in and support the merger, which would protect all of Bear's counterparties and bondholders. The FDIC was the only agency that had the authority to resolve failing financial institutions, and that authority was limited to banks, which we insured, not securities firms, which were outside the safety net of deposit insurance and Fed discount window lending. In the past, when securities firms had gotten into trouble, they had been acquired or recapitalized by private-sector entities, or they were placed into bankruptcy. Yet here the NY Fed was, putting government money at risk to protect Bear's counterparties and creditors; even Bear's shareholders would get a little something out of the deal.

It was all the more amazing given the fact that the FDIC was strictly prohibited from providing government assistance to keep a failing institution open. Under our rules, if a bank failed, it was put into our resolution process, which, like bankruptcy, imposed losses on shareholders and creditors. If we wanted to "bail out" an institution, that is, provide government money to keep it open and protect its stakeholders from loss, we had to invoke something called the "systemic risk" exception. That was an extraordinary procedure whereby supermajorities of the FDIC board and the Federal Reserve Board had to certify that putting a bank into our bankruptcy-like resolution process would cause "systemic" ramifications—that is, resolution would result in broad, adverse consequences for the larger economy. Once the FDIC and Fed boards made that determination, we had to seek approval by the Treasury secretary and the concurrence of the president himself. It was an extraordinary process, as was appropriate. Protecting a mismanaged financial institution and its stakeholders from the consequences of their own actions with government money was, needless to say, a step that should rarely, if ever, be taken. In fact, prior to the 2008 financial crisis, the FDIC had never invoked the systemic risk exception. But here we had the NY Fed going out on its own and deciding to bail out a relatively small investment bank, a perimeter player at best. It was very curious to me, and I was concerned about the precedent the NY Fed was setting. But I had no jurisdiction to object, and at that point I had other, more pressing matters to worry about.

Insured banks and thrifts with large exposures to subprime and nontraditional mortgages were starting to deteriorate markedly. On March 26, 2008, I convened a meeting with the heads of the other banking agencies to review our staff's analysis of insured banks and thrifts with more than $10 billion in assets that we believed were at heightened risk of failure. There were thirteen such institutions, with the biggest threats being WaMu, with $300 billion in assets and $190 billion in insured deposits; National City (NatCity), with $138 billion in assets and $92 billion in insured deposits; and IndyMac Bank, with $32 billion in assets and $18 billion in insured deposits. Our staff projected that IndyMac would fail by the fourth quarter of 2008 and that the rest of the thirteen institutions were at heightened risk of failure. We asked the other regulators to intensify their supervision of these institutions and to have them increase their capital base. Most important, we asked that they make sure that insured deposits were not being used to fund high-risk mortgages previously funded through the securitization market, which, by that point, had completely dried up.

At the top of our worry list was WaMu, a $300 billion Seattle-based mortgage lender regulated by the Office of Thrift Supervision, given its size and fragile condition. Fortunately, in January 2008, Bank of America had already announced plans to acquire another troubled West Coast thrift, Countrywide. Contrary to popular belief, we played no role whatsoever in BofA's acquisition of Countrywide, and although I was relieved that a larger, more profitable commercial bank had taken it over, I was very concerned that the purchase price had been too high. Another national bank, Wachovia, had purchased a large California thrift, Golden West, at the top of the market in May 2006, and the losses associated with that pricey acquisition were already starting to weigh on Wachovia's balance sheet—indeed, it had experienced a 98 percent drop in earnings in the fourth quarter of 2007, and its stock price was down by more than 40 percent. But in early 2008, at least, it appeared that BofA could handle Countrywide's troubled-mortgage portfolio and that although Wachovia would suffer significant lost earnings from its acquisition, its solvency would not be threatened.

WaMu, on the other hand, was a completely different kettle of fish. If pride goeth before a fall, WaMu's management stood as a case in point. The thrift had grown rapidly from a smaller regional mortgage lender into one of the country's largest thrift institutions, with branches scattered throughout the country and a heavy exposure to California's overheated housing market. WaMu's management was viewed by many in the market as unsophisticated and not up to the task of managing an institution of that size. The bank had long been viewed as a takeover target, but its management had persistently fended off potential suitors, determined to maintain both their jobs and their autonomy. And notwithstanding the institution's rapidly rising delinquencies and charge-offs on its troubled-mortgage portfolio, management refused to see the necessity of finding a larger, healthier partner to help it ride out the storm, as the more savvy executives at Golden West and Countrywide had done.

The other problem with WaMu was its too-close relationship with its primary regulator, the OTS. Having lost two of its three major charters (Countrywide and Golden West) to national banks that were regulated by the OCC, I feared that OTS would work to prevent an acquisition of WaMu to preserve its one remaining major charter. Those fears were confirmed when we were alerted by JPMorgan Chase that WaMu CEO Kerry Killinger had refused to talk with it about a possible acquisition because of JPMorgan's (understandable) desire to conduct due diligence on WaMu's loan portfolio before making an offer. That was outrageous. WaMu could not afford to be picky any longer. Its fourth-quarter loss of $1.9 billion had surprised analysts. Its stock price was down by 67 percent, and though its credit rating was still investment grade, it had been subject to a series of downgrades by all the major ratings agencies. The local press in Seattle was running stories trying to reassure depositors about the safety of WaMu's FDIC-insured deposits. And as if its mortgage problems weren't enough, its credit card losses were among the highest in the industry.

Where had WaMu gone wrong? Its problems had begun in 2005, when it had shifted its mortgage business away from traditional fixed-rate loans to subprime loans and option ARMs to compete with Countrywide. Internal memos written by WaMu officials in 2006 estimated that profit margins on subprime loans and option ARMs were six to ten times as profitable as traditional mortgage products. To ramp up the volume even further, WaMu had originated a significant number of "stated income" or "low-doc" loans that allowed borrowers to simply write in their income on the loan application without independent verification. About 90 percent of WaMu home equity loans, 73 percent of its option ARMs, and half of its subprime loans were low-doc mortgages. Our examiners feared that those toxic loans would ultimately generate tens of billions of dollars' worth of losses for WaMu, far exceeding its capital base.

I contacted OTS head John Reich to determine the basis of JPMorgan Chase's complaints and let him know that we had been told that it was going to pull out of discussions if it could not conduct additional due diligence. I also made clear our view that an acquisition by a healthy bank, as opposed to an additional capital investment by private-equity investors, would likely provide a permanent solution to WaMu's problems. An additional capital infusion might or might not be sufficient to keep WaMu solvent, given the uncertainty about the scope of its losses. I was particularly concerned that Killinger, given his desire to maintain control over his institution, would skew his presentation of options to the WaMu board toward a private-equity group, TPG Capital, led by David Bonderman, who was close to Killinger and had served on the WaMu board in the past. From the standpoint of the shareholders, it seemed clear to me that an acquisition by Chase was the better course. Shareholders would not have to accept dilution, as they would with the TPG proposal, and it would remove any risk of a WaMu failure. At that time, Chase was probably the strongest bank in the world. In my email, I told Reich:

This is something the WaMu board and ultimately the shareholders need to decide, with input from their regulators on prudential considerations associated with the various options. I think the discussion yesterday emphasized the advantages of an acquisition in assuring adequate infusions of capital on a long-term basis, as well as the stabilizing impact it could have on market perceptions of WaMu. As WaMu's insurer and backup regulator, I look to you as their primary regulator for help in assuring that WaMu will fully and fairly present all options to its board and that OTS will evaluate all options with the management and board from a safety and soundness standpoint.

Unfortunately but predictably, Reich responded that he did not necessarily agree with the FDIC view. He argued that the willingness of a private-equity firm to make a capital investment indicated that WaMu was in a stronger position than Chase's offer suggested. In the end, the WaMu board rejected Chase's offer of $8 a share. Instead, the company sold TPG $7 billion worth of newly issued common and preferred stock. The TPG deal also allowed the Killinger management team to keep their jobs and reinstated Bonderman to the WaMu board.

Though I was not convinced that the WaMu board had fully considered both options, I was very relieved to see a fresh $7 billion capital infusion. Earlier reports we had received from the OTS had indicated that TPG would invest only $5 billion, which our examiners believed was far too low to provide an adequate cushion against WaMu's escalating mortgage losses. The market also reacted positively, though analysts' commentary included a healthy dose of skepticism about whether $7 billion was enough capital to see WaMu through. Indeed, for context, another bank on our "worry list"— NatCity—acting under intense pressure from the OCC—had also raised $7 billion in new capital, even though NatCity was half WaMu's size.

For a while, at least, the situation at WaMu seemed to be stable. We increased our backup examination presence at WaMu while concentrating on some of the other regional thrifts that were deteriorating fast. We were also busy monitoring the growing number of community banks that were getting into trouble with their commercial real estate loans. The FDIC kept a list of "troubled banks," which essentially was a list of banks whose primary regulator had assigned a CAMELS supervisory rating of 4 or 5. They were banks we viewed as being at heightened risk of failure and requiring more intensive supervisory attention. Each quarter we published the number of banks on the list as well as the total amount of banking assets represented by the group. In 2006, when I came to office—at the tail end of the "golden era of banking"—the list stood at fifty, representing $8 billion in assets. By the end of 2007, the list had jumped to seventy-six, representing $22 billion in assets, and we predicted that it could go as high as $885 billion by the end of 2008. We had already experienced three failures in 2007 after nearly three years of no bank failures at all and projected that another eleven banks would fail before the end of the year.

I had mixed feelings about our troubled-bank list. On the one hand, I thought the public had a right to know about the basic health of the banking industry, and our troubled-bank list was a long-used public indicator. On the other hand, the list could be misleading, as it was clear that it lagged the true health of the industry. Indeed, we thought our failure projections in the first quarter of 2008 were aggressive, but as it turned out, they understated the risks significantly. One problem was that the list was based on examination ratings, which were refreshed only once a year for most institutions, in accordance with examination schedules. But more important, it was clear to me that the OCC and OTS were reluctant to downgrade their larger institutions. Downgrading a bank was, to some extent, an acknowledgment of weakness in the examination program. Ideally, if examiners were on their toes, they would intervene and take measures to stabilize a bank before it ever reached troubled status. (Such interventions typically included regulatory orders for banks to raise capital, stop weak lending practices, or hire new management.) In addition, because we publicly disclosed the total dollar amount of troubled-bank assets, placing a large bank on the troubled list could start a market guessing game about which large institution had been added. And in retrospect, it is clear to me that the OCC was not giving us information that truly reflected the severity of problems at two of its biggest banks, Citi and Wachovia.

An early case in point of that phenomenon was IndyMac Bank, yet another OTS-regulated West Coast mortgage lender. IndyMac was everything an insured bank shouldn't be. It had very little in the way of "core" deposits, meaning that it didn't have many true bank customers who actually had a relationship with the bank; rather, most of its deposits came by offering above-market rates on deposits through third-party brokers. It also borrowed excessive amounts of money from the Federal Home Loan Banks (FHLB) system. And it made some of the most toxic mortgage loans in the country. It specialized in interest-only loans and option ARMs originated through mortgage brokers with little or no income documentation. Though by the end of 2007, our staff projected that it would fail before the end of 2008, OTS had failed to downgrade it to troubled status.

We did finally convince OTS to downgrade IndyMac in the second quarter of 2008 and began planning a resolution strategy for the fourth quarter. However, on June 26, John Reich and I received letters from New York Democratic Senator Chuck Schumer stating "I am concerned that IndyMac's financial deterioration poses significant risks to both taxpayers and borrowers" and that the bank "could face a failure if prescriptive measures are not taken quickly." The impetus for that provocative letter and Senator Schumer's decision to make it public remain a mystery. However, it spooked the heck out of IndyMac depositors and prompted a major bank run. Between June 27 and July 11, depositors pulled out $1.3 billion in deposits. In addition, the Federal Home Loan Banks pulled IndyMac's credit lines. IndyMac was quickly running out of cash. We worked with the OTS on an emergency closing on Friday, July 12. Without time to auction the bank in advance, as was our usual practice for bank failures, we set up a "bridge" institution to keep the bank operational and preserve what little franchise value it had. It was extremely difficult to find buyers for the institution, given its high-cost deposits and toxic mortgage loans. The ultimate price tag for IndyMac's failure: more than $7 billion, by far the most expensive bank failure for us of the crisis.

IndyMac was a major learning experience for me on a number of fronts.

First, I learned that we should never let the primary regulator close a bank before the close of normal business hours. OTS had decided to close IndyMac three hours early to give John Reich time to call members of Congress while they were still in their offices. Waiting until IndyMac's normal closing time of 6 P.M. Pacific Time would have meant that he was calling congressional members at nine at night. (It was common courtesy for regulators to notify the chairmen and ranking members of the banking committees of significant bank failures.) When told of this plan by our resolutions team, my chief of staff, Jesse Villarreal, questioned the timing, noting that people would still be going to the bank, expecting it to be open.

I wish I had intervened with OTS, because Jesse was right. As it turned out, word of the closure spread like wildfire as soon as the OTS and FDIC staff showed up to take the institution over. The news media showed up within minutes. Customers expecting the bank to still be open were terrified by the locked doors and media circus filming their every move. Throughout the weekend, the cable news played a video of a panicked, tearful woman banging on the door trying to get in to close her account. That never would have happened if we had just told OTS to wait until the bank closed. After IndyMac, I put a firm policy into place that no banks would be closed before their regular closing time.

Second, I learned how sensationalistic and irresponsible the media could be—particularly those that are not accustomed to covering financial issues. Driven in large part by the media hype, by Saturday morning, bank customers were lined up for blocks in the California heat, trying to withdraw their deposits. Incredibly, we were seeing a bank run after it had already closed and was under FDIC control. At that point, it was probably the safest place in the world for depositors to keep their money.

Many of those in line were uninsured depositors. Unfortunately, there was a significant amount of uninsured deposits at IndyMac, about $1 billion. Those deposits were going to have to take some losses, or "haircuts," under our rules to help cover part of the FDIC's costs. Insured deposits were paid out immediately, but half of the uninsured money was held back. There were some really heartbreaking stories about many of those uninsured accounts: the mother of an Afghanistan soldier killed in action who had deposited all of his life insurance, a policewoman who had just sold her home and had deposited the proceeds. Yes, our rules—which were governed by statute—required us to impose losses on uninsured deposits, and it is incumbent on people to know the FDIC deposit limits and stay below them. (But, as will be discussed later, the same can be said for the bondholders and counterparties of large financial institutions. They should have expected to take losses. Instead, they were bailed out in full.)

Andrew Gray, our head of public affairs, was on the phone continuously with the press trying to get it to balance its stories with a public reassurance that FDIC-insured deposits were safe. The FDIC has a very strong record in this regard. No depositor has ever lost a penny of insured deposits. Never. We had already launched a media campaign celebrating our seventy-fifth anniversary. Given the increased public uncertainty about the safety of the banking system, we thought the seventy-fifth anniversary would provide a good opportunity to remind people about the FDIC's rock-solid guarantee that would protect their insured deposits no matter what. After the IndyMac failure, we redoubled our efforts to educate the public to counter the fearmongering that we were seeing among some of the more ill-informed members of the press corps.

Not only were those fearmongers seizing on the increasing fragility of the financial system, they were also starting to scare people about our financial

capability to fully protect depositors in the event of wide-scale bank closings. The IndyMac failure was horrifically expensive and had put a huge
dent in the fund we maintained to cover the cost of bank failures. Over
industry opposition, upon assuming office, I had forged ahead with increasing deposit insurance premiums to build our financial resources, but by the
summer of 2006, it was too late to accumulate a meaningful extra cushion
before the mortgage crisis hit and our losses started to mount.

Under our accounting rules, the FDIC projects the number of likely
bank failures over the next twelve months and their cost, and then deducts
that amount from the fund we maintain to back our insurance guarantee.
In the second quarter of 2008, the Deposit Insurance Fund had declined to
$45.2 billion from $52.4 billion just a year earlier. However, we had already
set aside more than $7 billion to cover our likely losses from IndyMac and
other banks and thrifts that we thought would fail over the next year. That
money was in a special account called a "contingent loss reserve" (CLR).
Families do much the same thing when they know they have an upcoming expense such as school tuition, an insurance payment, or property
taxes. From the perspective of managing a household budget, it sometimes
helps to put committed money into a separate account to make sure it is
not used for other purposes. Our contingent loss reserve served a similar
purpose.

The media would consistently ignore the amount we had in that special account—the CLR—and instead focus on the DIF, which was declining rapidly. (By the end of 2008, it had plummeted to $17.3 billion, and by
2009, it was in negative territory, though our total reserves, which included
the CLR, always remained positive.) It was a more sensational story to suggest that the FDIC was running out of money than to accurately account
for our total resources, which included the CLR. Of course, even if we had
run out of money (which we never did), we had the power to impose additional assessments on the industry as well as borrow from the Treasury.
The FDIC guarantee is statutorily backed by the full faith and credit of the
United States. We *were* the government, and the only way we could run out
of money was if the Treasury Department or Congress refused to honor our
"full faith and credit" obligations. That would be tantamount to a U.S. government default, and it just wasn't going to happen.

But all of that was overlooked in the sensationalistic coverage of the burgeoning financial crisis. Dealing with media and public inquiries about our
financial resources became a daily task for me and our press office. I will
never forget getting onto a plane to go to Phoenix to speak to a community

banking group. I was sitting in coach, as I always did on domestic flights. (Those movies showing senior government officials in first class and private planes are la-la land.) Another passenger boarding, a young man in his twenties, stopped in the aisle, looked down at me, and asked if I was Sheila Bair, the chairman of the FDIC. When I said yes, he stated in a quite loud voice, "Holy cow! You must be running out of money if they have you sitting in coach." I replied in an equally forceful voice, "No, we have plenty of money. Your deposits are safe, and I always ride coach."

Early in my tenure at the FDIC, the late William Seidman, the legendary FDIC chairman who had steered the agency through the S&L crisis, told me that my success in the job would rise or fall on how successfully I handled the media. His words echoed loudly in my head when, every morning, I would peruse our press clips and see at least one article saying that the FDIC was going broke. I gave speeches and media interviews and took a road show through seven major cities to explain our financing to the public and local media. We had a perfect track record in protecting people's money through thousands of bank failures over our seventy-five-year history.

I also reached out to Suze Orman, who had a strong brand and trust relationship with the public based on her straight-talking, commonsense approach to personal financial management. Suze agreed to help us set up a new website devoted exclusively to explaining to people how FDIC insurance worked. She and her staff spent days with us providing free help in making the site as user-friendly as possible. She also agreed—again for free—to appear in a series of public service ads (PSAs) assuring people about the safety of their insured deposits. I met her in New York in August 2008 to film the ads. She, of course, had a coterie of wardrobe/makeup/hair specialists (at her own expense) to help her pretty up for the glaring lights and cameras. I, on the other hand, had my teenage son, Preston, with me to hold my purse while we did the shoot. She offered to let her "beauty team" work on me. I said sure. I'll never forget her hairstylist, a Russian gentleman. He asked me if it was okay to take a little off the sides of my below-chin-length hair. I said sure. After thirty minutes—and a significant amount of my hair tumbling to the floor—he pulled out his blow-dryer and started styling away. My back had been to the mirror the whole time, and when he was finished, he whirled me around so that I could see the masterpiece. My hair was exactly the same style as Suze's except parted on the other side. If you watch the PSAs, you can see that we look like the mirror image of each other. My kids called it my "Suze-do."

Ultimately, our public education campaign was successful. Not only did people leave their insured deposits in the banks, but insured deposits started growing as a result of the public's faith in us. However, other bank creditors who were not protected by us, including uninsured depositors, started to withdraw their money from institutions viewed as being at risk of failure. That was particularly true for institutions that, like IndyMac, had large exposures to high-risk mortgages on the West Coast.

WaMu was hit particularly hard. Deposit outflows averaged $1.2 billion a day during the first week after IndyMac's failure; the following week they averaged $750 million a day, tapering down to average withdrawals of $550 million a day the week after. Wachovia (because of its misguided purchase of Golden West) was also hemorrhaging deposits, but for whatever reason, its primary regulator, the OCC, did not alert us to that fact until much later on. (By July, we had put our own monitors into WaMu but not Wachovia, based on the OCC's assurances that it was in sound condition.) WaMu's deposit outflows tapered off after the fourth week but continued at elevated levels. In addition, depositors started restructuring their uninsured deposits into insured accounts, by, for instance, setting up trust accounts or separate accounts in other family members' names. To make up for the lost funds, WaMu started borrowing much more heavily from the Federal Home Loan Banks.

Receiving daily reports about WaMu's deposit outflows made me physically ill. All of those events would dramatically increase the FDIC's costs if WaMu failed.

A bank can essentially fail in one of two ways: It can become insolvent, meaning that the amount of capital it has is insufficient to cover its losses on its loans and other assets. That is why regulators watch each bank's capital ratios very closely; when it dips below 2 percent, federal law requires that the regulators close the bank within ninety days, unless it can raise more capital. As we learned during the S&L crisis, insolvent institutions need to be closed quickly to minimize losses. If a failed institution is left open, the management will typically get deeper and deeper into high-risk lending in an attempt to generate fat returns to dig their way out. But those high-risk loans end up generating even more losses. That is exactly what happened during the S&L crisis, and the cleanup cost the taxpayers more than $125 billion.

A bank can also suffer a liquidity failure. That essentially means that it runs out of money to meet its obligations, including deposit withdrawals. A bank nearing insolvency will frequently fail because it runs out of cash, even though it is technically still solvent. The market anticipates that its capital base is insufficient to absorb likely losses, so creditors will try to pull out early, before the failure occurs. Some creditors—such as insured depositors and those holding collateral to secure their loans—are protected in an FDIC resolution. However, unsecured creditors, including uninsured depositors, are not. So they are the first to try to pull out when it looks as though a bank is running into trouble. They want to escape whole because they know they will take a haircut if the FDIC has to take over. That increases the FDIC's costs in two ways.

First, in an FDIC resolution process the failing institution will typically have to replace the uninsured deposits or unsecured loans with other sources of funding that are protected from loss: in the case of WaMu, uninsured deposits and unsecured loans were being replaced with insured deposits and loans secured with collateral. For instance, the FHLBs lend only on a secured basis and typically demand a bank's best loans as collateral for their lending. When the bank fails, the FDIC must turn all of that collateral over to the FHLB. We cannot sell those high-quality assets to recoup our losses, so our costs for a bank that relies heavily on FHLB loans are typically quite high, as we saw with IndyMac.

Second, once the market perceives that a bank or thrift is on a failure trajectory, it will start losing franchise value. This means that the longer we wait to resolve an institution, the lower the price we will receive when we sell it off. No one wants to do business with an institution that looks as though it will fail. So valuable business customers leave and find new banking relationships. It becomes more expensive for a failing institution to fund itself. It may have to pay high interest rates to keep even insured deposits. As its access to unsecured lending dries up, it will have to tie up good assets to post as collateral for loans. All those things make a bank unattractive to potential buyers.

That was precisely what was happening to WaMu. Its valuable deposit franchise was being eroded through massive withdrawals. It was losing business customers and having to turn to more expensive ways to fund itself to meet its obligations. Fortunately, through our public outreach and aggressive media campaign, we were able to stabilize its insured deposits. I thank my lucky stars to this day that notwithstanding the media hysteria, people kept faith in us and left their insured money in the bank. However, stabilizing the insured deposits was a mixed blessing in the case of WaMu, as it increased our exposure significantly.

WaMu CEO Kerry Killinger called me at the end of July, pleading for help, but there was not much I could do. I instructed our public affairs staff to increase our public information campaign on the West Coast, and we saturated WaMu's major service areas with ads extolling the FDIC's long, perfect track record of protecting insured deposits. At Killinger's request, I also called Christopher Cox, the chairman of the SEC, to complain about a short selling restriction the SEC had just slapped on the shares of the country's biggest banks. The restriction had stanched the short sales in the stocks of behemoths such as Citigroup and Goldman Sachs, but it had also redirected short-selling activity to the smaller, publicly traded banks such as WaMu, and WaMu's share price was taking a beating. Depositors saw WaMu's shares taking a nosedive, and that was scaring them even more. Without taking a position on whether the SEC should restrict short sales, I complained that by protecting only the big institutions, it was creating more downward pressure on the shares of smaller institutions. Cox said that he was generally sympathetic but his commissioners would not support a broader ban. (Of course, the alternative was to remove the short-sale ban completely, but as with so many of the other policies pursued during the crisis, we protected the big guys and let the smaller ones fend for themselves.)

Frankly, I had little sympathy for Killinger. He had had a chance to sell his institution at a fair price in the spring to a strong acquirer, which would have permanently stabilized his institution. Instead, he had raised speculative capital from a private-equity fund. The market was now telling him that it was not enough to provide confidence in his institution's solvency. Our examiners were reaching the same conclusion. I told him point-blank that he needed to either go back to his investors and raise more capital or sell the institution. I reminded him of the harshness of our process and the fact that if we stepped in, his shareholders would almost certainly take a complete loss. He had an obligation to them to right his institution. Unfortunately, his primary regulator, the OTS, was not pushing him in the same direction. It was not pushing him at all.

As WaMu's problems mounted, I started receiving "gentle" inquiries from both the Fed and the Treasury Department about what we were doing to deal with the situation. I was trying to get our resolutions staff into WaMu to develop a contingency plan in the event that the deposit withdrawals got out of control and we had to have an emergency closing. Of course, we were being met with resistance by the OTS. On July 25, Donald Kohn, the vice chairman of the Board of Governors of the Federal Reserve, contacted me to let me know that Chase CEO Jamie Dimon had been making the rounds with Hank, Ben, and Tim Geithner to let them know of Chase's continued interest and that Wells Fargo had contacted Janet Yellen, the head of the

San Francisco Federal Reserve Bank, to say that they were interested in a potential acquisition of WaMu. That was a huge relief. My nightmare scenario was that we would have a sudden liquidity failure at WaMu and either have to set up an expensive bridge institution or sell it to JPMorgan Chase at a steep loss. If WaMu could not be sold prior to failure, we would at least have two potential acquirers. I didn't have a lot of personal experience with bank failures, but one lesson I had already learned was we got a much better price for a failed bank if we sold immediately *and* we had multiple bidders in the confidential auctions that we ran prior to a bank's failure. If Chase thought it was the only bidder, it could really gouge us. Having Wells in the mix was a real godsend.

Our strategy was to ask troubled banks to hire an investment adviser and start soliciting bidders' interest—essentially putting themselves up for sale. For the FDIC, the strategy was about maximizing the probability of desirable outcomes. Frequently, the process would result in an "unassisted" sale, meaning that the bank would find a buyer or investor to acquire or recapitalize the bank without our having to get involved—the best outcome from our perspective. But if the bank was not successful and ended up entering our resolution process, we would have a ready cadre of potential buyers who had already conducted due diligence on the bank and were prepared to make an informed bid. Even so, in this case we were unlikely to get a very good price unless Chase and Wells had the opportunity to conduct due diligence on WaMu prior to making a bid. If they had to bid blind—without the benefit of being able to analyze WaMu's loans and deposit franchise carefully—both would lowball their bids because of uncertainty about what they were really buying.

I had already told Killinger when he had called on July 25 what I thought he needed to do. On July 29, I received a message from John Reich informing me that Killinger would be coming to Washington and wanted to give both of us a briefing on WaMu's capital and liquidity positions. Instead of acting on my request, my guess was that Killinger was going to try to convince us that its condition was sound and it didn't need to sell itself or raise more capital. Of course, Killinger wanted to have this meeting jointly with his primary regulator, who, he knew, would be sympathetic to his position.

Our examiners were increasingly convinced, however, that the thrift would fail without significant new capital. I agreed to take the meeting but advised John Reich that I would be bringing two staff members, Sandra Thompson, our head of supervision, and John Corston, the head of our large-bank examination unit. In a strategy meeting with them before the briefing, I told them that we should first hear Killinger out, but then I wanted John to lay out the staff's supervisory concerns and reiterate our view that WaMu needed to raise capital or sell. I decided to have John, a tough career examiner, make the case, because I knew John Reich would try to personalize our concerns about WaMu's growing problems to me if I led the discussion. Whether that was strategic on his part or whether he was really blind to WaMu's problems, I was never sure. But throughout our struggles with OTS on WaMu's failing condition, John repeatedly tried to denigrate the FDIC's concerns by suggesting that it was all just an effort on my part to concentrate more power in the FDIC. (As Citigroup's primary regulator, Tim Geithner would try to use the same strategy against us later as Citi's condition deteriorated and we felt that more aggressive action was needed on his part.)

On July 30, we held the meeting in John Reich's office. Representing WaMu were Kerry Killinger; Thomas Casey, the CFO; and Robert Williams, the treasurer. The group presented an analysis showing an outer range of cumulative losses through 2010 of $31.1 billion. However, even their "high-loss" scenario assumed that the economy would continue growing and the bank would continue to grow its revenues, assumptions that we viewed as unrealistic and indeed laughable now, given how badly the nation plunged into recession and the steep losses WaMu's mortgage portfolio continues to generate. As scripted, John Corston told the WaMu team as much, then reiterated our view that the institution needed to raise capital or sell itself. Those words were barely uttered when John Reich angrily cut him off, stating that his comments were "inappropriate."

A few days later, I followed up with an email to John Reich after consulting with Fed Vice Chairman Don Kohn. I told him that I wanted to have further discussions about WaMu contingency planning during an upcoming weekly call held among the principals of the four bank regulators to review conditions at high-risk banks. I told him we needed a contingency plan in the event of a sudden WaMu liquidity failure, and that would have to involve reaching out to potential acquirers.

Again he responded strongly, opposing the idea of having such a conversation, even among regulators. In an exceptionally argumentative email, he reflected a fundamental misunderstanding of the FDIC's authorities and responsibilities. That was surprising to me, since he had served as the FDIC vice chairman for several years before being appointed to head the OTS. Indeed, he stated that the "FDIC has no role until the [primary regulator] (OTS) rules on insolvency and the PFR utilizes PCA." In fact, the FDIC does have backup authority to close an institution, and those grounds can include the institution's insolvency or inability to meets its liquidity obligations. In short, if a bank runs out of enough cash to meet deposit withdrawal demands or other cash obligations, the FDIC most certainly has authority to close it. Once again, he personalized the discussion, stating that "the FDIC is behaving as some sort of super-regulator—which you and it are not." Interestingly, he threatened to meet with Ben Bernanke and Hank Paulson to complain, even though both the Fed and Treasury had been nudging us on contingency planning. I forwarded his email to Don Kohn, who responded that Ben would be "glad to talk to him, but John won't like the message."

I had no desire to go to war with the OTS. For better or worse, we needed its help in monitoring a number of very sick thrift institutions. So instead of contacting potential acquirers directly, which in retrospect I wish we had done, I held off and kept trying to work through the OTS. We proceeded to downgrade WaMu to troubled status and pressed the OTS to do the same. We also pressed hard for the bank to replace its management and, most important, to hire an investment adviser for help in raising capital or merging with another institution. The two were related, as we did not think that WaMu would be able to interest investors or acquirers on an open-bank basis with the current, poorly regarded management team. However, as the Senate Permanent Subcommittee on Investigations would later document, the OTS was, at best, not on top of the severity of the institution's problems and the extreme risks it posed to the Deposit Insurance Fund or, at worst, was completely captive to the only remaining major institution that it regulated. Indeed, our internal analysis showed that if WaMu had failed without an acquirer and we were forced to liquidate it, it would have cost us a whopping $40 billion.

It was not until September 7 that the OTS forced a management change at WaMu. Exasperated, I called the new CEO, Alan Fishman, on his first day at work, to let him know that he needed to take steps to raise capital or sell the institution. I notified him that the FDIC had placed WaMu on our troubled-bank list during the third quarter. That meant that early in November, when we publicly updated our troubled-bank list, we would add another $300 billion in assets, which, of course, everyone in the market would know was WaMu. Amazingly, neither the current WaMu management nor the OTS staff had told him that the FDIC was downgrading WaMu. I notified John Reich of the call after I made it, which prompted his now-famous email to one of his staff stating "I cannot believe the continuing audacity of this woman." If only OTS had spent as much energy regulating WaMu as it had fighting us, we might have been able to avert a failure.

But time was running out. The deposit runoff continued, with uninsured money fleeing or being converted into insured accounts. The ratings agencies were downgrading WaMu's debt to junk or near-junk status, and its stock price continued to plummet. To offset deposit withdrawals, WaMu was offering high-rate, fully insured CDs and borrowing heavily from the FHLB. On the week of September 8, WaMu lost one of its largest commercial depositors, with $800 million in deposits. On September 11, its share price dipped as low as $1.75 a share, and the cost of buying insurance against a WaMu default skyrocketed. Deposit withdrawals for that day hit $1.6 billion. Within a week, deposit withdrawals would be hitting more than $3 billion per day.

To Fishman's credit, he did act swiftly to hire an investment adviser as the death watch continued. Working in coordination with Fishman, we also started reaching out directly to potential acquirers, contacting Chase, Wells, and Santander, a large Spanish bank. (Surprisingly, we also heard from Citigroup. I questioned whether Citi was financially strong enough to acquire WaMu, but both the Fed and the OCC—its two primary regulators—said it was strong enough.)

Chase initially refused to participate in the process. I called Jamie Dimon, at Fishman's request, and asked him to work with Fishman on an open-bank, unassisted transaction. It was clear that Dimon was more interested in doing a closed-bank resolution. That was, of course, the result we were trying to avoid. I was concerned that he thought we would arrange a deal in the same way that the NY Fed had arranged his acquisition of Bear Stearns. I advised him that if it came to that, we ran a competitive process, and we expected multiple bidders. If he really wanted WaMu, the only way to guarantee the acquisition was to work with Fishman and be the highest open-bank bidder.

Unfortunately, as bidders came in to look at WaMu's loans and "kick the tires," they didn't like what they saw. One by one, the investors' interest withdrew—there were simply too many toxic loans on WaMu's books and too much uncertainty about the scope of the losses. Chase and Citi were the last two to remain in, but when Lehman Brothers filed for bankruptcy on September 15, market conditions worsened significantly and WaMu experienced another $10 billion in deposit withdrawals. It was unlikely that WaMu would survive unless it started borrowing from the Federal Reserve Board's discount window. However, Fed lending—like FHLB lending—is heavily collateralized, meaning that the more a bank borrows from those sources, the more expensive it becomes for the FDIC to resolve. For that reason, the law prohibits the Fed from lending to a failing institution, and as a matter of courtesy, the Fed typically consults with us before lending to a troubled bank and does so only with our consent.

As WaMu continued to hemorrhage deposits, David Bonderman reached out to Fed Governor Kevin Warsh for help. Kevin referred the call to Don Kohn, who had been our primary contact on the WaMu situation. Don and I held a conference call with Bonderman on Saturday, September 20, and I was shocked at the combative way Bonderman pressed Don for access to Fed lending. Don held firm. We told Bonderman that he needed to continue with efforts to sell or recapitalize the bank. We also told him that given WaMu's rapidly deteriorating condition, it had to have firm commitments in place by Sunday evening. The next evening, we received an update from Bonderman. All interested buyers had pulled out. In a last-ditch effort to avert a failure, I told him that if TPG would put in $8 billion of new capital, we believed that would be sufficient to stabilize the institution, but if it could not raise that amount of new capital, we would have to go to Plan B.

But instead of being willing to commit new capital, Bonderman and the WaMu team had come up with gimmicks and accounting tricks to try to convert outstanding debt into equity. It was highly questionable whether they could execute the plan, since it relied on the cooperation of the debt-holders. Moreover, from the FDIC's perspective, their plan did little to protect us from loss because the unsecured debt instruments they proposed to convert were subordinate to the FDIC's claims in a resolution. That is, they were simply rearranging the proverbial deck chairs on the *Titanic*. In a resolution, unsecured debt and equity are fully available to absorb FDIC losses. The only way to reduce our risk was to put in additional loss-absorbing capital. But TPG did not want to risk any more money, even though it was happy for the government to get in deeper through Fed lending to keep the sick institution afloat. As a result, I said no to their gimmicks and accounting tricks and instructed our resolutions staff, led by Jim Wigand, to begin our confidential auction with an eye to closing the thrift on Friday, September 26.

Throughout the open-bank marketing process, our resolutions staff had carefully stayed away, as was our usual practice. However, once it became clear that there would be no open-bank solution, Jim and his team sprang into action. They worked the phones over the weekend, setting up Monday meetings with Chase, Wells, Santander, and Citi to review the FDIC resolution process in the event that WaMu failed. By Tuesday, it was clear that WaMu would not make it through the week, so we opened our "data room," which contained bid instructions, and notified the companies that we would be taking bids Wednesday evening.

However, at the end of the day, only Chase submitted a serious bid. Wells offered to take the deposits and a few of the high-quality assets but would not touch the rest of the portfolio without "significant support through loss sharing." Similarly, Citi would not take the loans without significant FDIC support. In contrast, Chase offered $1.8 billion to purchase all of the assets and all of the deposits, both insured and uninsured. Chase would also fulfill all of WaMu's obligations to its general creditors. The only stakeholders to take losses would be WaMu's shareholders (WaMu was wholly owned by its holding company, WMI) and its bondholders. Losses would be absorbed by bondholders and shareholders, not the government.

Press speculation about WaMu's imminent failure was becoming more and more intense, and we were concerned that continuing media speculation would only spur additional deposit withdrawals. Indeed, we already had one inquiry from Damian Paletta at *The Wall Street Journal* saying that he had heard we were auctioning WaMu, but thanks to some fancy footwork by Andrew Gray, he never ran the story. However, we had no desire to tempt fate further, so the OTS moved to close WaMu on a Thursday, one day earlier than our usual Friday closings. The transition was seamless, the deposits were stabilized, and the press coverage was generally favorable and reassuring. The day after the closing—by far the largest in FDIC history—the Dow Jones Industrial Average was up almost 200 points.

I was particularly relieved that the Chase acquisition protected all of the uninsured depositors, particularly given some of the heartbreaking instances of uninsured depositors at IndyMac. However, two groups were not happy: WaMu bondholders and WMI shareholders. WaMu's failure forced the bankruptcy of WMI within days of the bank closing. WaMu and its parent, WMI, had been in declining health for so long, most of the shares had been dumped onto the market and purchased by speculators, who were betting on a government bailout. That expectation was reinforced when Hank Paulson and Ben Bernanke had gone to Congress several days before, requesting $700 billion to provide troubled-asset relief for U.S. financial institutions. Our phones started ringing off the hook the week following the WaMu failure, mostly irate flippers. I fielded some of the calls myself and couldn't believe what I was hearing. They were at least honest; they told me that they had purchased WaMu stock at a steep discount when they had seen in the news that Paulson was seeking Trouble Asset Relief Program (TARP) funds and had been expecting to profit when WaMu was bailed out! (At that point, Congress had not yet approved TARP. In fact, the House of Representatives initially voted it down. It was not approved until October 3.)

That is not to denigrate those who took losses from the WaMu failure. And there were some bona fide purchasers of WaMu stock who took losses. But a lot of people suffered loss as a result of the crisis, and there was no defensible reason for the FDIC to bail out WaMu's shareholders and creditors, shifting the losses from WaMu's stakeholders to the government. As has been repeatedly documented by the Treasury and FDIC IGs, the Senate Permanent Subcommittee on Investigations, and the Financial Crisis Inquiry Commission, WaMu had been horribly mismanaged and was a major player in the kind of abusive, unaffordable, and at times potentially fraudulent lending that had driven the subprime mortgate crisis. WaMu's bondholders and shareholders had a duty to monitor risk taking at the institution and assure management's accountability. The responsibility was theirs, not the taxpayers'.

It is amazing to me that those who lost money on the WaMu failure tried to assign blame to the FDIC and Chase, instead of the WaMu management. In truth, Chase stepped up and took a very sick institution off our hands when none of the other bidders would touch it without significant financial support from the FDIC. To be sure, Dimon was acting in the interests of his bank, and he still believes the acquisition was a positive one for Chase. However, there is no doubt that the WaMu acquisition was risky, and dealing with its troubled-mortgage portfolio has been a challenge for the Chase management. If Chase had not acted, the FDIC would have suffered tens of billions of dollars in losses.

Another criticism of the WaMu resolution—as well as other government-facilitated mergers during the crisis—was that we made already big institutions bigger and thus made the too-big-to-fail problem worse. As a leading critic of the too-big-to-fail doctrine, I am obviously sensitive to this argument, but I think the WaMu transaction has to be viewed in the context of available alternatives. We had no legal authority to bail out the institution absent a systemic risk exception, which required the consent of the Fed, Treasury, and president. I did not think that poorly managed institution should have been bailed out. We could have set up a bridge institution and operated it for a period of time, but eventually we would have had to sell it;

the FDIC is not in the business of running banks, nor should it be. Finally, though we were making Chase bigger, we were adding only to its traditional banking operations; WaMu took deposits and made loans. As will be discussed later, the too-big-to-fail phenomenon is more a function of interconnectedness and complexity than of size. A bank—even a very large bank—that is in the business of taking deposits and making loans is "resolvable" without systemic implications because of the ease with which mainstay banking can be transferred to other institutions. So yes, we made Chase bigger, but we did not make it more complex or more difficult to resolve if—down the road—it should ever get into trouble.

CHAPTER 8

The Wachovia Blindside

On the Friday morning after the WaMu failure, we had our weekly conference call from other regulators on the status of high-risk institutions. I was particularly worried about Wachovia, primarily because of its pricey acquisition of Golden West. Golden West had the same type of exposure to toxic mortgages on the West Coast that had brought down IndyMac and WaMu. Amazingly, even after Wachovia had purchased Golden West in 2006, it had continued to make high-risk mortgages. Indeed, the performance of the mortgages Wachovia had originated after the acquisition was significantly worse than that of the loans it had taken over from Golden West. Wachovia had other problems as well. It had made a large number of commercial real estate loans that were experiencing heavy losses. In addition, it had gotten itself into trouble with the SEC by selling high-risk investments called "auction rate securities" to small businesses, charities, and other less sophisticated investors. In August, it had announced a settlement with the SEC that forced it to buy back nearly $9 billion of these investments.

In June, the Wachovia board had replaced its longtime CEO, Ken Thompson, with Bob Steel, formerly at Goldman, who had served as undersecretary for domestic finance. The bank had also raised $7 billion in new capital over the summer. However, those steps proved to be too little, too late. Wachovia had suffered $32 billion in losses over the previous three quarters. Its share price had plummeted, and its CDS spreads—the cost to an investor of buying insurance protection against a default by Wachovia—had widened considerably. During that Friday-morning call, when we turned to Wachovia's primary regulator, the OCC, for an update on Wachovia's position, OCC's staff told us that the bank's liquidity was stable. I was surprised but relieved. Having just resolved the $300 billion WaMu, I had no desire to turn around and tackle an $800 billion institution.

My relief was short-lived. Late Friday evening, I was contacted by OCC head John Dugan, who had been abroad and had not participated in the earlier call. He told me that Wachovia was having some problems and we needed to talk over the weekend. That was followed by an email I received from FDIC senior staff member John Lane early Saturday morning, who had been notified by his counterpart at the OCC, Michael Brosnan, that Wachovia was in serious trouble. Its board had held an emergency meeting on Friday and determined that Wachovia either had to raise capital or merge with either Wells Fargo or Citigroup, both of which had expressed an interest in an acquisition. It had also determined that a capital raise was not feasible, given the current market conditions. Brosnan told John Lane that "the market has turned on them" (counterparties refusing to do business with them) and that the FDIC "should start thinking about contingency planning as Mike said they could only last a couple of weeks on their own." That was followed by an email from OCC Senior Deputy Comptroller Douglas Roeder to me informing me of a 10:30 A.M. conference call with the OCC, the Federal Reserve Board, and the New York Fed to discuss the Wachovia situation. I asked him if we should include our resolutions staff on the call. He said yes.

The 10:30 A.M. call was full of surprises. As a number of market analysts had been saying for some time, Wachovia was having serious problems. Tim Geithner, then the head of the New York Federal Reserve Bank, was pushing an FDIC-assisted transaction for Citi to acquire Wachovia. It was obvious that Citi had already had extensive conversations with the NY Fed. Citi even had a specific proposal. It wanted to acquire the institution, with the FDIC providing a "ring fence" over Wachovia's more troubled assets and absorbing losses if they went over a certain threshold. The proposal sounded to me like a "twofer"—a bailout for Wachovia and a bailout for Citi.

I was astounded. First, why had the OCC and Fed taken so long to alert us to Wachovia's problems? Second, why was the NY Fed in discussions with Citi about a Wachovia acquisition, based on the understanding—not shared by others—that the FDIC would help it cover its losses? Wachovia's CEO, Bob Steel, was in active conversations with Wells Fargo for a privately negotiated acquisition that did not involve any government support. And I was very concerned that word of the NY Fed's active engagement with Citi about an FDIC-assisted deal would get out and disrupt the discussions with Wells. Why would Wells want to buy Wachovia completely on its own dime if it thought it could get some help from the FDIC?

Steel was supposed to have breakfast in New York with Wells Chairman Dick Kovacevich on Sunday morning. After hearing how fragile Wachovia was, I contacted Steel and asked him to keep me posted on the status of the discussions. After the breakfast, Steel reported back that it had gone well. He and one of his top executives, David Carroll, had broken bread in Kovacevich's suite at the plush Carlyle hotel. The talks had been positive, and Kovacevich had ended the conversation by talking about the share price offer, which he said "could not be in the twenties." Steel took that to mean that the offer from Wells would be between $15 and $20 a share. He felt good about the breakfast but was disappointed that they had not yet closed the deal.

I was worried.

As I relayed in an email to Ben, Don Kohn, John Dugan, and Tim Geithner after my call:

> Just got off the phone with Bob Steel. Things are still going in the right direction with wells, though they are hampered by uncertainty that this perhaps could be a government facilitated deal. It doesn't help that Citi has told everyone they are looking for government assistance.
>
> I think it is important for both the fed and the OCC to make clear to both potential bidders that this institution has significant value and the transaction should occur on an open bank, unassisted basis. That is certainly our view.

To be polite but somewhat pointed about the New York Fed's advocacy for an assisted deal, I added, "You probably have already done this but I would encourage you to make this clear as soon as possible."

For once, John Dugan and I agreed on something. He responded with support: "Understood. . . . We will continue to make these points with both bidders."

Steel had asked me to call Kovacevich directly to encourage him to close the deal. I think that Steel, one of the savviest people I have ever met, also feared that the NY Fed might be trying to push Wachovia into Citi's arms as a backdoor way to bail it out, though the deal would be camouflaged as a way to help Wachovia. If that was the game plan, it would not want a Wells acquisition to go through. My getting involved would help counter the NY Fed. But the risk was that I might compound the problem if I talked to Kovacevich. He might try to engage me about the prospect of FDIC assistance, and I wanted the acquisition to go through without FDIC support. Up to that point, at least, Kovacevich had not even hinted that Wells would need government help. I decided not to make the call.

How would a Wachovia acquisition help Citigroup? Citi had forayed deeply into the subprime and CDO markets, which were in severe distress. It had suffered four consecutive quarters of losses. It also had a highly unstable funding base; much of its funding came from deposits overseas, which were not covered by strong deposit insurance guarantees similar to those provided by the FDIC. It had very little in the way of domestic deposits that we insured, so our direct exposure to it was quite small. Funding its U.S. assets with foreign deposits kept its deposit insurance premiums low. However, at the same time as Citi's problems mounted, those foreign uninsured deposits had become highly unstable. Citi needed a domestic insured deposit base to provide it with a stable source of funding. In that regard, Wachovia's $450 billion in U.S. deposits was highly attractive. But that would also dramatically increase the FDIC's exposure to Citi.

I waited all day for word as to whether the Wells acquisition was going through. Little did I know that shortly after Kovacevich's breakfast with Steel, he had initiated a call with the OCC, NY Fed, and Federal Reserve Board to let them know that he was unwilling to move forward without government assistance. Indeed, I knew nothing about the call until I read about it in David Wessel's book *In Fed We Trust: Ben Bernanke's War on the Great Panic.* It is amazing to me that given the fragile state of Wachovia and the need for FDIC intervention if the Wells deal came off the table, none of the primary regulators bothered to call and give us a heads-up. (I hasten to add that Ben Bernanke was not on the call and was unaware that we had not been notified.) Was it gross incompetence or unbelievable disrespect? Or was it just the all-boys network wanting to make the decisions among themselves, as many commentators have speculated? Maybe the boys didn't want Sheila Bair playing in their sandbox. Or, equally likely, they may have wanted to force us to bail out both Wachovia and Citi without imposing losses on market participants, as we had with WaMu. The longer they waited to notify us, the more difficult it would be for us to prepare for a bank closing and find a buyer. Without enough preparation time, a bailout would have to be the default option.

Late Sunday afternoon, after contacting Steel, who had also been left in the dark, I decided to contact Wells directly. If the deal had gone sour, we needed to start to prepare. I called Warren Buffett to get contact information for John Stumpf, Wells' CEO. I had always found Stumpf to be professional and direct in my dealings with him, unlike Kovacevich, a former marine, who was known for his combative, confrontational style. Stumpf told me that the deal was off and acted somewhat surprised that I had not been notified. I thanked him for the information and headed in to the office.

With the markets coming unglued and Wachovia's liquidity highly unstable, I felt we had no alternative but to act to facilitate a stabilizing merger before Wachovia opened for business on Monday morning. We could not afford the risk of a disorderly failure if Wachovia could not meet the withdrawal demands of its creditors, including depositors, once it reopened its doors. A bank run on Wachovia could have very well precipitated widespread panic. I notified the other regulators and the FDIC resolution staff that we would be contacting Wells and Citi to solicit bids for an FDIC-facilitated transaction.

No sooner had I reached the office than I received separate calls from Ben Bernanke and Josh Bolten, President Bush's chief of staff. The men informed me that the Fed and White House, respectively, would support a systemic risk exception for Wachovia. This was their polite way of telling me not to try to close Wachovia as we had done with WaMu. The argument that Tim and other bailout advocates were making was that because we had imposed losses on WaMu shareholders and bondholders, we had destabilized the market, so we should be prevented from imposing any further losses on bank stakeholders, particularly bondholders. Of course, the facts did not bear that out. The WaMu closing had been virtually a nonevent. They pointed to the fact that the stock market had fallen precipitously on Monday, four days after we closed WaMu. But that had been in reaction to Congress's failure to pass the TARP legislation, not the WaMu closing, as contemporaneous market analysis clearly demonstrated. If there was a relationship between WaMu's failure and Wachovia's problems, it had nothing to do with the fact that WaMu's bondholders had taken losses; it was because Wachovia had the same type of exposure to toxic loans on the West Coast that had brought WaMu down.

But that was only the beginning of a profound philosophical disagreement between me and Tim Geithner. He did not want creditors, particularly bondholders, in those large, failing financial institutions to take losses. I did. For years, those poorly managed institutions had made huge profits and gains from their high-flying ways, and large institutional bond investors had provided them with plenty of cheap funding to do so. Their primary regulators, the NY Fed and OCC, had stood by as bond investors extended credit to the behemoths based on the implied assumption that if anything went wrong, the government would bail them out. But we do not have an insurance program for big bond investors. They are sophisticated and well heeled and can fend for themselves. There is no reason for the government to protect them. We do have an insurance program for Main Street bank depositors through the FDIC under a system that requires the FDIC to impose losses on uninsured depositors and other creditors for "nonsystemic" institutions. We charge banks a premium for that insurance coverage, which inevitably is passed on to consumers. Why should the mother of a soldier in Afghanistan or a policewoman making $50,000 a year have to take losses on their uninsured deposits, while the FDIC bails out big banks and those who have invested in them?

Late Sunday afternoon, I instructed FDIC staff to talk with Citi and Wells about bidding on either an open- or closed-bank basis. I wanted to at least have some sense of whether a closed-bank deal was possible and what it might look like, to compare against the cost of bailing Wachovia out. However, there were a number of impediments to a closed-bank transaction. For one thing, Wachovia was a bigger and more complex institution than WaMu. It had multiple bank charters and significant operations outside its insured banks, most notably several retail securities brokerages. Using FDIC resolution powers on Wachovia would require that we split up the franchise, resolving the banks and likely sending the holding company and brokerages into bankruptcy. But perhaps more important, the main bank's primary regulator, the OCC, whose job it was to revoke the charter of a failing institution, flatly refused to do so. John Dugan clearly did not want the embarrassment of a major national bank being closed on his watch. (Indeed, months later, after massive bailouts were required to stabilize two of his largest charters, Citigroup and BofA, he would publicly criticize community bank failures for causing losses to the FDIC while boasting that none of his major banks had been closed.) Given the opposition of the OCC to closing Wachovia, it is hardly surprising that both Wells and Citi refused to bid on a closed-bank basis in defiance of the wishes of their primary regulator.

Much misinformation has been written about that long night as we worked with Wells and Citi to come up with firm bids. Both Wessel and Andrew Ross Sorkin, in his book *Too Big to Fail: The Inside Story of How Wall Street and Washington Fought to Save the Financial System—and Themselves,* erroneously allege that the night was spent with the other regulators wrangling with me over whether to close Wachovia. Hank Paulson (who was not involved at all in the discussions) asserts that the night was spent with my trying to get the Fed or the Treasury to foot the bill for the bailout. Neither version is true. Having received calls early Sunday evening from both the chairman of the Federal Reserve Board and the White House chief of staff making clear that they wanted a bailout, I saw the writing on the wall. My efforts to try to see what closed bids would look like were quickly stymied by Citi's and Wells' refusing to entertain a closed-bank transaction. So I gave up early, and the main reason the negotiations took all night was that Wells took several hours to come forward with a bid and then hours more had to be devoted to analyzing the competing bids and working through the legal and accounting issues associated with the transaction. Our head of resolutions, Jim Wigand; Art Murton, who headed research; and our COO, John Bovenzi, had been in phone communication with Wells all night as Vice Chairman Marty Gruenberg and I sat in my office waiting for the staff to notify us of the winning offer. Finally, I got on the phone with the Wells people directly and, frankly, let them have it. (I get cranky when sleep deprived.) Less than twenty-four hours earlier, the chairman, Dick Kovacevich, had been talking about an acquisition of potentially $15 to $20 a share with no government support. How could things have changed so dramatically since then? I told them I wanted a firm offer and I wanted it then, or else we would go with a competing bid.

That competing bid, of course, was from Citi. Consistent with the proposal that the NY Fed had been pushing on Saturday, it submitted a bid of $1 a share, with the FDIC providing protection on a $312 billion pool of high-risk mortgage and commercial real estate assets for losses in excess of $42 billion. In return for providing loss protection, the FDIC would receive $12 billion in preferred stock and warrants. On its face, the latter aspect of the offer looked like a good deal for the FDIC, and if Citi had been a healthy institution, it might have been. But the truth was—as we were only starting to fully appreciate—that Citi was a very sick institution, and it was happy to pay us a generous amount in stock for our assistance because the NY Fed and OCC would let it count that $12 billion as capital, thereby improving its sagging capital ratio. That was unbelievable to me. The main purpose of regulatory capital requirements is to protect the FDIC from losses should an institution fail. But there was no loss protection if we were the ones holding the shares of stock. (We had asked for a commitment from Citi to go to the market to raise $15 billion in real capital issuance, but the Fed and OCC had not supported our request, and Citi had refused.)

After my conversation with the Wells team, they also came up with a bid that was less favorable to the FDIC under our least-cost test. Under our authorizing statute, we are required to pursue the bid that imposes the least cost on the government, and we have established procedures and methodologies for making the least-cost determination. Wells proposed that the FDIC provide protection on a smaller pool of $127 billion of Wachovia assets. Wells would take the first $2 billion in losses; after that, the FDIC would cover 80 percent of the losses, but our total exposure would be capped at $20 billion. That bid was better from the perspective that Wells was a much healthier and better-managed company and, as a California-based lender, had much more experience than Citi managing mortgage assets on the distressed West Coast. It was also better in protecting our "tail" risk; that is, we knew we would likely have to pay out some amount in loss protection, as losses on that $127 billion portfolio were likely to exceed $2 billion, but we also knew our maximum exposure would be $20 billion. With the Citi deal, we were much less likely to pay anything on the loss protection because Citi would be covering initial losses up to $42 billion, a very high amount. However, if losses turned out to be catastrophic, there was no cap on our exposure, which theoretically could run up to $270 billion. And of course, there was always the risk that Citi itself would run into trouble, even with Wachovia's stabilizing deposit base. In that case, the whole mess would be back in our arms and that $12 billion in premiums would amount to nothing. Standing alone, Citi's insured deposits were only about $125 billion. But with that deal, its insured deposits would balloon to nearly $600 billion.

However, under the rules we follow in determining least cost, we could not take into account the relative health and risks of the acquirer, and both the OCC and the NY Fed had approved Citi as healthy enough to acquire Wachovia. But our examiners did need to evaluate the probability of FDIC losses in both deals to confirm that the projected losses from the Citi deal would be less costly than the Wells proposal. Because of the lateness in being notified of Wachovia's problems, our examiners were not familiar with the quality of Wachovia's assets, and it took them some time, working with the OCC examiners, to complete their analysis. They had to rely heavily on the OCC supervisory staff but finally concluded there was minimal likelihood that the losses on the $312 billion pool of assets would exceed $42 billion, and thus Citi should win the bid.

The other problem we encountered was an accounting one. If our examiners turned out to be wrong and we did end up having to pay out on the Citi deal, our only source of available cash was the Deposit Insurance Fund. But under our statutory scheme, losses associated with systemic risk determinations are supposed to be paid for through a special assessment that falls primarily on large institutions, not the DIF, which is there to protect insured deposits, not bail out big banks. So we asked Treasury if they would be willing to set up a separate line of credit that we could borrow from to make Citi payments, which would be repaid through the special assessment, should the unexpected happen and losses exceeded $42 billion.

I was trying to avoid the prospect of dipping into our declining reserves to support this bailout package. But we were asking only for a special line of credit, which the FDIC would repay in full. We did not ask Treasury to cover possible losses on the Citi deal.

In truth, it was the first time the FDIC had completed a transaction under the systemic risk exception, and we received little advance notice or cooperation from other regulators. FDIC staff worked tirelessly all night to work through the analytical, legal, and accounting issues to get the deal done, and instead of being thanked, our efforts were met with snide, off-the-record criticism that Wessel and Sorkin took at face value without contacting us for a response. Ben Bernanke, ever the gentleman, sent an email to me on the morning of Tuesday, September 30, congratulating us on our "extraordinary actions" on Sunday night and the "ability of your staff to accomplish this in practically no time. I don't think the markets appreciate the size of the bullet that was dodged—although everyone will understand it when the history is written." Hope you are right, Ben.

My board, the Fed, the Treasury, and the White House all approved the Citi deal early Monday morning, and it was announced before the markets opened. Ben Bernanke and Hank Paulson hailed the deal as reinforcing the government's commitment to financial stability. I thought our work was done; all that was left was approval by the Citi and Wachovia boards. But by Wednesday morning, Citi still hadn't closed the deal, and in fact, it was renegotiating key provisions of its transaction with Wachovia without even consulting us. Then, on Wednesday afternoon, I received a call from Hank Paulson advising me of a rumor that Wells was going to come back in with an offer to buy Wachovia without government assistance. He called back on Thursday to confirm that Wells was ready to make an offer. I was a bit perplexed that I still had not heard directly from Wells, so I contacted Bob Steel to see if he had heard from Kovacevich. He had not and was getting ready to board a plane, so he asked me to contact Jane Sherburne, Wachovia's general counsel.

In the interim, I received a call from Dick Kovacevich, who finally notified me that Wells was getting ready to make an offer for Wachovia. I couldn't believe it! After jerking Bob Steel and the Wachovia board around during the weekend, then tormenting us all Sunday night and Monday morning as

we waited for them to make a bid, I was concerned that he was just mess-
ing around again and wasn't fully committed to making a serious offer. He
somewhat sheepishly told me that Wells had had more time to analyze the
risks associated with Wachovia's loans. He also referenced a recent tax ruling that made the economics of the deal work better. I did not know anything about the tax ruling he was referring to (which later became quite a
controversy), but it did not surprise me that he was referring to the tax consequences of the deal. Tax considerations frequently drive merger decisions,
whether they are of banks or any other entities.

He asked me if I had any objection to Wells moving forward. Since Wells
was not asking the FDIC for assistance and since Citi had left itself vulnerable by not yet completing its own transaction, I really didn't have much
leverage to object, even had I wanted to (which I didn't). I did tell him, however, that he should not move forward unless he had a written, irrevocable,
firm offer approved by his board. Wachovia was still a highly unstable institution, and it should not move forward unless they were serious and could
execute quickly.

I then called Sherburne, gave her a heads-up about the Wells offer, and
reaffirmed, once again, that they shouldn't even talk to Wells unless it had
a firm written offer. I also advised her of the FDIC's "nonobjection" posture
and wished her good luck.

Later that night, I would receive calls from both Steel and Sherburne, giving me updates on the discussions and seeking my input on what to do in
what was clearly a highly unusual and unprecedented situation. I felt that
I was walking a fine line. Regardless of my personal views, it was really up
to the Wachovia board. Its institution was failing, and one of these transactions had to go through. I told Steel and Sherburne that they needed to act
in the interests of their shareholders, but I also stated the obvious: that, at
$7 a share, the Wells deal was clearly the better offer.

Around 5 A.M., Steel and Jane notified me that their board had approved
the Wells offer. Steel asked me if I would join him on the call to Citi's CEO,
Vikram Pandit, to deliver the news. I agreed. I didn't want Citi trying to
relitigate Wachovia's decision with me, so being on the call to make clear we
weren't going to get in the way of this seemed to make sense. Pandit grog-
gily answered the phone, and Steel got straight to the point. The silence was
deafening. Talk about a rude awakening! Pandit asked me if I would get off
the phone, which I did. I can only imagine the conversation he had with
Steel after I hung up.

Then my phone rang. It was Pandit. He wanted to up the Citi offer to $7 a share, but he wanted the FDIC to continue to support the deal with the loss-sharing arrangement. I told him we had committed to his $1-a-share deal and would stick with that if the Wells deal did not go through. (The Fed still had to approve the Wells acquisition.) But we were not going to subsidize his getting into a bidding war with Wells, particularly since Wells was not seeking government assistance.

The Wells deal was announced early Friday morning. Over the next several hours there was a flurry of calls and emails that culminated in a very heated exchange on Friday evening among all of the regulators. The Fed wasn't sure that it wanted to approve the Wells deal. Instead of being pleased that Wells had agreed to buy Wachovia without government help, Tim Geithner was arguing that the Wells acquisition would hurt the credibility of the government in backing transactions. At the behest of the Fed, we issued a statement, also on Friday morning, stating that we would stand behind the original Citi deal if the Wells deal did not go through.

During the Friday evening call, Tim Geithner was apoplectic. He wanted us to object to the Wells transaction and support Citi in making an enhanced bid of $7.50 a share. That would increase the cost of the transaction for Citi by another $15 billion, which was a huge stretch for it. It was amazing to me that Tim wanted us to take that additional exposure when there was another offer on the table that required no government support. He used that familiar saw: if we didn't support Citi, it could destabilize the system. I was incredulous. Both offers provided full backing of all depositors and his precious bondholders. Why would they run, knowing that under any scenario, they would be protected? In any event, the Fed, not the FDIC, approved mergers. The transaction was out of our hands. If the Fed wanted to disapprove the Wells offer, we would stand behind the original Citi deal.

Of course, Tim wanted to use the FDIC as cover for the Fed blocking the transaction. I was not going to let my agency be used. It was clear that the Fed did not have the will on its own to block it, and Fed Vice Chairman Don Kohn supported us in our unwillingness to increase government support just to help Citi. I suggested that the Fed try to broker a compromise between Wells and Citi. What Citi really needed was Wachovia's stable domestic deposit base. Wells' interest was in its lending platforms. Perhaps Wells could sell some of Wachovia's deposit-taking branches to Citi, while keeping the assets. The Fed agreed, and Kevin Warsh was dispatched to try to work it out. The negotiations lasted all weekend, but the gap between the two institutions was just too great to bridge. The Fed approved the Wells deal.

CHAPTER 9

Bailing Out the Boneheads

As we at the FDIC were dealing with WaMu and Wachovia, the Fed and Treasury were dealing with the broader aftermath of the collapse of Lehman Brothers, a $600 billion investment bank, which filed for bankruptcy on September 15, 2008. Lehman's failure had created major disruptions in the markets and acute liquidity problems, particularly for other investment banks that did not have stable deposits. I believe that stemmed from a combination of factors.

First, the bankruptcy defied market expectations. Bear Stearns had been bailed out, and most market players assumed that the government would step in with Lehman as well, given that it was a much bigger institution. Markets hate uncertainty, and the Lehman failure confused them. Was the government going to bail everyone out or not?

Second, Lehman's balance sheet was nontransparent to the market, primarily because of accounting rules that allowed Lehman to hold complex mortgage-related investments at valuations that really bore no reality to their true worth. Because of that flexible accounting treatment for complex securities, Lehman looked as if it was much stronger than it really was. The lack of transparency about Lehman's true financial condition immediately created suspicion about other financial institutions that also held opaque, complex mortgage investments on their books. As a consequence, the institutions with the biggest exposures, such as Merrill and Citigroup, started having problems accessing credit even from other financial institutions, as did Morgan Stanley and Goldman Sachs to a lesser extent. (It is always amazing to me that as the major financial institutions started running from one another, retail depositors kept their heads and their money in the FDIC-insured deposits. If they had not, the system really would have fallen apart.) But probably the biggest problem related to a fairly technical provision of bankruptcy law that gave all of Lehman's derivatives counterparties the right to cancel their contracts and liquidate any collateral

Lehman had posted with them. As a consequence, Lehman's counterparties canceled billions of dollars' worth of derivatives contacts and dumped the collateral—primarily mortgage-backed securities—onto the market, which put further downward pressure on market valuations of those securities and created even further suspicion about the value of similar securities held on the books of other financial institutions. (As will be discussed later, if there is a single thing Congress could do to make the bankruptcy process work for financial institutions, it would be to eliminate this unusual right of derivatives counterparties to cancel their contracts and liquidate their collateral.)

In any event, the fallout was severe.

A large money market mutual fund, the Reserve Primary Fund, which had invested heavily in Lehman Brothers, suffered significant losses and had to "break the buck." This piercing of money market funds' veneer of safety—one that the industry had fostered to compete with banks for deposits—had the predictable result of leading to widespread withdrawals from money market funds. Money market fund investors were waking up to the reality that their money was not government-insured and that, unlike with FDIC-insured deposits, it was possible that they could lose some of their cash. Hank Paulson and his team made up an emergency guarantee program for those funds that—unlike with insured bank deposits—had no limit on government coverage. I give them credit. They created the program pretty much out of whole cloth (the fund they used, the Exchange Stabilization Fund, was supposed to be used to stabilize the dollar in world trade). Unfortunately, they did not consult with us and did not even consider that the unlimited coverage would create liquidity issues for banks. For weeks, we had been watching runs on uninsured deposits at weaker banks. Now, with a new government program providing money market funds with generous, unlimited guarantees, we were afraid that even the healthy banks would start losing their uninsured deposits, which stood at $2.7 trillion.

On September 17, I was in New York on one of our deposit insurance public education tours, scheduled to ring the opening bell at the NYSE and conduct a series of press interviews. Up at six, I made some coffee with the machine in my hotel room and opened the papers that had been delivered to my door. *USA Today* had a front-page story on Treasury's plans to announce this unlimited program, probably leaked by the money market fund industry, which had been pushing for it. I hoped against hope that the leaks were not true. If they were, we would soon start hearing the giant sucking sound of uninsured deposits draining out of banks and being deposited in money market funds, which, of course, were sponsored by giant mutual funds and retail brokers such as Merrill Lynch. I called my chief of staff, Jesse Villarreal, who was with me on the trip, to try to verify the validity of the reports before I called Hank to protest. He connected with David Nason, who confirmed that unlimited coverage was the game plan. By seven o'clock, I was on the phone with Hank, still in my PJs. He was annoyed at first but heard me out. I didn't try to talk him out of the program—clearly something needed to be done—only to place some limits on coverage to keep bank deposits stable as well as to protect the Treasury from unnecessary exposure. He agreed with my suggestion to limit coverage to individual account balances at the close of business that day. So if a money market fund investor had $300,000 on deposit at the close of business on September 17, his insurance coverage would not exceed $300,000. That had the desired effect: it stabilized money market funds without destabilizing bank deposits.

Hank and Ben Bernanke had also started meeting with congressional leaders to seek approval of legislation authorizing $700 billion for the purchase of illiquid mortgage-backed securities and other "troubled assets," aka the TARP bill. We were not involved in those early discussions and were not consulted in any meaningful way about what needed to be done. However, the bill failed spectacularly on Monday, September 29, and the Dow Jones Industrial Average tanked by 778 points. The congressional leadership told Hank and Ben that they needed to demonstrate a more tangible benefit to "Main Street" depositors if they were ever going to secure enough votes to pass the TARP bill.

So they came back to us with the idea of increasing deposit insurance coverage from the current limit of $100,000 to $250,000. I was not opposed to the idea, but I also didn't think it would make much of a difference for either Main Street depositors or banks. There were already a number of fairly simple ways for depositors to secure coverage in excess of $100,000, and after IndyMac's failure, we had seen massive amounts of uninsured deposits being restructured to obtain full coverage. For instance, a married couple could have three separate accounts, each with $100,000—two individual accounts in each of their names and a joint account. They could easily obtain another $500,000 in coverage by setting up a trust account with five different beneficiaries. At that point, the depositors who really needed additional protection were small businesses, whose bank checking accounts would periodically balloon well over our limits when they would deposit large sums to meet payroll or other cyclical obligations. Those business accounts were being pulled from smaller banks and being deposited in too-big-to-fail institutions such as Bank of America. I suggested temporary unlimited coverage for business checking accounts, and others, such as the conservative economist Larry Lindsey, supported that view. However, Hank, Ben, and Tim would not support me; they always thought they knew better. Sometimes I wonder why they even bothered to ask, except for appearance's sake. Their reasoning was that such a move would lead to "distortions," with foreign depositors putting their money into U.S. banks to take advantage of the higher limits. I thought that was somewhat ironic, given just a week before, they had been going to give securities firms unlimited coverage for their money market funds (and would later ask me to guarantee the debt of all financial institutions without limit).

I also asked for their support in raising the FDIC's borrowing limit from the U.S. Treasury. At that point, there was a tremendous amount of focus on our declining Deposit Insurance Fund, and our backup line at Treasury of $30 billion was, I thought, woefully inadequate to provide a credible backstop for guaranteeing more than $5 trillion in insured deposits. We managed our resources carefully during the crisis and, as it turned out, *never* had to borrow from Treasury. But I was very worried that should we have a very large failure, our short-term funding needs could easily blow through the $45 billion we had in reserves plus the $30 billion credit line. The credit line had not been raised since 1991, when insured deposits had been around $2.4 trillion. It was important to me that we have enough money on hand that depositors would have uninterrupted access to their accounts. We saw the instability that had occurred in the United Kingdom after one of its major mortgage lenders, Northern Rock, had gone down. One of the reasons for the deposit run on Northern Rock was the fact that it could take months for depositors to access their insured deposits in the UK. People expected ready access to their bank deposits; they needed that money for paying bills, loans, medical expenses, what have you. And in truth, I was starting to worry a bit about Bank of America. I thought it had overextended itself with acquisitions, including the planned purchase of Merrill Lynch. BofA's deposit base was over $800 billion. If the press started seriously scrutinizing our ability to protect the depositors of an institution that size with only a $30 billion credit line, we were going to have a serious public confidence problem on our hands.

But I received only token support for raising the credit line from the Treasury and White House, and in the end it was not included in the bill either. It felt like all they wanted from us was the appearance that they were doing something for Main Street, and raising the insurance limit to $250,000 was an easy sound bite. They weren't interested in having a serious discussion with us about other measures we felt we really needed. Of course, though I didn't know it at the time, they had probably already decided that they were going to bail all the big banks out with the $700 billion they were getting from Congress, so BofA failing was not really something they were worried about. But the word I got back from the White House was that Congress felt it was already providing enough of a bailout with the $700 billion. I couldn't believe the mixed-up priorities. Seven hundred billion for a big bank bail-out. Zero for the deposit insurance system.

Raising the deposit insurance limit helped Hank and Ben garner the votes they needed to finally get TARP passed on October 3, 2008, but as soon as the bill passed, the plan changed from buying troubled mortgages and mortgage-related investments to guaranteeing the debt of big finan-cial institutions and giving them capital injections. On Tuesday, October 7, Jesse was contacted by Christal West, Hank's assistant, asking that I attend a meeting at Hank's office on Wednesday morning. Jesse emailed back, "Do you want to discuss TARP? Just want to be prepared." Christal responded, "I'm not sure. I'll get back to you once I can raise with Hank," but she never did.

I showed up at Hank's office at ten, still not knowing what the meeting was about. He was sitting in a chair. Ben Bernanke was sitting on a couch. In between them was a table with a conference phone. Tim Geithner was on the line. It was an ambush. They told me that they wanted me to publicly announce that the FDIC would guarantee the liabilities of the banking sys-tem. They had even already prepared a script for me:

> It is the policy of our federal government to use all resources at its disposal to make our financial system stronger. In light of current conditions, the FDIC, with the full support of the Fed and the Treasury, will use its author-ity and resources to protect depositors, protect unsecured claims, guarantee liabilities and adopt other measures to support the banking system.

So, after failing to support my efforts to get our line of credit raised, now they wanted me to stand up and say that the FDIC was going to be guaran-teeing everybody against everything in the $13 trillion banking system— and the Treasury and the Fed would be right behind me.

It was an overreach of the worst sort, and there was no doubt in my mind that Tim Geithner was the instigator. For months, he had been arguing that the federal government should guarantee all the debt of U.S. financial institutions, but no one had taken him seriously—until now. I decided to play for time. Yes, of course, I wanted to work with them on financial stability, but a step of this magnitude would have to be discussed with my board.

I took the language back to my office and shared it with my two internal board members, Marty Gruenberg and Tom Curry. They were as incredulous as I. On the other hand, how could the FDIC turn down a direct request from the chairman of the Federal Reserve and the secretary of the Treasury? I reviewed the proposal with our staff to see if we couldn't come up with an alternative program that would help stabilize funding in the financial markets without requiring that the FDIC take such a huge amount of risk.

On the following Friday, October 10, I sent Hank a counterproposal. We would guarantee the *newly issued debt* of the banks we insured at 90 percent of face value. Current bondholders did not need our protection. They had already made their investment and were stuck with it. We acknowledged that there was a problem for banks in being able to reissue debt as outstanding bonds matured, and we were willing to address that problem, but for only 90 percent of the obligation; we still wanted bondholders to take some risk. We also wanted to charge a fee for the guarantee, as we did with deposit insurance. We weren't going to give away that government benefit for free.

For viable insured banks, we also proposed a variety of other measures. First, we wanted to launch a program of temporary, unlimited deposit insurance for business transaction accounts; that had not been addressed in the TARP bill, but a lot of otherwise healthy community banks were under distress due to trying to meet the deposit withdrawal demands of those valuable business customers. That was serving the purposes of the too-big-to-fail banks that were getting the deposits, and I was still angry that Treasury had not supported us during the congressional consideration of TARP. In addition, we proposed our own troubled-asset relief program for viable banks: we would set up a "bad bank" to acquire their assets at a steep discount and restructure them as needed. Finally, we were willing to provide capital injections, so long as they were accompanied by management changes and increased supervision. All of those programs would support FDIC-insured institutions and would be paid for through assessments on the industry. We were willing to take on the task and the attendant risks of cleaning up the insured banking sector, which was our responsibility, but we did not think we should be stretched to bail out investment banks and insurance companies, particularly now that Treasury had its $700 billion in TARP funds.

Hank called me and, after some discussion, agreed to our guaranteeing only new debt and charging a fee, but he pushed back hard on limiting the guarantee to FDIC-insured banks and then guaranteeing only 90 percent of the principal. He told me that the Europeans were moving toward guaranteeing holding company debt at the full amount and that we needed to coordinate our actions with the global community. Pointedly, if the Europeans provided full guarantees and we provided only partial guarantees, it would put our financial institutions at a big disadvantage. He invited me to attend a dinner he was hosting that night of the G7 finance ministers and central bank heads. All of the world's leading financial powers would be there.

It was a smart move on Hank's part because it helped me understand the broader, global dynamic and fears among the world's central bankers and finance ministers. Like Congress, I had been expecting Treasury to use TARP to buy troubled assets, Treasury's stated purpose. But during the G7 meeting, it became clear that no one had a plan to put a troubled-asset program together quickly enough. Debt guarantees and capital investments, however, could be put into place within a matter of days. It was also clear that the Europeans were going to be providing full guarantees for bank holding company debt. Since Treasury had requested that Congress give it the authority to buy troubled assets, the legal authority for Treasury to make capital investments was ambiguous at best and nonexistent for debt guarantees. The FDIC, with our authority to provide systemic risk assistance, was the Treasury's best bet.

We continued wrangling over the issue throughout the weekend. During marathon meetings in the Treasury Department's large conference room, my team—Jesse; John Thomas, our deputy general counsel; Jason Cave, my senior adviser; and Art Murton, our head of insurance and research—went back and forth with lawyers from Treasury, the Fed, and the OCC. As was typical, we were surrounded; it was amazing how eager and willing other agencies were to expose us to risk. Lawyers at the Treasury Department and Federal Reserve insisted that we did have the authority to guarantee holding company debt; our lawyers thought their interpretations were a stretch but couldn't definitively determine that we were legally prohibited from doing so. After a weekend of negotiations, we finally achieved agreement on a debt guarantee program that would be limited to reissuance of expiring debt and for which we would charge a fee. Amazingly, Tim Geithner argued for minimal fees, his reasoning being that we were trying to save the system, so financial institutions shouldn't have to pay for system stability. My view was that many of them were responsible for the crisis and that since they were on the ropes, we should make them pay dearly for that government benefit. At the same time, I realized that if we charged too high a fee, it could undermine the economics and effectiveness of the program.

The first problem I saw was one of adverse selection. The truth is, there were only three major institutions at that time that were clearly insolvent with no options for accessing capital from nongovernment sources: Merrill Lynch, Citi, and AIG. Morgan Stanley and Goldman Sachs were having problems, but they had been able to access additional capital from "deep pockets" (Warren Buffett for Goldman Sachs and the giant Japanese bank Mitsubishi for Morgan Stanley) and probably could have bumbled through. I was starting to worry more about BofA, but the other major financial institutions—JPMorgan Chase, Wells Fargo, Bank of New York, and State Street—were in reasonably good shape. All had remained profitable, even though everyone's funding costs had spiked after Lehman's collapse. But if we made the fees too punitive, those healthy institutions would not participate. Thus we would be stuck insuring the high-risk institutions without benefit of fee revenue from the healthy institutions to protect us against losses.

But the other, more important reason for not making the fee structure too punitive was that we were trying to get funding costs down to minimize disruptions to the credit flows supporting the real economy. Credit spreads, which reflect the cost to banks of borrowing to fund their operations, had widened dramatically. If there was a reason to provide the debt guarantee (indeed, the only reason to provide the debt guarantee), it was to keep the banks in a position of continuing to lend. Make the guarantee too high, and you defeat your purpose. So we decided to charge a fee that would replicate banks' funding costs in a normalized market environment.

The other question was how long the FDIC was willing to take exposure. Views on that question were all over the place. I finally decided on a three-year time frame. A key source of instability for large institutions during the crisis was their excessive reliance on short-term funding. The investment banks and Citigroup in particular had relied heavily on unstable, short-term funding, which had quickly evaporated at the first sign of trouble. I did not want to reinforce that by putting short time limits on the maturity of the debt they could issue. Moreover, we didn't know how long it would take until the debt markets normalized. If we had tried to cap the maturity at six months or a year, we would have been confronted with the specter of all those major institutions having to replace huge amounts of government-guaranteed debt at the same time. So we settled on a three-year time horizon to provide more stable long-term funding as well as sufficient breathing room for a gradual, orderly transition out of the program.

We were also finally able to convince Treasury and the Fed that something needed to be done to guarantee business transaction accounts. Ironically, some at the Treasury were concerned that an unlimited guarantee for those accounts would destabilize money market mutual funds! We assured them that our target was business transaction accounts and agreed to limit the guarantee to accounts that paid no or nominal interest. Those types of accounts would not be attractive to money market fund customers, who were looking primarily for investment returns, not payroll and other types of transaction services.

We were not, however, able to convince Treasury and the Fed to support a systemic risk exception so that we could provide troubled-asset relief to viable banks via a good-bank/bad-bank structure. At that point, Treasury itself was still mulling over eventually launching a troubled-asset program, and I think turf issues were a factor here—they wanted to run the program, not us. Of course, Treasury never did launch such a program for troubled loans, and I think the lack of a cohesive, centralized government program to effectively deal with troubled mortgages and commercial real estate loans continues to hinder the recovery of the real estate market to this day. In contrast, during the Great Depression, the government launched the Home Owners' Loan Corporation (HOLC) to buy up and restructure troubled mortgages; similarly, in the aftermath of the S&L debacle, the government had created the Resolution Trust Corporation (RTC), under the direction of the FDIC, to clean up the mess. But it was easier and faster to write fat checks to big banks to stabilize the system in the short term, and the harder work of cleaning up the loans still hasn't been done.

It was not until that long weekend that we were formally informed by the Treasury and the Fed that they were going to launch a TARP capital investment program. The first inkling we had of it was a press leak on Thursday, October 8. We were not consulted in the decision to select the banks that would receive the first round of TARP money—that was done by Tim Geithner in consultation with John Dugan—nor were we consulted on the amount. In fact, we were surprised to find out that the program would include mandatory investments in all of the major commercial banks because, with the exception of Citigroup, they had seemingly strong capital levels and were nowhere near being insolvent. My strong suspicion was that they were making those capital injections to provide cover for propping up the investment banks and Citi, though both the Fed and the OCC insisted that all of the nine institutions to receive the TARP money were solvent. (Of course, later, Citi would need more rounds of support, as would BofA as the acquirer of Merrill Lynch's toxic assets and unstable balance sheet.) Frankly, I was taken aback when I was invited to a meeting on Sunday, October 12, with Tim, Ben, and Hank, where they strategized over how to force all of those banks to take TARP capital. They were particularly worried about the cooperation of probably the two strongest banks, Wells Fargo and Chase. I kept my head down and mouth shut during that prep session except to say that I thought the banks should be required to commit to loan modifications for troubled borrowers. Hank and the group readily agreed to extract a general commitment from them but did not want to go so far as to impose specific obligations.

The CEOs of the nine largest banks were summoned to the Treasury Department the next day, Monday, October 13, and ordered to take the TARP capital.

The meeting concluded with most of the CEOs saying they would check with their boards and get back to Hank by the end of the day. As I exited the Treasury Building after the meeting, I confronted a wall of reporters as well as a handful of protesters standing in a Treasury parking lot, deriding fat cats and bailouts. Apparently mistaking me for a fat cat, one of them shouted at me as I walked past the group, "How much did that suit cost that you have on?" (His jaw dropped when I responded truthfully that it had cost $139 at Macy's.)

By the end of the day, all the CEOs had notified Hank that they would participate in the government's programs. At 7:30 A.M. on the following Tuesday, Hank, Ben, and I, along with the rest of the regulators, met with President Bush in the Roosevelt Room to brief him on the programs and the buy-in by the nine banks. The president actually personally thanked me for offering the debt guarantee program; it was obvious to me that there had been considerable debate within the White House about the legal authority to launch the program and the scope of the FDIC's authority. After being relentlessly pressured and pushed around, I was gratified that at least the president was acknowledging the brave step the FDIC was taking.

The meeting with the president was followed by a press conference in the Treasury's Cash Room, a beautiful room of marble and gilt, styled in the fashion of an Italian palazzo, where, in the late 1800s, banks and members of the public could redeem securities or cash government checks in exchange for the bills and coinage kept in Treasury's vaults. Hank, Ben, and I were the only three to have "speaking parts." I was exhausted from the events of the weekend, and the crowds of reporters and glaring lights of the TV crews were daunting. The weight of the decisions I had made and the unknown risks that I had assumed on the part of my agency weighed on me heavily. I had prepared my remarks carefully and decided that the best approach was to express optimism and confidence in our country and our banking system. The FDIC was all about public confidence, and as the head of that agency, I felt it was my job to tell the country that I thought it was going to be okay. The banks they relied upon to keep their money and make them loans were going to hold up and continue to provide those services. The programs we were announcing were designed to make sure that was the case.

The press conference was followed by the issuance of a joint statement by the Treasury, Federal Reserve, and FDIC, seeking to explain the benefits to the public of supporting bank lending. At our request, the press release also noted that the banks "have also committed to continued aggressive actions to prevent unnecessary foreclosures and preserve homeownership." Consistent with our usual high standards of operational excellence, the FDIC expeditiously and efficiently fulfilled our obligations under the program. By October 23, the program was in place and approved unanimously by the FDIC board of directors.

Regrettably, throughout implementation, we had to struggle against the efforts, primarily by Geithner, to make the program more generous.

Tim wanted us to guarantee the debt not only of banks and their regulated holding companies but also of any affiliate organizations within the holding company structure. I flatly refused. There were tens of thousands of such entities, and we had no way of evaluating the risks of such a bold move. Fortunately, the United Kingdom's debt guarantee program was limited to one entity within each financial holding company structure, which helped us fend off his arguments for broader coverage. But of course, all that was being driven by Citi's special needs; unlike most banks, which used their holding companies to issue debt, Citi issued its debt through a variety of affiliate structures. Unfortunately, Don Kohn, who was usually helpful to us, supported Tim in his desire to have us guarantee affiliate debt. But Don was willing to compromise, so we agreed to let banks apply for special permission to issue guaranteed debt out of an affiliate if they received approval from the Fed (which, of course, Citi did).

We also excluded most thrift holding companies from our guarantee program, because the OTS could not give us an accurate count of all its thrift holding companies and frankly, we did not have confidence in the quality of the OTS's holding company supervision. For instance, we had no intention of guaranteeing the debt of AIG, which was a thrift holding company. However, that also excluded GE Capital from the debt guarantee program, and GE—which was heavily funded with senior, unsecured debt—quickly found itself at a huge competitive disadvantage to bank holding companies, which could now offer an FDIC guarantee to bond investors. GE CEO Jeffrey Immelt called and came to see me, explaining the disadvantage his company confronted. And of course, he had the strong backing of his regulator, as well as Hank Paulson. I asked our examiners to take a look at our credit exposure. The report back was favorable on both GE's capital position and its risk management and information controls. I decided to approve it once Immelt agreed to have the commercial side of GE—the one that makes everything from lightbulbs to jet engines—guarantee us against loss. Both its financial arm and its commercial arm were triple-A-rated. It was inconceivable that we would take losses on the guarantee except in an Armageddon scenario. And the fee revenue from GE promised to be substantial, which would bolster our reserves against the higher risk of losses from weak institutions such as Citi.

The Temporary Liquidity Guarantee Program (TLGP) was the least controversial of the initiatives announced on October 14, probably because it was industry funded (unlike TARP) and the amounts involved, though substantial, paled in comparison to the trillions of dollars the Fed was throwing at financial firms. Trying to be the good soldier, I got out there with Hank and Ben in an effort to explain the public benefit of the programs. But the public backlash was substantial. Public ire was trained primarily on TARP, because of its use of taxpayer money. Antibailout sentiment continues to influence the political landscape in the United States. This anger is justifiable. Participating in those programs was the most distasteful thing I have ever done in public life. But we clearly had to do something, and they did achieve their intended short-term objective of stabilizing the system.

Looking back, I don't think the capital investments would have been necessary if the government had had the legal tools to wind down the truly sick institutions in an orderly fashion. Citi, Merrill, and AIG (which was being bailed out in a separate effort run by Treasury and the Fed) were insolvent and should have been put into our bankruptcy-like resolution process, but we didn't have the legal authority at the time. The Lehman experience demonstrated that bankruptcy was not an option for the orderly resolution of large, interconnected financial institutions. The government needed a process similar to the one we had for insured banks. Later, largely through the FDIC's advocacy, we would secure resolution tools in the Dodd-Frank financial reform law to resolve both bank and nonbank systemic entities. We also secured a statutory ban on bailouts of insolvent institutions.

But we did not have the resources, clout, or response time to try to push Congress in that direction in the fall of 2008. Frankly, from where we sat—looking primarily at what was going on inside insured banks—things didn't look that bad. Yes, we had our weak institutions, but, with the exception of Citi, they had been successfully resolved through acquisitions or the FDIC's resolution processes. As I stated in an October 9, 2008, email to Hank and Ben, "Our best available information, gathered in consultation with other bank regulators, is that projected bank failures remain manageable and within the capabilities of our industry-funded resources." Citi was a problem, but the FDIC's direct exposure was limited, given Citi's small insured deposit base. Unfortunately, we did not have a good picture of what was going on in the nonbank sector, and the Fed and Treasury—to the extent that they had better information—were feeding it to us in spoon-sized portions, and only when they needed our participation in the bailout efforts. Some of our staff strongly suspected that Tim's push for us to guarantee all bank holding company debt was more about protecting derivatives dealers from having to pay out huge sums on credit default protection than the protection of bondholders.

To this day, I wonder if we overreacted. Like the rest of the country, I was appalled that all of those institutions paid out big bonuses to their executives within months of receiving such generous government assistance. The Treasury would eventually invest $165 billion in nine institutions (most of it going to Citi and to BofA to support the Merrill acquisition) and that doesn't count all of the indirect assistance provided to them through the hundreds of billions in government support given to AIG (which was a counterparty to most of them) and plowed into Fannie Mae and Freddie Mac, which protected them from losses on their GSE debt securities. The FDIC would guarantee $330 billion of their debt, and they would receive trillions of dollars in special programs set up by the Federal Reserve to provide them with loans on terms far more generous than those available in the market. Were we stabilizing the system, or were we making sure the banks' executives didn't have to skip a year of bonuses?

Yes, action had to be taken, but the generosity of the response still troubles me. We dialed back considerably what the Fed and Treasury had originally asked us to do, and yes, on a cash-flow basis we made money off of our guarantee program. But does that justify the bailouts? How many other smaller businesses and households could also have survived intact if the federal government had been willing to give them virtually unlimited amounts of capital investments, debt guarantees, and loans? Granted, we were dealing with an emergency and we had to act quickly. And the actions did stave off a broader financial crisis. But the unfairness of it and the lack of hard analysis showing the necessity of it trouble me to this day. The mere fact that a bunch of large financial institutions is going to lose money does not a systemic event make. And the rationale—to keep them lending—didn't meet expectations. Yes, the steps taken prevented a more severe credit contraction, but the big banks still pulled back. Indeed, between 2008 and 2010, they pulled trillions of dollars in credit lines and their loan balances fell significantly. Throughout the crisis and its aftermath, the smaller banks—which didn't benefit from all of the government largesse—did a much better job of lending than the big institutions did.

CHAPTER 10

Doubling Down on Citi: Bailout Number Two

October 14 was not the end of it. By November, the supposedly solvent Citi was back on the ropes, in need of another government handout. The market didn't buy the OCC's and NY Fed's strategy of making it look as though Citi was as healthy as the other commercial banks. Citi had not had a profitable quarter since the second quarter of 2007. Its losses were not attributable to uncontrollable "market conditions"; they were attributable to weak management, high levels of leverage, and excessive risk taking. It had major losses driven by their exposures to a virtual hit list of high-risk lending: subprime mortgages, "Alt-A" mortgages, "designer" credit cards, leveraged loans, and poorly underwritten commercial real estate. It had loaded up on exotic CDOs and auction-rate securities. It was taking losses on credit default swaps entered into with weak counterparties, and it had relied on unstable, volatile funding—a lot of short-term loans and foreign deposits. If you wanted to make a definitive list of all the bad practices that had led to the crisis, all you had to do was look at Citi's financial strategies.

It had suffered losses of $9.8 billion in the fourth quarter of 2007, $5.1 billion in the first quarter of 2008, $2.5 billion in the second quarter of 2008, and $2.8 billion in the third quarter of 2008. Its head-in-the-sand management was projecting a fourth-quarter loss of $2.8 billion (in fact, it turned out to be $8.29 billion). Even after receiving TARP capital of $25 billion, it was one of the most thinly capitalized big banks in the nation. What's more, virtually no meaningful supervisory measures had been taken against the bank by either the OCC or the NY Fed. A smaller bank with those types of problems would have been subject to a supervisory order to take immediate corrective action, and it would have been put on the troubled-bank list. Instead, the OCC and the NY Fed stood by as that sick bank continued to pay major dividends and pretended that it was healthy. Indeed, in 2007, Citi was the third highest dividend payer among S&P 500 companies, paying out a whopping $10.7 billion. In 2008, it was still near the top—at number fourteen—paying out $3.5 billion, an outrageous sum given the economic conditions at that time and the bank's rapidly declining health.

Citi's CEO, Vikram Pandit, was a former hedge fund manager. His selection as the CEO had been strongly supported by Citi's titular head, Robert Rubin, to replace Chuck Prince in late 2007. Prince, Citi's former general counsel, had served as CEO since 2003. He had done the right thing by resigning (albeit with a $38 million pay package) as Citi's losses began to mount, but Rubin, who also shared the responsibility, was indifferent to his culpability. Not only did he continue in his role, but he handpicked Prince's successor. (He finally stepped down from his position with Citi in 2009.) The selection of Pandit simply reaffirmed that Citi was no longer a bread-and-butter commercial bank. It had been hijacked by an investment banking culture that made profits through high-stakes betting on the direction of the markets, in contrast to traditional banking, which focused on making loans to people based on their ability to repay. Pandit had started his career as an investment banker with Morgan Stanley but had been forced out in 2005. He had begun his own hedge fund, Old Lane Partners, which had delivered break-even performance until its purchase by Citigroup in July 2007 for $800 million. Pandit had reaped at least $165 million out of the deal. He was named CEO of Citi in early 2007. A few months later—and less than a year after Citi had spent nearly a billion dollars to buy his hedge fund—the fund was closed.

Citi had essentially bought into all the gimmicks to generate short-term profits: poorly underwritten loans, high-risk securities investments, and short-term, unstable liquidity. It desperately needed an experienced, traditional commercial banker to right the ship. Pandit had no experience in commercial banking and wouldn't have known how to underwrite a loan if his life depended on it. But he was the guy Rubin wanted and the NY Fed and the OCC acquiesced, so he got the job.

With the typical lack of adequate notice, I was not notified by the Treasury and the Fed that they wanted to do another bailout of Citi until Friday, November 21, when the institution was on the brink of collapse. My weekend was spent in a round of conference calls with Hank, Ben, Tim, and John Dugan. Citi wanted the government to ring fence about $300 billion in troubled loans and other investments. It would take losses up to a certain amount, with the government covering the rest. None of us thought that the ring fence by itself would stabilize the institution. To my mind, it was just another example of cluelessness on the part of Citi management. Citi's share price had dropped to below $4, and its CDS spread (the cost to a creditor insuring against Citi defaulting on its obligations) had grown significantly. Citi officials were getting numerous inquiries from their creditors about their solvency, and foreign depositors were withdrawing their money at an increasing rate. Citi funded about one-fifth of its balance sheet through foreign deposits. That had been a cheap way for it to fund itself, since foreign deposits were not FDIC-insured and thus Citi did not have to pay insurance premiums on them. However, as the institution's condition deteriorated, those deposits started to run, substantially contributing to Citi's financial distress.

Many people have asked why Citi's foreign deposits were not protected under foreign deposit insurance systems. Not all of them were insured. For instance, China has no deposit insurance system, and even in countries that do have deposit insurance, they are generally weak systems with low insured limits and the prospect of substantial delays before paying out. Another key lesson of the crisis is that many foreign deposit insurance systems need to be strengthened to provide depositor confidence. Indeed, the lack of a strong, central deposit insurer for Eurozone countries has led to massive deposit withdrawals from banks domiciled in weaker countries, further contributing to instability in Europe's fragile banking system.

As our discussions about how best to stabilize Citi began, I took the position that we should at least consider the feasibility of putting Citibank, Citigroup's insured national bank subsidiary, through our bankruptcy-like receivership process. That would have enabled us to create a good-bank/bad-bank structure, leaving the bad assets in the bad bank, with losses absorbed by its shareholders and unsecured creditors.

My request that we at least look at using our receivership powers was met with derision by the other regulators. Hank Paulson and Tim Geithner mockingly accused me of saying that Citi was "not systemic."

That was a mischaracterization of my views. I did not question that proactive, forceful action was needed to stabilize that badly mismanaged behemoth and prevent a systemic impact. But I did think we should have at least analyzed all of the tools we had at our disposal to mitigate that impact, including receivership authority to impose some of the loss burden on shareholders and creditors. I also wanted them to understand that the FDIC's exposure to insured deposits at Citi—given its reliance on uninsured foreign deposits—was limited and the FDIC should not be expected to bear the brunt of the exposure. But the other regulators were dismissive. To them, pretty much anything that was big and in trouble was systemic and if it was systemic, that meant it was entitled to boatloads of government money and guarantees. The whole tenor of the conversation was that the government owed it to Citi to get it out of trouble. As Hank said in his book, "If they go down, it's our fault."

In addition to being outnumbered, I was as usual operating in an information vacuum. That was because Citigroup's management information systems were so poor that we really couldn't be certain which operations were in the bank, and thus subject to the FDIC's powers, and which were outside the bank, and thus beyond our reach. Tim Geithner, of course, was pushing Citi's case forcefully. Not only did he want a bailout, but he wanted the FDIC to take the lion's share of the exposure. It was clear that part of that was payback for his failed Citi-Wachovia deal. At that point, the newly elected Obama administration had announced its decision to nominate him to be the next secretary of the Treasury. Given his pending nomination, he ceased communications with the institution, though he continued to advocate strongly for Citi in our internal discussions.

The conversations were intense and continued nonstop through the weekend. A brief reprieve came during a somewhat heated conversation on Saturday evening. I was on the phone in our upstairs bedroom when our discussion was interrupted by a click and then the sound of someone punching numbers into our touch tone phone. My eight-year-old daughter, Colleen, had picked up the downstairs extension and was trying to call her friend Katherine. We heard her sweet little voice come on the phone: "Hello?"

"Colleen, Mommy's on the phone," I replied. She hung up, and after a three-beat pause, we all started laughing. It eased the tension, albeit briefly.

When I was unable even to start a discussion on creating a good-bank/bad-bank structure using our receivership powers, I suggested that we at least set up a facility that would be generally available to all banks to purchase their troubled assets and liquidate them over time. I was tired of the attempts to provide special help to Citi. Both the OCC and NY Fed refused to accept the reality of just how sick the institution was. With the other major failures—Bear, Lehman, AIG, Fannie, and Freddie—the OCC and NY Fed had had no significant regulatory responsibilities, so they could rightfully say, "Not on my watch." But Citi was a completely different story. It had long been the "premier" charter for both the OCC and the NY Fed. It had a huge international presence, and as such its failure would be not just a domestic but an international embarrassment for those two regulators. What's more, Tim Geithner's mentor and hero, Bob Rubin, had served as the chairman of the organization and, as the Financial Crisis Inquiry Commission would later document, had had a big hand in steering it toward the high-risk lending and investment strategies that had led to its downfall. I frequently wonder whether, if Citi had not been in trouble, we would have had those massive bailout programs. So many decisions were made through the prism of that one institution's needs.

If I was going to be stuck with another bailout, I at least wanted the same kind of support available to other banking institutions, large and small. A programmatic approach would address the public perception that the government was just helping the big, politically connected institutions. It would also obviously be more fair. But the other regulators refused to engage on setting up a generally available program as well. I couldn't even get them to agree to require management changes at Citi.

I finally acquiesced. We were all fearful of what would happen to an uncontrolled failure of Citigroup. I tried to posture a bit, suggesting that we might move to close it (that got a nice rise out of Hank and Tim), but at the end of the day, I couldn't maintain the bluff. We couldn't let it slide into a messy, uncontrolled failure à la the Lehman debacle.

We did at least reach agreement on compensation and dividend restrictions, as well as specific requirements that Citi restructure the residential mortgages in the ring fence (but not its other mortgages). With those weak conditions in place, we settled on a bailout package that included the $306 billion ring fence, with a second capital infusion of $20 billion from TARP.

The negotiations over how the losses on the ring fence would be apportioned were difficult, to say the least. Part of the problem was that Citi could not definitively identify the assets it wanted in the ring fence, so it was difficult for our examiners to evaluate the extent of the likely losses. But at that point, all it was looking for was an announcement of the bailout—a signal to its creditors that the government would not let it go down—and it was happy to work out the details later.

We finally agreed that Citi would have to absorb the first $37 billion in losses. TARP would absorb the next $5 billion in losses, followed by the FDIC at $10 billion, with the Fed assuming any "tail" risk for losses above that. We were to be given $3 billion in preferred stock to compensate us for our exposure. The Treasury would get $4 billion in preferred stock. The OCC and NY Fed were happy to let Citi add that $7 billion into its capital base, along with the $20 billion from TARP, to make it look as if it had a higher capital ratio than it actually did.

Late Sunday, I convened my board to approve the systemic risk exception required by law before the FDIC could provide bailout assistance. In presenting the case, our staff dutifully presented the arguments that had been laid out by the NY Fed and the OCC. Those arguments essentially stated the obvious: that Citi was big and internationally active. That wasn't the issue, to my mind. The question was why Citi's shareholders and unsecured creditors couldn't assume some of the burden. During the meeting, John Reich—who was resentful of the fact that WaMu hadn't received a bailout—had pressed John Dugan on why the OCC still had Citi rated as a CAMELS 3 when it was on the verge of failure. I was incredulous at John Dugan's response: he essentially said that since the government was bailing Citi out, the OCC did not plan to change its supervisory rating. "Is that the standard now that people get a '3' if with government assistance they can have adequate liquidity?" I asked. "Well, I think it has been the actual standard," he answered. ". . . [T]hey already have a certain amount of government assistance already, and now they have more." He was certainly right about that. With the second bailout, Citi had $45 billion in TARP capital, the $306 billion ring fence, about $77 billion in our new guaranteed debt program, and access to hundreds of billions of dollars' worth of cheap loans from the Federal Reserve. "[W]hat is your supervisory strategy?" I asked him. "[T]he government's obviously very deeply on the hook now." And I continued, "I think this institution has some significant problems and it's going to require a very aggressive supervisory strategy or we are going to be back in writing some more checks." His response: "We will continue to work hard to address the problems of Citigroup. We are not committing to a particular strategy now. We don't know what the situation will be once this gets addressed, and when it is, we are looking at all kinds of alternatives. And we will keep you posted."

I couldn't believe it. All those hundreds of billions of dollars of government aid to stabilize this institution, and the OCC had no supervisory strategy—but it was going to keep us posted.

We—the Fed, the Treasury, and the president—all approved the bailout, as required by law, and it was announced at midnight that day. The market reacted positively in the short term, with a 65 percent boost in Citi's stock price. But it turned out not to be enough. Citi's toxic assets, combined with its weak management and thin layer of "real" common-equity capital, would later require more extraordinary action by the government to keep it afloat.

Then, of course, as Citi had gotten that "special deal," Bank of America head Ken Lewis approached Hank and Ben a month later, wanting a similar one. He was having buyer's remorse over the high price he had agreed to pay for Merrill Lynch, without doing enough due diligence. Though the Fed had already approved the acquisition, it wasn't scheduled to close until the first quarter of 2009. Hank and Ben felt that if the deal didn't go through as agreed, it would have a destabilizing impact on the system. I was skeptical. Lewis did not approach them until late December, when the aftershocks of Lehman had subsided and markets had calmed down, soothed by the massive government aid programs we had announced on October 14. Frankly, I wasn't wild about the idea of BofA buying Merrill Lynch. I didn't think its management and board knew much about running a major securities firm, and Merrill had really loaded up on toxic mortgage investments. My view was that holding companies and their subsidiaries should be sources of strength for insured banks, not the other way around. Like so many of the other major securities firms, Merrill had relied excessively on short-term, unstable funding and had taken on extremely high levels of leverage. It needed BofA, with its stable insured deposit base and thicker capital cushion, not the other way around.

Discussions with the Fed and Treasury started on December 21 and continued on through January. On one call, Hank got a big laugh when he referred to the toxic assets BofA proposed to ring fence as "the turd in the punch bowl." I pushed back, questioning whether there was a need for the bailout and, if so, why the FDIC should be involved since at that point in time, the problem was with Merrill, not BofA, and it was not the FDIC's business to bail out securities firms. I was also disillusioned by the steps we had already taken. They were not producing the hoped-for lending activity, nor were the big banks doing much to restructure mortgages. There were clear benefits from the bailouts for shareholders, big institutional bondholders, and derivatives counterparties, but not much for Main Street.

I wanted to try a different approach: instead of participating in another ring fence as we had with the Citi deal, I suggested that the FDIC provide debt guarantees beyond the caps imposed on our TLGP program and for longer terms, but only if the debt was used to finance new loans. Our specific proposal was for BofA to create what is called a "covered bond" structure. It could issue new debt, which we would guarantee, but it could use that money only to make new loans, which in turn would be put into a special pool and serve as collateral for our guarantee. With that type of structure, the FDIC's risk would be reduced (by having collateral to secure our guarantee) and we would be assured that the support we were providing went to new lending.

But Treasury and the Fed were bound and determined to do another ring fence. I think that they had decided months before that that would be their approach, and they weren't going to entertain any new ideas from the FDIC. I continued to resist, and Hank, reaching the point of exasperation, told me that they would proceed without the FDIC. In retrospect, I wish I had kept the FDIC out of that unnecessary bailout. But he agreed to limit our exposure to $2.5 billion on a ring fence of $115 billion, given that the vast majority of assets subject to the guarantee were coming out of Merrill Lynch, not the insured bank. For our portion of the guarantee, we would receive $1 billion in preferred stock from BofA. He also agreed to support another systemic risk determination that would allow us to offer guarantees on our proposed covered bond structure. He never followed through on that latter commitment.

The bailout was announced on January 16, 2009, but BofA never put the ring fence into place. As I had said, it was unnecessary, though we made it pay a $425 million termination fee, of which $92 million went to the FDIC.

And as we were spending all of this time on big-bank bailouts, not much was happening to help home owners. Two days after the October 14 Cash Room press conference, I gave an interview to *The Wall Street Journal*'s Damian Paletta to explain the programs and the FDIC's role. During the broad-ranging interview, I vented my frustration at the massive bailouts for institutions but timid, at best, responses for borrower relief. "Why there's been such a political focus on making sure we're not unduly helping borrowers but then we're providing all of this massive assistance at the institutional level, I don't understand it. It's been a frustration to me."

That one quote became an above-the-fold article on the front page of *The Wall Street Journal* the next day: "FDIC Chief Raps Rescue for Helping Banks over Homeowners." It would be the opening volley in our continuing battle with the Treasury over getting a comprehensive program into place to deal with the heart of our financial system's problems: bad mortgages.

Hank did ask the regulators, at our urging, to issue a statement asking banks to use the programs to continue lending. We pushed for language to tell the banks not simply that they needed to use the programs to lend but that if they didn't do so, it would lead to supervisory action. We also wanted language promising vigorous enforcement action against banks that used the programs inappropriately to pay dividends, as well as language requiring a moratorium on foreclosures where the bank had not first considered a borrower for a loan restructuring. As usual, the OCC and OTS fought us on those changes, but Ben Bernanke personally intervened and helped us toughen up the language, though, like most of our interagency products, it was still too weak.

Public outrage over the bailouts helped elect a Democrat to the White House, one calling for profound change in the special-interest ways of Washington. Even though I am a Republican, I was hoping that the new administration would bring in some fresh perspectives. The relationship between Washington and Wall Street had become too cozy, and too many of the people involved in handling the crisis—at both the senior and staff levels—had been responsible for some of the regulatory errors and missteps that had brought us the crisis to begin with. They weren't bad people, but they were human, and instead of looking forward to needed reforms, many were still looking backward, trying to justify and rationalize their past mistakes.

CHAPTER 11

Helping Home Owners, Round Two

Treasury was able to secure passage of the TARP legislation through the votes of liberals, as well as a good number of conservatives, who thought the government would use the TARP money to support the restructuring of distressed mortgages. Senate Banking Committee Chairman Chris Dodd—long an advocate of loan modifications—had specifically included language in the law authorizing Treasury to "use loan guarantees and credit enhancements to facilitate loan modifications to prevent avoidable foreclosures." When the Treasury abruptly shifted strategy from loan purchases to capital investments—without specific commitments from recipient banks to do loan mods—key members of Congress began to question whether those expectations would be fulfilled. I wondered too. I had received assurances from Hank that the Treasury would construct a program to help home owners.

Neel Kashkari, Hank's point man on TARP, had initiated conversations with us on October 7 and had received a detailed proposal from our chief economist, Rich Brown. However, as soon as TARP passed and we publicly committed to the debt guarantee program, Treasury's attitude changed dramatically. Notwithstanding the clear language of the TARP legislation, Hank and Neel questioned whether they had the legal authority to use TARP funds to promote loan modifications! (On Main Street, that might be called a "bait and switch.")

Members of Congress who had voted for the bill solely because they thought it would provide relief to borrowers were incredulous. Chairman Dodd called Hank to press him on the Treasury's plans for a loan-restructuring program. During an October 23 hearing before the Senate Banking Committee, Dodd again pressed Neel Kashkari, stating that he had received a commitment from Hank to launch a program and he wanted to know the status of Treasury's efforts. Unbelievably, to this day, Hank Paulson blames me for stirring up trouble for him in Congress over the Treasury's failure to do anything under TARP to provide relief for home owners. Either he didn't know, or his lobbyists failed to tell him, that the only reason TARP was passed was that key members thought it was going to provide comprehensive relief to borrowers.

Treasury's insistence that it lacked legal authority was followed by a pattern of attacks against the FDIC in the media. After we had in good faith provided a written loan modification proposal to Treasury and the White House, the document was promptly leaked to the press, accompanied by a whispering campaign that our program was really another hidden bailout for the banks! Reporters rightfully viewed the charge against us with some skepticism and called us for a response. Put on the defensive, we went ahead and made our program public, explaining its design and expected impact in some detail. The press leaks backfired, and the coverage was overwhelmingly favorable to our position. Then our opponents at Treasury attacked us for going to the press during negotiations.

What was our initial proposal? It was based on a loan modification program we had successfully launched when we had served as conservator of IndyMac Bank. The only good thing to come out of the IMB failure had been our ability to practice what we preach by pioneering a systematic approach to loan modifications in contrast to the one-by-one negotiations being used by most mortgage servicers at the time IndyMac failed. But the truly pioneering aspect of the IndyMac program was our success in getting mortgage-backed securities investors to support it. Up until that time, servicers' indifference, coupled with resistance by MBS holders, had impeded wide-scale loan restructurings. But once we obtained control of IndyMac, we were able to make loan mods a higher priority for servicers albeit with some foot-dragging by the IMB staff. To keep the pressure on, I insisted that they personally give me weekly status reports on the number of loans they had modified. We were also able to convince the investors who owned most of IMB's loans to support our systematic approach.

Regrettably, some compromises had to be made as part of those negotiations. For instance, investors would not agree to principal write-downs. In addition, they initially wanted to keep the debt-to-income ratio at 38 percent—far too high—but we were subsequently able to convince them to lower it to 31 percent. The approach we used was to modify the loan with three different approaches, used in sequence. We would first reduce interest rates, followed by extending the term of the loan, and finally principal "forbearance"—as opposed to forgiveness. That meant we could lower the amount of principal used to calculate the borrower's monthly payment but the borrower would still have to repay his or her loan in full if he or she sold the house or refinanced. For the problems that we were seeing in the summer and fall of 2008—unaffordable mortgages, as opposed to underwater mortgages—the plan worked well.

But it was an uphill climb to convince investors, and here was the main problem: they said they were reluctant to agree to loan modifications because of redefault risk. As discussed in earlier chapters, in a flat market, there is not much risk in trying a loan restructuring first because if it works, you have preserved substantial economic value and if it redefaults, you still have the option of going to foreclosure and recovering what you can. However, in a declining market, waiting to see if a loan mod works runs the risk that you will end up having to foreclose several months later, at a steeper loss because of further home price declines. And in 2008, home prices were going down dramatically. That led to a "rush to foreclosure" phenomenon where mortgage investors would try to repossess and sell properties quickly, before prices went down further. But the dumping of millions of properties on the market at one time was becoming part of the problem, as it made prices go down even faster. Like a dog chasing its tail, mortgage investors rushing to liquidate properties to get higher prices were actually forcing those prices to drop more rapidly. It was that vicious, self-reinforcing cycle that needed to be broken.

Our idea was this: if investors would agree to support systematic, sustainable loan modifications—and insist that their servicers devote the time and resources necessary to achieve wide-scale loan restructurings—the government would agree to absorb half of the losses from redefaults due to declining home prices. That would accomplish several things.

First, it would qualify more borrowers for loan modifications. Most troubled borrowers were being denied loan modifications because they failed to pass something called the net present value (NPV) test. That test, included in virtually all securitization agreements, required a servicer to determine that a modified loan would have more value for investors than the likely recovery if the borrower were put into foreclosure. But in making that calculation, servicers would lower the value of the modified loan based on the chance that it could redefault later on. Servicers were assuming very high loss rates from redefaults, particularly in areas of the country where home prices were falling rapidly—which, of course, were exactly the areas of the country where borrowers needed the most help. By agreeing to insure half of the loss from subsequent home price declines, we could increase the value of the modified loan and change the NPV calculation to help many more borrowers qualify.

Second, by producing more modifications and fewer foreclosures, we would slow downward pressure on home prices by disrupting the self-destructive dog-chasing-tail cycle of investors rushing to foreclosure to try to get ahead of home price declines.

Finally, we would create powerful economic incentives for investors to support loan modifications. If they refused to participate, they would leave money on the table, something they hated to do. And yes, we said it would be expensive—we estimated the cost at $38 billion—but it would also prevent 2.1 million foreclosures in 2009 and 2010. You get what you pay for, as they say, and real money was needed to counter the economic incentives relentlessly driving borrowers into foreclosure.

Our critics at the White House and the Treasury Department tried to attack us in the media by saying that our insurance program would result in payments to investors, not to borrowers. (That was quite a mode of attack after the government had happily shoveled out $125 billion to nine large banks.) That was, of course, true, but investors would not be eligible to participate in the program unless they agreed to lower borrowers' payments significantly, to affordable levels. The program required that Main Street home owners get some specific benefit, unlike the TARP infusions, which were accompanied only by vague, general commitments to make and restructure loans.

In truth, I think Hank was generally sympathetic to a loan modification program, but he was caught between two administrations. The new Obama Administration wanted its own program. The hard-line free-market economists at both the Treasury and White House did not want to make more than token public relations efforts to help borrowers. Hank had only a few months left in office, and he didn't have the focus or commitment to override the naysayers and simply launch the program. Instead, he asked me to work with the White House economic staff to try to get their sign-off, which proved to be a hopeless task.

We dutifully attended a series of meetings at the White House. Between some of the Treasury and White House free-market economists, it was death by a thousand cuts. Unbelievably, they rejected the notion that foreclosures had much of anything to do with downward pressure on home prices. "Eliminating even all foreclosures is unlikely to qualitatively change the amount of inventory" was the conclusion of a policy options paper presented by senior White House economists. It was unbelievable. According to RealtyTrac, 2.3 million homes had received foreclosure filings in 2008, an 81 percent increase from 2007 and a whopping 225 percent increase from 2006. One in every fifty-four homes had received a foreclosure filing. Home prices were already down by 20 percent, and respected experts such as Robert Shiller were predicting declines even greater than the 30 percent drop the nation had experienced during the Great Depression.

Without explanation or analysis, they said our program would cost $76 billion, not $38 billion, and would help at most 700,000 borrowers. The whole discussion was maddening, rigged from the beginning, I felt, to lead to inaction. Not a single White House or Treasury staff person sitting around that table had ever modified a loan or read a pooling and servicing agreement. Not one had ever visited a foreclosure-plagued low-income neighborhood. This was Washington at its most myopic, concluding against all the evidence to the contrary that the burgeoning number of foreclosed, empty houses had nothing to do with declining home values. We did get some constructive input and support from James Lockhart, the head of Fannie and Freddie's regulator, the Federal Housing Finance Agency (FHFA). But the rest had already decided they were going to block us, and the meetings were simply a staged process designed for them to be able to say that they had taken a serious look at our proposal before they turned it down.

At least I wasn't alone. During the meeting they also trashed other proposals made by the noted conservative economists Martin Feldstein, Larry Lindsey, Glenn Hubbard, and Charles Calomiris. All of those distinguished economists had proposed separate measures, which frankly were much more aggressive (and expensive) than ours. But they also recognized the urgency of major action to staunch the tidal wave of foreclosures and excess inventory washing up on our shores. In contrast, none of the economists at the White House or Treasury got it—nor did they want to. After the worst financial crisis since the Great Depression, they were still mired in the ideology of government laissez-faire and "self-correcting" markets.

But the markets would not correct on their own. Securitization had created conflicting and skewed economic incentives among the owners of the mortgage-backed securities as well as the servicers who had the frontline responsibility to mitigate losses through restructuring. In past crises, the market had worked because the owners of loans had also serviced those loans. Now responsibility for loan mods was in the hands of understaffed and undercompensated servicers who made more money from foreclosing than modifying. Investors were not pressing them to mitigate losses because of conflicts and perverse economic incentives among the different tranches.

Toward the end of the White House discussions, a new proposal popped up, concocted by Phillip Swagel, a Bush-appointed economist at the Treasury Department with close ties to the White House hard-liners. I had not dealt with Swagel directly but had received negative reports from my staff that he had been a key obstacle in discussions of our proposal and had also worked to undermine Hope for Homeowners, an FHA program Congress had authorized to help distressed home owners. Instead of an insurance program, his proposal involved Treasury contributing some money to each borrower's interest payment reduction. The idea was that Treasury would pay down a portion of a distressed borrower's interest, while the lenders or mortgage-backed investors would agree to absorb further interest rate reductions to get the borrower's payment down to an affordable level. In that way, Treasury would pay only for success by subsidizing reduced payments to borrowers so long as they paid on their restructured mortgages.

Desperate to get something done, I asked our staff to analyze the proposal. Could it be another way to get foreclosure rates down? But as we delved deeper into it, we became convinced that it would not work.

For one thing, it was an administrative nightmare, requiring the government to track monthly cash flows on potentially millions of mortgages to ensure continued borrower and servicer compliance. If the borrower became delinquent, the government's payments would have to stop, but if the borrower "cured"—that is, eventually made up the late payments—the government would start up the payments again. The subsidy would be good for only five years, with the borrower reverting back to the original higher rate at that time, promising another wave of defaults down the road. Moreover, the subsidy was bigger the higher the interest rate on the current loan, meaning that investors in the most abusive loans—those high-rate 2/28s and 3/27s—would get the biggest subsidies.

But most important, by not addressing redefault risk, the proposal failed to meaningfully change the NPV calculation. The majority of borrowers would still not be able to pass that crucial test and thus would not even qualify for a loan mod. The program was significantly cheaper—we estimated it would cost about $8 billion, as opposed to $38 billion for our program. But you get what you pay for, as they say, and our economists were convinced that the program wouldn't deliver. Investors would keep pressing for speedy foreclosures, and "robo servicers" would comply. They were operating within their contractual rights—rights that the government could not constitutionally abrogate. Unless the government made it economically worth their while to stop, they would continue to foreclose.

I communicated my concerns to Hank, but it was Treasury's program, and he was obviously free to do what he wanted. TARP was his, not ours. Indeed, through Treasury's lobbying efforts, we had been excluded from the oversight board that would oversee how the TARP money was used. I had no control of or power over the outcome of the discussions other than the strength of our arguments and Hank's moral commitment to me and Congress to implement a loan modification program. The White House meetings ended without reaching a decision. The participants basically bucked the issue back to Treasury. We continued our discussions with Treasury staff and kept agreeing to pare our proposal back in response to their criticisms. We agreed to require six months of performance on a modified loan before the loan would qualify for redefault insurance. We agreed to exclude GSE loans. We agreed to exclude mortgages on homes that were deeply underwater. Finally I suggested that since Treasury remained unconvinced, it should fund a small pilot program to test it. But it refused to do even that.

Media and congressional pressure continued. Even the American Bankers Association weighed in with support for a variation of the FDIC's loan modification program. Treasury and the White House continued blaming us for the criticism they were receiving, preferring to ignore the reality that the administration itself had set up expectations for a major loan-restructuring program when securing votes for TARP. Yes, the press was playing us up as the "good guys," but that was because it agreed with our policy position, not because we were feeding it stories.

The hardliners in the administration went back at us in the press, and again, it backfired. Even the *Washington Times*—a newspaper known for its conservative bent—was sympathetic to our position and was pursuing a story, which the White House killed, that the administration had orchestrated the leaks to discredit me. Then, early in December, I was participating on a regulatory panel with John Dugan, John Reich, and Randy Kroszner, who was still on the Fed board at that point, at a housing conference sponsored by OTS. The moderator asked me for my reaction about a report from the OCC showing redefault rates in excess of 50 percent on loans modified by national banks. I was flabbergasted. I had no idea what she was talking about, but she had been given a copy of that surprise OCC report, as had other panel members. I had been left out of the loop. I told her honestly that I had not seen the report but that redefaults were driven heavily by whether the modification resulted in meaningful payment relief and that in any event, even at 50 percent redefault, you were still keeping the other

50 percent of borrowers in their homes (and the houses off the market). The boys on the panel were all smiling broadly.

After the conference, we obtained a copy of the OCC report and couldn't believe the lengths the OCC had gone to generate high redefault rates. First, it counted anything that changed the mortgage terms as a modification. As it turned out, more than half of the "modifications" included in its initial report included repayment plans that actually increased the borrowers' payments by adding in delinquent amounts, late charges, and other fees. Second, it included as a redefault any payment that was more than thirty days late. But the vast majority of thirty-day delinquent loans "cure"—that is, the borrower usually catches up in the next month. By including repayment plans that increased mortgage payments, as well as short-term delinquencies, the OCC was able to make it appear as if even when borrowers were helped, most of them defaulted again. By comparison, a report prepared by Credit Suisse, which used a sixty-day delinquency rate for redefault (the industry norm) and looked only at borrowers who actually received interest rate reductions, found a 15 percent redefault rate.

The OCC press office went into overdrive promoting the report. But as its obvious weaknesses became apparent, the report was discredited, and the OCC was eventually embarrassed into changing its reporting metrics to differentiate between early and late delinquencies and whether the borrower's payment had actually been reduced. Two years later, of course, the agency would have egg on its face as private litigants and investigators unearthed wide-scale improprieties in the way banks regulated by the OCC serviced mortgage loans.

But the lowest point in the whole miserable affair occurred when our press office was contacted by Charles Duhigg at *The New York Times*, who had clearly been fed the Treasury line that I was a power-grabbing self-promoter who just wouldn't play nice. Yes, the narrative was that the Treasury had been unable to launch a program that would help home owners because I was "difficult." Duhigg had all of the propaganda that had been launched against us, OMB's over-the-top cost estimates, the OCC's inflated redefault rates, and lots of unkind comments from anonymous sources at the Treasury and White House. The notion was ridiculous—that somehow I was stopping the Treasury from making a decision. It didn't need me. We had a proposal, but it was free to do something else if it wanted. If it didn't want to work with me, there were plenty of smart people out there in the academic community who could have helped it. I liked Martin Feldstein's program (which was a variation of our original HOP loan proposal) as much as our insurance guarantee, but I didn't try to push it because the cash outlays would have been much more substantial than the $38 billion we were asking for and because I assumed that MBS bondholders—an important Treasury constituency since the firms also bought government debt—would just shoot it down again, as they had earlier in the year. The reality was that the free-market die-hards in the administration didn't want to do anything but wanted it to look as though the reason for their inaction was my being difficult.

As nasty as that whole episode was, I don't think Hank personally encouraged it. Rather, it was being driven by free-market hard-liners in his press office and economic staff. And Tony Fratto, the head of the Bush White House press office, worked with us constructively to try to counter the troublemakers. With Tony's help, the Duhigg piece turned into a reasonably balanced profile, though it still included venomous quotes from unnamed sources within the outgoing administration. The tragedy of all of that was that nothing got done. I turned my hopes to the new administration. Elected on a "change" agenda, the new administration, would presumably bring fresh perspectives and a stronger commitment to helping Main Street. But on that score, my expectations proved dead wrong.

CHAPTER 12

Obama's Election: The More Things Change . . .

Both John McCain and Barack Obama had embraced major programs for housing relief for troubled borrowers during their campaigns, so I was hopeful that a change of administration would bring stronger action. A lifelong Republican, I had voted for John McCain. I knew him from my Senate days and had deep respect for him. I also had deep respect for Barack Obama, particularly his amazing organizational capacity for grassroots campaigning, his promise of fundamental change in Washington, and his considerable oratorical skills. What's more, outrage over the financial mess we were in and the generosity of the TARP bailouts had clearly helped catapult him into office. I had high hopes that his administration would bring greater separation from the financial community and more independence of judgment.

Soon after Obama was elected, the president-elect announced that John Podesta would be the head of his transition team. I had known John for decades, dating back to the early 1980s, when he and I had served together as legal counsels on the Senate Judiciary Committee. I had been working for Senator Bob Dole at the time, and he had been working for Vermont Democrat Patrick Leahy. We had also been neighbors for many years.

From November 7 to 10, we communicated by phone and email. I pitched him on our loan modification proposal. (He had been highly supportive of our efforts.) I offered my agency's help with the transition and also took the liberty of suggesting that Mr. Obama make Paul Volcker his first secretary of the Treasury. I thought at the time (and still do) that some of the key decision makers during the 2008 crisis were too close to Wall Street leaders and that we needed more independent perspectives to deal with the substantial problems confronting the financial sector. We needed someone with gravitas, someone like Volcker who could stand up to those CEOs. The immediate crisis was over, but much cleanup work remained. Now was the time to start imposing some accountability on financial institutions' management and force the institutions to clean up their balance sheets, even if that meant that they needed to realize substantial losses.

I never heard back from John, but a few weeks later, Obama announced his choice of Tim Geithner to become Treasury secretary. It was like a punch in the gut. I did not understand how someone who had campaigned on a "change" agenda could appoint someone who had been so involved in contributing to the financial mess that had gotten Obama elected. Tim Geithner had been the bailouter in chief during the 2008 crisis. If it hadn't been for my resistance and the grown-up supervision of Hank Paulson and Ben Bernanke, we would have spent even more money bailing out the financial bigwigs and guaranteeing all their debt. As president of the NY Fed, Tim had been responsible for regulating many of the very institutions whose activities had gotten us all into trouble.

The only explanation I could think of was that Bob Rubin had pushed him. Rubin had been a major fund-raiser for Obama's general election campaign. Indeed, as subsequent economic appointments were announced, they were a veritable hit parade of individuals who had served in Bob Rubin's Treasury. Lawrence Summers, his deputy, who would go on to serve as Treasury secretary, would head the National Economic Council; Gary Gensler, his colleague at Goldman Sachs who had later served as his undersecretary at Treasury, would head the CFTC; and Michael Barr, who had served as a lower-level deputy assistant secretary, would serve as Summers's lieutenant. (Barr would later be appointed to my old job as assistant secretary for financial institutions at Treasury.) Without a team of his own, this new, inexperienced president was turning to officials in the former Clinton administration to staff his own administration. In certain areas, that made great sense, particularly at the State Department with the appointment of Hillary Clinton as secretary of state. But it made no sense to turn to the Bob Rubin team to implement much-needed reforms in the financial sector. President Clinton himself said that Rubin was wrong in urging deregulation of derivatives. Notably, Gensler, at least, has now become a strong advocate for derivatives regulation.

Obama also announced that Rahm Emanuel, a congressman from the Chicago area, would serve as White House chief of staff. Several months before, Rahm had reached out to me in his capacity as an Illinois congressman to express support for my efforts on loan modifications and, in classic Chicago-style semantics, to assure me that he "had my back." Rahm had also worked in the financial sector, but in Chicago, not New York, and I did not view him as one of the Rubin clique.

So I called him to let him know that I was willing to stay but that I was also willing to go if that was what the president wanted. Though the FDIC is an independent agency and I had a fixed term extending to 2011, I had no desire to continue serving against the president's wishes. I would be hopelessly compromised if I did not have the president's support to continue in my job. Rahm was very reassuring, telling me that he would talk with Larry and Tim, but the whole tenor of the conversation was that the new administration wanted me to be part of its team.

A few days later, on December 4, a story was leaked to a Bloomberg reporter that "Timothy Geithner, President-elect Barack Obama's choice for U.S. Treasury Secretary, is seeking to push FDIC Chairman Sheila Bair out of office." The second paragraph cited Geithner as arguing that "Bair isn't a team player and is too focused on protecting her agency rather than the financial system as a whole." It attacked me for having weakened Citigroup by refusing to block the Wells acquisition of Wachovia and "holding out for concessions" during the November Citigroup bailout. As a clear warning shot to me, the story went on to say that "Even if Bair remains at the FDIC, the Obama economic team has decided that she won't play a central role in policy."

I decided to reach out to Tim to see if he would at least tell me to my face that he was trying to oust me. I had a business trip already scheduled to New York the following day, so I sent him an email asking if he would have some time to get together. To try to take some of the edge off, I also let him know that my nine-year-old daughter, Colleen, would be traveling with me. Would it be possible, I asked, for her to have a tour of the New York Fed's famous vaults, where they stored one of the biggest caches of gold in the world?

He readily agreed to the meeting and the tour for Colleen. It was chilly and overcast when Colleen and I went to the NY Fed's mammoth stone building in the heart of Wall Street late on the morning of December 5. The coldness and sterility of the architecture served as an intimidating backdrop for a homeless person who was rummaging through a trash can on the corner. The scene seemed an apt metaphor for the bailout strategies: reinforcing the biggest and most powerful while leaving the little guys to fend for themselves. Colleen and I were promptly ushered through the NY Fed's elaborate security systems and taken upstairs to separate receiving areas. She was guided to a room with a television, while I was taken to a small anteroom outside of Tim's office, which he entered after a few minutes. He would not meet with me in his office. A bad sign, I thought.

The meeting was short. As politely as possible, I referenced the press leaks that he wanted to force me out. I asked him if he could discuss his concerns with me. He talked in generalities about the need for everyone to support the system, not individual agencies, but we didn't really get into the meat of the issues between us and nothing was really resolved. Tim seldom engaged with me directly, the main exceptions being when he was advocating for Citi and needed my help. (For instance, he had apparently railed against our decision to close WaMu but had never said a word to my face.) He was polite but unwilling to have much of a substantive discussion, so after fifteen minutes or so, there wasn't much else to say. I left to join my daughter for the gold tour.

Whoever was responsible, leaking the Bloomberg story turned out to be a stupid thing to do. Though obviously the strategy was to weaken my hand by portraying me as an unwanted holdover, the strategy backfired. Without any prodding from me, Senate Banking Committee Chairman Chris Dodd and House Financial Services Committee Chairman Barney Frank immediately wrote a vigorous letter to the president-elect on my behalf. Frank was famously quoted as saying "We have several regulators up in the tree house with a 'no girls allowed' sign." I waited several weeks without hearing anything back from Rahm. Then on Wednesday, January 7, 2009, the president-elect all but endorsed my retention by answering a question about housing policy during a CNBC interview by responding "I do think that the FDIC and Sheila Bair have had the sense of urgency about the problem that I want to see." On Thursday, January 8, *The Wall Street Journal* ran an article titled "FDIC's Bair Gets Nod to Stay, Address Housing Mess," citing Mr. Obama's quote and congressional sources.

As the question of my future was resolved, we entertained a steady stream of Obama transition team members who came to visit us about our operations and programs, including our ideas on foreclosure prevention. They included Shaun Donovan, who eventually became the secretary of housing and urban development, and Michael Barr, who had been asked by Larry Summers to come up with a loan-restructuring program. Larry also asked to meet with me. We were happy that they were reaching out, but at the same time, we had the impression that they were going through the motions because of the president's public embrace of our efforts. My guess is that behind the scenes, Larry and Tim were working hard to make good on the leaked threat that I would have no real role in or influence on policy.

My skepticism was heightened by the tenor of some of the questions the transition team asked about our IndyMac program. They were obsessed with the "high redefault rates" at IndyMac, even though none of our Indy-

Mac loan mods had redefaulted. We had operated the program for only three months. It was true that the loan mods tried by the IndyMac management before we took over had had very high redefault rates, but that was because the bank had mostly raised payments, similar to the redefaulting loans in the OCC study. When we took over IndyMac, there were thousands of "modified" loans that had redefaulted and had been delinquent for several months. We tried to salvage them, but for most, it was too late. The new mods that met the parameters of our program, those modified within three months of delinquency and reduced to a 31 percent DTI ratio, did perform in accordance with our redefault predictions. We gave Summers's people studies that showed low redefault rates when payments were meaningfully reduced, but they kept focusing on "high redefault rates" at IndyMac, even though, as we told them repeatedly, at that point the redefault rate was zero.

Daniel Tarullo, a professor of law at Georgetown University, also came by for a long visit, not to talk about housing policy but rather to discuss our opposition to Basel II. It was not a perfunctory meeting but rather a sincere desire on his part to be briefed on our concerns and analysis showing that Basel II would result in precipitous drops in capital levels at most of the major U.S. banks. As an academic, Dan had been a leading critic of the Basel II advanced approaches. I truly rejoiced. Finally, I would have an ally in the new administration in resisting that idiotic approach to bank capital. No longer would the FDIC and I be fighting alone. I was very pleased when the president announced that Dan would be nominated to serve on the Federal Reserve Board of Governors. Dan would later play a pivotal role in changing the whole dynamic of the Basel Committee away from letting banks set their own capital to setting much stronger capital standards. Not only was he an ally in domestic discussions, he also redirected the Fed so that at last the Fed and the FDIC would be aligned.

Unfortunately, though, the new administration's economic team was much more aligned with the previous one when it came to helping troubled home owners.

CHAPTER 13

Helping Home Owners, Round Three

Geithner was nominated and confirmed by the Senate on January 26, 2009, by a vote of 60 to 34. Most Republicans voted against him due to his failure to pay Social Security and Medicare taxes for several years. A few Democrats also opposed him because of his perceived favoritism to the big financial institutions and his weak record as a regulator when he headed the NY Fed. Once ensconced in office, and to his credit, Tim initiated an aggressive series of meetings with the heads of the major agencies as well as senior White House economic staff (Larry Summers, Michael Barr, and Christina Romer, the new head of the Council of Economic Advisers). Other attendees included Mary Schapiro, the new head of the SEC (due to delays in Senate confirmation Gary Gensler, the new head of the CFTC, would later join in May); Ed DeMarco, the acting head of the FHFA; the regulator of Fannie Mae and Freddie Mac; John Dugan, the holdover head of the OCC; William Dudley, Tim's choice to succeed him as the head of the New York Fed; Ben; and me.

The meetings were useful in the sense that they pulled everyone together to discuss financial stabilization measures, as well as the need for legislative reforms to strengthen the financial regulatory structure. However, they were not the "real meetings." As per usual, key decisions were made by Tim, Larry, Ben, and their key staffs, working behind the scenes. Separately, we were in continued dialogue with Larry Summers and Michael Barr on a loan modification program. Given the outreach and President Obama's supportive public statements, I was hoping we would reach consensus on a meaningful program that could have a real impact on foreclosure rates.

But the Bush free-market economists who had stymied our efforts were still working at the Treasury and, amazingly, had the ear of Larry and Tim. On February 3, an article was leaked to Bloomberg quoting Geithner ally John Dugan describing in detail "administration discussions" on loan mod programs, mentioning our insurance guarantee program but also the pay-

147

ment subsidy approach that Phil Swagel had proposed, which we knew was administratively unworkable. The article was remarkable in that John Dugan was the cited source, even though I was unaware that he had had any role in the loan modification discussions nor should he have had, given his unabashed championship of large national banks and disingenuous efforts just months earlier to manipulate redefault data to undermine support for loan workouts.

After seeing the article, I contacted Larry Summers and was not reassured by what I heard. Yes, the White House was leaning toward pursuing the same plan that Phil Swagel had proposed during the Bush administration. I requested a meeting and contacted Michael Barr in a panic, pleading for help. Michael had a good reputation on consumer issues, and I thought he would respect the views of our two top experts, Rich Brown, our chief economist, and Mike Krimminger, my chief legal adviser, on why, from both the economic and legal/operational standpoints, that program wouldn't work. Unfortunately, in that case as well as others later, Michael would be working against us.

Larry met with me on Friday, February 6, along with Michael and Larry's senior adviser, Diana Farrell. I laid out our concerns about the Swagel payment subsidy plan and told him that I would not publicly criticize them if they decided to go down that route, but that I would also not support it. I told him point-blank that the program had been devised to make it look as though the administration was doing something with the smallest amount of money possible. At most, the program would result in $8 billion worth of subsidy payments and have no meaningful impact on countering the countervailing economic incentives that were driving millions of borrowers into foreclosure.

He listened politely, but clearly his mind was already made up. However, I did detect discomfort when I mentioned the low dollar amount the program would likely provide to foreclosure prevention, as well as my refusal to support them publicly if they launched this program. Clearly, my only leverage with Larry was the new president's respect for my commitment to foreclosure prevention and desire that I be a part of the program development team (even if Larry and Tim wanted to exclude me). Obviously, the president of the United States was not going to be happy with an $8 billion program that I refused to support.

Larry suggested that we continue the discussions. I asked Mike Krimminger to work with Michael and Diana to see if we couldn't achieve some meeting of the minds. Unfortunately, Larry and his staff were much more willing to throw additional money at the program than they were will-ing to revisit its basic structural flaws. They agreed to allot $5 billion to a much narrower and more complex version of our insurance program, while sweetening other subsidies to reach a total price tag of $48 billion. They allotted $21 billion for the Bush program interest subsidy, another $10 bil-lion for a principal reduction program, as well as $12 billion to pay servicers to help cover their additional administrative costs. We were horrified by the administrative complexity of the program. We knew from our experience with IndyMac that the servicing operations were bare bones, with poorly trained and compensated staff. The program had to be simple, or the ser-vicers wouldn't be able to operationalize it. But Summers and Barr didn't want to hear that. We were equally horrified to learn that they were going to put Fannie Mae and Freddie Mac in charge of the program. That was akin to putting the fox in charge of the chicken coop. Fannie and Freddie were the biggest holders of the Triple-A subprime mortgage-backed securities. Every interest rate that was reduced for a distressed borrower could potentially eat into their returns. They were hopelessly conflicted.

Larry and I met again in his office on Presidents' Day, February 16. Again, I ran down our concerns, but I also realized that that was the best I was going to be able to do. I asked if they would at least set up an over-sight board where I could serve and help with program implementation. He said no, but they would be willing to set up quarterly advisory meetings. He also said that the president wanted me to join him when he announced the program, implying that he had already achieved sign-off. The tables were turning: if I refused to participate, I would be turning the president down.

So, notwithstanding our concerns, I agreed. On February 18, 2009, I went to Phoenix to join the president, along with Tim and HUD Secretary Shaun Donovan, to announce the loan mod program, named the Home Afford-able Mortgage Program (HAMP), as well as another program to make refi-nancing more broadly available to borrowers whose mortgage was for more than their house was worth, so-called underwater mortgages. Even while I was traveling to the announcement, Mike Krimminger was continuing to negotiate with Michael Barr in a last effort to have a fuller test of our simpler insurance program. Unfortunately, as was often the case, our program was never implemented and the Treasury's more complex program became the only approach allowed.

At the Phoenix announcement, the president was masterful in announc-ing the program, though I cringed as he threw out what I considered to be wildly inflated numbers on the programs' impact. The Treasury and White House staff had told him that 3 million to 4 million borrowers would be helped under the program. Even with our own, more aggressive proposal, we had estimated the number of successful modifications at 2.1 million tops.

Tim, Shaun, and I all flew commercial aircraft to the event, though the president asked us to fly back with him on Air Force One. It had to be awkward for Tim as I joined him on the plane, sitting in the same area that was reserved for senior administration staff. The space was furnished with overstuffed beige leather chairs and glossy wood tables. Paper place mats, napkins, and cardboard coasters, all embossed with the presidential seal and the name Air Force One, were scattered about, and yes, I took a few as souvenirs and stuffed them into my purse (for the kids, of course). About halfway through the flight, after a gourmet lunch had been served, I settled in with a copy of Peter Bernstein's *Against the Gods: The Remarkable Story of Risk,* sipping a Diet Coke and popping nuts out of a small Air Force One china bowl.

"What are you reading, Sheila?" came the president's voice. I looked up and saw him standing in our staff area. Everyone straightened up, a few jealous glances casting my way. "It's a book about risk," I said and smiled— an apt topic and, thank goodness, a substantive book. What would he have thought if I had been reading a Stephanie Plum mystery novel? "Come on back," he said with a big wave. I started to get up and plopped right back down, forgetting that I still had my seat belt on. I released the metal buckle, successfully rose from my seat on the second attempt, and followed him to his personal office, a spacious room near the front of the plane.

We must have talked for a good twenty to thirty minutes. He wanted to hear about our work on loan modifications and my prognosis on the health of the banking system and the overall economy. We talked about credit availability and small businesses. He was certainly focused on all of the right issues, and I was impressed with his sincerity, the depth of knowledge reflected in his questions, and his obvious desire to learn about what was going on in the banking sector and housing market from the frontline vantage point of the FDIC. It was such a contrast from the conversations with his senior economic team, where the attitude was that they already had all the answers and were talking to us only because the president wanted them to.

If his strategy was to motivate me to help him achieve his foreclosure prevention goals, it worked. As frustrated as I was with the arrogance of his economic advisers and their failure to even listen to any criticism of their programs' fundamental design flaws, I decided to do everything I could to try to make the programs work. I spoke in favor of them and instructed our staff to provide whatever technical assistance the administration requested. Unfortunately, after the big announcement, program implementation went from bad to worse. The Treasury Department was paying much more attention to Fannie, Freddie, the OCC, and the Fed than it was to us. It kept making the program more, not less, complicated. Primarily at the behest of the OCC and GSEs, it imposed extensive documentation requirements on borrowers, requiring detailed reports on income as well as monthly bills and expenses and credit card and other debt obligations. And it would not give a borrower a permanent modification until all of those documents were in. What it was essentially requiring was that the servicers requalify the borrower as if a new loan were being made. That was exactly the loan-by-loan process we had tried to avoid at IndyMac. The loan had already been made. The borrower had already bought the house. New money was not being provided to the troubled borrower. It was already out the door. To require every borrower to essentially prove that he or she could qualify for a new loan was stupid—the loan had already been made. And given the huge number of loans that needed to be reworked, as well as the problem of ill-trained, understaffed servicers, the cumbersome process was doomed to failure.

What's more, it cheated borrowers. Because Treasury wanted to demonstrate quickly that huge numbers of borrowers were being modified, it let borrowers enter into "trial modifications" whereby they would start making reduced payments pending completion of all of their paperwork. But many of the borrowers could not provide all of the extensive documentation required by the program, so they would be put into foreclosure even though they had been making timely payments for months! At IndyMac, we used a streamlined approach. We relied principally on electronic confirmation of borrowers' previous year's tax return from the IRS. That could be supplemented with two pay stubs and the name and contact information of their employer, whom we called to verify their income. Based on that information, we would take their mortgage payment down to 31 percent of their documented income. Once they provided that information and the first month's check, they had their loan modification. That was it. Treasury and others criticized the approach because we didn't look at the borrowers' entire debt load when making the modification. But in point of fact, it worked, and the modifications we did at IndyMac, lowering mortgage payments to 31 percent of income using this streamlined approach, have performed as well as if not better than HAMP loans.

As we had predicted, the financial incentives were not enough. By the end of 2010, nearly two years into the program's operation, only about 522,000 successful permanent modifications had been completed. The government had spent about $2 billion on the program. The number of proprietary modifications—those that banks and servicers had done on their own outside of the program—was four times as high. (Of course, many of these provided no meaningful payment relief.) In the spring of 2011, Tim finally publicly acknowledged that the HAMP financial incentives were not strong enough to achieve the program's ambitious objectives but failed to announce any meaningful reforms to the program. And he essentially blamed the servicers for the program's failures. At the same time, neither Treasury nor the big servicers' primary regulator, the OCC, took any effective action to punish those servicers and make them hire enough staff and training to execute the program effectively.

Treasury never implemented our insurance program, nor did it ever institute quarterly meetings to review the program's process. Tim and Larry had gotten what they wanted: my public support. I doubt if they ever had any intention of following through on their promises. For the next two years, I stood by as they flailed around with a fundamentally flawed program. Occasionally, I would get bits of information from Mary Schapiro, who, as head of the SEC, served on the TARP oversight board. She would fill me in on the HAMP briefings it received from Treasury staff. "Loan restructuring isn't the SEC's expertise," I remember her saying. "Why don't they have you on this board?"

It was a good question.

In retrospect, it was apparent that Larry and Tim were determined to keep me out of the design and operation of any of the programs from the very beginning. As I learned years later, Larry had dismissed our program to the president in December 2008, even though he had led me on in discussions well into February. In January 2012, the White House released the economic transition memo that Summers had prepared for the new president on December 15, 2008. In that memo, Summers had recommended the Bush economists' subsidy program, though he had failed to inform the president of where the proposal had come from and its pitfalls, which we had well documented, and had frankly misrepresented our program to the president in recommending against it by citing nonexistent "scary redefault numbers coming out of IndyMac."

HAMP was a program designed to look good in a press release, not to fix the housing market. Larry and Tim didn't seem to care about the political beating the president took on the hundreds of billions of dollars thrown at the big-bank bailouts and AIG bonuses, but when it came to home owners, it was a very different story. I don't think helping home owners was ever a priority for them.

CHAPTER 14

The $100 Billion Club

The loan modification program was not the only new initiative to be undertaken by the young Obama administration. Secretary Geithner was trying to take bank bailouts to a whole new level.

My assumption was that now that the system had stabilized—given the trillions of dollars we had collectively thrown at it—it was time to roll up our sleeves and do the hard work of cleaning up bank balance sheets. The best way to do that would be to set up a government facility to buy troubled assets at a discount from financial institutions, rework them, and sell them back to the private sector. That was essentially what the Resolution Trust Corporation had done successfully to clean up the mess from the savings and loan crisis. Similarly, during the Great Depression, the government had set up the Reconstruction Finance Corporation (RFC) and the Home Owners Loan Corporation to acquire and rework troubled mortgages and other distressed loans sitting on bank balance sheets.

However, the New York Fed and Federal Reserve staff had another idea. They wanted to conduct "stress tests" on the nation's biggest banks, harkening back to another initiative undertaken during the Great Depression, when President Roosevelt had ordered a "bank holiday"—a euphemism for closing all of the nation's banks to halt the deposit runs that were causing widespread bank failures. Government examiners entered each bank and conducted a thorough analysis of its books and records. Each bank that was determined to be solvent by the government examiners was allowed to reopen.

The Fed's proposal was somewhat different. All of the banks would remain open. Obviously, with the public maintaining confidence in the FDIC's guarantee, there were no bank runs to stop. But the Fed's examiners, assisted by the other bank regulators, would "stress" the balance sheet of banks larger than $100 billion to make sure they had enough capital to remain solvent and continue lending even if the economy deteriorated significantly. If the examiners determined that they needed more capital to survive a much more adverse economic environment, the banks would be forced to issue new common stock or take TARP government capital.

As Fed staff presented the idea, it was obvious to me that they and the Treasury had already decided that they were going to do the stress tests, though in fairness, they did seek our input on how to construct them. My initial reaction to the idea was one of ambivalence. Many banks definitely needed to bolster their capital levels to continue lending in an economic downturn, but capital by itself—particularly if it was government capital— wouldn't be enough to keep them lending in a severe recession. With hundreds of billions of dollars of toxic mortgage and other real estate assets sitting on their books—and substantial uncertainty about the amount of losses they would ultimately have to absorb given the rapidly deteriorating real estate market—previously profligate banks would be reluctant to lend while those assets still sat there rotting on their balance sheets. Just propping up banks with additional capital, without also making them get rid of their toxic assets and take their losses up front, did not work. Japan had used exactly that strategy during its banking crisis of the 1990s, and it is reeling from the consequences of its banks' profligate lending with moribund economic growth to this day.

However, trying to be a team player, I did feel that the stress tests might be a good start if we used them as a catalyst to get banks to clean up their balance sheets. The banks would be in a much better position to attract new investment capital if they first cleared their books of toxic loans. Why would anyone want to invest in Citigroup, for example, with well over half a trillion dollars' worth of distressed loans and other investments sitting on its balance sheet? And even the Fed and the Treasury seemed to agree that the stress tests would be only part of a broader strategy to strengthen the financial sector. The goal was for the major banks to build "fortress balance sheets," meaning that they would have enough capital to continue to lend even in a severe downturn. Everyone seemed to agree that we needed a way to deal effectively with troubled assets—the original goal of the TARP legislation.

Everyone also seemed to agree on the type of facility that the government would use to buy the bad assets. At our suggestion, the plan was to use a combination of TARP capital and private capital to buy the bad assets, using a competitive auction process. Private investors would be responsible for managing the troubled assets, with the government sharing in any profits once they were reworked and sold off. Such public-private investment partnerships (PPIPs) had been used by the FDIC during the savings and loan crisis with good results, and we had already been working on a similar structure to deal with the loans we acquired from failed banks. Moreover, mainstream investors such as Warren Buffett and Bill Gates had expressed an interest in participating in the facilities, a huge plus. The last thing I wanted to do was set up a facility that only hedge funds and other Wall Street types would use.

Early discussions on the stress tests were tense. We wanted a clear connection between the stress test results and requiring banks to sell their troubled assets into the PPIPs. We had to have a lever to force them to sell their bad assets. The banks did not want to face reality. They were carrying the assets at inflated values, and selling them at competitively set "real" market prices was not something they would want to do. We worked to develop effective ways to achieve market prices that would better reflect the intrinsic value of the assets rather than the unrealistically discounted values in the deleveraging market. However, at each discussion, Treasury seemed increasingly determined to undermine any approach that would lead to the banks cleaning up their balance sheets as a primary way of regaining market confidence. The Fed, Treasury, and OCC were clearly much less committed to forcing banks to sell bad loans and other investments.

There was also disagreement over how severe the stress scenario should be. The Fed's adverse scenario showed GDP growth slowing to a half a percentage point and unemployment rising to 10.3 percent in 2010. We viewed that scenario as a highly likely one, not an extreme stress environment. Our head of insurance and research, Art Murton, ran internal stress tests to determine how an extreme recession might impact bank failures and losses to the Deposit Insurance Fund. For that purpose, we assumed a 13 percent unemployment rate. (In fact, the unemployment rate peaked at 10.1 percent in October 2009.)

There were even more disagreements about what we would do with the banks that failed the stress tests and needed more capital. The OCC and its general counsel, Julie Williams, questioned whether the regulators had the legal authority to require banks to maintain their capital above the regulatory minimums. I thought that was shortsighted and indicative of the narrow, pro–big bank focus of the OCC. Congress had given the banking regulators broad authority to define and enforce safe and sound banking practices. The banks needed to be prepared for a downturn and show that they could keep lending. The whole purpose of deposit insurance was to make sure that banks would have funds to keep lending. With deposit insurance and its tremendous government benefits, banks large and small had an obligation to support the credit needs of the real economy. The fact that the OCC would even question our authority to tell the banks to raise their capital cushions above the bare-bones regulatory minimums spoke volumes about that agency's skewed priorities and inability to see beyond the needs of its largest banks. Bank regulators, including the OCC, routinely forced smaller banks to maintain capital ratios higher than the regulatory minimums.

Tim was eager to announce the initiative. I was reluctant to go public with any such proposal until the details had been worked out, particularly on the PPIP. And I thought the markets would be surprised by the stress test announcement because they were expecting a troubled-asset program.

But Tim was eager to move ahead. So on February 10, he held a major press conference to announce his Financial Stability Plan. The lead announcement was Treasury's new Capital Assistance Program, under which the banking regulators would stress test the balance sheets of the nineteen bank holding companies with assets in excess of $100 billion and would be provided with additional TARP capital if the stress tests indicated that they needed it. Our PPIPs to buy troubled assets were given short shrift—two paragraphs in the announcement—but the Fed's programs to buy mortgage-backed securities from banks were given prominence. At Tim's insistence, we had agreed to extend the TLGP an additional four months, through October 2009, so that it would sync up with the expiration of some of the Fed's emergency programs. The announcement also included somewhat stronger conditions on lending and executive compensation, including a prohibition on common stock dividend payments absent approval from the Treasury and the Fed.

It was Tim's first major news conference as Treasury secretary, and he was visibly nervous as he explained the program to a roomful of reporters. Notwithstanding our differences, I felt bad for him. The secretary of the Treasury needed to be a commanding figure, someone who exuded confidence and strong leadership. Tim had always played a staff role. Even as the head of the NY Fed, he had basically been the mechanic who had engineered the bailout programs. Hank and Ben treated him almost like staff. He had been elevated to the role for all of the wrong reasons, boosted by Bob Rubin, who no doubt had had every expectation that Tim would continue his Citigroup-friendly policies. That ill-fated choice was painfully apparent as he struggled to get the words out, his voice at times quivering, his eyes darting nervously back and forth across the room. He looked like a scared little boy.

The market reaction was devastating. The Dow Jones Industrial Average sank nearly 382 points after the announcement. Tim's rollout was universally criticized as lacking content and detail. Bank stocks were roiled. Ironically, Citi and other weak banks were hit the hardest as investors speculated over which banks would or would not pass the tests. Everyone assumed that Citi would be forced to raise significantly more capital, which would further reduce the value of its already decimated outstanding shares.

With bank stocks under severe pressure, Tim decided that the banking regulators needed to issue a reassuring statement. So on February 23, we all joined in another statement that essentially said that the chosen nineteen would be propped up by the government no matter what: "[T]he capital needs of the major U.S. banking institutions will be evaluated under a more challenging economic environment. Should that assessment indicate that an additional capital buffer is warranted, institutions will have an opportunity to turn first to private sources of capital. Otherwise, the temporary capital buffer will be made available from the government."

Many traditionalists, including Warren Buffett, lashed out at the stress tests as wrong and unnecessary. He was quoted in the *Financial Times* complaining that Citigroup's high-profile problems had tainted the entire industry. Most of the banking institutions were relatively healthy, he said, and in any event, fourteen of the nineteen banks being stress tested could easily be resolved under the FDIC's normal processes if they got into trouble.

Buffett was right. But the truth is, I had no place to turn to find allies to fight these ill-conceived ideas. I had hoped that the new administration would be tougher on the banks. Instead, it was bailing out all the big guys. That meant that neither the OCC nor the Fed would have to suffer the embarrassment of an FDIC resolution of any of the big banks they regulated. The little banks would be subject to our harsh process if they failed, but who cared about them? No one at Treasury, the Fed, or the OCC was going to challenge that. I was alone. There were a few token conversations about moral hazard, and we tried to include language suggesting that the government would support only new investors. But Tim was going to get what he had always wanted—the propping up of all the big banks. Some shareholders would have to accept a reduction in the value of their shares, but big institutional bondholders, who should have been subject to the discipline of the market, would be fully protected.

So I put my hopes into at least getting a bad-bank facility up and running to force the sick banks such as Citi to sell off their assets and take their losses, even if the government would backstop them with capital to keep them open. And I instructed my FDIC troops to do everything they could to keep the OCC and the Fed honest in applying the stress tests rigorously and evenhandedly to all of the nineteen banks. I didn't want to see the process manipulated to help "favored banks." Jason Cave was my point person, helped by John Corston and his team of examiners, with Art Murton and his economists providing analytical support. But the stress tests were of the bank holding companies, not the banks, so the Fed—as the primary regulator—had the lead. We didn't even have backup authority for those holding companies (a situation I remedied later in Dodd-Frank). But Jason et al. pushed anyway. We argued for more aggressive loss rates. We argued for harsher stress scenarios.

When the preliminary results from the stress tests came back in mid-March, they matched what we had expected to see: Citi (even with its $45 billion in government capital) and a few others would be insolvent under the stress test assumptions. Citigroup still needed tens of billions of dollars' more capital. However, if it raised that amount of additional capital, it would lose a very valuable tax break called a deferred tax asset (DTA). Citi could raise only a few billion more in additional capital before it would lose its DTA. That DTA was worth about $50 billion to Citi.

The preliminary numbers were rough, and everyone agreed that they needed more analysis. But as the Fed continued to review and refine the numbers, an interesting pattern emerged: the amount of capital Citigroup needed to pass the stress test was getting lower and lower. In fact, in some cases, the Fed and the OCC were using numbers regarding likely losses that were more optimistic than those of the better-managed banks. In one situation, they assumed losses would be only half of what one of the stronger banks was estimating.

The Fed and OCC decided to give the banks such as Citi credit if they planned to sell assets as a way to improve their capital ratios, even though the banks had no firm, legally enforceable agreements to sell them. Citi was also given special credit for its ring-fenced assets. And finally, the Fed and OCC made some very optimistic assumptions about Citi's and other banks' future earnings growth. The result: when the final stress test results were announced on May 7, lo and behold, Citi's capital need was $5.5 billion— just below the amount it could raise without adverse tax consequences.

The total amount of capital required by the stress tests for all nineteen banks was $75 billion, $33.9 billion of that attributable to Bank of America, which was reeling from its overpriced purchases of Merrill Lynch and Countrywide. But the incongruous results for Citi stood out like a sore thumb. Indeed, Wells Fargo, one of the best-managed banks in the country, was told to raise $11.5 billion, twice as much as Citi. And much to our disappointment, the announcement of the stress test results did not include any firm commitments to review the managements and boards of directors of the institutions that needed to raise capital. I issued a separate statement announcing that I looked forward to working with the Fed to review "capital plans and corporate governance structures" at the impacted institutions and put the other regulators on notice that we would continue to push for management changes at the weaker banks.

We did prevail on some important issues. For instance, with Ben Bernanke's help, we were able to raise the banks' common-equity requirement—the highest-quality capital—to 4 percent under stressed conditions, as opposed to the 3 percent favored by the OCC. Again with Ben's help, the Fed publicly committed to consult with us on the evaluation of each bank's capital plan. Given our hundreds of billions of dollars of exposure to those holding companies with our debt guarantee program, it was amazing that we even had to fight for that, but we did.

All of the institutions, with the exception of GMAC and Citi, were able to immediately raise additional capital from the private sector to comply with the stress test requirements. In that sense, the stress tests were a success. But I fear the main reason investors were willing to buy more shares of stock in those banks was not that they had confidence in our stress tests; rather, it was that the government pretty much said it wouldn't let any of the banks fail. It was a reaffirmation of too big to fail, taken all the way down to institutions with $100 billion in assets or more.

And what happened to PPIP, our bad-bank legacy loan program? On March 23, 2009, Tim had announced the program over my objections. As discussions over the structure of the PPIP had progressed, it had become clear that Tim and his senior advisers were primarily interested in setting up programs that would allow banks and other financial institutions to sell securities that they held on their balance sheet at market value. Because the PPIPs would provide favorable government financing to investors to purchase those securities, they could produce prices above the current market values. Thus, selling institutions might be able to book a profit.

Treasury wanted to exclude the FDIC from any involvement in the PPIP for securities; they would be run by the Fed and Treasury. Tim wanted the FDIC to handle only PPIPs for loans. As previously discussed, accounting rules allow banks to hold loans at book value (essentially the unpaid principal balance). That value is typically much higher than a loan's value if it is sold on the open market. Because the PPIP would require banks to sell their loans at market prices, as established by a competitive bidding process, the banks would most certainly take big losses in selling them. It would take real strength of will for the government to force the banks to sell the troubled loans; Tim had no stomach for it. The PPIP for securities was a potentially lucrative opportunity for banks and investors, and Wall Street was licking its chops to get in on the action. I was fearful that if the loan program and these now-separate securities programs were announced together, the public reaction would be adverse.

I was right. Commentators and liberal pundits such as Paul Krugman attacked the programs as more government giveaways, while more thoughtful analysts such as Mark Zandi were favorable, recognizing that if we were to avoid our own "lost decades," à la the Japanese experience, we would have to find a way to get the toxic loans off banks' books. But the worst attack on PPIPs came from *New York Times* columnist Andrew Ross Sorkin.

In early April, Sorkin contacted our press office to say he was doing a story on the Public-Private Investment Program and wanted to interview me. Consistent with our open-door policy, I agreed. The PPIP was the subject of much misunderstanding, and Sorkin had a reputation for understanding market mechanics. I was hopeful that we could get a dispassionate piece from him explaining the program.

Our staff took substantial time to conduct a briefing for him on the PPIP. Then he interviewed me by phone on the afternoon of April 6. I thought the interview had gone fine. He hadn't seemed hostile to the program, and I expected to get a fair and balanced story. However, when Sorkin's column came out the next day, it was very negative—not just about the program but about me personally. (Notably, it said nothing about the Treasury-run program for securities; he bashed only our program for loans.) The column started snidely with the notion that the FDIC was supposed to do only the "simple job" of insuring deposits, ignoring our long record of cleaning up troubled loans. It accused me of saying that the PPIP had "no risk"—which I had most certainly never said—and, in a particularly low blow, compared me to Joseph Cassano, the head of the Transaction Development Group at AIG. It cited "unnamed sources" attacking the program and repeatedly and erroneously said I was putting taxpayers at risk, giving only passing reference to the fact that we were funded by the industry.

I had flown to Kansas City immediately after the Sorkin interview to hold a town hall meeting the next day on deposit insurance. Because of personal threats I had received after the WaMu failure, I traveled with a security detail provided by the FDIC inspector general (usually Agents Matt Alessandrino and Gary Sherrill, who I owe for keeping me safe and secure throughout my term). Two IG agents picked me up at my hotel at 5:30 A.M. to take me to some local morning news shows. Andrew Gray was sitting in the backseat of their SUV as I climbed in. He handed me a coffee and a sheaf of newspapers, with *The New York Times* on top. He looked grim. I read the Sorkin piece and couldn't believe it. I felt as if we had been misled. Sorkin had not shown his hand during the interview. Usually when reporters are going to take a negative angle, they tell you up front.

I was stressed and sleep-deprived. Yes, I've been known to use an expletive now and again, though rarely and then only in front of close aides. However, I let 'er rip after reading Sorkin's piece, and let me take this public opportunity to apologize to those two IG agents who were sitting in the front seat of the car when I unleashed my four-letter-word diatribe.

Andrew, as upset as I was, emailed a somewhat stern protest to Sorkin, who read it on his BlackBerry while he was appearing on *Morning Joe* and announced on air that Andrew was threatening him (he wasn't). Later that morning, I got on the phone with Sorkin and his editor, Larry Ingrassia, and I didn't hold back. We pointed out the blatant inaccuracy that I had said that the program was "no-risk" as well as the over-the-top comparison of me to the guy who had driven AIG into the ground. Sorkin didn't have any good responses, but he also didn't acknowledge that he had done anything wrong. Exhausted, I went from my heated exchange with Sorkin and Ingrassia to sitting down for a previously scheduled interview with Alison Vekshin of Bloomberg News, and then appearing at a public roundtable discussion on deposit insurance. It was a challenging morning, to say the least.

After a few months of fits and starts, the Treasury and Fed launched the securities purchase program, but it never really took off. It was easier for the banks, if they wanted to sell, to simply do so directly through the Fed. Also, the few banks that did sell securities in the PPIP took losses, suggesting that they were not carrying the securities at true market prices.

Our loan program—which required both Fed and Treasury approval—languished. Though Ben was supportive and the Fed had approved the launch of our program, Tim twiddled his thumbs. In fact, despite repeated attempts on my part, he never approved the launch of the program as required under the statutory process. By the fall of 2009, in the face of growing congressional opposition to PPIPs (fed in part by the Sorkin piece), I gave up. We did use a PPIP structure to sell loans we acquired from failed banks, with good results. But we were never given the opportunity to launch a wide-scale program to remove bad loans from the balance sheets of the major banks. Our staff, led by Mike Krimminger and Joe Jiampietro, had worked countless hours to design the program. But it was just another example of Tim refusing to cede authority to us over cleanup programs, even though we had the best experts in the world on the subject. I think the recovery would have been much stronger if he had just let us do our job.

CHAPTER 15

The Care and Feeding of Citigroup: Bailout Number Three

Though Tim successfully stymied our efforts to launch a bad-bank program for the purchase of toxic loans, he did for a time show a lot of interest in how the structure would work. In fact, he invited me to two separate meetings in his office to discuss the subject. However, both of those meetings quickly digressed into how the bad-bank structure might work for Citigroup.

Throughout the early months of 2009, as the stress tests were being launched, there was more behind-the-scenes maneuvering on Citigroup. The bank had a terrible fourth quarter in 2008, with losses of $8.3 billion. As I had feared, the November bailout, which had provided a second capital injection and a ring fence agreement for the government to absorb potential losses on $300 billion in assets, was not enough to calm market fears.

The institution continued to lose deposits and was under severe pressure from key trading partners. To try to calm the markets, Citi's management was eager to formally execute the legal documents regarding the ring fence. That would give it another vehicle for making an announcement to remind nervous depositors and others of the bank's government support. But they still hadn't decided on the assets they wanted to include in the ring fence, which made closing the deal difficult. Daniel Frye of the FDIC staff pushed hard to include in the final deal a ban on bonuses if the government took any losses on the ring fence, but the other regulators would not support us. On January 15, 2009, we announced the execution of the deal.

The announcement didn't do much good. The ratings agencies were threatening further downgrades, citing Citi's low levels of high-quality capital—tangible common equity—and not giving much credence to the government's preferred stock investments. They also cited Citi's poor earnings prospects and the fact that it hadn't put its most toxic securities into the ring fence.

Then, on January 16, without any consultation or advance warning to us, Citi's management announced a "restructuring" of Citi into a "good bank" and a "bad bank." That was nothing more than a publicity stunt. It identified about $864 billion in "bad" assets that Citi said it eventually planned to sell off. There was no fundamental restructuring, not even a concrete plan on how to sell those assets without raising additional capital to absorb the losses, just a happy-face announcement that it was going to get rid of all the stupid loans and investments it had made over the past several years. The market took it for what it was.

Clearly, more needed to be done. As I had predicted in November, the second round of capital investments and the ring fence were not enough. We wanted Citi really to sell off its bad assets—not just announce that it planned to do so—and major management changes were also clearly needed. I was particularly concerned about Citi's CEO, Vikram Pandit. He had no commercial banking experience, yet he was running one of the world's largest commercial banks. In addition, Citi management's performance during the crisis had not been impressive. They had had a very difficult time making decisions and then executing once the decisions were made. Their dithering and ultimate failure to quickly close the Wachovia deal had given Wells the unexpected opening to come in with a competing bid. They frequently couldn't answer even basic questions that I had—for instance, it took them weeks to tell me how much of their foreign deposits were covered by foreign deposit insurance schemes. They had a terrible time deciding what assets to put into the ring fence. They had a reputation in the market of being the gang that couldn't shoot straight. From what I saw, it was well deserved. They had brought in Richard Parsons to be the new chairman of the board on January 21. I was skeptical when Parsons's selection as chairman was announced. I viewed him as a politically connected insider, not someone who knew much about running banks. But I give him credit; on the surface at least, he seemed to want to have a good working relationship and once appointed, he actively reached out to us and the other regulators to try to get on top of the management problems and correct them.

Indeed, I was surprised when Tim started reaching out to me directly on the possibility of doing a good-bank/bad-bank structure for Citi. Initially, he raised the idea of the FDIC setting up and funding a bad bank, without imposing any loss absorption on shareholders and bondholders. I was flabbergasted. Why in the world would the FDIC take all of the losses and let Citi's private stakeholders take all of the upside with the good bank? During the second meeting, we discussed a proposal to have the common equity and some of the preferred shareholders help absorb losses. Our view was that all of the private preferred shareholders should convert and that the bondholders should take some losses as well. That was only good policy—the private sector should take losses before the government—and it was clear that given the size of Citi's toxic assets, both shareholders and bondholders would have to pony up to keep the bad bank solvent.

That was a nonstarter for Tim. He wanted the FDIC to take a hit. I reminded him that our statute clearly gave us priority over bondholders. I wasn't going to budge. Given Citi's highly unstable condition, Tim felt that he needed to go ahead with something, so he decided to convert $25 billion of the government's preferred shares into common equity to raise Citi's all-important tangible common-equity ratio. We felt strongly that Treasury should require all of the preferred securities holders to convert to common shares before Treasury converted, but Tim thought that was too harsh. He argued that the preferred shareholders would never go along.

We had also hoped that Tim would impose conditions on Citi related to disposing of its toxic assets as well as seek strong commitments on management changes. Though language along those lines was included in early drafts of the press release announcing the third bailout, it was dropped in the final release. Treasury agreed to convert its preferred shares to match private preferred conversions up to $25 billion. The release also stated that a majority of Citi's board would be replaced. There was no mention of dealing with Citi's troubled assets, nor was there a hint of management changes.

It was unbelievable to me how little Treasury was asking of the institution to right itself. The government had considerable leverage. With the common-stock conversion, it owned more than a third of the institution. In addition, the FDIC had the legal authority to close Citibank—Citi's $1.3 trillion insured-bank subsidiary—which would surely have forced the rest of Citi into a bankruptcy. In that event, the preferred shareholders would likely have been wiped out. That was a high-risk course, granted, but a tool that we could have threatened to use to extract more concessions from shareholders and bondholders. But Tim's interest was just the opposite: he was anxious to make good on Citi's too-big-to-fail status. He wanted to appease those stakeholders. I wanted them to share the pain.

Citi never paid back that $25 billion. It was the only major bank that did not pay back its TARP grant in full. Instead, Treasury eventually sold its $25 billion stake to other investors. It should be acknowledged that Treasury did sell those shares at a profit—a point repeatedly made to defend against critics of Tim's generous treatment of that institution. Of course, Tim did not know whether Treasury's investment would pay off at the time, and it still troubles me that he could so readily subordinate the government's interest to those of private shareholders. The larger issue was the fundamental unfairness of the vast lengths the government went to to protect this institution and its management, shareholders, and bondholders.

Treasury's conversion of $25 billion of its shares did help stabilize Citi, though it was still a very sick institution. Our FDIC examiners were aghast that the OCC had kept Citi's CAMELS rating at a 3 even though it had required three separate bailouts.

In January, I received a heads-up from Jason and John that they were in discussions with the OCC about the need for a downgrade. The Federal Reserve had already lowered its rating of Citi's holding company to a 4—though that was nonpublic and, unlike a bank downgrade, had no severe repercussions. A downgrade of Citibank to a 4, on the other hand, would put its $1.3 trillion in assets on the troubled-bank list, which at the time included 305 banks with total assets of $220 billion. A downgrade would also entail a formal enforcement order against the bank that would be public, as well as a significant increase in the deposit insurance premiums it paid.

Though the OCC examiners in the field had moved to downgrade the bank in tandem with the Fed's downgrade of the holding company, on January 21, Jason notified me that the OCC was wavering. The argument was again that with all of the bailout assistance, Citi wasn't in a troubled condition.

There was no doubt in my mind that our examiners were right. Citi was a troubled 4 by every established standard used to measure bank health. At the same time, I was worried about the impact of adding $1.3 trillion to our troubled-bank list; everyone would know that it was Citi. Citi was highly vulnerable to a bank run because of its heavy reliance on foreign deposits. There was a real chance that those foreign depositors would withdraw en masse once they saw the inevitable headlines: "Citi Added to FDIC Troubled-Bank List." So I decided to see if we could avoid a downgrade by using the threat of it to effectuate real changes at Citi.

I convened a meeting with Don Kohn, John Dugan, and Bill Dudley from, respectively, the Fed, OCC, and NY Fed, on Friday, February 20, to discuss our concerns about Citigroup. I wanted to make sure that senior officials at the other agencies were aware of our concerns and the threat of a Citi downgrade to the FDIC troubled-bank list. I also wanted to call their attention to what we considered to be grossly inappropriate use of the TLGP by Citi. We had made very clear when launching the program that funds raised through FDIC-guaranteed debt issuance were to be used to support lending activities. Yet my examiners reported that Citi was using the program to pay dividends to preferred shareholders, to support its securities dealer operations, and, through accounting tricks, to make it look as if funds raised through TLGP debt were actually raising capital for Citi's insured bank.

I informed my colleagues that I supported our examiners in their view that Citi was a 4 but wanted to work with them to see if we could avoid a downgrade by taking more concrete steps to return the bank to health. Specifically, I told them that we wanted Citi to raise its tangible common-equity ratio to 7 percent by converting all of its preferred shares, as well as some of its subordinated debt, to common equity. In addition, we wanted to have an experienced commercial banker running Citigroup. With those two requirements, I essentially told them that we could avoid the downgrade. However, without significant improvement in Citi's management and capital position, we would have no alternative but to downgrade the institution and also seriously restrict its use of TLGP.

The following day, I sent an email to Don, Bill, and John formalizing our concerns in writing.

At that point, the FDIC had $167 billion in insured deposits and another $70 billion in debt guarantees, as well as $10 billion worth of exposure on the ring fence agreement. But did those gentlemen acknowledge the legitimacy of our concerns and pledge to work with us? No. They didn't even respond to my email.

A few weeks later, as Citi continued to wobble, Tim convened a conference call to review emergency strategies if Citi experienced another run by its creditors. The NY Fed had circulated proposals to provide all-out support to Citi, with the FDIC guaranteeing all of its debt, including its half-trillion dollars in foreign deposits! However, the NY Fed also conceded that the Citi management team should be replaced if another emergency bailout was needed.

During the call, I once again pressed for a more fundamental restructuring to force Citi to sell off its bad assets into a bad-bank structure that would be funded by private shareholders and bondholders. We had significant leverage, given the FDIC's resolution powers over the bank and Treasury's ownership interest. But no one on the call would support me; they were all worried about how the markets would react. I thought the markets would respond quite positively. It wasn't exactly a secret that Citi was on the edge. My proposal would actually fix it.

Couldn't we at least bring in an experienced commercial banker to run the place? I asked. Tim resisted, offering a bone instead: that Vikram could hire some more commercial bankers to work for him. I doubted that many senior commercial bankers would be willing to work for Vikram, given his weak reputation, but no one was going to buck Tim. The call concluded after an hour. I would later read in Ron Suskind's book *Confidence Men: Wall Street, Washington, and the Education of a President* that Tim had consulted with Vikram prior to our call and had talked with him again afterward about where things stood. Looking back, I have to wonder. Tim seemed to view his job as protecting Citigroup from me, when he should have been worried about protecting the taxpayers from Citi.

The next day, out of the blue, I received a call from Larry Summers, wanting to know how we would set up a good-bank/bad-bank structure for Citi. I explained our plan to force Citi to sell its $800 billion of toxic assets into a PPIP structure. The losses would be funded with the existing privately held equity and debt. I did not push to "close" Citi; I assumed that Tim was speaking for the administration when he kept saying that the government had to save Citi at all costs. Surprisingly, Summers said he didn't think that removing $800 billion of bad assets from Citi's balance sheet would do it. He thought the place was in even worse shape than we did. It was a confusing conversation because his comments seemed completely opposite from what I was getting from Tim. Again, only later would I learn (by reading Ron Suskind's book) that Summers had been pushing to nationalize Citi and break it up. If only he had let me know, we could have worked with the White House to impose some accountability on the institution. It would have completely changed the political dynamic and the growing anger and resentment against the government's seemingly endless willingness to throw money at big institutions. The public justifiably wanted retribution. Citi should have been led to the pillory.

But I didn't know Summers's views, so things stayed confused and unresolved. However, we maintained tight controls on Citi's use of TLGP, and our examiners continued with their downgrade. On May 26, 2009, our head of supervision, Sandra Thompson, sent a letter to William Rhodes, the CEO of Citibank, notifying him that FDIC examiners had downgraded Citibank to a CAMELS 4, citing the institution's weak capital and liquidity position and the failure of its management to correct its inadequate controls against excessive risk taking. That same day, I received a call from Ben Bernanke, asking that the FDIC not downgrade Citi. I asked him how the Fed could reconcile downgrading the holding company but not the bank. He was surprised to learn that the Fed examiners had downgraded the holding company. Whoever had asked him to call me had left out that crucial fact. I think he was miffed that he had not been fully briefed before calling me, but that worked to my advantage. Throughout the difficult negotiations with Citi and the regulators, Ben, more than anyone, helped us secure some meaningful management and other changes to that institution.

Within a few days, I also received a call from Dick Parsons, requesting a meeting the following week. Parsons had been staying in regular contact with us and with our strong encouragement had added two career commercial bankers to the Citi board, Jerry Grundhofer, the highly successful former CEO of U.S. Bancorp, and Michael O'Neill, a former CEO of Bank of Hawaii. I had been pushing hard for Grundhofer to replace Pandit, and I believe Jerry would have stepped in if Tim had asked him to. But Tim would not take decisive action to replace Bob Rubin's handpicked choice for CEO, Vikram Pandit.

We scheduled the meeting for June 22, to give Parsons and his board members time to prepare. Because we did not have the support of Citi's primary regulators, the OCC and the NY Fed, I was not optimistic that he was going to willingly offer us much. Then, on June 5, all hell broke loose as a front-page story in *The Wall Street Journal* headlined "FDIC Pushes Purge at Citi" with the subhead "Bair Wants to Shake Up Management, Sought to Cut Rating of Bank's Health."

I was horrified. There is nothing more sacrosanct at the FDIC than the confidentiality of the supervisory process and the identity of banks that go onto the troubled-bank list. Throughout my five years at the FDIC, we never had a run on a failing bank because of a leak of supervisory information or downgrade. Our whole mission is to try to avert bank failures and to make sure that when a bank does fail, it is a planned and orderly resolution. Nothing goes deeper in the culture of the FDIC. Yet as soon as the article hit, Citi officials were pointing their fingers at us.

That was ridiculous. The article itself cited on- and off-the-record sources at Citi who accused me of trying to use a downgrade as leverage to remove Vikram Pandit. Ned Kelly, the bank's combative CFO, was on the record disparagingly calling us its "tertiary regulator." My assumption was that Citi, fearful of being put on the troubled-bank list, leaked the story preemptively to try to make it seem as though the downgrade was all about personalities and power struggles, not about the health of the institution. But that strategy had backfired badly. Citi was a very fragile institution, and the FDIC had a huge exposure. We were doing our job, and the story came out that way. The irony was that I was trying to work out a package of measures that would keep Citi off the list, but the inept management—fearful of losing their jobs—had panicked and gone public instead of meeting with us to work out the problems.

If there was any question about the leaks being orchestrated by Citi, they were put to rest by a Bloomberg article that appeared the following day, headlined "Citigroup Gains Geithner Backing as Pandit Bucks Bair." The message was clear: Geithner would protect Pandit at all costs. And going from ridiculous to ludicrous, the article accused us of blocking Citi's efforts to convert $25 billion of preferred shares to common shares, which the Treasury would match with its own conversions. Yes, that was the plan that had been announced in February; Citi had still not executed on it. The reason for the delay had nothing to do with us. Citi simply had not yet obtained all of the approvals it needed from the SEC. (That was acknowledged by Citi's counsel, as well as the SEC.)

Citi had also failed to raise the $5.5 billion required as a result of the stress-test results conducted by the Fed in May. In contrast, the rest of the banks had moved quickly and efficiently to raise capital after the stress tests. The stress tests had been announced on May 8, and within a month, all of the banks needing to raise capital, with the exception of Citi and GMAC, had substantially completed their capital raising with new common-equity issuance and conversion of preferred shares. That was just another in a series of examples of Citi management being unable to execute in a timely way.

I met with Parsons, Grundhofer, and O'Neill on June 22 to discuss their willingness to boost capital and change management. They showed willingness to make some management changes, but resisted further capital raising. Grundhofer, whom I trusted, basically said he thought it would be the end if we put Citi on the troubled-bank list. That was my problem: my only leverage was a potential nuclear bomb, the troubled-bank list. If I detonated it, it would be in direct defiance of the Treasury and Federal Reserve Board. That was a huge risk for the FDIC to take. And they knew it.

The situation was becoming more and more about power and control and less about righting Citi's ship; it was turning into a classic Washington turf battle. My fear was that instead of helping us, Geithner, the OCC, and the NY Fed were, behind the scenes, encouraging Citi not to give too much.

Throughout the ensuing negotiations, Ben Bernanke, Dan Tarullo, and others at the Fed would play a constructive role, while Tim's close ally at the NY Fed, Bill Dudley, took the lead in opposing our downgrade. (Because it was a supervisory matter, Tim was prohibited from being openly involved in the process.) With Ben's help in particular, we were able to get significant management changes. A strong board, separate from the Citigroup board, was appointed to oversee the operation of the FDIC-insured bank. Jerry Grundhofer was made the chairman of that board, and Citi brought in a new CEO, Gene McQuade, another experienced commercial banker, to run the bank. Ned Kelly was removed as the CFO and replaced with John Gerspach, who was well respected by our examiners.

Citi also agreed to hire an independent consultant to review its management from the top down and benchmark their qualifications and performance against other banks'.

I had no doubt that Pandit would compare unfavorably to deeply experienced bank CEOs such as Jamie Dimon at JPMorgan Chase, John Stumpf at Wells Fargo, Richard Davis at U.S. Bancorp, and James Rohr at PNC. These gentlemen were not perfect, but they did have decades of experience running commercial banks. They had all done a good job steering their institutions through the 2008 crisis and avoiding much of the high-risk activity in the years leading up to the crisis that got Citi and others into trouble. What astounded me was why the Citigroup board hadn't gone higher for a respected, experienced commercial banker. It could have done so much better than Pandit. In the past, Citi had been led by well-respected industry titans such as John Reed and Walter Wriston. Bringing in a top-name CEO would have been a huge boost to market confidence in the Citi franchise.

On the basis of those changes and commitments, I asked our examiners to review their downgrade to determine if it was still appropriate. In late June, I invited John Corston to have lunch with me. I laid things out for him. I thought we had gotten a lot in terms of management improvements, not enough but a lot, and there was a risk, given Citi's huge foreign deposit base, that we would have a nasty run on the bank if it went on the troubled-bank list. As chairman of the FDIC, I had to consider the broader risks involved with a downgrade. Neither of us liked it, but our choices were between bad and very bad. Shortly thereafter, Citi was restored to a 3. Since both the downgrade and subsequent upgrade occurred in the same quarter, Citi never went onto the list. To this day, I question whether we made the right decision.

At the end of July, Parsons requested a meeting with me and the other regulators to review the progress they had made in carrying out the agreement and discuss the next steps, including the management review. Ben deferred to me in setting up and hosting the meeting. On August 10, Parsons, with three new board members, Grundhofer, O'Neill, and Diana Taylor, the well-regarded former head of banking supervision in New York State, came to the FDIC. We were joined by Ben, Dan Tarullo, John Dugan, and Bill Dudley. The meeting was held in my large conference room across the hall from my office. It was amicable. The fighting was over. We had done the best we could.

Pandit ended up staying at Citi. When the "independent consultant" report came back in the fall, it compared Pandit to small European bank CEOs and gave him glowing marks. As for its review of the rest of Citi's management, it gave high grades to Pandit loyalists while criticizing those who were not viewed as part of the Pandit team. One of the first to go was a solid, experienced commercial banker—and one of the few senior women at Citi—Terri Dial. Pandit had hired her in 2008 but, for whatever reason, had cooled in his support for her. It has bothered me that as a result of the crisis, too many management "improvements" at Citi and elsewhere have really been attempts by weak management teams to circle the wagons, promoting their closest supporters and axing those who are more independent. And because women executives are frequently outside top management's inner circle, far too many have lost their jobs.

That was my first and last experience in asking bank consultants to assist regulators in reviewing bank operations. They are hopelessly conflicted, given their desire to secure future consulting work at those big banks. The consultants clearly considered their primary client to be Vikram Pandit. Indeed, they reported to him regularly on their review and sought his input until we found out about it and objected. The whole review violated the spirit of the agreement we had reached with Citi. But Citi's primary regulators, the OCC and NY Fed, didn't seem to mind one bit.

CHAPTER 16

Finally Saying No

Tim's zeal for bailouts didn't stop with the nation's largest banks. He was equally determined to get the FDIC involved in the bailout of General Motors. That was really a stretch. It was bad enough that we had been dragged into guaranteeing the debt of big securities firms such as Goldman Sachs and Morgan Stanley; now we were being asked to extend our scarce resources to help an automotive company.

In February 2009, Tim and Larry had hired a New York financier, Steven Rattner, to be the lead in the administration's bailouts of General Motors and Chrysler, both near bankruptcy. Though it was not made public at the time, Rattner and his private-equity firm, Quadrangle Group, had been the subjects of investigations by both the New York State attorney general and the SEC. The charge was that they had paid bribes to New York State Comptroller Alan Hevesi and his political consultant, Henry Morris, in return for lucrative business managing the New York State Common Retirement Fund. In 2011, Hevesi and Morris were sentenced to prison, and Rattner ended up paying substantial fines out of his personal pocket to both the SEC ($6.2 million) and the New York State Office of the Attorney General ($10 million), though he refused to acknowledge culpability. The SEC also banned Rattner from the securities business for two years.

I didn't know much about Rattner other than his questionable reputation when I was summoned to meet with him on April 28, in Tim's office. The meeting was billed as a "principals plus one," which meant that I could bring one staffer. My choice was Christopher Spoth, the FDIC deputy in charge of overseeing our supervision of some five thousand FDIC-insured state-chartered banks. One of those banks was Ally, the insured-bank subsidiary of General Motors Acceptance Corporation (GMAC), the financing arm of General Motors.

During the go-go days of the subprime crisis, Ally had not dramatically lowered its underwriting standards and was thus in reasonably good shape as the crisis took its toll. On the other hand, another of GMAC's nonbank subsidiaries, ResCap, had gotten itself deep into high-risk subprime lending and was teetering on the edge. Similarly, GMAC's portfolio of automotive loans was not performing well. Chris's supervisory strategy had been to try to keep the relatively healthy, FDIC-insured Ally Bank insulated from the broader problems of GMAC and GM. Moreover, because GMAC was in such bad shape, we had prohibited it from using the TLGP to guarantee its debt.

Geithner and Rattner wanted us to allow GMAC to move billions of assets from its other subsidiaries into the insured bank. That type of transfer is explicitly prohibited by a statutory provision known as "23A." The Federal Reserve Board has the authority to grant exemptions from 23A, and Ben was prepared to exercise that authority, but he didn't want to proceed over our objections. Hank Paulson had asked me to agree to a 23A waiver for GMAC in December 2008. I had half jokingly told him that we would agree to move $6 billion in loans into the bank if he would put $3 billion of capital into the bank to protect it against losses. He never seriously pursued the idea.

But Tim, unlike Hank, was unable to take into consideration the FDIC's point of view. He was undeterred by and indifferent to the increased risks to the Deposit Insurance Fund. In addition to the 23A waiver, he was particularly determined that we guarantee several billions of dollars' worth of GMAC debt. We had already guaranteed about $330 billion in debt through TLGP, and it was keeping me up at night. If we took any losses on that program, I would have to immediately assess insured banks—including thousands of community banks—to cover the losses, placing more stress on fragile banks. Our reserves were declining steadily, and our ability to borrow from the Treasury was limited to $30 billion; it had not been raised since 1991. By that point, we were insuring more than $5 trillion of insured deposits, in addition to the $330 billion in debt guarantees. An unexpected major bank failure would easily wipe out our reserves and the Treasury line of credit. We had no statutory authority to tap the big holding companies such as GE, Citigroup, Goldman Sachs, and Morgan Stanley for cash to cover our losses on the debt guarantee program. Even though they were the big users of it, if one of them defaulted, it would be thousands of community banks that paid. On March 19, at my request, Tim and Ben had given me a "comfort letter" saying that the Fed and Treasury would use their best efforts to protect us from losses on TLGP debt guarantees. But it was not clear to me that they had the tools to protect us, and in any event, it was the big financial institutions that needed to be on the hook for losses, not they.

I was pushing hard to get our line of credit raised, as well as legal authority to impose an assessment on big bank holding companies to cover TLGP losses. I had had several conversations with Chris Dodd, the chairman of the Senate Banking Committee, about getting the legislation through. He was highly supportive, but he told me point-blank that we would not get it passed in the Senate unless Tim made it clear that the Treasury Department wanted it done. Though Tim had written a letter in support, I took the cue from Dodd to mean that behind the scenes, he was telling senators that it was not an administration priority.

I was not going to take any more exposure on TLGP until I had a bigger Treasury line of credit as well as the authority to make sure the big institutions covered any losses. I told Rattner and Geithner as much at the meeting. Both were indignant. Rattner clearly thought that he was entitled to whatever help he wanted from the FDIC, and he and Tim both threatened to publicly bash me for getting in the way of the GM deal.

In a candid back-and-forth, I told them that if the legislation went through, I was willing to work with them to try to help get GM back on its feet, but our examiners' safety and soundness concerns had to be addressed. That was the FDIC's bottom line. At the top of our list was a commitment to maintaining the insured bank's capital at 15 percent, the same commitment that Treasury had given the Fed for holding company capital. It was ludicrous that government support for bank capital should be weaker than holding company capital.

I held firm, and after some additional negotiations between Chris and Tim's staff, we got what we wanted. On May 20, 2009, legislation was enacted with the authority we needed, and we followed through on our end by agreeing to the 23A waiver and guaranteeing about $7 billion in GMAC debt. Shortly before the legislation passed the Senate, Tim called me, still trying to browbeat me into backing down. But I had also put Rahm Emanuel into the loop, and I knew that the White House supported our position. So, with administration support, we got our legislation passed.

In the end, everyone got what they wanted, but Rattner lived up to his nasty reputation by attacking me in his book *Overhaul: An Insider's Account of the Obama Administration's Emergency Rescue of the Auto Industry.* His version of events was that I was some Washington insider trying to wheel and deal for power and advantage, while he ridiculed Chris, a career public servant with a stellar reputation, as being a clueless bureaucrat. He clearly felt that the government purse was supposed to be readily available to him, and anyone who got in his way was the target of scorn and derision.

The next bailout candidate was CIT, a commercial lender that owned a small insured bank. We regulated the insured bank jointly with the state of Utah. During the fourth quarter of 2008, the Federal Reserve Board had made CIT a bank holding company and had approved it for a $2.3 billion TARP capital investment. We were surprised by that, because after the nine big banks were approved for the first round of TARP, an interagency process had been set up to handle applications and all regulators were supposed to have a vote in whether the applications were approved. However, with CIT, Chris Spoth and his staff had received only perfunctory inquiries from Fed staff about the health of the bank as part of its review of whether CIT should become a bank holding company. Chris told the Fed that although the small bank was stable, he thought that the holding company was not viable. His staff also notified it that there were unresolved consumer issues at the bank that would ordinarily slow down a bank holding company application. The Fed approved the application anyway, and Treasury followed with the TARP investment.

In January, CIT filed an application with us to participate in TLGP. Our staff was highly skeptical. Then, in March, the *Financial Times* reported that the FDIC was "delaying" approval of CIT's request that we guarantee about $10 billion of its debt. The story had obviously been fed by CIT officials trying to put public pressure on us to give them their bailout. But the result was the opposite of what was intended. I had no patience for financial institutions trying to lobby us in the media. I met with CIT's CEO, Jeffrey Peek, and told him that if he wanted to litigate his request in the media, he could withdraw his application then and there.

I also had no interest in the FDIC bailing out CIT. After reviewing the facts, it was clear that our examiners were right: the place was not viable. A century old, CIT had once been a safe, stable source of credit for small retailers. However, Peek, a former asset manager at Merrill Lynch, had taken over in 2003 and soon gotten the company into high-risk commercial lending and subprime loans. CIT had grown quickly under Peek—too quickly—its assets increasing by a whopping 77 percent from 2004 to 2008. He also changed the company's public profile from stodgy to flashy, moving its global corporate headquarters from an office park in Livingston, New York, to the CIT Building, a newly constructed 300,000-square-foot tower in central Manhattan.

As we had made very clear when we announced it, the debt guarantee program was supposed to be for viable institutions, which CIT was not. The only other possible rationale for supporting CIT was to avoid systemic risk. But CIT was not systemic. It had assets of about $75 billion, and our analysis indicated that its lending activities could be easily picked up by other, healthier institutions. So I was disinclined to help it, and our examiners felt the same way. However, if we didn't guarantee CIT's debt, it would likely enter bankruptcy and the $2.3 billion investment that Treasury had erroneously made would be wiped out.

I was sick of bailouts and wanted to just say no. But a $2.3 billion Treasury loss troubled me. So we continued discussions through July with CIT and Treasury to try to see if we could responsibly guarantee some of CIT's debt without posing risks to the FDIC. We tried to explore whether CIT could give us collateral against our guarantee, but it insisted that it did not have legal authority to do so. Lee Sachs, Tim's point person on the bailout programs, had been in contact with me about our plans for CIT but had been careful not to pressure us. In deciding to invest in CIT, Treasury had not gone through the usual interagency process for TARP approvals, and it had not consulted us before making the TARP investment. Thus it was on thin ice. (It should be noted that Lee had not been involved in the TARP approval. That had been done before he arrived at Treasury.) After several discussions, in July, I finally told Lee that our first preference was to deny the application, but to try to help Treasury, we would consider granting it *if* CIT could demonstrate its market viability by issuing at least $1.5 billion in new common stock. We would also need collateral to protect us from risk. And finally, I needed to hear from Tim that it was important to him before I would proceed.

As I suspected, CIT was too weak to meet our conditions. Potential investors knew how sick it was and would not have committed a dollar of new common equity. So then I suggested to Treasury that it try to find an acquirer. Goldman Sachs seemed a possibility. It was a major creditor of CIT, and it had benefited mightily from all of the bailout programs. It was time for it to give something back. I actually called Goldman CEO Lloyd Blankfein myself to see if he would be interested, but he assured me that Goldman had collateral to cover the loans it had made to CIT and he didn't think CIT's business was a good fit for his firm.

With no other acceptable options, we denied CIT's application, and at the end of October, it filed for bankruptcy. It had reached agreement with its creditors in advance on how to restructure the company and how much would be paid to claimants—what is known in industry parlance as a "prepackaged bankruptcy." For an institution the size of CIT with no significant derivatives positions, the bankruptcy process worked just fine. We were right: the failure was not systemic. As other lenders picked up some of CIT's business, it reemerged from bankruptcy in December. There were no major disruptions in credit availability.

It appeared that we had finally stopped the bailout mania. Our refusal to throw good money after bad in the case of CIT was hailed as a turning point in the government's rescue efforts—at last an institution had been left to fend for its own in the private markets, and lo and behold, solutions had been found that salvaged the viable parts of CIT while shareholders and creditors took their losses. Our resistance to GMAC and denial of the CIT application also sent a message to Tim and his team: the gun they had kept putting to our heads—the threat of systemic risk—was no longer loaded. We had let one fail. No big deal.

Though I couldn't change the past, I was determined to make sure that going forward, the FDIC would have the tools it needed to put large, interconnected institutions into our bankruptcy-like process. Never again did I want to see the FDIC given the Hobson's choice of bailing out a bank or "letting the system go down." In my quest to secure new resolution tools for the FDIC, I would find an unlikely boost in the AIG bailout and a welcome, if unexpected, ally in President Obama.

CHAPTER 17

Never Again

I was driving in to work on Monday, March 16, when my BlackBerry started ringing. I answered (in hands-free mode). It was my assistant, Benita Swann, saying that Tim was on the other line. Would I take the call? Of course. I heard a click as it came through. Tim's voice was warm and friendly. He could be very charming when he wanted to be. The president wanted to see me ASAP. Could I come to a meeting at 10:30 in the Oval Office? Again, of course. Another click.

The call took me aback, and I didn't have the presence of mind to ask what it was about. When I arrived at the West Wing receiving area shortly before 10:30, I was ushered right in. The president was waiting for me in his office, standing by one of two chairs that sat in front of the fireplace. Tim and Larry were there as well, each sitting across from each other on the couches that stood in parallel between the fireplace and the president's desk, which stood at the other side of the Oval Office. Rahm was also there, standing next to one of the windows several feet away. The president motioned for me to come sit next to him in one of the two chairs. Tim and Larry looked uncomfortable, their eyes downcast. I slowly walked over to the president and took my seat, my mind racing. What was this about?

"Have you seen the headlines on the AIG bonuses?" the president asked. Yes, of course I had. *Everyone* had seen them. AIG—the troubled insurance giant that had gotten itself into trouble by selling insurance against losses on high-risk mortgage-backed bonds—had received $170 billion in taxpayer bailout money and was by that time 80 percent owned by the government. On Sunday, *The New York Times* had broken the story that AIG management planned to pay out $165 million in bonuses, mostly to the employees of the financial products division—the division that had gotten the company into trouble to begin with. The explanation was that AIG was contractually committed to paying the bonuses. Tim had known about the bonuses and had not objected to them. He had also not given the president a heads-up.

I was aghast when I read the story. Why hadn't they just fired those people? There was some suggestion that they needed to pay the bonuses to retain those folks to help them unwind all of the dumb transactions they had previously entered into. Really? Who in the world would want to hire those yahoos, who had brought one of the world's largest insurance companies to its knees? They should have been working for free to clean up the mess they'd made. I couldn't believe they had anywhere else to go.

"Do you have any thoughts on how to stop these bonuses?" the president asked. He was visibly angry. Hmm. I wanted to say, just fire them. But I didn't have all of the facts, and maybe there were reasons unknown to me why Tim and the AIG management thought they needed to retain those folks. I decided that I wouldn't second-guess Tim's decision; with him sitting there, we would have just gotten into a debate about it. I thought that my precious time with the president could be used more constructively. So I took the opportunity to tell him about our resolution process. A big disadvantage of keeping an institution open, I explained, was that the government preserved all of the legal rights of the employees, creditors, shareholders, and other stakeholders. With our bankruptcy-like resolution process, we could break all of those contracts. We could pick and choose the staff we wanted to keep and decide for ourselves what we needed to pay them. Shareholders and creditors had to get into line to be paid in accordance with an established claims priority. And yes, to keep the franchise operational, key staff frequently did have to be paid to stay and help run the bank until it could be sold. But with our process, the government was in control and the bad apples could be terminated immediately.

I then suggested that as part of financial reform, the president should push for FDIC-like powers to resolve all large financial entities, not just insured banks, as was currently the case. I told him my view that the AIG bailout had been necessitated because the FDIC lacked the legal powers to resolve big nonbank entities. If he wanted to make sure the government was never again put into that type of position, he should seek statutory changes designed to give us the authority to unwind all of the big institutions.

He liked the idea, and Larry and Tim were nodding too. Frankly, I had given the president a constructive idea for moving forward in a way that did not criticize or question their actions on AIG. You would have thought they would be grateful, and for a time the Treasury did embrace empowering the FDIC with powers to close down large nonbank firms. But later Tim would backtrack from the understanding we reached in the Oval Office that morning. Fortunately for me, Rahm was there as a witness, and he would help us later on.

I left the meeting elated. The Hill was already actively engaged in discussions with us about setting up new resolution tools to handle large, interconnected financial institutions when they got into trouble. The president's personal commitment of support would all but guarantee that it got done.

On March 19, Chris Dodd publicly proposed empowering the FDIC with expanded resolution authority. Citing the Fed's regulatory failures in consumer protection and supervising bank holding companies, he went even further and said that the Congress should take away the Fed's power to regulate big, systemic entities and give it to the FDIC.

Dodd's House counterpart, Barney Frank, the chairman of the House Financial Services Committee, had also been in contact with us about new resolution authority. The Fed staff had been talking with him too, and they were pushing hard for the Fed to get the authority. They had already given him draft language—as "technical assistance," which, of course, gave the Fed most of the power.

On March 25, nine days after the White House meeting, Tim went public with a Treasury proposal for new resolution tools. They were a far cry from what we had in mind. Though it created new resolution tools that were "modeled" on the FDIC's, it also gave the government huge latitude to keep doing bailouts. The Treasury secretary and FDIC, acting on recommendations by the Fed, could decide to put an institution into our bankruptcy-like process, or the government could provide "financial assistance measures," which included all of the bailout measures we had used during the crisis. What's more, instead of funding resolution activities through assessments on financial institutions in advance—the FDIC model—the bill had the Treasury Department funding the measures using taxpayer dollars, with any losses paid by assessments on the industry later over time. That approach would—once again—make taxpayers the first line of defense if a large financial institution failed and would also have the perverse effect of imposing the ultimate burden of loss on the surviving institutions. The failed firm would pay nothing.

At least the proposal had us directly involved in the decision making and in charge of the resolution process, but, based on past experience, I was afraid that when it got down to a crunch, the Fed and Treasury would try to avoid a resolution and instead opt for a bailout and put severe pressure on the FDIC to go along. I wanted a requirement that all failing financial institutions would have to be put into our resolution process, where their shareholders and creditors, not the taxpayers, would have to absorb the losses.

We held our fire and worked behind the scenes with Treasury staff and Chairman Frank's office to try to make sure that the Treasury draft legislation would end bailouts, with no loopholes. The Fed and OCC were fighting us and each other. All the agencies were jockeying for the new resolution power, and that included me. But not because I was trying to feather my own nest; I had no intention of serving past the expiration of my five-year term. I wanted the FDIC to be in control of the resolution process not only because we had the greatest expertise in dealing with failed financial institutions but, most important, because by culture, I knew, the FDIC would be the most resistant to bailouts.

After resolving failed banks for eight decades, the FDIC had prescribed rules for handling them, which we followed religiously. The process we used was the same for all institutions and their creditors. We provided extensive public information about our resolutions, we were audited annually by the GAO, and we received a lot of tough-love oversight from our inspector general's office—by far the largest and most robust among the banking agencies. We watched every dime because we couldn't print money like the Fed, nor could we tap taxpayers or issue public debt, as could the Treasury (and we didn't want to). Everything we did was paid for by assessments on the industry. I wanted a statutory framework that, long after I was gone, would prevent a repeat of the ad hoc responses the government had used in 2008 and was still using in 2009, even after the crisis had passed. Those responses had resulted in overly generous bailout programs, favoritism for institutions such as Citigroup, and, worst of all, a reaffirmation of market perceptions that investing in big financial firms was safe because the government wouldn't let them go down. Giving the new resolution power to the FDIC would be the best way to make sure that we wouldn't see a repeat of the bailouts.

Amid all of the agency scrambling, Chairman Frank asked me to meet with him privately on April 20. It was a unique opportunity. I've always liked and respected Barney Frank. He's been repeatedly bashed for his support of Fannie and Freddie, and he's acknowledged making mistakes on GSE policy, but I think the criticisms have been overblown. Overall, Frank's legislative record has been impressive, and he has taken some courageous positions over the years. For instance, he was one of the few in Congress brave enough to take on Wall Street and mortgage brokers by pushing for strong national lending standards in the early 2000s. He is the preeminent expert in Congress on financial policy, and, notwithstanding his liberal reputation, I've always found him to be pretty middle of the road. He's a brilliant, short, frumpy, Jewish, gay guy who succeeded in the rough-and-tumble world of Massachusetts politics by being emotionally as tough as nails. He's never been one to want to spend quality, personal one-on-one time with professional colleagues. I was honored to be meeting with him privately.

Whenever I had met with Frank before, I had sat in a straight-back chair facing him across his desk. He usually liked to keep his distance when meeting with people. However, that time, as I entered his office, he came around from his desk, shook my hand—also rare—and took a seat next to mine. I thought he wanted to talk about resolution authority, so I launched into our priorities of banning bailouts and making sure that the FDIC's process applied consistently and evenly to all. I also pitched him hard on giving the FDIC the power to assess big financial institutions to build a prepaid fund that could be tapped to provide working capital. He was receptive to all those points, but what he really wanted to talk about was the need for a new systemic risk regulator and who that should be.

Dodd had already gone public in wanting to take supervision of large holding companies away from the Fed. Frank hadn't proposed stripping the Fed of its current powers, but he was also disinclined to give the Fed any new authority. As we talked through the issues, I told him I thought he needed to differentiate between the agency that supervised the large, systemic entities—that is, the agency responsible for examining those institutions and enforcing safety and soundness standards against them— from the entity that would have the power to say which institutions were systemic and write rules that would address systemic risk. For the supervisory function, I thought that the Fed, with all its shortcomings, was the best equipped. The SEC was not a safety and soundness regulator, and it had allowed the large investment banks to take on far too much leverage. The SEC's strength and core mission were to protect securities investors, not to prevent large-bank failures. I felt that the OCC was too narrowly focused on protecting its large banks instead of regulating them. Though I felt the Fed also had its issues with regulatory capture, given its role as a central bank, it had another important function that gave it greater separation from the behemoths.

I think I surprised him when I told him that I didn't want the FDIC to be the systemic regulator. Having both resolution authority and supervisory powers over large financial institutions was, I feared, too much for the agency to bite off. As a check against the Fed's laxity, however, I suggested that he give the FDIC backup authority for large institutions that would help us keep the Fed honest. If one of the big guys got into trouble again, the FDIC could come in itself if it didn't feel the Fed was adequately addressing the problems. Clearly the Fed had its shortcomings as a regulator. Citigroup was Exhibit A. So having the FDIC looking at the banks with a second set of eyes was, I thought, a good idea and would also give the FDIC direct legal authority to address problems with management where warranted—authority that we had lacked with Citigroup.

We then turned to the question of how nonbank systemic entities should be designated. That was a huge issue. It was one thing for a financial institution to decide voluntarily that it wanted to own an insured bank and be a bank holding company, with all of the regulatory requirements that entailed. It was quite another thing for the government to order a financial institution to be regulated by the Fed. Someone had to have that authority; otherwise we would not be able to fix the problem of regulatory arbitrage that had led up to the crisis. Bear Stearns, Lehman, Merrill Lynch, and AIG had all escaped tighter capital and regulatory standards by operating as "shadow banks." I suggested that an independent council of regulators, chaired by a presidentially appointed head, be formed to make that kind of systemic determination. I also suggested that the council have the ability to write rules to address risks that spanned individual regulators' jurisdictions. For instance, the oversight of money market funds was clearly a matter that concerned both bank regulators and the SEC. Finally, the council should be able to step in with its own rules when an individual regulator was not doing its job. For instance, as I envisioned it, in the early 2000s, the council would have been able to step in and write mortgage-lending standards when the Fed failed to act. It would also have had the power to set higher capital standards for securities firms in 2004 and 2005 as those firms started taking on so much leverage after the SEC relaxed its capital requirements.

Frank liked my idea of a systemic risk council and said he would bring it up with the Treasury and the Fed, which he did. Both the Treasury and the Fed initially resisted the idea. The Fed wanted to have all of the power over both designating and regulating systemic institutions, and it certainly didn't want a new council with authority to write its own rules to address systemic risks when the Fed failed to act. Tim, who still had a strong allegiance to the Fed from his seven years as president of the NY Fed, was of a similar view. But the reality was that even if Frank had wanted to give the Fed those major new powers, he probably didn't have the votes to do so. The members of his committee were still quite angry about the Fed's regulatory failures leading up to the crisis, and there was a growing popular resentment against the Fed and its role in the bailouts. The political winds were in favor of stripping the Fed of power, not giving it more.

Once Tim heard that I had met with Frank, he reached out to me. He didn't like the council idea, but I told him I could not support giving the Fed unfettered new powers. For decades it had been at the forefront of the deregulatory movement that had given us the crisis. We needed a council to be a check on it. I reiterated that I would not support resolution authority that allowed the government to bail out mismanaged institutions such as Citi and AIG. I told him that I could support legislation that gave the FDIC and the Fed the power, in periods of severe market distress, to provide systemwide support through lending and debt guarantee programs that were generally available to all healthy institutions—no special favors for anyone. But if an institution was failing, it could not use those programs and would have to be put into resolution.

Though I could support systemwide programs for healthy institutions in times of crisis, I also wanted an extremely high bar for the government to provide this type of systemwide support. Supermajorities of the FDIC board and Federal Reserve Board should be required, as well as the approval of the Treasury secretary and president. I was appalled at the trillions of dollars the Fed had seemingly willy-nilly lent, directly or indirectly, to scores of large banks, hedge funds, and asset managers, as well as foreign institutions. There were virtually no requirements that it publish an explanation of why the programs were needed, how eligibility was determined, and, most important, who was profiting and by how much. It was completely off on its own. Indeed, it would not be until late 2011 that it would fully disclose the true extent of the lending programs that it had launched during the crisis, and that was only after it was forced to do so by the courts in response to a lawsuit filed by Bloomberg News.

I thought I was making some progress with Tim and was trying to meet him halfway by agreeing to systemic support programs while insisting on a ban for individual bank bailouts. Unfortunately, instead of relying on the many excellent career staff at Treasury, Tim had recruited Patrick Parkinson from the Fed to develop a white paper that would provide the president's blueprint for reform. I was surprised by his choice. I had known Pat for years; he was a great guy, smart, thoughtful, and sincere. But as a career Fed staffer, he was very close to Chairman Greenspan and was known for his antiregulatory views. During the Greenspan years, he had been Will

Rogers in reverse when it came to regulation: he'd never met one he liked. He'd had a role in opposing CFTC Chairman Brooksley Born's attempts to regulate the derivatives markets. And he was a Fed partisan. Whether consciously or not, his loyalties were there. Soon the process of writing the white paper devolved into backroom Fed and Treasury discussions. Tim and Pat stopped sharing drafts of the white paper. Tim would simply hold meetings and discuss concepts in the abstract. He said he was worried about press leaks (a favorite excuse at both the Treasury and the Fed when they didn't want to share information).

Throughout the spring and early summer of 2009, we continued our multiple-track discussions with the Treasury Department and the Hill. The Senate was particularly interested in new resolution authority. Two of the Senate's smartest members, Mark Warner, a savvy Democrat from Virginia, and Robert Corker, a down-home Tennessee Republican, contacted us about helping with a bill to give the FDIC new resolution powers. Chairman Dodd scheduled a hearing on the need to end too big to fail, asking me and Minneapolis Federal Reserve Bank President Gary Stern, a long time TBTF critic, to testify. (It should be noted that the NY Fed was the only Fed regional bank with much enthusiasm for big-bank bailouts. Other regional bank heads, including Stern, Dallas's Richard Fisher, Richmond's Jeff Lacker, and Kansas City's Thomas Hoenig, have been staunch critics.) But the best public platform I had to advance the need for resolution authority was at the Economic Club of New York on April 27. I knew that unless I could convince at least some in the New York financial community to support resolution authority, we would never get it. The opposition of the weak, bailed-out banks would be too strong. So I laid out all of my arguments but made my strongest pitch based on basic economic and capitalist principles: "Everybody should have the freedom to fail in a market economy. Without that freedom, capitalism doesn't work. In the longer term, a legal mechanism to resolve systemically important firms would result in a more efficient alignment of capital with better managed institutions. Ultimately, this would benefit those better managed institutions and make the financial system and the economy stronger."

Some of the better-managed banks, such as JPMorgan Chase, did end up supporting resolution authority. We also received strong support from smaller banks. In April, Camden Fine, the president and CEO of the Independent Community Bankers of America (ICBA), wrote a letter to Secretary Geithner vigorously endorsing giving the FDIC the ability to resolve large nonbank entities—and for good reason. Why should the little banks be subject to that harsh process but not the big guys?

We were also starting to make some headway on the council. SEC Chairman Mary Schapiro had endorsed the idea. Rahm Emanuel invited me to lunch on May 27, and we discussed the concept in detail. Indeed, I gave him several suggestions on how regulatory authorities might be realigned in a way that would be fair to all of the agencies but make the U.S. regulatory system more streamlined and efficient. But I also made an important concession: I told him I could live with the Treasury secretary chairing the council, instead of an independently appointed head.

Tactically, that was the right move. With the prospect of chairing the council, Tim's views on it started to change. In early June, Tim acknowledged in Senate testimony that in reference to the Fed, "I don't believe it's necessary or desirable for us to concentrate all authority for dealing with future risks to the system in one agency." Dodd and Frank were also clearly sympathetic to the council and were pushing it behind the scenes. The Fed was becoming increasingly isolated in its resistance. But the trade-off in letting Treasury head the council was that it compromised the independence of the financial regulatory process. Treasury was a part of the administration and was bound to promote the president and his policies. Financial regulators were supposed to be independent of those considerations. In my public statements, I would continue to speak out in favor of an independently appointed chairman, but I did not make it a priority. (The final legislation ended up creating a council headed by the Treasury secretary.)

Frankly, I had my hands full trying to steer the reform efforts on resolution authority. Treasury and the Fed were still pushing for regulators to have maximum flexibility to do future bailouts. That was amazing to me. They seemed impervious to the public outrage and cynicism caused by the bailouts. I think the White House truly wanted to end bailouts, but it was relying on Tim and Pat Parkinson to put together the technical proposal.

On June 12, the heads of all the major agencies received an invitation from Larry Summers's office to attend a meeting with the president on June 17 ahead of an announcement later that day of the administration's reform measures. We were not given a copy of the final white paper until shortly before the meeting, so my staff and I had little time to review it. Much to my surprise (and contrary to the express representations that had been made to my staff), instead of ending bailouts, the white paper essentially ratified them as legitimate and empowered the secretary of the Treasury to carry them out unilaterally in the future. The white paper removed the FDIC from any meaningful role in the resolution of a large bank, except if asked by the secretary of the Treasury. It was the bailout advocates' dream. Now even the FDIC—the only agency that had tried to curb the bailout excesses and impose some meaningful structural and management changes on mismanaged institutions—would be disempowered. As my chief legal counsel, Mike Krimminger, stated in his analysis:

> UST [U.S. Treasury] would vest in itself both the power to decide whether to resolve a failing institution using the systemic process and how to resolve that institution. . . . UST's claim to plenary authority to decide on how to resolve the firm without any clear constraints increases the likelihood of TBTF. . . . There are no provisions in the legislative draft that tie UST's hands by an obligation to minimize costs compared to a receivership or liquidation process. The white paper simply notes that UST should consider the action's costs to taxpayers. Second, in a crisis, . . . the uncertainties will likely push for loans, guarantees or other tools that avoid closure [of the institution]—and UST asserts authority to make this decision alone. Nowhere is there any recognition of the troublesome moral hazard or exit strategy issues created by some of these tools or of the stringent conditions that should be, but in practice have not been, placed on institutions receiving such assistance. While there has been much discussion of compensation limits . . . the real tools of restructuring, management changes, or sales of assets have—by and large—not been pushed by UST or other regulators, other than the FDIC.

In other words, instead of ending bailouts, the white paper embraced the status quo. Tellingly, it didn't even meaningfully address the AIG bonuses that had troubled the president so greatly in March!

It was clear to me at the meeting and subsequent announcement that the president thought he had a proposal to end bailouts, when in fact, it did the opposite. It was also clear to me that Tim and Larry had engineered the meeting to make it look as though all of the regulators supported the white paper, when in fact few of us had had even seen the final version more than twenty-four hours in advance. Feeling blindsided but unprepared to respond to a document I had not yet analyzed, I remained silent, though seething, while the president talked about the importance of financial reform. The private meeting with the regulators took place in the Roosevelt Room, a stately conference room just outside the Oval Office. After that meeting, I, along with the rest of the agency heads, trooped into the East Room for his press announcement. I listened quietly, without expression, as he described what he called "a comprehensive regulatory reform plan to modernize and protect the integrity of our financial system."

Notwithstanding Larry and Tim's hardball tactics, I tried to keep my public comments constructive while educating members of Congress of our concerns behind the scenes. I also let Rahm know that we had not been given a chance to review the white paper in advance. We didn't have to do much to discredit the white paper. Without any prodding from us, Hill staff were referring to it as "codifying TARP." A few weeks later, Corker and Warner introduced their bill, which really would have ended bailouts, and on July 27, at Senator Corker's invitation, I met with a bipartisan group of senators to talk with them about the FDIC resolution process. The meeting went very well.

If anything, we were being too successful from Tim's standpoint. On Friday, July 31, he summoned all of the major agency heads to his conference room and proceeded to give us an expletive-laced tongue-lashing about talking to people on the Hill. The arrogance and disdain he showed for the agency heads, who also included Ben Bernanke and Mary Schapiro, was astonishing. He ignored the legitimate policy issues that stood at the heart of most of our disagreements, seeking to portray anyone who disagreed with him as interested only in protecting his or her own turf. I believe the tirade was probably mostly aimed at me, though Tim was also upset over the Fed's continued resistance to the council and the SEC, which, like us, wanted the council to be a more powerful check on the Fed's power. I patiently listened to his rant and then pointedly told him that the problem was one of his own making as he had failed to adequately brief and consult with the other regulators before going public with a proposal. Tim wanted to have it both ways: he didn't want to make the changes needed to get other agencies on board, yet he wanted everyone to fall into line and support him.

His meeting accomplished nothing other than the creation of resentment, hard feelings, and a bad press story. (No, we were not the leak, but, as with everything that made its way into the press that Tim didn't like, he blamed us.) Even if we had wanted to stop separately communicating with the Hill, we couldn't have. Members of Congress were reaching out to all of us directly. The administration's white paper had had little traction in Congress, whose members were going to write their own bill. And in the House, things were definitely going our way, with growing support for a tough ban on bank bailouts, strong resolution authority for the FDIC, and assessments on large financial institutions to pay for it.

Unfortunately, things took a bad turn in the Senate. Chris Dodd's staff started pushing the idea of a single "superregulator" for all banks. Supposedly the idea was to create a completely new bank regulator, stripping authority from the Fed, FDIC, OCC, and OTS. Though I believe that Dodd and his staff were sincere in pushing a single regulator as a way to strengthen bank supervision, in reality, that would have served the interests of the biggest banks by consolidating power in the OCC, their friendliest regulator. The single-regulator concept was exactly what the big banks had been pressing for since the early 2000s. As one commentator put it, "For big banks like JPMorgan Chase and Bank of America, a single regulator would be like a dream come true." They wanted to move toward a single, monolithic regulator patterned after the United Kingdom's Financial Services Authority (FSA), a model that had been thoroughly discredited during the crisis as weak and a captive of the industry it regulated. The two main lobbying groups for the biggest banks—the Financial Services Roundtable and the Financial Services Forum—were all for it. But the idea quickly ran into opposition from Barney Frank, who went out of his way to say that his committee would not support taking regulatory authority away from the FDIC.

I have no doubt that Chairman Dodd was well intentioned in pushing for that. I think he truly felt that he would be getting rid of the OCC in favor of a stronger regulator. But I firmly believe that the opposite would have happened, with the captive OCC becoming the dominant core of the new regulator. Moreover, Dodd's premise was wrong; he viewed the crisis as having been caused by FDIC-insured banks "shopping" for the weakest regulator. To be sure, the OTS had not provided sufficient oversight of insured thrift mortgage lenders, and there was general agreement that the agency needed to be abolished. However, for the most part, regulatory "shopping" had occurred between banks and nonbanks, with unregulated mortgage brokers originating high-risk mortgages with funds provided by the big securities firms, most of which operated outside of the tougher prudential standards we had for insured banks. Our three biggest problem institutions among insured banks—Citigroup, Wachovia, and WaMu—had not shopped for charters; they had been with the same regulator for decades. The problem was that their regulators did not have enough independence from them. Consolidating all of the power with the OCC, the weakest regulator along with the OTS, would make things worse, not better.

We had seen some sporadic instances of smaller banks trying to change charters to escape supervisory actions. However, earlier in the year, as the chairman of an interagency group of bank regulators, I had successfully pushed for an agreement binding us all to one another's CAMELS ratings and enforcement actions so that banks could have no hope of derailing supervisory actions by converting charters. If a bank wanted to change charters, any pending supervisory actions would now follow them to its new regulator.

Moreover, a single regulator would have meant the end of smaller, state-chartered banks that compete with the big banks for loans in their local communities. As I wrote in an op-ed in *The New York Times* in August, a single regulator would inevitably be biased toward the largest banks, hurting the ability of smaller institutions to compete and leading to even more industry consolidation. And putting all of our regulatory eggs into one basket would be a disaster if that regulator were weak and a captive of the largest institutions. Indeed, if it hadn't been for the FDIC blocking the Basel II capital standards, FDIC-insured banks would have been able to take on excessive levels of leverage, as had the securities firms, which had only one regulator to convince, the SEC.

That was a prime example of how influential industry lobbyists can contort reform efforts to achieve policy results that will weaken, not strengthen, regulation. Creating a single regulator made for a good sound bite. But in truth, the result would have been to take the FDIC—a strong voice for prudence, given its trillions of dollars' worth of insured bank deposits—out of decisions governing the conduct of the banks we insured.

Eventually, we were able to convince Senator Dodd not to pursue the single-regulator idea, and in that effort we allied with both the Fed and the nation's community banks. However, fending off the proposal divided our time and resources. We had to fight a rear-guard action at the same time we were pushing hard for real resolution authority to end too big to fail.

Then we ran into another obstacle on resolution authority: House Republicans, armed with the permissive language in the white paper, tried to paint the effort to create new resolution tools as a codification of bailouts. And notwithstanding our successful efforts to help Chairman Frank write legislation that really would end bailouts, the stigma of the white paper stuck. Bankruptcy attorneys seized on the controversy to argue that the failure of large financial institutions should be dealt with through only bankruptcy and began lobbying against our efforts, trying to convince members of the House Judiciary Committee—which had jurisdiction over bankruptcy law—to weigh in. The lobbying effort was led by Harvey Miller, the lead attorney in the Lehman Brothers bankruptcy. Mr. Miller, a highly influential member of the New York bankruptcy bar, was vigorously arguing the self-interest of his profession. As of this writing, legal and other fees associated with the still unresolved Lehman bankruptcy have topped $1.5 billion. In addition to the massive economic disruptions it caused, it has served Lehman's creditors poorly. The company's assets—which stood at $639 billion in the fall of 2008—dissipated to $65 billion by the end of 2011. As of the end of 2011, its creditors had still not been paid, and when they are finally paid, the senior creditors are expected to recover only about 21 cents on the dollar.

Why has the Lehman bankruptcy proven to be so costly? There are three reasons. As previously discussed, one problem is the preferential way the bankruptcy code treats derivatives trading partners. They are given the ability to cancel their contracts immediately and take ownership of the collateral the bankrupt firm has posted with them. In practice, what happens is that as a firm becomes weaker, derivatives trading partners will demand more and higher-quality assets as collateral. When the firm finally fails, many of the good assets have already been transferred to those trading partners and thus are no longer available to pay the claims of other creditors. The second problem is that there is no way in bankruptcy to ensure continuous funding of operations. Unlike a commercial entity that has plant, equipment, and physical inventory that maintains value even in bankruptcy, a financial firm's assets have to be funded continuously or their value is severely impaired. With bankruptcy, funding comes to a full stop as creditors cease lending to the institution. Finally, bankruptcy is a highly litigated process, meaning that fighting over what little value is left in a financial institution is protracted. It can take years for creditors to finally be paid. In contrast, the FDIC process is grounded in the public interest. It ensures continuity of credit availability to support economic activity and protect the public purse. For that reason, we put a high priority in getting banking assets back into the private sector as quickly as possible.

In 2011, the FDIC staff did an analysis of how Lehman Brothers could have been resolved using our standard resolution tools. The analysis indicated that Lehman's senior creditors would likely have recovered 97 cents on the dollar. What's more, given our ability to plan in advance and auction a failing institution quickly, the healthy parts of Lehman's operations would have continued uninterrupted and creditors would have been paid much more quickly. Another contrast between the FDIC process and the bankruptcy process is provided by the WaMu failure. We were able to auction and sell WaMu's insured thrift immediately. There was no disruption to WaMu's customers, depositors, and borrowers. General creditors also suffered no losses. But WaMu's holding company, WaMu Inc. (WMI), is still mired in bankruptcy proceedings. For three years, billions of dollars in cash and tax benefits have sat at the holding company. As with Lehman Brothers, these billions are just sitting in litigation instead of being deployed to support economic activity. That is not the fault of the bankruptcy courts; they do an amazing job, given all the legal avenues available to claimants to litigate. It is a problem with the adversarial nature of the judicial process and the way litigants are able to exploit it to their own advantage. Bankruptcy courts exist to protect creditors. The FDIC process exists to protect the public interest.

Fortunately, through the exceptional work of my chief legal adviser, Mike Krimminger, and Paul Nash, a seasoned Washington pro whom I had hired to head our External Affairs office, which included our legislative operations, we were able to beat back the assault on resolution authority. We convinced House Judiciary Committee members that the government needed the new resolution tools if we were to end bailouts. The irony was that continued reliance on the bankruptcy code to resolve large financial institutions would be an affirmation of the bailout status quo. After contending with the severe disruptions caused by Lehman's failure, no government official in his or her right mind would allow a large, interconnected firm to enter that process again. The government would do another bailout before allowing the system to seize up as it did following Lehman's bankruptcy filing.

Chairman Frank and his staff continued their discussions with us and the other regulators. I tried desperately to engage House Republicans to support *our* version of resolution authority. If promarket Republicans should be about anything, they should be about letting the market work to punish mismanaged, inefficient institutions. I reached out to Spencer Bachus (R–Ala.), the committee's ranking Republican, and Jeb Hensarling (R–Tex.), one of the committee's more influential conservative members, and met with them over the summer to try to convince them that, with our revisions, the new authority really could end bailouts. But they had it in their minds that it was all about ratifying bailouts, and in truth I think they wanted to keep the issue alive to bang over the administration's head. Tim had made

a terrible mistake with the white paper. Given his perceived close association with Bob Rubin and the too-big-to-fail institutions, the GOP smelled
an issue, and it wasn't going to give it up.

Unfortunately, Tim, and his financial reform point person, Michael Barr,
continued to press Frank for flexibility to do future bailouts, as did members
of the Fed staff. We were fighting for the souls of Barney Frank and his staff.
Draft legislation that Frank floated in October still did not ban bailouts, nor
did it give us the power to assess large institutions to build up a resolution
fund. On October 29, I testified forcefully before Frank's committee:

> Congress should also prohibit open company assistance that benefits share-
> holders and creditors of individual institutions. The ban should apply to
> any assistance provided by the government including lending programs
> provided by the Federal Reserve Board. . . . The government should not
> be in the position of picking winners and losers among poorly managed
> firms that can no longer function without government assistance. Those
> institutions should be placed into receivership, and their shareholders and
> creditors, not the government, should be required to absorb losses from the
> institution's failure.

I also insisted that the resolution mechanism be funded in advance
through assessments on the big industry players:

> To be credible, a resolution process . . . must have the funds necessary to
> accomplish the resolution. It is important that funding for this resolution
> process be provided by the set of potentially systemically significant finan-
> cial firms, rather than by the taxpayer. To that end, Congress should estab-
> lish a Financial Company Resolution Fund (FCRF) that is pre-funded by
> levies on larger financial firms. . . . We believe that a pre-funded FCRF has
> significant advantages over an ex post funded system. It allows all large
> firms to pay risk-based assessments into the FCRF, not just the survivors
> after any resolution, and it avoids the pro-cyclical nature of requiring repay-
> ment after a systemic crisis.

In other words, collecting money from the industry in advance, as we did
with our deposit insurance, would make sure that all potentially impacted
firms, including the one that failed, paid into the fund. Collecting the money
in advance would also mean that the government would have it when it was
needed and was not put into the position of trying to collect money from

the industry in the midst of a crisis. Most important, it would provide an added measure of protection for taxpayers: going forward, I didn't want to see a penny of taxpayer money used to clean up big financial institution messes if I could help it. We acknowledged that some temporary borrowing authority from the Treasury was needed as a backstop, as was the case with the FDIC's Deposit Insurance Fund. But Treasury borrowing should be available only as a last resort; the first line of defense should be a prepaid industry fund.

The hearing was a huge success for us. Paul Nash immediately received inquiries from committee members wanting help to draft amendments to ban bailouts and set up a resolution fund. On November 3, Frank told reporters that he planned to revise his legislation to include a resolution fund. It would apply to nonbank financial institutions with $10 billion or more in assets. (Insured banks would continue to pay into the FDIC fund.) When asked about the size of the fund, he responded that he hoped it "gets enormous." Subsequently, his staff gave us his new draft bill, which also included our long-sought ban on bank bailouts, mandatory receivership for insolvent institutions, and FDIC backup authority for large systemic institutions.

We were succeeding in the House in closing off the bailout loopholes in the bill and securing authority for a resolution fund. Chairman Dodd's staff was also coming our way on how resolution authority should be structured, much to the consternation of Tim and Michael Barr. But Frank was sticking with the Fed in having a very weak council, with most of the new regulatory authority over systemic institutions going to the Fed. Frank's Democratic committee members were still nervous about GOP attacks that the new resolution authority was bailout authority. In point of fact, over Treasury's objections, the Frank staff had included our language expressly prohibiting bailouts. All failing institutions would have to be put into resolution. Frank asked me to meet with his committee Democrats on Saturday, November 7, at 2 P.M., after the president's scheduled remarks to the Democratic Caucus. I readily agreed.

Paul Nash accompanied me to the meeting. It was held in the committee's cavernous wood-paneled hearing room. More than thirty members, plus their staffs, were sitting in their tiered seats waiting for a briefing from Frank on the status of the financial reform bill. After providing his members with an update, Frank turned to me and asked me to talk about the new resolution authority. Although I had testified in the room many times, Barney asked me to address the committee from the chairman's seat atop the dais.

Having him turn over the meeting to me in that way underscored that we shared the same priorities in truly ending bailouts. Barney and his staff had accepted our amendments that closed off the loopholes Treasury and others were pursuing. That gave me the ability to assure the committee that the bill banned future bailouts of failing institutions. I walked them through the resolution tools we used at the FDIC to impose losses on shareholders and creditors. I complimented them on their courage in authorizing the resolution fund. I knew that the Treasury Department, under Tim and Michael Barr's direction, had been working behind the scenes to kill it, but I put my credibility on the line to convince them that Barney had the right approach.

Frank's committee convened to consider the bill and on December 2, 2009, approved it on a party-line vote of 31 to 27. I was very disappointed that the bill did not attract GOP support, as I believe that with our strengthening amendments, it gave regulators the tools to end too big to fail. The legislation was then sent to the full House, where it was combined with other reform measures previously approved by the committee, including bills to create a new consumer bureau for financial products, provide for regulation of so-called over-the-counter (OTC) derivatives (those not traded on regulated exchanges), and ban abusive mortgage-lending practices.

Our language on resolution authority enjoyed widespread support among House Democrats. Unfortunately, there was continuing controversy over the new consumer protection agency—which we also strongly supported—even within the Democratic Party. Most damaging was an amendment to reinstate the OCC's power to block states from enforcing their consumer laws against national banks. On Tuesday, December 8, I was having my monthly luncheon with FDIC economists when I received a call from Chairman Frank asking me to contact certain centrist Democrats and Republicans to oppose the amendment. I obliged but wondered why the Treasury Department wasn't doing it; overturning the OCC's preemption of state consumer laws, I thought, was an administration priority. In any event, I was happy to help and made the calls.

The full House passed the bill on December 11 by a narrow vote of 223 to 202, again along party lines. The final version included a $150 billion resolution fund, to be assessed against hedge funds with greater than $10 billion in assets and other nonbank financial firms with assets greater than $50 billion. All of our antibailout language was included. We were even successful in securing an amendment offered by Congressmen Bradley Miller (D–N.C.) and Dennis Moore (D–Kans.) to impose losses on secured creditors that had extended short-term credit based on complex, hard-to-value assets as collateral. The purpose of the amendment was to discourage the precrisis practice of poorly managed firms such as Bear, Lehman, and Citi funding their operations with short-term loans and posting toxic mortgage securities as collateral. Creditors who extended credit on those terms would be at risk if the institution failed. Here again, the Treasury Department under Tim's direction vigorously (but unsuccessfully) opposed this amendment.

Shortly before the final vote in the House, I received an irate call from Tim saying that the resolution authority was a "mess" and that the "whole thing" needed to be fixed in the Senate.

Yes, from Tim's perspective, it was a "mess" because it didn't permit endless bailouts at his discretion.

After getting that call, I knew we were winning.

But I also knew we would have a real fight on our hands in the Senate, squeezed between the industry and its Senate allies on the one side and the Treasury Department on the other.

CHAPTER 18

It's All About the Compensation

As we pressed our case in Congress for legislation to permanently ban future bailouts, we struggled with other regulators over how to unwind the 2008 bailouts.

In the summer of 2009, the Fed, as the holding company supervisor, permitted nine members of the $100 billion club to repay their TARP capital investments. We did not object to the repayments. The nine banks had all passed the stress tests and, with the exception of Morgan Stanley, were in relatively strong condition. Morgan Stanley was still wobbly, but it had successfully issued a significant amount of new common equity before it exited TARP, suggesting that there was some market confidence in its financial strength. In addition, it had the deep pockets of the Japanese banking giant Mitsubishi standing behind it.

However, the eight institutions that showed an additional capital need under the stress tests, including Citi, were not allowed to exit. In October, Tim began convening meetings on how the rest of the TARP bailout recipients could exit the program, a surprising reversal of the TARP bailout support he had generously promised to any institution over $100 billion a few months earlier. He asked the Fed, in consultation with us and the OCC, to devise criteria for the standards to be used to approve TARP repayments by the weaker banks before the end of the year.

That was a serious matter for the FDIC. At the Fed and Treasury's strong urging, we had taken significant exposure in guaranteeing the debt of the giant holding companies, but it had been part of a coordinated action that relied on continued support from both the Fed and the Treasury to protect us against losses. If the weak banks repaid their TARP money without raising significant new capital to replace it, it would leave them in a weakened condition. The banks had originally been required to keep their TARP money for three years, but earlier in the year, the industry, working with the Treasury Department, had convinced Congress to pass legislation allowing them to repay sooner. But when launching TLGP, we had agreed to a three-year debt guarantee, so we would continue to be exposed long after the Treasury got out.

On the other hand, I had acquired a deep dislike for the capital investment program. It was enormously controversial, and as a capitalist, I just didn't like the idea of the government owning banks, even as a preferred-equity owner. The new resolution framework we were pushing on the Hill would ban government capital investments. Moreover, if the banks were required to replace their government capital with new, privately held common equity, it would strengthen their capital position and, at the same time, reduce the government's involvement.

But could some of the weak banks raise that much common equity? The Fed thought that requiring them to raise one dollar of new common equity for every repaid TARP dollar was too harsh. Instead, its staff circulated a proposal to require "1 for 2," meaning that a bank would have to issue one dollar of new common equity for every two dollars it repaid in TARP. So, for instance, Bank of America, which had received $45 billion in TARP capital, would need to issue $22.5 billion in new common equity.

Given the major capital raises that many of the banks had already completed over the summer after the stress tests, we were comfortable with the 1-for-2 construct for all of them, except Citi. Citi had been required to raise only $5.5 billion after the stress test. As previously discussed, we viewed this as a "lowball" number that had helped Citi keep its tax benefits. We insisted that Citi's TARP repayment had to be at least dollar for dollar. Citi had already been given a special break when the Treasury had converted $25 billion of its original $45 billion of TARP into common equity, planning to sell those shares off to private investors. Citi would never have to pay back that $25 billion. As a consequence, even with a 1-for-1 standard, Citi would have to raise only $20 billion to repay the remaining $20 billion in TARP funds. It needed every penny of that capital.

We also insisted that the capital increase be done with common equity newly issued to the open market. That was the only way we could be sure that the TARP exit process actually strengthened the banks. We didn't want to see gimmicks such as issuing stock as additional compensation to employees or measures that could actually weaken the banks, such as selling good, income-producing assets. We wanted full market validation of each bank's strength by requiring that it convince private investors to commit substantial amounts of new capital to it.

The Fed purported to agree with us on those points, and on November 3, it finalized its guidance along these lines. However, while giving us verbal assurance that they would require at least 1-for-1 repayment of Citi, the Fed dropped a footnote we had asked for saying that some banks would be required to repay on a dollar-for-dollar basis. It did, however, agree to consult with us and the OCC before approving any individual bank's TARP repayment plan.

I thought we had a solid agreement with the Fed and Treasury, one that was motivated by a desire to help the government start exiting the bailout programs but in a way that would ensure a stable financial system. Looking back, I see that I was naive. I think what was really going on was that Citi and BofA—the two biggest bailout recipients—were desperate to get out of the special restrictions on executive compensation that had been placed on them when they received their second round of TARP money.

Indeed, within just a few weeks of issuing the guidance, the Fed and OCC were pushing us to loosen its parameters. BofA had proposed a repayment plan that was laughably short of the principles in the guidance. Its original proposal would have raised only $9.25 billion in common equity, with another $4 billion in trust-preferred securities, which are essentially a form of debt. We pushed back hard, demanding the full $22.5 billion. After several more proposals, BofA proposed raising $14 billion in new common equity, $3.5 billion in trust preferred, $8.8 billion in assets sales, and $1.7 billion in employee stock compensation.

At that point, the Fed notified us that it wanted to give BofA flexibility to conduct assets sales as part of the capital raise, in direct contravention of our agreement. Again we demanded a full $22.5 billion in newly issued common equity. We presented an analysis that had been prepared by our outside investment adviser, Perella Weinberg Partners, that a capital raise in excess of $20 billion was achievable, though the shares would have to be sold at a steep discount. That, I suspected, was the real reason BofA did not want to go to the market with a huge capital raise; it did not want to dilute current shareholders' assets. On November 21, I circulated the analysis to my colleagues, stating that dilution of shareholders' assets should not be our concern. Our job was to ensure the safety and soundness of the institution. The Fed and OCC dug in. The Fed insisted that BofA could not sell that amount of common equity and that a failed offering would undermine confidence in the institution. I replied that if it couldn't complete an offering of that size, it wasn't strong enough to exit TARP.

I also cautioned against the precedent the Fed would set if it gave BofA that flexibility. In an email to Don Kohn and Dan Tarullo, I wrote,

"Acceptance of this . . . proposal will have repercussions beyond [Bank of America]—as other banks see that the [government] has loosened its repayment standards and will expect to get a similar deal." I went on to conclude, "None of us liked the TARP program, but let's not compound the error now by allowing a weak institution to prematurely exit."

But my arguments fell on deaf ears. The Fed let it be known that it was prepared to go ahead and approve the repayment plan over our objection.

Upon hearing that from my staff, I responded that we would need to notify the bank directly that we objected to its plan, a communication that BofA would likely have to disclose to investors under securities rules. Fortunately, the Fed did not force our hand and continued discussions with us.

I then made a counterproposal: that BofA raise $15 billion to partially redeem $30 billion of its TARP investment and that Treasury give it some flexibility under its compensation restrictions, solely for the purpose of recruiting a new CEO. BofA's longtime CEO, Ken Lewis, had been forced out of his position, and the BofA board was having a hard time finding a strong replacement. Obviously, it was in the FDIC's interest for BofA to bring in a well-qualified CEO, and we were willing to support flexibility on pay and bonus restrictions solely for that purpose.

We and the Fed reached agreement on this counterproposal. When the Fed presented the plan to BofA, the bank flatly rejected it. But instead of telling BofA it was that or nothing, the Fed came back to us to negotiate some more! I later discovered that the Fed had also been consulting with Lee Sachs at the Treasury Department, Tim's close advisor, who was disdainful of our concerns and siding with the bank. I still refused to give.

Fortunately, Fed Vice Chairman Don Kohn started to question BofA's analysis and pushed the bank harder to explain why it couldn't do the full $22.5 billion. On November 25, two of BofA's board members came to see me to plead their case. Again, I told them we needed the full $22.5 billion in common equity. On December 1, BofA came in with its tenth repayment plan, which had it issuing $18.8 billion in common stock and $4 billion in trust preferred, which we again rejected.

Its last and final offer was to raise the remaining $4 billion in asset sales. We agreed to that on the condition that BofA fully exercise what is called a "green shoe" up to $3.5 billion. What that meant was that if it had investors willing to buy more than the $18.8 billion offered, it had to sell them additional shares up to $3.5 billion. I received verbal assurance from both the acting CEO and the chairman of the board that they would exercise the green shoe, and we notified the other regulators that this was key to our agreement. Based on Perella Weinberg's analysis, I was confident that BofA would have sufficient investor demand to raise the full $22.5 billion.

I was right. Demand for the offering was far in excess of the $18.8 billion. BofA easily sold the $18.8 billion and could have sold $3.5 billion more. But in violation of its commitment, it sold only an additional $500 million of the green shoe. I do not believe that BofA would have defied us if we had had the other regulators' support. However, the Fed and OCC already had egg on their faces, given the ease with which BofA raised so much new capital. Making BofA go all the way to $22.5 billion would have fully vindicated us, and the OCC and Fed were not going to let that happen.

As I predicted, giving BofA flexibility on the 1 for 2 encouraged other banks to seek similar flexibility. We had to fend off similar attempts by Wells Fargo and PNC to raise substantially less than the 1 for 2. But, as usual, the biggest fight was yet to come from Citigroup.

Our examiners felt that Citi actually needed to raise more than $20 billion to exit the program. They put the number at closer to $35 billion. The Fed eventually settled on $25 billion, but there again, as was the case with BofA, the Fed was willing to be flexible as to how the capital was raised. But the real agenda with regard to Citi's repayment did not become known to me until the night of December 3, 2009. At Paul Volcker's invitation, I attended a dinner meeting of a prestigious international banking group known as the G30. The dinner was being held at the NY Fed building. Bill Dudley was also at the dinner, and at its conclusion, he asked me to meet with him privately in his office (not the anteroom, but of course, he wanted something from me). We settled into his paper-cluttered office, and he got right to the point. Citi wanted to get rid of its $300 billion ring fence so that it could be free of all government support and the compensation restrictions that went with it. The NY Fed wanted to let it do so.

I rolled my eyes in disbelief. Citi's bungling management had just finished identifying the assets that were going into the ring fence a few weeks earlier. Yes, it had taken them nearly a year to decide which toxic assets they wanted to ring fence. Now they wanted to get rid of the ring fence? I had heard through the grapevine that Vikram was telling stock analysts that Citi was going to repay its TARP money and exit the ring fence so that it would have flexibility to pay bonuses to keep employees. He was also boasting that at some point it would start paying dividends again. We had laughed those stories off as delusional. Later, I found out that Citi had been having discussions with the NY Fed about terminating the ring fence going back to September.

I had underestimated the NY Fed's and Treasury's determination to make Citi look healthier than it was. They wanted to bolster its ability to compete against the better-managed banks. I essentially told Bill that was a non-starter. Again, our outside financial adviser Perella Weinberg thought that the market liked the ring fence. The market knew how sick the bank was. Exiting all the government programs would not make Citi look stronger; no one would buy that. It could, however, weaken the markets' perceptions of the institution by eliminating all of its government support. I hated the bailouts and I hated the TARP capital investments, but we had gone down that path and the FDIC had guaranteed a significant amount of Citi's debt—at the Fed's and Treasury's urging—to keep it from failing. Now the Treasury and Fed were happy to pull out while leaving us exposed with the debt guarantees. And if Citi got sick again, there was no going back, because TARP was ending.

In addition to terminating the ring fence, Citi wanted to raise only $15 billion in new common equity to repay its $20 billion in TARP. I pushed back hard. "Sorry, this is all about compensation," I said to Dan Tarullo in a December 10 email. "I'm not going to be jammed on hasty negotiations so they can pay their execs more money." But as usual, we were isolated in our opposition, and it was clear to me that the Fed would approve Citi's exit without us. So, aided by Jason Cave and John Corston, we negotiated the best deal we could. We were able to get the common equity offering up to $17 billion, with a commitment to sell another $2.5 billion if the offering was oversubscribed. Citi did not reach the $2.5 billion for lack of investor interest, so the Fed required that it issue additional trust-preferred shares. Treasury also agreed to keep Citi under compensation restrictions for another year. The FDIC kept the $3 billion in preferred securities that Citi had paid us for agreeing to take $10 billion in exposure on the ring fence. Given the FDIC's continued exposure to Citi on the debt guarantee program, I insisted that we keep those securities, which pay an 8% dividend, until all of Citi's guaranteed debt expires.

Citi blamed Wells Fargo for its failure to raise the full amount, essentially accusing Wells of timing its own offering to interfere with Citi's capital-raising efforts. (Wells had no problem raising its $12.25 billion in new common equity.) Ironically, Wells was not in a hurry to exit TARP and I think would have been willing to keep the capital and repay it over time, dollar for dollar, through retained earnings. However, the Treasury and Fed had pressured all of the institutions, including Wells, to exit the program, which meant that they were all going to the market at about the same time, competing with one another.

The special inspector general for TARP (SIGTARP) conducted a thorough review of the TARP exits and justifiably criticized the regulators for easing the terms of the 1-for-2 guidance, as well as pressuring the banks all to exit at the same time. However, it commended the interagency process, finding that "interagency sharing of data, vigorous debate among regulators, and hard-won consensus increased the amount and improved the quality of the capital that SCAP institutions were required to raise to exit TARP. . . . FDIC, exposed through its deposit insurance fund and its emergency lending program, was by far the most persistent in insisting that banks raise more common stock. The checks-and-balances that resulted from this interagency coordination helped to ensure that the nation's largest financial institutions were better capitalized upon exiting TARP than prior to TARP."

That was a prime example of why we needed more than a regulator. If it had not been for the FDIC, there is no doubt in my mind that the Fed and OCC would have settled for substantially less capital raising from all of the institutions.

Not that it was a happy relationship. SIGTARP's original report contained numerous quotes of my emails pushing back against the other regulators on TARP repayment. SIGTARP reluctantly agreed to delete a number of them at the insistence of the Fed's general counsel, while noting in its report that "exclusion of such information unnecessarily inhibits transparency, and is a missed opportunity to shed additional light on transactions that involved billions of dollars in taxpayer money." I agree and thus have included in this chapter some of my excluded quotes.

We demanded, and got, significantly more capital from the banks, but the banks also got what they wanted. By January, they were announcing bonuses that rivaled the amounts they had paid before the crisis. It made me wonder whether all of the bailout measures had been to protect the system or make sure those guys didn't have to skip their bonuses. As John Reed, the well-regarded former CEO of Citigroup, stated at the time, "There is nothing I've seen that gives me the slightest feeling that these people have learned anything from the crisis. They just don't get it. They are off in a different world."

The year 2009 put me at the center of many battles with the larger banks. I knew I was making myself unpopular, but I was astonished to read a major article in *The New York Times* on October 11, 2009, that Citigroup Chairman Richard Parsons had hired Richard Hohlt, a Washington lobbyist with a checkered reputation whose job, according to anonymous sources at Citi, was to "blunt" the pressure we were putting on Citi to improve its management and operations. As the story recounted, Hohlt is infamous in Washington for the role he played as the well-paid point man for the savings and loan industry in the 1980s. He was a key player in beating back regulators' efforts to effectively deal with the S&L debacle, which ultimately cost the taxpayer hundreds of billions of dollars. William Black, the lead congressional investigator of the savings and loan mess, was quoted in the article as saying "It is singularly obscene that any recipient of taxpayer assistance through the TARP program during the current financial crisis would hire one of the most infamous lobbyists in the world to represent them."

Hohlt denied that he was hired to "lobby" the FDIC, which was technically true, but beside the point. Citi had a very competent Washington, D.C., office. In any event, we were dealing directly with the board and senior management. Hohlt had no sway with anyone at the FDIC (just the opposite, in fact). He would have added nothing to the mix. People such as Rick Hohlt have other skills. One is to create trouble for government regulators by feeding negative stories and information to Hill staff and reporters. Being a "background source" for Washington-based media was one of Hohlt's fortes, as *The New York Times* noted. For instance, during the perjury trial of Vice President Cheney's aide, Scooter Libby, Robert Novak, who wrote the column "outing" Valerie Plame, testified that he gave the column to Hohlt prior to its publication. Hohlt, in turn, gave it to Karl Rove, the White House political director. So here was an institution (Citi) that had received $45 billion in TARP capital from the government and had issued about $70 billion in FDIC-guaranteed debt using its funds to hire a well-known hired gun to "blunt" the FDIC. In addition to his relationship with Citi management, Hohlt had another ax to grind with us: he had been a longtime lobbyist for Washington Mutual and even told the *The New York Times* that he had lost thousands of dollars in WaMu stock when it failed.

A few months later, Andrew received a provocative call from Keith Epstein and David Heath of the Huffington Post Investigative Fund, which operates independently of the much-better-known Huffington Post news blog led by Arianna Huffington. They were working on a story that suggested I had received special treatment from Bank of America in securing two mortgages from that bank during the same time I was working on BofA's "rescue." Andrew was aghast, as was I. I didn't know what the heck they were talking about.

As I explained in earlier chapters, when Scott and I moved the family to Washington in 2006, we were not certain that it would be a permanent move. So we signed a three-year lease for a house in the D.C. area while renting out part of our home in Amherst to help pay the bills. We are not wealthy people, having spent most of our careers in government or the non-profit sector. It was financially challenging for us to keep up the mortgage on the Amherst property while also paying rent in the expensive D.C. market. When the lease came due in July 2009, we decided to make the move permanent. Thus we started looking for a house to buy in D.C. and put our Amherst house on the market. Unfortunately, we could not find a buyer for our Amherst house, and after months of looking, the only house we could find to accommodate our needs in Washington had a million-dollar price tag (which in D.C. is not viewed as that expensive). To afford the mortgage on the D.C.-area house, we needed to reduce our monthly payments on the Amherst house, so we decided to refinance out of our fifteen-year mortgage into a thirty-year mortgage.

My husband worked with our real estate broker in finding financing for the D.C.-area house. (I stayed completely out of these discussions.) Since it was a jumbo loan, she advised us that financing was readily available only from the bigger banks and gave Scott the names of loan officers at both BofA and Wells Fargo. We already had a banking account at BofA, reflecting a customer relationship that went back to the 1980s. BofA and Wells were offering comparable deals, so Scott went with BofA. At the same time, we contacted our local lender in Amherst, Florence Savings Bank (FSB), and asked if it would refinance our fifteen-year mortgage into a thirty-year loan, explaining that we still used part of the house as a second home for weekend trips and summer vacations. The Florence Savings Bank loan officer confirmed in writing that it could refinance the house as a second home, but at that time, it was offering only variable-rate financing.

We wanted a fixed-rate loan, so Scott went to the BofA loan officer, explaining again that we used part of the Amherst house as a second home, and asked if BofA could refinance the Amherst mortgage as well. It was obvious that the Amherst house was not our primary residence, as BofA was also financing the purchase of our primary home in the D.C. area. Both loans were considered prime, low-risk mortgages. We could have easily secured comparable financing from a number of lenders. My husband and I have high FICO scores and have always paid our mortgage on time. We were putting more than 20 percent down on the D.C.-area house and had built up 70 percent equity in the house in Amherst. If anything, we were doing BofA a favor by taking our business to it, not the other way around.

The FDIC has strict rules forbidding FDIC officials from owning bank stocks, but it does not restrict us from getting credit cards or mortgages from insured banks; pretty much everyone has a credit card and mortgage. We are forbidden from getting those loans from FDIC-regulated banks, which are mostly the smaller, state-chartered community banks. Hence, FDIC officials go to national banks or thrifts, where we have no primary supervisory responsibilities. Of course, all of our banking relationships, including loans, credit cards, and deposit accounts, are publicly disclosed each year in annual financial reports. The two mortgages were to be disclosed in the next reporting cycle.

The mortgages did not violate the ethics rules, and they were both clearly consistent with the market rates being provided by other lenders at the time. So where was the story? There wasn't one.

The first tack the reporters tried to take was that it was simply inappropriate for me to do business with BofA when I was involved in "negotiating the bank's bailout." They overlooked the fact that BofA had received its bailouts long before my husband had started looking for a mortgage for us. In any event, Hank Paulson, as recommended by BofA's primary regulators, not the FDIC, had decided to invest $45 billion in TARP funds and provide other government support. I had resisted BofA's second bailout. I thought it was unnecessary, and I was proven right.

Then the reporters tried to argue that it was inappropriate for me to have been negotiating the terms of BofA's TARP repayment, having gotten two mortgages from the bank. They also tried to make something of a short courtesy call on me from one of BofA's executives, Gregory Curl. This type of "meet and greet" is held all the time in Washington. No business was conducted. In any event, the mortgages were approved and locked in well before the meeting occurred and before we had any inkling that BofA wanted to repay its TARP.

The idea that I might be handing out favors to BofA because I had gotten two market-rate mortgages from it was laughable. Anyone familiar with the record knows that I fought tooth and nail for BofA to raise much more capital than the other regulators would have required. If I had recused myself, I shudder to think what the outcome on its TARP repayment might have been. With both approaches, the reporters tried to make it look as if I were leading the charge to help BofA, while the facts clearly showed just the opposite.

In addition, the idea that BofA was giving us any special deal was ridiculous. On the contrary, we experienced the same kind of problems with BofA's mortgage operation as have many other customers. It lost our paperwork, pulled me out of an important meeting a day before we were supposed to close to get additional documentation, and then, when we and the sellers arrived at the settlement table, the officers didn't have all the papers necessary to close and we had to reschedule. About a year later, as mortgage rates plummeted, we tried to refinance. The bank charged us $700 to lock in a rate and then let the clock run out before the paperwork was done. It kept our $700, and we never got our refi.

The reporters focused a lot on the fact that BofA had erroneously designated our house in Amherst as a primary residence on our mortgage. They argued that by doing this, we had received a more favorable interest rate. My husband clearly told the BofA representative that part of the house in Amherst was being rented and we used the other part as a second home. The proof of insurance we gave the bank clearly showed that it was partially rented. It had to know that it was not our primary residence because it was financing the D.C.-area house, which was. When our IG looked at it, he found that the Amherst mortgage complied with established market guidelines and published rates. Actually, the rate BofA had given us was 5.62%, when the average for a thirty-year loan at the time was 5.26%. That was a paperwork error, and in fact, we paid a rate that was higher than the average rate.

The reporters could not have known any of that personal financial information about me without a professional investigation of our mortgages and family circumstances. I seriously doubt that on a whim they had just started looking at my home finances. Someone had had to dig deeply to find out that we owned two houses, that we had recently taken out two mortgages, that BofA had erroneously designated our Amherst house as our primary residence (we didn't even know that), and that we were renting part of our house to tenants. I have to assume that someone with expert knowledge of the mechanics of mortgage finance dug the information up, contrived a way to interpret it in the worst possible way, and provided it to them. I can only speculate where the story came from. I am happy to report that no other media outlet would touch it. It died a quick and well-deserved death.

CHAPTER 19

The Senate's Orwellian Debate

After the House passed its financial reform bill at the end of 2009, the effort moved to the Senate, where we were still engaged with Senator Dodd and his staff on the single regulator. It was a frustrating dialogue with Senator Dodd. We shared the same goals of wanting a stronger, more independent prudential supervisor for the nation's largest banks. Yet we were completely at odds as to how it should be done. Since his bill technically abolished the OCC, he truly felt that the new agency—to be called the Financial Institutions Regulatory Agency (FIRA)—would provide better oversight. Our fear was that the new agency would just be the OCC with a new name, except that we would no longer have a seat at the table to keep an eye on it.

The OCC staff was gleeful at the prospect of getting the FDIC and Fed out of bank supervision, and we strongly suspected that they were behind the scenes supporting this. Indeed, so enamored were some of the Dodd staff with consolidating power in the new, morphed OCC that at one point they actually proposed giving it the job of consumer regulator as well. In a truly strange twist, an alternative was proposed by Senator Richard Shelby, who suggested making the FDIC the new consumer regulator. We continued to strongly and vocally support the creation of a new, independent consumer agency. (Though I must say, if the Senate had decided to keep consumer regulation with an existing bank regulator, I think it is obvious that we would have been a more vigilant protector of consumer rights than a renamed OCC.)

After extensive discussions with Dodd and his staff, we finally convinced them to leave regulation of state-chartered institutions with us. Indeed, according to a draft his staff gave us on March 13, he proposed to give us primary responsibility over all state-chartered institutions with less than $50 billion in assets *and* their holding companies, taking that authority away from the Fed. For institutions with more than $50 billion, the new

FIRA would have authority over both the insured bank and its holding company. In that draft, the Fed would end up with nothing.

The Fed pulled out all the stops to keep its supervisory authority over holding companies intact. Senator Dodd, working with Senator Corker, then developed another proposal that would have given the Fed supervisory responsibilities over the largest twenty-five bank holding companies, with the rest divided up by size between us and the FIRA. But at that point the OCC and large institutions were starting to lose interest, and the community banks weighed in heavily in support of keeping the Fed's authority intact. Many smaller, state-chartered community banks had long-standing relationships with the Fed's regional banks, whose only real function was bank supervision. If the Fed lost its supervisory authority, the Fed regional banks would have had nothing to do.

I had no interest in trying to wrestle turf from the Fed. My priority continued to be ending too big to fail, and we were still butting heads with both the Fed and the Treasury, which wanted the government to have the flexibility to bail out failing institutions. I saved my influence for that issue. Dodd finally relented and dropped the FIRA proposal completely.

I had my hands full with resolution authority. Dodd's office was being heavily lobbied by Tim and Michael Barr for more flexibility to do bailouts, but Rahm Emanuel had told me that the administration would not work against the resolution fund, so I assumed that we were at least safe there. In addition, Dodd was consulting with us, as well as Mark Warner and Bob Corker, in writing the resolution sections of the bill. My staff spent numerous weekends at the negotiating table with those three Senate offices. One of the real advantages the FDIC enjoyed was the excellent reputation of its professional staff. We offered technical assistance in drafting legislation and amendments that no other agency could offer. Our team was trustworthy and fast. When we drafted something, congressional offices knew there was no hidden agenda; they were getting what they asked for. The same did not always hold true of the other agencies. That gave us a real advantage in knowing what the important priorities were for the key players.

In March, Dodd released a draft that kept the resolution fund, albeit at a reduced level of $50 billion. But at the behest of the Fed and Treasury, he had included a provision giving the Fed the authority to provide support to failing "financial market utilities" under the Fed's so-called 13(3) authority. The term "financial market utility" was broad enough to essentially encompass all of the megabanks in the country.

The provision completely negated other provisions we had worked hard for to ban bailouts of individual failing firms. We tried to convince the Dodd staff to take the language out, but they refused, given the pressure from the Fed and Treasury to keep it in. So I reluctantly went public with my concern that it was a backdoor bailout. In a March 19 speech to the Independent Community Bankers of America in Orlando, I criticized the provision, stating, "If the Congress accomplishes anything this year, it should be to clearly and completely end too big to fail. Never again should taxpayers be asked to bail out a failing financial firm. It's time that the big players understand that they sink or swim on their own."

That same day, Dodd announced that he was taking the provision out of the bill.

Dodd had tried hard to produce a bipartisan bill, going so far as to divide the committee membership into teams of two—one Democrat and one Republican—to give him recommendations in all of the key areas, such as resolution authority, derivatives regulation, and governance issues. He drew from those recommendations in devising his bill. (Fortunately for us, Warner and Corker had been assigned to resolution authority.) But in the end, he could not convince committee Republicans to vote for his proposal. So he reported his bill out of committee on March 22 on a strict party-line vote. Under Senate rules, he had to get 60 votes to end debate and bring his bill to a final vote on the Senate floor. He likely had 56 Democratic votes, meaning he needed at least 4 Republicans. He hoped to get many more.

The ranking Republican on the committee, Richard Shelby, was really the key to a bipartisan bill and, at least on resolution authority, he was ready to make a deal. On the positive side, he was in sync with the FDIC in closing off loopholes for individual bank bailouts, including restrictions on the Fed's ability to lend to entities other than solvent banks. In responding to Dodd's draft, he wanted language tightened further on any suggestion that the FDIC would use our new authority to favor particular counterparties or groups of creditors, as had been done with AIG. We were only too happy to oblige.

Senator Shelby also wanted to tighten restrictions on the FDIC's and Fed's ability to use its emergency lending programs to provide generally available assistance to solvent institutions in the event of a systemic crisis. We also agreed with him there, but his staff did not follow through. Instead, they drafted language that allowed the Fed to provide such assistance with the approval of only the Treasury secretary. In contrast, they required congressional approval for the FDIC to offer such programs. So they tied the hands of the FDIC, the one regulator that had resisted the bailouts, while imposing minimal constraints on the Fed.

But the really bad news was that Shelby decided to make elimination of our resolution fund a make-it-or-break-it issue. He wrote Tim on March 25, calling the resolution fund a "slush fund." He charged that "the mere existence of this fund will make it all too easy to choose a bailout over bankruptcy. This can only reinforce the expectation that the government stands ready to intervene on behalf of all large and politically connected financial institutions at the expense of Main Street firms and the American taxpayer."

It was interesting that the letter was addressed to Tim, not to Dodd. Indeed, Shelby's arguments against the resolution fund echoed the same arguments that I had heard in private meetings from both Larry Summers and Geithner. Larry, known for his ties with big hedge funds that would have had to pay into this fund, liked calling it a "bailout fund." I suspected that Tim and Larry were behind the letter, even though that would have been in violation of Rahm's statement to me that the administration would not work against the fund. It was also interesting that the letter had come from Shelby alone. Senate GOP Leader Mitch McConnell was also publicly opposed to the fund and attacked it on the Senate floor. However, Senator Corker strongly countered McConnell, pointing out that the fund helped protect taxpayers, not the other way around. In a subsequent letter in which McConnell spearheaded some forty Senate Republicans expressing opposition to the Dodd bill, the prepaid fund was not mentioned.

On April 13, my suspicions were somewhat allayed when Tim's top deputy, Neal Wolin, defended the fund in a conference call with reporters. But apparently Neal didn't get the memo from Tim, because on April 16, the Associated Press reported that "Obama administration officials want Senate Democrats to purge a $50 billion fund for dismantling 'too big to fail' banks from legislation that aims to protect against a new financial crisis." Dodd's staff alerted us to the story and told us that Treasury was behind it but that Dodd was going to stick with the fund. I forwarded the story to Rahm and asked for confirmation that the administration was not working against the fund. He reconfirmed that that was the administration's view.

But in apparent defiance of the White House, Tim was behind the Republican opposition to the fund, as became patently clear. On April 18, during the Sunday-morning talk shows, CNN reporter Candy Crowley tried to pin McConnell down on how an industry paid fund could be a "bailout fund." McConnell testily told her that Obama should go talk to his Treasury secretary, who agreed with McConnell. Similarly, Senator Susan Collins said on the Senate floor that Geithner had told her that he supported elimination of the fund.

That was hardly a fair fight. The irony was that Tim was obviously teaming up with Senate Republican partisans, who were overtly using the bailout-fund rhetoric to criticize his boss, President Obama. Why? The fund was going to be paid for through an assessment on large financial institutions. Polls showed that the public was cutting through the bailout-fund rhetoric and supporting the fund. Congressional Democrats in both the House and the Senate strongly supported it.

So why were Tim and Larry siding with some in the GOP who wanted to use the fund as a partisan issue? Indeed, there were press reports that the GOP was using the issue for fund-raising.

I think there were several reasons.

First, I think they were trying to protect the big institutions from having to pay assessments. In January 2010, after the House had passed the $150 billion resolution fund, the administration had proposed a new "TARP tax" to raise about $90 billion over a ten-year period. Supposedly, the tax was designed to cover the projected costs of TARP. The TARP tax was dead on arrival, and Tim never seriously pushed it. My assumption was that it was a tactical ploy to divert support from the resolution fund. Indeed, more recently, Tim has worked against proposals in Europe and the United States to impose a transactions tax on financial firms. In doing so, he has revived his going-nowhere TARP tax as an alternative—this time at a reduced $30 billion over ten years. He pulls it out as an alternative whenever momentum builds for a meaningful assessment on high-risk financial firms.

Second, I think it was petty. They didn't like the influence we were exerting on the new resolution authority and wanted to beat it back just because it would be beating us back.

But finally, and perhaps most important, Tim wanted leverage against us. That is because he and some of the Republicans, while calling the resolution fund a "bailout fund," were proposing that the fund be replaced by a line of credit with the Treasury Department. That's right: they were arguing that our proposed resolution fund, which would be built from assessments on big hedge funds, investment banks, nonbank mortgage lenders, and others, would be a "bailout fund," but that giving the FDIC a line of credit from taxpayers to support resolution activities would be fine. Got that? It was an argument straight out of George Orwell's *1984*. Big Brother couldn't have said it better.

It was nonsense. The resolution fund was designed to provide a barrier between failing institutions and taxpayers. As Andrew Sorkin observed in a May 25, 2010, column supporting the fund, "the prepay model, as unattractive as it may be for Wall Street, may be the only way to truly protect taxpayers."

But protecting taxpayers wasn't Tim's priority. Having control over the resolution process was. And of course, under the Shelby proposal, Treasury would control the line of credit. By forcing the FDIC to have to come to Treasury for money to conduct the resolution, Tim's ability to influence the FDIC would increase.

All sides agreed that to achieve an orderly resolution of a large financial institution, some temporary funding had to be provided to continue operations. Even Harvey Miller and the bankruptcy advocates were arguing that the Federal Reserve Board should provide funding to bankrupt financial entities to preserve the franchise. (And I can't think of anything more dangerous than to have the Fed or any other government entity lending money into a bankruptcy proceeding, as private litigants spend years squabbling over who gets what.) The question was always where the money would come from.

As I stated in a letter to the editor in *The Washington Post* on April 29:

> The real question is not whether some liquidity funding is necessary, but where it comes from: pre-funding from the industry, Fed lending (which would impose no burden on the industry) or a Treasury line of credit that would be repaid by the industry after the fact. The FDIC feels strongly that large institutions should be required to pay risk-based assessments up front to make large firms internalize the costs of resolutions and make sure that the riskiest institutions pay the most.

That was another important facet of a prepaid fund: our ability to assess institutions on the basis of risk. And we were planning to base the assessments on exactly the type of activities that fueled the crisis. Firms that funded themselves with short-term debt, took on maximum leverage, made high-risk loans, and invested in complex, hard-to-value securities would have paid the most. Financial firms that used stable, longer-term funding and made prudent loans and investments would pay less. In addition, by adding to the funding costs of large financial institutions, the assessment would have helped level the playing field between large and small banks. As a result of the bailouts, banks perceived as being too big to fail were having to pay much lower rates on their deposits and other borrowings than were community banks. Depositors and other creditors demanded higher rates of return from the smaller banks because they knew their money was at risk. With the larger banks, the assumption was that the government would protect them.

Dodd stuck with us in support of the fund, notwithstanding Tim's shenanigans. McConnell also backed off somewhat. But Shelby wouldn't budge. He essentially told Dodd that if Dodd agreed to drop the fund and incorporate his other changes (which we mostly supported), he would endorse the resolution section of the bill and acknowledge that it would provide the means to end bailouts. Recognizing the importance of Shelby's support to achieving financial reform, Senator Dodd finally relented. We had no choice but to go along. As Dodd pointed out, we could claim victory in that our language banning bank bailouts was in and in fact had been strengthened by Senator Shelby. I agreed to support the Dodd-Shelby compromise, while preserving our right to push for the prepaid fund again when the House and Senate met in conference to reconcile their bills.

Dodd and Shelby offered their amendment on the Senate floor on May 5, and it was approved by an overwhelming margin of 93 to 5. At least the support for resolution authority was bipartisan, another goal of mine.

Though the fight over the resolution fund was disappointing, we preserved the ban on bailouts and were winning key battles on other fronts. Most important, we were successful in our support for an amendment sponsored by Senator Collins to require that minimum capital levels set by regulators for large banks could not be lower than the minimums generally applicable to smaller banks. That was a knife in the heart of the Basel II standards, and it came none too soon.

On April 22, 2010, Senator Collins invited me to join her for breakfast in the Senate Dining Room to talk about the financial reform bill and ways it could be strengthened. Prior to her election to the U.S. Senate, Senator Collins had served in the Maine cabinet and had overseen state banking supervision, among other responsibilities. As a consequence, she understood the essential importance of strong capital standards in a stable financial system.

At that breakfast, I shared with her our Basel II woes and suggested that she sponsor an amendment mandating that large-bank capital requirements stay at least as high as the requirements generally applicable to smaller community banks, the kind she had overseen when in state government. I further suggested that it would help protect the FDIC from losses if her amendment required that bank holding company capital standards be at least as strong as those applicable to insured banks. I thought that was the only way to make sure that bank holding companies were truly a source of strength for the insured banks they owned. During the crisis, we had in fact found the opposite to be true: due in part to the weaker capital standards the Fed had in place for bank holding companies, FDIC-insured banks had ended up supporting the holding companies, not the other way around. At one point in the breakfast, Senator Harry Reid, the Senate majority leader, came by our table to encourage us to work together to help build bipartisan support for the financial reform legislation. Like Senator Dodd, Reid understood the critical importance of locking in Republican support.

Collins agreed that mandating higher capital requirements was paramount to financial reform, and Paul Nash and her legislative director, Mark LeDuc (both of whom were at the breakfast) formed a partnership that helped drive the Collins Amendment through to enactment. Our capital expert George French provided technical assistance to the Collins staff, and several days later, Collins sent the amendment to Dodd and Shelby, asking for their support. However, as soon as he got wind of the amendment, Tim visited Collins and pushed back against the amendment, saying that it would hurt smaller banks! Tim's strategy, also backed by the Fed, was to keep capital standards out of the legislation. The Fed wanted flexibility to write capital standards as it saw fit, working with the Basel process. Given our past experience with Basel II, we wanted some statutory constraints on it.

The amendment was anathema to the large financial institutions, which were still hoping they could take on more leverage under Basel II after memories of the crisis started to fade. Big foreign banks that owned U.S. bank holding companies were also opposed to the amendment. The Fed routinely granted holding companies owned by foreign banks exceptions from capital requirements. As a consequence, foreign-owned bank holding companies held very little capital. Indeed, one actually had negative capital, according to our staff analysis.

The Fed's rationale for granting the exceptions was that foreign banks could infuse additional capital into their U.S. banks if needed, so it was not necessary to require their U.S. holding companies to be well capitalized. We were skeptical of that argument, given the high level of leverage of European banks and the likelihood that if one of them got into trouble, their foreign regulators would want it to keep any excess capital at home, not send it to the United States. Our concerns about foreign-owned holding companies proved to be prophetic, as the European sovereign debt crisis has more recently caused widespread distress in that banking sector, creating questions about the financial strength of European banks.

The big banks and the Treasury Department, as well as the Fed, were all working to oppose or water down the Collins Amendment. However, a number of market analysts and commentators spoke well of it, as they had seen firsthand how lax capital regulation at the holding company level had failed during the crisis. As *The Wall Street Journal*'s David Reilly put it, "Sen. Collins' amendment was right to end this charade. Neither she nor the Senate should backtrack on it."

Most important, Senator Collins stood up to all of the naysayers, recognizing that her job was to protect the public from financial instability, not cater to industry special interests. Given her background overseeing bank regulation, she understood the role of excess leverage in causing the crisis and the need to put some basic statutory capital standards into place. She knew her vote would be key to whether the financial reform bill passed in the Senate. She had her own "leverage," and she masterfully used it in sponsoring this amendment.

But we ran into an unexpected snag from community banks. Keeping large-bank capital minimums at the same level as community banks' would help the smaller institutions, not hurt them. But the part of the Collins Amendment that required bank holding capital standards to be as high as those for the insured banks did have some impact on smaller institutions. Many community banks had holding companies that had issued hybrid debt instruments to raise capital. Those instruments were not recognized as good capital at the insured-bank level, so they would be disallowed under the Collins Amendment, and for good reason: we had extensive research showing that holding companies, both large and small, that used hybrid debt as capital were more likely to fail, and when they did fail, they generated more losses for us.

Given that the amendment was targeted primarily at large institutions, we agreed to support a change to Senator Collins's proposal to let community bank holding companies continue counting hybrid debt that they had already issued as good capital—known as a "grandfather provision"—though, going forward, any new securities that they issued would have to be pure equity to count as capital. With that change, Dodd and Shelby agreed to accept the amendment, and on May 13, it was approved on the Senate floor by a voice vote, without opposition.

But we knew that Tim and some of the big banks would make another run at the Collins Amendment when the House and Senate met to reconcile their two bills. Indeed, I was summoned to a meeting with Tim and Ben at the Treasury on the day the Collins Amendment passed the Senate and subjected to a stern lecture from Tim about being a team player and that capital standards should be set by regulators, not Congress. Fortunately for the future stability of our financial system, that view did not prevail. I believe that the Collins Amendment will stand as one of the crucial reforms of the Dodd-Frank Act.

A war was also brewing over the Volcker Rule, named for its chief proponent, Paul Volcker, the legendary former chairman of the Federal Reserve Board. The Volcker rule was designed to ban FDIC-insured banks and their affiliates from making speculative bets on the markets, instead of serving customers.

Here again, Michael Barr, under Tim's direction, was trying to water it down. Fortunately, the two chief sponsors of the provision, Senators Carl Levin (D–Mich.) and Jeffrey Merkley (D–Oreg.), held their ground.

Tim and the Fed's general counsel, Scott Alvarez, continued trying to sneak bailout language into the bill, and they succeeded in securing one loophole. At their behest, Dodd included in his bill a provision to let securities and derivatives clearinghouses borrow from the Fed at its discount window. We had successfully opposed that provision in the House but were becoming increasingly isolated in the Senate. Both the CFTC and SEC, initially skeptical of the provision as a potential Fed intrusion into their oversight of clearinghouses, came to support it. And the clearinghouses that they regulated were drooling at the prospect of having access to loans from the Fed.

I thought it was a terrible precedent and still do. It was the first time in the history of the Fed that any entity besides an insured bank could borrow from the discount window. Clearinghouses had performed well during the crisis, and they have never posed a serious threat to financial stability. That is because they are tightly regulated and managed and have high financial qualification standards for their members. In the past, clearinghouses and their regulators understood that if they ran out of money to stand behind their trades, the consequences would be disastrous for both them and their members. But with the bailout loophole, the market discipline that had previously kept clearinghouses tightly and prudently managed was seriously diluted. Now if the clearinghouses run out of money, they can just borrow from the Fed.

The Fed already had authority under the Dodd bill to make assistance generally available to healthy clearinghouses during a systemic crisis. The provision went further and gave it the flexibility to bail out individual outliers that were in trouble due to their own mismanagement. That unwarranted authority created a classic "moral hazard" for clearinghouses, which will be protected from realizing the negative consequences of risky decisions while still able to reap profits. Paradoxically, that increases the likelihood of clearinghouses engaging in risky activity, adding an element of potential instability to an area where it had not previously existed.

The consumer agency proved to be the biggest fight of all. The Senate GOP had insisted that the responsibility for consumer issues stay with one of the bank regulators, citing the concern that an overly zealous consumer agency would not be sufficiently attentive to safety and soundness issues and risks to the Deposit Insurance Fund. So Dodd cleverly made the consumer agency a division of the Fed and required the Fed to fund it, but he also wrote the law so that the director of the new agency had near-complete discretion to run it as he or she saw fit. The chairman of the Fed and the Fed board were forbidden from interfering with the new agency, called the Consumer Financial Protection Bureau (CFPB). So the CFPB was technically a part of the Fed, a banking regulator, but it had the same degree of autonomy as an independent agency.

The proposal, while clever, outraged the Republicans and made it all the harder to get the 60 votes needed to bring the bill to a vote on the Senate floor. To this day, I wonder if perhaps consumer advocates and their congressional allies were a little too clever with the proposal, given continued GOP opposition, even among moderates, to the consumer agency as it is currently constituted. We had suggested that the new consumer agency be run by a five-person board, with two bank regulator representatives. We also suggested that though the new agency should have exclusive authority to write consumer rules, it should share responsibility with the bank regulators for examinations and enforcement of those rules on banks. Sharing examination and enforcement functions for FDIC-insured banks would have allowed the new bureau to focus greater resources on examining nonbank financial services providers, such as payday lenders and check cashers, which had had no federal oversight. We had prevailed with that argument at least with the community banks. Both the House bill and the Dodd bill gave the banking regulators responsibility for examinations of and enforcement for banks with less than $10 billion worth of assets. The CFPB was given backup authority to enforce its rules if we didn't do our job. But given the OCC's past abysmal record on consumer protection, the consumer groups were bound and determined not to let it have any role in enforcing consumer rules against big banks. Who could blame them?

Dodd persevered, and he was able to convince four Republicans and 56 Democrats to secure the 60 votes necessary to end debate and bring the bill to a Senate vote. Republican Senators Chuck Grassley of Iowa, Susan Collins and Olympia Snowe of Maine, and Scott Brown of Massachusetts—the late Ted Kennedy's surprise successor and the first Republican to win a Massachusetts Senate seat since 1972—voted with Dodd. On May 20, the Senate passed the bill.

But the fight was far from over.

Tim was still unhappy with the restrictions on bailouts in the bill and was hoping that in the conference, Michael Barr would be able to rewrite the resolution authority more to his liking. That was a very real threat to us. House-Senate conferences—when key members of the House and Senate meet to reconcile differences in the bills they have passed—are notoriously opaque, closed-door processes. Without the bright spotlight of media and public scrutiny, we were fearful that the reform bill would revert to the bailout approach of the white paper Tim had released a year earlier.

Fortunately, we had excellent relationships with Dodd and Frank, as well as a number of other Republican and Democratic conferees. Our legislative and legal team attended every minute of the two-week conference. Kym Copa and Roberta McInerney from our general counsel's office worked around the clock, providing technical help and answering questions for the conferees. Fortunately, Dodd, Frank, and most of the conferees were aligned with us and our antibailout perspective. They kept us plugged in, and we were able to fend off further efforts to dilute the bailout ban in the bill.

We had a real fight on our hands to fend off Tim's and the industry's attempts to eviscerate the Collins Amendment. The American Bankers Association lobbyists were bordering on hysteria, going so far as to send my board members an inflammatory analysis basically saying that the amendment would destroy community banks. My board ignored them.

So did the House.

As *The Wall Street Journal's* Damian Paletta reported on June 17:

You might hear a collective "Uh Oh" on Wall Street today.

Big banks had figured surely lawmakers would strip out a controversial provision in the Senate bill that would force bank holding companies to hold more capital and essentially prohibit them from counting hybrid securities as Tier 1 capital. . . .

So on Thursday, there were collective gasps when the House came back with their proposed changes to the provision and instead of offering to kill it, they are essentially proposing to tailor it in such a way that it would only affect banks with more than $15 billion of assets.

In an apparent act of desperation, Bob Diamond, at the time a top official of Barclays, one of the biggest banks in the United Kingdom, made the outrageous accusation that the Collins Amendment would cut credit to U.S. bank customers by "as much as $1.5 trillion." There was no basis in fact for the assertion, and it surprised me as I've always viewed Diamond as a levelheaded CEO. But in that instance, his arguments were over the top, even compared to the exaggerated claims of other industry groups. For example, a leading international trade association had been arguing that eliminating hybrid debt and substantially raising capital ratios globally for all banks would contract lending worldwide by $1.3 trillion. All of that was self-serving nonsense too. Numerous government and academic studies have shown that stronger capital standards will have, at best, a negligible impact on lending while producing tremendous benefits by reducing the risk of large-bank failures and the huge credit contractions we experienced in 2008.

The conferees ignored Diamond's hyperbole. We were ecstatic. In the face of opposition from Tim, the Fed, the big banks and their trade groups, the provision stayed in with only minor modifications. Recognizing the importance of Senator Collins's support for the overall legislation, Chairman Dodd instructed his staff to keep her amendment intact. Though she was not a conferee, Dodd would oppose any changes to her amendment that Collins herself did not support. The House and Senate conferees both understood that Senator Collins was a "must-have" vote for final passage of the reform bill. She played that card masterfully, but not to appease Wall Street bigwigs or fill her campaign coffers with financial industry money; she used the leverage for the public benefit, to secure what was really the only concrete provision in the bill to improve the quality and quantity of capital held by large U.S. financial institutions.

Indeed, most of the provisions of the House and Senate bills that we supported were approved by the conference committee.

The conferees agreed to several provisions to permanently raise the deposit insurance limit to $250,000 and provide a two-year authorization of the Transaction Account Guarantee (TAG). That was the program we put into place during the crisis to provide unlimited coverage for large, non-interest-bearing checking accounts held by businesses and local governments. I was a bit ambivalent about those provisions, as they expanded the government safety net. At the same time, they were important to the stability of community banks, which rely heavily on insured deposits for their funding. The conferees also agreed to give the FDIC discretion to build our reserves to high levels during the good times, to provide more of a cushion to draw on them during downturns. Under prior law, we had to manage our fund within a range of 1.15 to 1.5 percent of insured deposits, which was too low.

The conferees further agreed to provisions in both the House and Senate bills that changed the base we use to calculate assessments. Under the old system, we could look only to insured deposits in charging premiums. That gave large institutions incentives to game their premiums by obtaining funds from other sources, such as foreign deposits, which are highly volatile, or secured loans, which are costly to us in the event of a failure because they tie up good assets. Under the new law, we could look to all of a bank's borrowings in determining its premium. The effect of that change was to shift a much higher portion of the FDIC assessment burden to banks with more than $100 billion in assets, providing a significant reduction in community banks' FDIC premiums.

The conferees preserved all of the FDIC's safety and soundness regulatory authorities, as well as our ability to examine and enforce consumer rules for institutions with less than $10 billion in assets. And thanks to Senator Dodd and his chief staff aide, Amy Friend, the conferees included the House provision that gave us backup authority over bank holding companies and other systemic institutions, notwithstanding vigorous opposition by the Fed.

But we lost the battle on the resolution fund, again primarily to the relentless efforts of Tim Geithner and Michael Barr. The House strongly advocated for the fund, and Dodd, working with Bob Corker, valiantly tried to keep a small fund in the bill. On June 25, Paul Nash reported to me that it looked as though there would be agreement on a $19 billion fund. That would give us some ability to impose assessments on the high-risk nonbanks, while the interest we earned on the fund would provide enough money to support staff salaries and other operational expenses for the new office we would need to create that would be dedicated to nonbank resolutions. But Geithner and Barr fought tooth and nail against that as well, at one point even suggesting that we would have to seek appropriated funds to support resolution authority. They didn't want us to have any autonomy in carrying out our new resolution responsibilities.

Even though Shelby's staff was working in tandem with Geithner, other key Republicans, including Corker, were not opposed to a small fund to support FDIC operations. So Geithner went to Senator Scott Brown, a key swing vote, and, in a true devil's deal, reached an agreement with him to delete the $19 billion fund and to water down the Volcker Rule as well. Specifically, Geithner agreed to support an exception from the Volcker Rule to allow insured banks and their affiliates to invest in speculative hedge funds and private-equity funds so long as those investments did not exceed certain limits. Tim was eager to make the changes, and he used Brown as the vehicle for doing so. Brown could then claim victories for Boston's financial sector, while President Obama's secretary of the Treasury would give him cover with the Democrats.

On Monday, July 12, Brown announced that he would support the financial reform bill with that change to the Volcker Rule and the elimination of the $19 billion "bank tax."

Of course, the assessment would not have been a "tax" on "banks," which already paid fees to the FDIC. It would have been a risk-based assessment on large nonbank financial players.

Dropping the fund created a new complication: there was no way to pay for the implementation costs of the bill without relying on taxpayers. Under congressional rules, new legislation must contain sources of additional revenues to offset any costs associated with it.

So how did Congress decide to pay for the financial reform bill? It raised the FDIC's minimum reserve requirements. That's right—the costs of the new resolution authority and other provisions of the bill, now known as "Dodd-Frank," would be offset by raising the minimum amount we had to assess insured banks with more than $10 billion in assets. Investment banks, finance companies, hedge funds, and other "shadow bank" highflyers who contributed to financial instability would not pay a dime.

Some Republicans balked at that accounting artifice, and rightfully so. I did not have an objection to the policy behind raising the minimum reserve requirements for FDIC insurance. We should have had more of a cushion going into the crisis, and we were planning to build our reserves substantially higher over time. The existing statutory minimum of 1.15 percent was far too low. But I did object to using the Deposit Insurance Fund to pay for reforms that were targeted mostly at the nonbank sector. You would have thought that the groups representing insured banks would have supported an assessment on nonbanks to pay for the bill, but did they? No, they did not. The American Bankers Association, which is supposed to represent the interests of traditional, FDIC-insured banks, vigorously lobbied against the resolution fund, making me wonder who it was representing.

Dodd pressed me hard for a letter supporting the higher minimum reserve requirement. He was afraid that if I did not support it, he wouldn't be able to keep all of his swing Republican votes, and the whole bill would fall on the issue. I thought it was better to have a bill than not have a bill, so I reluctantly wrote him the letter he requested but gave him only half a loaf: I told him in the letter that I supported raising the FDIC's reserve minimum but did not express a view on whether that was the appropriate way to pay for the bill.

The conferees finished their work in late June. On June 20, the House approved the bill reported by the conference committee on a 237–192 vote. The Senate did not vote until July 15, as Chairman Dodd struggled to line up the 60 votes he needed to bring the report to a vote. In the end, Senators Collins, Snowe, and Brown were the only three Republicans to vote with him and all but one Democrat, Russ Feingold, who opposed the bill because he thought it was too weak.

On July 21, the president signed the bill in a widely attended ceremony. It was held in a large auditorium at the Ronald Reagan Building and International Trade Center, but notwithstanding the bipartisan venue, only one Republican member of Congress attended: Joseph Cao, a newly elected congressman from New Orleans. I was invited, as were all the other major agency heads. Only two industry CEOs attended, and guess who they were? Vikram Pandit, the head of Geithner's favorite bank, and Bob Diamond, who had carried Tim's water in savaging the Collins Amendment.

Ben Bernanke and I sat side by side in the front row as the president extolled the legislation. No, it was not a perfect bill. Legislation never is. But it gave the government important new tools and authorities that had been missing during the crisis and that, if properly used, could prevent a repeat of the terrible events of late 2008. I was particularly pleased that in speaking about the importance of the legislation, the president highlighted the resolution authority we had worked so hard for:

And finally, because of this law, the American people will never again be asked to foot the bill for Wall Street's mistakes. (Applause.) There will be no more tax-funded bailouts—period. (Applause.) If a large financial institution should ever fail, this reform gives us the ability to wind it down without endangering the broader economy. And there will be new rules to make clear that no firm is somehow protected because it is "too big to fail," so we don't have another AIG.

That sounded like the president I had heard during the meeting in the Oval Office on AIG more than a year before. I believed that was how he felt, but I didn't think his Treasury secretary felt the same way. As I sat there, I couldn't think of one Dodd-Frank reform that Tim strongly supported. Resolution authority, derivatives reform, the Volcker and Collins amendments—he had worked to weaken or oppose them all. Yet Obama had left the legislative battles to him. For instance, Senator Dodd had spoken to Obama only three times during the entire legislative process. Dodd-Frank was a good bill, but for that President Obama had to thank Chairmen Dodd and Frank and legislators such as Senator Collins, who were willing to rise above partisan posturing and industry pressure to protect the country.

CHAPTER 20

Dodd-Frank Implementation: The Final Stretch (or So I Thought)

The battles over financial reform did not end with the president signing Dodd-Frank. Virtually all of the reforms in the new law relied on agency rule makings for implementation. So as the industry redirected its army of lobbyists to the rule-writing process, I decided to try to outrun them. I knew that the longer regulators waited to finalize the rules, the greater the risk that they would be watered down. There was also another need for expediency: I had barely a year left in my five-year term. I wanted to make sure we finished the rules on resolution authority, deposit insurance, and the all-important Collins Amendment before I left office. I also wanted to complete rules that we had initiated containing important reforms to the securitization process.

Already amnesia was setting in about how bad the crisis had been. The Tea Party—born of outrage over the 2008 bailouts—was redirecting its ire toward government. Instead of providing political support for common-sense measures such as higher capital requirements, resolution authority, and mortgage-lending reform, it was bashing government and regulations for impeding the economic recovery, forgetting that the recession had been caused by the excesses of many large financial institutions. That, of course, was playing into the hands of industry, and it frustrated me no end. As a market-oriented Republican, I was outraged at the way some of the big firms had come running to Washington to be bailed out of problems of their own making. They had been worse than the proverbial welfare queen. Yet the narrative in some (not all) conservative circles was becoming that the crisis had been the government's fault; folks at those poor big financial firms had been forced to do all those stupid things and be paid all of those big, multimillion-dollar bonuses because the government had wanted poor people to have mortgages. Right.

With less than twelve months left in my tenure, I had a very full plate. I moved quickly on organizational changes to implement the new law. We created an Office of Complex Financial Institutions (CFI). The office would take responsibility for backup supervision and resolution of bank and non-bank institutions with more than $100 billion in assets. I promoted Jim Wigand, who had been a superstar in handling our bank failures, to be in charge of the new office. Jason Cave was installed as his deputy in charge of creating better systems to monitor big banks. During the crisis, we had learned the hard way that we needed to keep a closer eye on them.

We also created a new division focused solely on consumer protection, consolidating our public education programs for deposit insurance and community outreach with our consumer examination functions for institutions with less than $10 billion in assets. To head the division, I hired Mark Pearce, who had overseen bank supervision for the North Carolina banking department and before that had worked at the Center for Responsible Lending. I wanted us to have a better consumer focus and a more cohesive examination strategy for ensuring compliance with consumer laws. I've always prided myself on being proconsumer, but during the crisis, I found that consumer issues—as is all too often the case—took a backseat to our safety and soundness responsibilities. To be sure, we had a good consumer record during my tenure at the FDIC. We had great consumer compliance examiners, second to none among the banking agencies. We initiated a number of high-profile consumer enforcement cases and also pioneered research to support banks in their efforts to offer safe, simple products to less sophisticated populations, such as low-cost small-dollar loans and low-fee checking accounts. Retail banking products had become far too complicated for many consumers. With a new division, headed by a strong leader like Mark, consumer issues would always stay front and center before the FDIC chairman and board. Mark's shop would also be responsible for coordinating with the new Consumer Financial Protection Bureau on its rule makings related to FDIC-insured banks.

For the Dodd-Frank rule writings, I organized the FDIC staff into implementation teams and scheduled weekly meetings to receive progress reports. Helping me in this endeavor were our deputy general counsel, Roberta McInerney, and her top lieutenant, Kym Copa. Kym was one of our brightest attorneys, a whiz at drafting legislation and rules. She and Roberta had worked tirelessly during the congressional consideration of Dodd-Frank.

I also instituted a new transparency policy: we would adhere to an open-door policy for anyone who wanted to meet with us on pending rule makings. Industry groups, consumer groups, reform advocates, all would get an equal hearing. But we would publish on our website the names and affiliations of people who met with us and the topics they discussed. To try to preempt industry lobbying, I organized roundtable discussions on important rule-making topics that we could control in terms of who came and the topics discussed. The roundtables provided an excellent way to get technical input from the industry and others, but in an open and transparent way; we webcast all of them. We were the first to propose a transparency initiative, but soon thereafter a number of other agencies did the same.

The rules related to deposit insurance were the easiest to accomplish because we had sole authority for getting them done. For instance, the rule to implement the higher deposit insurance limits was completed on August 10. The more complicated rules related to the way we charge banks' deposit insurance premiums were proposed in early November. Consistent with Dodd-Frank, the rules allowed us to look at all sources of a bank's funding in determining the amount of its insurance premium, and they also improved the way we adjust large banks' premiums on the basis of risk. We looked back at the attributes of weak banks such as Citi, Wachovia, and WaMu several years before the crisis to find common predictors of risk. We wanted to see what they had looked like before their problems became prominent to reduce the procyclicality of our assessment system. Our goal was to assess risk throughout the cycle, not just penalize mismanaged banks once they started experiencing losses. In that way, we hoped our risk-based premium system could deter risk taking before big problems emerged.

The combined effect of the rules was to shift about 80 percent of the assessment burden to large banks, reducing small banks' assessment burden by 30 percent. Thanks to the outstanding work of Art Murton, Diane Ellis, and their team, the rules were promptly finalized in February 2011.

Another area in which we had exclusive authority related to how we viewed securitizations during a bank failure. A late-2009 accounting change had created confusion about whether loans a bank sold into a securitization were the property of securitization investors or the FDIC if the bank failed. The securitization industry was lobbying us to provide relief on the issue. They basically wanted us to issue a carte blanche rule that said we would not try to claim ownership of any failed banks' securitized assets that met the old accounting standard. I was willing to approve that kind of relief—called a "safe harbor"—for old securitizations. In fairness, they had been issued when the old rules applied and investors had purchased the mortgage-backed securities based on the expectation that the FDIC would not try to claim ownership of the underlying mortgages. However, for future securitizations, I wanted better standards to apply. Securitizations had provided the fuel for the conflagration that had consumed our housing market and our economy. I wasn't going to facilitate a return to the old ways. We needed better safeguards in place.

In December 2009, we provided temporary relief, saying that we would continue to apply the old standards until March 2011. But we also requested comment on additional conditions that might be imposed to address the misaligned incentives in securitizations that had caused so much damage. After receiving comments, in May 2010, we proposed a rule imposing a number of conditions. The most important of them was "risk retention"— the idea that those who issue mortgage-backed securities to investors have to keep some of the risk of losses if the mortgages go bad. A 5 percent risk retention requirement was already included in the Dodd-Frank bill, then still wending its way to final passage, so we also proposed a 5 percent risk retention requirement in our rule. The idea was that for every dollar of loss on a mortgage that went bad in a securitization, the issuer would have to absorb 5 cents. (I would have preferred 10 percent, but we went with the 5 percent standard.)

In addition, working closely with Chairman Mary Schapiro and her staff at the SEC, we conditioned the safe harbor on new disclosure rules the SEC had proposed in April. Those important rules would give investors better information about the quality of loans in securitizations and more time to review that information before making the decision to invest. Finally, we imposed conditions on how servicers are compensated to make sure they had incentives to restructure loans when it would minimize losses for all investors, to end the "tranche warfare" that had so impeded loan modifications. All of those reforms were carefully coordinated with the SEC so that all securitizers would have to abide by them. Our safe harbor would apply only to insured banks. The SEC rules could reach everyone else.

After receiving a second round of comments on the proposed rule, I decided to move ahead with finalizing it. The industry was apoplectic. Late in the Dodd-Frank legislative process, it had been able to secure a significant weakening of the risk retention requirement. Specifically, the final law said that securitizers did not need to retain any risk in the mortgages they securitized if the mortgages met very high lending standards. Dodd-Frank further directed all of the major agencies to develop the new standards jointly. Mortgages that met the new, higher "gold standards" were called qualified residential mortgages (QRMs). The industry now wanted us to hold off on imposing risk retention or any other condition on bank-issued securitizations until the regulators wrote the QRM rules.

Having been a regulator for most of my career, I knew how long the writing of interagency rules could take. We had been generous enough with the industry. I knew that it would just try to drag out and water down the QRM rules (and it has). In the meantime, no new standards would apply if we backed down. So I instructed our staff to continue moving forward, and I notified our board that there would be a final vote at our September 27 meeting. I also told our board members that we would include something called an "auto-conform" provision in our final rule. That meant that if and when the regulators finalized the QRM standard for risk retention, our rule would automatically conform to that rule.

On Sunday, September 26, at 7 P.M., the evening before our board meeting, in an astonishing assault on the FDIC's independence, Tim sent an email to the heads of all the major regulatory agencies asking for their views as to whether the FDIC should proceed with the final rule or whether we should grant the relief the industry sought, without conditions. The only agency head not included in the email was Ben. Instead, Tim sent it to a senior staffer at the Fed, a holdover from the Greenspan era. My jaw dropped when I saw the email. I was working at home, and I howled so loudly that my kids came running to find out what the problem was. Then I started receiving calls at home from other agency heads telling me that one of Tim's deputies, Jeffrey Goldstein, had been calling them, encouraging them to email back that they wanted us to delay our rule and extend relief without conditions, just as the industry wanted.

The Fed staffer responded immediately to Tim's email that the Fed wanted us to delay. Ben was traveling, and it was not until early the next morning that I could reach him. I emailed him tersely: "This rule has been in the works for a year. If you really want to get into the middle of this, I'd prefer a call and not hear through an intermediary." Ben had always been professional and courteous to me, and my guess is that the staffer was pursuing her own agenda. In the meantime both Ed DeMarco, the head of the Federal Housing Finance Agency, and Mary Schapiro weighed in favor of the FDIC exercising its "independent judgment." When I did finally reach Ben, he tried to finesse the issue by saying that the Fed would prefer that we delay but that he respected that it was our decision to make. The next day, my board voted to finalize the rule, with only one dissent, John Walsh—Dugan's chief of staff, who had replaced him on an interim basis as acting comptroller of the currency. The irony is that another board member, acting OTS head John Bowman, was unsure of how he would vote on the rule, but I think he decided to support it partly in reaction to Tim's heavy-handed tactics.

John Dugan stepped down as the acting comptroller of the currency at the expiration of his term in August 2010. I was surprised that the administration did not nominate a replacement for Dugan, as it was probably one of the most important jobs for Obama to fill if he wanted to have a stronger regulator for the big banks. As secretary of the Treasury, it was Tim's responsibility to recommend candidates for financial regulatory agencies to the White House; they would then be nominated by the president and confirmed by the Senate. But in the case of the OCC, Tim had failed to recommend a replacement. Instead, he exercised his statutory right to appoint Walsh. In doing so, Tim passed over the OCC's top career official, Julie Williams, who had been with the OCC for decades and had served as the acting comptroller in the past when temporary vacancies had occurred. Julie was controversial with consumer groups and reform advocates, as she was generally viewed as friendly to the big banks. Ostensibly, that was the reason Tim passed her over. But Walsh turned out to be as much a supporter of industry as Julie was, as I learned with that securitization vote. I suspect that the real reason Walsh was named was that Tim thought he could control him, while Julie—a smart, tough-minded lawyer—would be more independent.

As we put our own conditions on securitizations into place, we continued working with the other regulators on the Dodd-Frank risk retention requirement and QRM exception. We pushed hard for very stiff standards for QRMs. I believed—and continue to believe—that the best way to prevent lax lending is to make sure that those securitizing the mortgages are on the hook for losses. QRMs provided a way for securitizers to escape having any "skin in the game." As such, the QRM criteria needed to be narrowly drawn. We strongly supported a minimum 20 percent down payment requirement, as well as tough income documentation standards and a low debt-to-income ratio.

We also pushed for servicing standards in the risk retention rules along the lines of those we had included in our own securitization safe harbor. We wanted to end compensation structures that made it profitable to the servicer to foreclose and ban other conflicts that had skewed economic incentives and sent so many families into unnecessary foreclosures. Those standards would have applied prospectively to future securitizations, as we could not rewrite securitization contracts that were already in place. But going forward, we wanted to make sure that servicers were required to take prompt action to mitigate losses and act solely in the interests of maximizing recoveries for investors as a whole.

Here again, John Walsh fought us tooth and nail on including servicing standards in the risk retention rule, while the Fed remained neutral. Finally, after receiving letters from consumer groups and Congress and 12,000 signatures on a petition circulated by the naked capitalism blog, the Fed came our way and helped convince the OCC to agree to most of our requested changes. (The other regulators already supported us.) But disagreements over that and many other facets of the rule delayed its publication for comment by all of the agencies until April 2011. Regrettably, once the proposed rules were issued, the 20 percent down payment requirement met with a storm of criticism from many (but not all) low-income advocacy groups and the real estate industry. They grossly misrepresented the risk retention rules as requiring *everyone* to have a 20 percent down payment. For instance, Bob Nielsen, the chairman of the National Association of Home Builders, was quoted as saying:

> By mandating a 20 percent down payment on qualified residential mortgages, the administration and federal regulators are excluding those without huge cash reserves—which constitutes most first-time home buyers and many middle-class households—from a chance to buy a home.

Of course the QRMs, those requiring 20 percent down, were meant to be a small part of the market—the exception, not the rule. Mortgages that banks kept in their own portfolios or securitized while retaining 5 percent of the risk could have lower down payments. That controversy and others prevented the regulators from taking final action, and I am very fearful that in the 2012 election year, they will succumb to political pressure and lower the QRM standards. In any event, as I write this in the middle of 2012, the agencies have still not finalized that or any other major rules reforming the private securitization market. Our hard-fought safe harbor rule is the only reform that has been put into place, four years after the crisis.

We also had a completely gratuitous, time-wasting fight with the OCC over rules to implement the Collins Amendment. Our FDIC Basel team drafted a straightforward rule that set a floor on big-bank capital requirements based on the generally applicable standard to all banks. Julie Williams, representing the OCC, then argued that the Basel II advanced approaches were the "generally applicable standard" for the large banks, so that Basel II should set the floor. That, of course, would have nullified the plain language of the Collins Amendment, as well as Senator Collins's express intent in her remarks on the Senate floor. She did not want the regulators to allow the big banks to take on more leverage than was allowed for the rest of the banking industry. Basel II didn't yet apply to any bank; the FDIC had successfully delayed its implementation, and in any event, by definition, it was not generally applicable because it was meant to be available only to the largest banks.

The OCC and a few Fed staff then tried to argue that the Collins Amendment applied only on an aggregate basis, so that if the Basel II advanced approaches produced higher capital in aggregate, individual big banks could still lower their capital below the requirements that applied to the smaller banks. So, for instance, if BofA had a capital increase under Basel II, JPMorgan Chase could lower its capital, so long as the average was the same. That was also clearly against the plain language and intent of the amendment, which banned any big bank from taking on more leverage than would be permitted for smaller institutions. There again, thanks to the strong position taken by Dan Tarullo, the OCC and Fed staff backed away from that argument, and in February 2011, the three agencies jointly proposed a rule that was true to Senator Collins's intent. We finalized it in June 2011, less than a month before I left.

But the battle royal came with the rules implementing our new resolution authority under Dodd-Frank. I was eager to finalize rules reinforcing the antibailout language for which we had worked so hard. Dodd-Frank strictly prohibits the Fed and FDIC from providing support to an individual failing or insolvent institution. Such an institution must be placed into bankruptcy or the FDIC resolution process. In addition, Dodd-Frank forbids the FDIC from favoring one group of creditors over another; they must be treated evenly, in accordance with the same priority followed in bankruptcy, with equity shareholders absorbing losses first. The act allows the FDIC to differentiate among creditors in two narrow situations, both of which also exist in bankruptcy. First, it can make payments to continue essential operations. Critical employees, technology providers, and security and maintenance personnel are examples of creditors who need to be paid to continue operations. Second, it can differentiate when it will maximize recoveries as the failed institution is sold off. That is essentially a mathematical determination. For instance, when an insured bank fails, we find that the bank acquiring it will frequently pay us extra to cover losses we would otherwise impose on the uninsured depositors. Large uninsured depositors are typically among a bank's best customers, and the acquiring bank does not want to lose them. So it will pay us extra to make sure those big depositors are fully protected.

I wanted to issue a rule reinforcing that those would be the only two limited circumstances when we would ever differentiate and that, further, certain classes of claimants, including common- and preferred-equity shareholders and subordinated debt and term unsecured debt holders would *never* qualify for extra payments. Throughout our decades of resolving thousands of failed banks, no one at the FDIC could ever remember a situation when those groups of claimants had needed to be paid to maximize recoveries or continue essential operations.

I had discussed the rule with Ben, and he was comfortable with the approach we wanted to take. However, when I discussed it with Tim, he reacted very negatively. As usual, he was concerned about limits on the government's discretion to bail out bondholders, but he could not provide me with plausible scenarios where protecting them while imposing losses on other creditors would meet the statutory criteria.

Dodd-Frank required the FDIC to consult with the new Financial Stability Oversight Council (FSOC) on our rules implementing resolution authority. To that end, our staff had been having conversations with the staffs of the Fed, the Treasury, and other agencies since July 2010 on our plans to have very tight controls on differentiating among creditors. In addition, I circulated our proposal to the heads of all FSOC members a full week before our September 27, 2010, board meeting, when I had scheduled a vote to approve the rule for public comment. Nevertheless, John Walsh argued that we had not given FSOC members enough time for a meaningful consultation, even though there had been months of staff discussion. Moreover, the other agencies could continue providing input during the public comment process. In an effort to accommodate him, I had the staff brief the board on the proposed rule on September 27, but we waited until October 12 to actually vote. (For all my reputation as a tough, hard-nosed FDIC chairman, in retrospect it amazes me how much I bent over backward to accommodate board members.)

In early January, after receiving public comments, I decided to proceed to the final rule making. Again, we gave the other agencies several weeks' notice that we would finalize the rule with only minor changes. None of the agencies, with the exception of the OCC, expressed a substantive objection to the rule, and Ben and Dan Tarullo made it very clear that the Fed was comfortable with our approach.

Then the Treasury's legal counsel contacted Mike Krimminger, giving him a heads-up that Tim would be contacting me to discuss the interplay between Section 203 of Dodd-Frank, which gave Tim approval authority over FDIC rules governing the Treasury line of credit, and Section 209, which gave the FDIC authority to write rules implementing resolution authority. According to the Treasury legal staff, "Geithner feels that Treasury should have a larger role than it has had to date on what they view as a large policy issue on the extent to which FDIC would or would not make additional payments to creditors in a Title II orderly liquidation."

So there it was. As I had feared, Obama's Treasury secretary was trying to use the line of credit the Republicans had put into the bill as a way to try to get us to loosen our proposed restrictions on the payment of creditors. Tim pushed me hard on the rule, I pushed back, but here again, to accommodate him, I told him we would approve the rule as an "interim final." That meant that the rule would go into effect but we would solicit another round of comments on it and leave the door slightly ajar for further changes. So on January 18, the FDIC board did just that, with the OCC's new comptroller, John Walsh—whom I had come to view as Tim's mouthpiece—complaining that we shouldn't be limiting our discretion to pay long-term bondholders and that we would be discouraging investors from buying long-term debt.

The back-and-forth with Tim over the Treasury's role in our rule making continued. On March 21, I sent him a polite letter explaining that the proposed rule did not involve policies and procedures governing the use of Treasury funds and thus they did not have to be acceptable to him. The second round of comments gave us nothing new, so in June 2011, we made the rule permanent. Perhaps because the Fed was supportive of our approach, Tim ultimately dropped his objections to it. (Or maybe he hoped to undo it after I left.)

Another extremely important rule related to resolution authority was the Dodd-Frank requirement for large financial institutions to file so-called living wills with both the Fed and the FDIC. Specifically, it required them to demonstrate to us and the Fed how their nonbank functions could be wound down in a bankruptcy process without systemic disruptions. (Insured banks remain subject to the FDIC's preexisting resolution powers. For large organizations such as Citigroup that have both bank and nonbank operations, the bank is resolved under FDIC's preexisting powers, and the nonbank affiliates are resolved by the FDIC under the new powers contained in Dodd-Frank.) If a large institution cannot show that its nonbank operation can be resolved in an orderly way in bankruptcy, the Fed and the

FDIC have joint powers to order it to restructure itself or become smaller through divestiture.

I viewed the living will requirement as a potent new tool in the regulators' arsenal to end too big to fail. Because of inherent flaws in the bankruptcy process, discussed earlier, I doubt that any large financial institution can make the required statutory showing. Thus, the regulators will likely have strong grounds to order divestiture or require that a failing behemoth reorganize into simpler, stand-alone subsidiaries that can be easily hived off and sold (or put into bankruptcy) without threatening the viability of the rest of the institution. Even more important, the living wills will be essential to improving information—which we lacked during the 2008 crisis—about the structure and location of major business lines, as well as the big institutions' exposures to one another. Each of the megabanks has thousands of different legal entities, making it virtually impossible to identify and locate all of the different entities that support each of the bank's business lines. Each institution is also required to identify every other institution to which it has a major credit exposure. During the crisis, we did not have good information about other institutions that might fail if, for instance, we put Citi into our resolution process and imposed losses on all of its unsecured creditors, including unsecured trading partners. Uncertainty about those types of interrelationships drove many of the decisions to bail out banks such as Citi and AIG.

However, under the statute, the first stage of the process is to give large financial institutions the opportunity to develop and present their plans. After that there needs to be a review process and a back-and-forth among the Fed, the FDIC, and the institution to determine whether it has shown that it can be resolved in bankruptcy in an orderly way. I thought that it would likely take at least a year before the Fed and FDIC would have final living wills, as well as the grounds, if necessary, to start ordering structural changes or divestitures. With Citi and BofA still in tenuous shape, it was essential to get the ball rolling.

But we had a tight time frame to work under, and the living will rule had to be joint with the Fed. I was already hearing that some of the Fed staff did not want to prioritize the living will requirement. Rather, they wanted to hold it back and issue it when the Fed issued other proposed regulations related to supervision of large financial institutions. So I reached out to Ben and Dan Tarullo, and both agreed to try to get it done before I left. We kept the pressure on the staff, but even with our efforts, the Fed and FDIC staff did not reach agreement until late March 2011. On March 29, we issued our joint proposed rule, with a forty-five-day public comment period. That would be barely enough time to finalize the rule before my scheduled departure on July 8.

Both Ben and Dan made yeoman's efforts to complete the rule before I left, but the time was too short. Ben promised me he would do everything he could to complete it by August. (They almost made it. It was approved by the FDIC on September 13, 2011, and shortly thereafter by the Fed.) I'm glad I pushed, because if I hadn't, the living will rule would have been held back and included in other Fed rules relating to large banks. Those were not proposed by the Fed until December 2011 and will be finalized in the summer of 2012 at the earliest. In contrast, because the FDIC and Fed acted early, the biggest banks should complete their first living will submissions by July 1, 2012.

My final board meeting was on July 6. Though the living will rule was not completed until after I left, I did complete action on another item of priority importance to me. That was a rule authorizing the FDIC to claw back two years' worth of compensation from officers or directors who had been "substantially responsible" for the failure of a financial institution. The rule created a strong presumption that senior executives and key board members were substantially responsible if they had been in charge when the institution got into trouble. I was dismayed, as were most Americans, at the way boards continued to hand out large bonuses and pay packages to senior executives of bailed-out financial firms. Even when the CEOs were terminated, they typically received a generous severance settlement. Never again. If there were to be a next time (and there likely will be; there will always be boneheads out there who somehow rise to the top of bank management), I wanted to make sure that not only would they lose their jobs but they would pay substantial personal financial penalties.

CHAPTER 21

Robo-Signing Erupts

I thought I was in the home stretch with the enactment of Dodd-Frank and the completion of priority rule makings. But by the fall of 2010, we were seeing clear signs that the major loan servicers—primarily owned by the nation's biggest banks—were failing to perform their basic obligations to borrowers, investors, and the government in dealing with troubled loans. At the beginning of 2010, I had started seeing scattered press reports of home owners challenging foreclosure proceedings based on faulty paperwork submitted by loan servicers. The most cited problem was "robo-signing"— a practice at some big bank servicers of having a single employee sign thousands of affidavits swearing that the borrower was in default and that the servicer had all of the documents necessary to prove legal standing to foreclose. When home owners challenged those affidavits, the courts were finding that the employee signing the affidavit had had no personal knowledge whatsoever as to the borrower's status or the adequacy of the servicer's documentation. Indeed, in some instances, the documentation was woefully insufficient, not even containing the mortgage note that proved that the servicer had the right to claim the house as collateral for the loan.

I would pass the articles along to my staff, but they seemed to be isolated cases, and in any event, the reports did not involve servicers that we regulated. Since 2007, we had made foreclosure prevention and loss mitigation an area of priority focus for our examiners. We had seen no problems of that type among the banks we oversaw (and I am happy to say that no FDIC-regulated banks were ever implicated in the robo-signing scandal). We assumed that any problems were being handled by the primary regulators of the major servicers: the OCC and, for a few servicers, the Fed.

But in September 2010, it became clear that the robo-signing controversy involved far more than a few isolated cases. On September 20, the press reported that GMAC Mortgage was suspending foreclosures in a number of states in order to review paperwork to make sure that foreclosures were being done correctly. That was followed by similar actions by JPMorgan Chase, Bank of America, and most of the other major servicers. The press went wild as the major servicers announced the foreclosure "moratoriums." As the media scrutiny intensified, there were immediate demands for federal investigations and actions.

On October 18, Chairman Dodd's staff demanded a briefing from the regulators. Though the OCC was the primary target of their questions, all of our staffs were asked to attend. During the briefing, the OCC acknowledged that it did not look at servicers' compliance with legal requirements outside of the requirements of the securitization trusts. The OCC and Fed also acknowledged that they had heard about the robo-signing problems from press reports, not the examination process.

Tim and HUD Secretary Shaun Donovan then convened a meeting at HUD on October 20 with all of the bank regulators and representatives from the Department of Justice, the Federal Trade Commission, the SEC, and the Federal Housing Finance Agency, the regulator of Fannie Mae and Freddie Mac. Elizabeth Warren was also invited in her capacity of special adviser to Tim and the president on setting up the new consumer agency. I was not surprised at Warren's presence. It made sense insofar as Dodd-Frank expressly gave the new consumer bureau authority to write mortgage-servicing standards. Even though the agency was not up and running yet, its views were obviously important, as in less than a year, it would have the lead role in overseeing big-bank servicing and treatment of borrowers.

Not much was accomplished at the meeting. HUD and the Treasury Department issued a statement that the meeting had occurred and detailed some of the individual initiatives each of the agencies was taking to hold mortgage servicers accountable. I was amazed to learn during that and subsequent meetings about the severity of penalties HUD could assess against servicers that did not comply with its strict loss mitigation requirements for mortgages guaranteed by the Federal Housing Administration (FHA), which is part of HUD. Theoretically, it could assess triple the amount of the insured unpaid balance on each mortgage on which a servicer had violated HUD rules. Given the pervasive problems we would later discover at some of the banks, if the FHA wanted to pursue the maximum penalties allowed by law, it could probably have threatened the financial viability of some of them.

Though we didn't have direct jurisdiction over any of the large servicers, a few of them had purchased failed banks from us under terms that required us to share the losses on the failed banks' mortgages. Those agreements gave us the authority to audit the servicing of mortgages since we were exposed to some of the losses if they defaulted. Our loss-sharing agreements required banks to restructure loans when doing so would mitigate our losses and also fully comply with foreclosure laws if foreclosure became necessary. As we learned more about the robo-signing scandal, it became apparent that robo-signing was simply one symptom of a much deeper problem: chronic underfunding and mismanagement of servicing operations by the major banks. So I asked our examiners, led by Stan Ivie and Frank Hartigan in our San Francisco regional office, to conduct detailed file reviews of loss-share banks to make sure they weren't foreclosing unnecessarily. Since the loss on a foreclosed loan could be 40 to 60 percent of the unpaid balance, we wanted to avoid it whenever a restructured loan would be a better economic alternative.

The OCC and Fed decided (obviously) that they needed to do a thorough review of all their major bank servicers to determine their compliance with foreclosure requirements, which are governed by state and local laws. As the deposit insurer, I was becoming increasingly concerned about the impact the controversy could have on the financial strength of the big banks. The maximum FHA fines by themselves could be a huge problem. And that was only the tip of the iceberg. State attorneys general were already launching investigations, and the trial bar was gearing up to challenge foreclosure actions en masse. Similarly, those who held mortgage-backed securities that were serviced by the big banks would have claims against them if they failed to adhere to basic standards of servicing competence.

Around the same time that the Fed and OCC began their reviews of the major bank servicers, they notified us that they wanted to start letting banks increase their dividend payments to shareholders. Since the crisis, we had kept a tight rein on dividends to make the banks conserve capital. I was concerned that letting banks raise their dividend payments at that point was premature. It would be better for the banks to hold on to their earnings, at least until we had a better idea of what their losses related to the robo-signing mess would be. In addition to the robo-signing controversy, the banks also had to contend with preparing to meet higher international capital requirements. Other jurisdictions, including Canada, were refusing to approve dividend increases until banks significantly raised its capital levels.

On November 5, 2010, I sent a letter to Ben strongly urging caution in approving dividend increases:

Given the continued uncertainty in the markets in which these institutions operate, we do not believe it is the right time to allow transactions that will weaken their capital and liquidity positions. The highly publicized mortgage foreclosure process flaws provide an example of how quickly material issues can arise in these institutions and how they are still exposed to the poor decisions made in the years leading up to the crisis.

I sent a similar letter to John Walsh, asking the OCC not to approve banks' dividends to their parent companies without first consulting with the FDIC. Once the money was at the holding company, I knew there would be pressure to let it pay it out to shareholders. In my letter to Ben, I pointed to research conducted by the Boston Federal Reserve Bank showing that regulators had been slow to curb dividend payments before the crisis, with $80 billion being paid out before and during the crisis. "[O]nce the level of dividends increases," I argued, "it is difficult to scale back."

The OCC and Fed agreed to consult with us on dividend payments. They also invited us to participate in their reviews of the fourteen largest mortgage servicers, twelve of which were regulated by the OCC. I reluctantly agreed. I was conflicted as to what our strategy should be. I didn't want us tainted by the foreclosure mess. The banks we regulated hadn't done those things. On the other hand, if we participated, we could perhaps push the OCC and Fed to take more aggressive action in correcting problems than they might otherwise be inclined to. There were reputational risks for us. If the OCC and Fed came out with weak orders, notwithstanding our advocacy, they would still expect us to sign on. Throughout the crisis, I had been frustrated by our lack of leverage in forcing more meaningful action to address the housing crisis. Here again, I had the same problem. Our only direct "hook" with those fourteen servicers was the fact that we were the primary regulator of GMAC's insured bank, Ally. Ally did not service loans, but it did originate conventional mortgages and contracted with GMAC Residential (regulated by the Fed) to service them. If not satisfied that GMAC Residential had taken appropriate corrective action, we could order Ally to stop doing business with it.

Notwithstanding my concerns, I decided that we should participate in the exams. Almost immediately, the disagreements began. We thought the OCC was being too narrow in how it was defining the scope of the exams—focusing only on the question of whether the borrower had been seriously delinquent before the foreclosure proceeded. Even if a borrower was seriously delinquent, the servicer still had to comply with the legal require-

On June 26, 2006, I was sworn in as the nineteenth Chairman of the Federal Deposit Insurance Corporation. I decided to pass on the big, formal ceremonies that frequently accompany a swearing in, opting for a low-key event with career FDIC staff. Delivering the oath of office is Robert Feldman, the FDIC's corporate secretary, and holding the Bible is Alice Goodman, who headed the FDIC's legislative affairs division. FDIC file photo

On September 19, 2008, I rang the opening bell at the New York Stock Exchange to celebrate our seventy-fifth anniversary. I was accompanied by FDIC staff whom we selected by lottery. It was an auspicious date. Coming only days after the collapse of Lehman Brothers and the implosion of AIG, markets were in free fall, and the confidence of the financial system was being tested. A few hours earlier, I had been on the phone with Henry "Hank" Paulson, negotiating the terms of an emergency program Treasury was putting together to protect money market funds, which were facing massive withdrawal requests. FDIC file photo

On October 13, 2008, CEOs of the nation's largest banks were summoned to the Treasury to meet with me, Hank Paulson, Ben Bernanke, Timothy Geithner, and other regulators. The message was simple: the banks were instructed to accept $125 billion in capital investments from the government. While some were reluctant to accept, others, like Citi CEO Vikram Pandit (on right, with Morgan Stanley head John Mack on the left) were quite happy to take the money. Citi would later need two more bailouts to avert failure in spite of the $25 billion it agreed to accept that day. Mark Wilson/Getty Images

On October 14, 2008, we lined up to announce financial stabilization measures, including debt guarantees and capital investments in the nation's largest banks. From left to right, Treasury Secretary Hank Paulson, Federal Reserve Chairman Ben Bernanke, me, then New York Federal Reserve President Timothy Geithner, Comptroller of the Currency John Dugan, Securities and Exchange Commission Chairman Christopher Cox, and Director of the Office of Thrift Supervision John Reich. Mark Wilson/Getty Images

As the crisis deepened, Congress became increasingly anxious about addressing what went wrong. Here I am testifying with Hank Paulson and Ben Bernanke at a November 18, 2008, hearing of the House Financial Services Committee where committee members were highly critical of Treasury's refusal to address mortgage restructuring as provided in the TARP legislation. My relationship with Hank, while often productive, was severely strained by our disagreements over the need for a loan modification program. Chip Somodevilla/Getty Images

I presided over the FDIC through the banking crisis, which proved to be one of the most tumultuous periods for the seventy-five-year-old agency. When the crisis hit we were immediately catapulted into the roles of fire chief and rescue squad. This picture, taken for a *Financial Times* article, featured me unwittingly standing in front of a giant eagle crest in the lobby of the FDIC. While I may have looked like an avenging angel, Robert Kuttner painted a less celestial image of me in the *American Prospect,* calling me "the skunk at the picnic" for my disagreements with my colleagues over what I considered to be lax regulation and overly generous bailouts. Brandon Thibodeaux

In September 2009, former President Bill Clinton asked me, along with JP Morgan Chase CEO Jamie Dimon, to participate in a panel discussion on the state of the banking industry. Dimon managed his bank well during the crisis, though in 2012 his bank would stumble badly on complex derivatives bets made by an errant trader. But in 2009, he was the king of the roost, with a fat, profitable balance sheet, while I was dealing with the challenge of maintaining reserves adequate to handle an increasing number of bank failures. My grimace was in response to his boast that he thought the FDIC was "creditworthy" and would be happy to lend to us any time.

Bloomberg/Getty Images

Here I am at a conference on small business lending, hosted by the FDIC. Small businesses were among the many victims of the 2008 crisis. Big financial institutions, with their highly leveraged balance sheets, pulled back drastically on small business loans. Community banks—which provided about 40 percent of bank small business lending—did a better job, but they also had to pull back as the economy deteriorated and loan losses grew. At the conference, I was joined by Ben Bernanke (to my right), Senator Mark Warner (D–Va.); Tom Donohue, the head of the U.S. Chamber of Commerce; and moderator Steve Liesman from CNBC (far left). FDIC file photo

Sitting next to President Obama at an April 10, 2009, meeting at the White House. The president held several meetings with all the major financial regulators early in his term, but I don't think Treasury Secretary Timothy Geithner (left) and NEC Director Lawrence Summers (center) liked us having access to him. By the time the summer of 2009 rolled around, the meetings had mostly stopped. Bloomberg/Getty Images

During the crisis, famed personal finance guru Suze Orman volunteered to help us reassure the public on the safety of FDIC insured deposits. Orman donated substantial personal time to our public education campaign, including appearing in four televised public service announcements (PSAs). When I arrived at the New York studio we used for filming the PSAs, she offered me the use of her hair stylist to pretty up before the shoot. After a considerable amount of clipping and blow-drying, the stylist gave me a mirror so that I could see the masterpiece. My hair was identical to Suze's, except that the part was on the opposite side. My kids called it my "Suze-do."
Courtesy of Suze Orman

In 2009, I was honored to receive the Kennedy Library's Profiles in Courage Award from Caroline Kennedy. My then eight-year-old daughter, Colleen, accompanied me to the ceremony. She had read picture books about Caroline growing up in the White House and riding a pony on the White House lawn. She had envisioned a young Caroline and was surprised to meet the grown-up one. Public Domain

Here I am testifying before the Senate Banking Committee in July 2009, proposing the creation of a systemic risk council, with SEC Chairman Mary Schapiro and Federal Reserve Board Governor Dan Tarullo. The SEC supported the council but the Fed initially resisted it. Congress did eventually approve the creation of a council, but it lacked the teeth I had originally envisioned. Chip Somodevilla/Getty Images

A May 2010 issue of *Time* magazine dubbed Elizabeth Warren (left), Mary Schapiro (center), and me "The New Sheriffs of Wall Street." I was somewhat amused that I was being called a "new" sheriff. Mary and Elizabeth came to office with the Obama administration, while I had been around nearly four years and had the battle scars to prove it.

After a long and contentious battle, the financial regulation bill known as Dodd-Frank was signed into law on July 21, 2010. I was honored to stand beside Ben Bernanke and my friend Elizabeth Warren, who had championed the creation of what would later become the Consumer Financial Protection Bureau, as the president spoke and greeted us. Dodd-Frank is a good, albeit imperfect law. Many of its provisions were watered down as a result of industry lobbying and, in some instances, at the behest of Timothy Geithner and his surrogates. Bloomberg/Getty Images

At my first meeting of the Financial Stability Oversight Council on September 30, 2010, expectations were high. I was joined by Ben Bernanke and Timothy Geithner—a potentially powerful alliance—but for all of the pomp and circumstance, the council still has not lived up to its promise. Brendan Hoffman/Getty Images

Here I am with my beloved family—my husband, Scott Cooper, and my son and daughter, Preston and Colleen—at my farewell party one day before I left office. Few people realize what incredible personal sacrifices public officials make to meet the demands of their jobs. A few months earlier, I had attended my son's high school graduation dinner. It broke my heart that I hardly knew any of his friends or teachers. Scott made substantial sacrifices to attend all the parental events that I missed. Because of him, our kids never resented their absentee mom but rather took pride in my work. FDIC file photo

ments associated with foreclosure. In particular, it needed to show that it held good title, which could be a challenge in some cases because the ownership of securitized mortgages changed hands many times. There were also many reported instances where servicers had charged borrowers inappropriate fees, then classified the mortgages as delinquent when the borrower refused to pay. Finally, and most important, we wanted to make sure that loan modification applications had been appropriately reviewed. Our ongoing review of the loan files of loss-share acquirers was revealing significant error rates in loan mod denials. Specifically, of the institutions we looked at, a number of borrowers had been denied a modification even though they had been entitled to one. In these instances the modified loan would have had greater value than a foreclosure. Yet the mod had been turned down.

The Fed was much more receptive and aligned with our thinking, again thanks to the efforts of Dan Tarullo. The disagreements came to a head during a December 1 hearing before the Senate Banking Committee on mortgage-servicing problems. All of the bank regulators, as well as the Treasury Department, were asked to testify. I did not want to testify at the hearing. We weren't perfect, but in this case, we had had nothing to do with the regulatory lapses that had led to the robo-signing scandal. If I testified, I feared, the FDIC would be lumped in with the OCC. But Dodd was insistent that I be there because he felt I would be more open about servicing problems and more proactive in pushing for action to address them.

Congressional hearings are a time-consuming process. It is a lot of work to write the testimony and prepare for all the questions that can come up. I had so much else on my plate in those final months of my tenure, I resented having to deal with this hearing. The night before my appearance before the committee, the staff and I were working late in my large conference room on preparation, and I just lost it. In the middle of the session, I stood up and said, "I DO NOT WANT TO TESTIFY AT THIS HEARING." I stomped out of the room, went into my office, slammed a few doors and drawers, took a deep breath, and counted to ten. Then I went back to the staff, sat down, and finished the prep. The staff just picked up and continued as if nothing had happened.

During the hearing, Dan and I were straightforward about the kinds of problems our examiners were seeing; Dan was even more pointed than I. "While quite preliminary," he told the committee, "the banking agencies' findings from the supervisory review suggest significant weaknesses in risk-management, quality control, audit, and compliance practices as underlying factors contributing to the problems associated with mortgage servicing and foreclosure documentation. We have also found shortcomings in staff training, coordination among loan modification and foreclosure staff, and management and oversight of third-party service providers, including legal services." He continued, "The servicing industry overall has not been up to the challenge of handling the large volumes of distressed mortgages. The banking agencies have been focused for some time on the problems related to modifying mortgage loans and the large number of consumer complaints by homeowners seeking loan modifications. It has now become evident that significant parts of the servicing industry also failed to handle foreclosures properly."

I watched Walsh stiffen as Dan testified. His testimony, in contrast, tried to minimize the issues as process-oriented and make it sound as though few, if any, borrowers had really been hurt. It was one thing for the FDIC to call out the national banks the OCC regulated; people expected that from us. It was quite another for the Fed to do so. Dan's testimony threw a monkey wrench into OCC's strategy of downplaying the problems.

The OCC's retaliation was swift. The day after the hearing, I heard from my examiners that the OCC no longer wanted us or the Fed participating in the servicing reviews because it was upset about our testimony. Several days later, our examiners were notified by the OCC that it would not be sharing their written exam findings with us or the Fed until December 23 and that it intended to begin discussions with the banks no later than January 3 to present those findings. I protested in a December 17 email to Walsh. "This will give us only one week over the holidays to review your findings and provide comments," I wrote. "Given holiday schedules and the fact that I, my board, and many of our senior officials will be out of the office that week, this 'offer' of information sharing is really no help at all." I demanded a briefing for the FDIC board and a copy of the OCC examiners' written reports.

Walsh responded with a token description of the OCC's findings that essentially recounted everything that we already knew—that policies, training, staffing, and so on were all "deficient." I fired back angrily, "I'm sorry but we cannot engage in a process in which our access to information has been delayed and impeded and in which we have had no meaningful input into decision making. . . . If that is all that is coming out of this, why in the world is it taking so long?"

Tarullo weighed in with similar concerns, and Walsh finally relented on allowing more time for interagency consultation.

As we began discussions over examination findings and what remedial action to require of the banks, the Treasury Department and HUD had initiated a parallel process to try to negotiate a global settlement among the major servicers and the various federal agencies that had enforcement responsibilities over servicing as well as the state attorneys general.

The idea—which I had advocated—was to negotiate an agreement among the major servicers and major enforcement agencies that would require the banks to significantly increase their servicing resources and loan workouts and provide redress to those harmed by wrongful foreclosures. In return, they would receive litigation relief from the state AGs and borrowers who were made whole. I viewed that type of agreement as crucial to the housing market recovery. Servicers needed to restructure loans when it made economic sense to do so. Because of the servicers' deficiencies, far too many loans were going to foreclosure when it would have been less costly to modify them. But we also needed a functioning foreclosure market. If the borrower was just in too big a house, we needed a process to move the property back onto the market. As numerous studies have documented, effective servicing can dramatically reduce mortgage losses and aid in the housing recovery. Ineffective servicing will cause unnecessary losses and delays. Because of skewed economic incentives and lack of adequate staffing, defective servicing had impeded our housing recovery. Now, because of all the servicing errors, the banks had opened themselves up to endless litigation that would further impede the clearing of the housing market.

As I stated in a January speech to the Mortgage Bankers Association:

If we are to successfully respond to today's foreclosure crisis, all parties involved must recognize some important principles. Loss mitigation is not just a socially desirable practice to preserve homeownership where possible. It is wholly consistent with safe and sound banking and has macroeconomic consequences. Fair dealing with borrowers and adherence to the law are not optional. They must be viewed as mandatory if our servicing and foreclosure process is to function in the interest of all parties concerned.

I went on to call for a major global settlement, noting that while industry would resist the financial costs of such a settlement, "this would be shortsighted. The fact is, every time servicers have delayed needed changes to minimize their short-term costs, they have seen a deepening of the crisis that has cost them—and the rest of us—even more."

I had been pushing for the FSOC to take a leadership role in resolving the foreclosure crisis. The growing backlog of foreclosed properties, combined with escalating litigation from servicer errors, presented a systemic risk, I thought, to both the financial sector and the broader economic recovery. A number of influential members of Congress, including Democratic Senator Jack Reed of Rhode Island, also called for the FSOC to exercise leadership. Tim scheduled a couple of discussions on servicing errors before the FSOC, including, at our request, a briefing from the FHA on the problems it had unearthed in their own reviews of servicers. But other than scheduling a few meetings, no one was showing any initiative. Some staff working groups had been set up and they were meeting frequently, but nothing was getting done. The Fed was also concerned about the inertia and had requested that Tim convene another meeting of principals. I decided to present a specific proposal to Tim for FSOC consideration. He would at least have to respond to our proposal, and even if he didn't like it, it would put pressure on him to come up with something on his own.

On February 7, I sent Tim an email suggesting a two-pronged approach to a global settlement with an estimated cost of $20 billion in cash outlays for the five major servicers. The first prong was to set up an independent claims commission for foreclosures occurring after January 1, 2008. The servicers would pay a nominal, standard amount for pure processing errors in exchange for the borrowers' waiver of claims. We estimated that a $1,000 payment for each mortgage would cost the servicers $3.3 billion. For borrowers who had suffered financial harm, i.e., those who had been wrongfully denied a loan modification, the independent commission would determine the appropriate amount of compensation. We roughly estimated wrongful foreclosures at 4 percent with an average award of $50,000 each, costing about $6.6 billion.

The second prong was what we called the "super mod." The idea was for the servicers to make a onetime, blanket offer to seriously delinquent home owners to write down their principal balance to below market value. A borrower could either complete a short sale at that reduced amount or try to resume mortgage payments at the reduced level. However, borrowers who redefaulted on their mortgage would have to contractually commit to relinquishing the property, ameliorating the need to initiate foreclosure. If at any point the house was sold, the borrower would have to give up any gain on the sale above the written down principal.

The super mod was designed to shock the market and create incentives for delinquent borrowers to sell their houses or start their mortgage payments again. Since the loan restructuring was based on a home's market value, not the borrower's income, all that the understaffed servicers needed was a current appraisal to make the offer. Moreover, since most of the seriously delinquent loans were virtually certain to land in foreclosure absent a modification, our super mod would save both lenders and mortgage investors money. Selling the house outside the foreclosure process, or letting the borrower stay with a reduced payment, would be significantly cheaper than liquidating the property in an increasingly lengthy, expensive foreclosure process. Thus the super mod would not cost the banks money, and we would not give them credit for writing the loans down. Instead, we proposed requiring incentive payments to investors and relocation and counseling expenses for borrowers that would total another $10 billion in cash outlays.

I told Tim that I wanted the opportunity to present those ideas at the next FSOC meeting. He never responded. The next thing I knew, Tim had asked Elizabeth Warren and her colleagues at the nascent consumer bureau to develop a proposal. Elizabeth and her team wanted to require the servicers to write down $25 billion in principal balances. That amount was cleverly based on the amount of money they estimated the servicers should have spent on servicing since 2007 but hadn't. But Tim was clearly trying to play us off each other. I asked Elizabeth to come to my office so that we could discuss our differences in approach. We had different perspectives, but we had a good working relationship and I think could have converged on a position. But we never got the chance. A few days later, a story broke on the front page of *The Wall Street Journal* that Elizabeth was pushing for $25 billion in relief from the big servicers.

All hell broke loose. The Republicans jumped all over her, accusing her of overstepping her authority. They charged that it was inappropriate for her to be involved in the global settlement discussions because the CFPB was not yet a functioning agency. (Dodd-Frank had given it a start-up date of July 1, 2011.) I couldn't believe it. Tim had invited her to the meetings, and he had asked her to give him a proposal. But he didn't do anything to defend her once the barrage started. Then, with Tim's blessing, the OCC, DOJ, and state AGs agreed to limit the global settlement discussions to the enforcement agencies (DOJ, HUD, and the AGs) and exclude the regulatory agencies, which, of course, took the FDIC and the CFPB—led by us troublemaking women—out of it.

The state AGs, led by Iowa's Tom Miller, also did not object to letting the OCC oversee the "lookback" process to make sure borrowers who suffered financial harm from wrongful foreclosures were compensated. That completely undermined our efforts to set up some type of independent remediation commission. The OCC argued against our proposal, saying that we would compensate only those who came forward to complain. Walsh argued that the OCC would require the banks to look at all the foreclosure files and require compensation for all victims, not just those who came forward. But of course, the OCC, not an independent commission, would be defining the scope of the lookback and determining whether compensation was required.

I do not understand why the state AGs acquiesced in that, as it played right into the hands of the OCC and the big banks. The only thing I can think of is that Tom Miller had his hands full trying to build consensus within his own ranks on the wisdom of a global settlement. Unlike the FDIC, the OCC did not want to put pressure on its big banks to come to the table and agree to something reasonable. The strategy suited the OCC well. I think it felt that the global settlement was worth doing if the big banks would have to make only token concessions. Otherwise, their attitude was that the big banks, with their deep pockets, could litigate the issues forever. We, on the other hand, as a deposit insurer, didn't want to take any chances that the litigation could get out of hand. We wanted it settled and resolved, and we were willing to put pressure on the banks to get there. That was shortsighted thinking on the OCC's part, as uncertainties about litigation exposure continue to weigh heavily on bank stocks. Ironically, I think that some of the banks would probably have been willing to make greater concessions. Based on my conversations with GMAC, Wells, and BofA, I believe they were willing to do much more to facilitate principal writedowns, but the OCC never pushed in that direction. There are decades of bad blood between the OCC and the state AGs. I seriously doubt that the OCC wanted the state AGs to succeed.

Our efforts to secure meaningful changes through the examination process were similarly stymied by the OCC's leadership, who seemed more interested in protecting the banks than regulating them. Unbelievably, the OCC would not even agree to require specifically that the banks provide the name and contact information of the individual who would serve as the borrower's single point of contact (SPOC). We thought an SPOC was essential to improving staff resources and accountability at the major servicers. Regulators had been inundated with complaints from borrowers about servicers losing their paperwork and putting them on hold forever when they called trying to reach a live person. We had also all heard numerous horror stories about when borrowers had been in the process of getting a loan modification from one division at the servicer while another division was sending them foreclosure papers. By requiring the servicers to have a single individual with both the authority and responsibility to handle a borrower's case from beginning to end, we would force the servicers to hire more staff as well as improve the quality of service. A single employee would be accountable for the proper handling of each loan, as opposed to the disorganized, uncoordinated process that many of the servicers were using.

Everyone, including the OCC, gave lip service to supporting the SPOC, but when it came down to negotiating the language of the orders we would give the banks, the OCC refused to require that a single person be identified and named. It wanted to give the banks flexibility to have a team of people serve as the single point of contact, which, of course, defeated the whole purpose. In contrast, the Fed's orders did require that servicers designate an individual employee to work with a borrower.

The OCC also failed to put any hard metrics into its orders. Early in the process, we had suggested that it make the banks develop quantitative objectives so that we would have some way to measure improvement. For instance, based on our loss-share reviews, we knew that one of the servicers it regulated had only about forty-four staff handling nearly 60,000 active loan files, or about 1,200 files per employee. Again the OCC refused, preferring instead to put vague standards into its enforcement orders. To this day, the OCC has failed to present any hard data that the servicers have significantly improved their operations with more staff, faster loan mod decisions, and fewer instances of lost paperwork and other processing errors. Whatever progress has been made has been due to the initiative of HAMP officials to publicly grade servicers, not anything required by the OCC.

Another problem was that the OCC treated all of the servicers the same even though the reviews showed variations in the quality of servicing operations. To be sure, all of the servicers had weaknesses, but the difference between, say, Wells' servicing operation and that of Bank of America, was the difference between night and day, as documented by published reports. But again, as was the case with the bailouts, all the banks were lumped together.

Most problematic was the way the OCC proposed to handle the lookbacks—that is, the process the banks were supposed to use to retroactively review the individual files of people who had already lost their homes to make sure that servicing errors had not resulted in wrongful foreclosures.

The OCC had fought our claims commission proposal based on the argument that all borrowers should have their records reviewed, not just those who came forward with a claim.

However, when it came to setting up the parameters of the lookbacks, the OCC decided to let the banks use their well-paid consultants to do it and also told the banks that they needed only to sample files! As previously mentioned, we had found significant error rates in loan mod denials in reviewing loss-share servicing records, so we suggested that they needed to conduct a 100 percent review, at least for borrowers who had applied for a modification and been turned down. Based on my bad experience in using bank consultants for the review of Citi's management, I did not think consultants could be completely trusted to conduct an independent review of foreclosure files. They relied heavily on the banks for their consulting business; why would they conduct a thorough review that could end up costing the banks a lot of money to compensate past victims? To keep the process honest, I suggested that the OCC, Fed, and FDIC jointly review and validate the consultants' work. Finally, I suggested that an independent hotline be set up to receive consumer claims and offered the considerable resources of the FDIC to operate it. (The FDIC has a highly regarded consumer call-in center with an excellent response time. I would occasionally test it by making an online inquiry, using my married name and my home email address. Within twenty-four hours, I always had a response.)

But time was running out on my tenure at the FDIC, and Walsh knew he could wait me out. In April, the orders were issued. They were vague and general. I issued a separate statement explaining the FDIC's limited role in the process and saying that the orders were only a first step. In early June, I sent an email to Walsh and Tarullo pleading for a 100 percent review of denied loan mod applications, borrowers' claims, and all loans to military personnel, who have special protections against foreclosure while they are on active duty. "[S]ampling alone will not ensure that all harmed borrowers are identified," I argued. I also pleaded for an interagency review process to validate the consultants' work. My pleas mostly fell on deaf ears. At the end of June, the OCC issued additional guidance to banks on complying with the orders. The guidance offered little new in terms of the specific remedial steps that banks were supposed to take. For the lookback, the OCC required 100 percent review for service members and those who came forward with a claim but expressly permitted sampling for everyone else. And instead of interagency oversight of the consultants, the OCC alone would be responsible for ensuring the independence of its work. The guidance provided no real clarity as to what the consultants were looking for and what would constitute financial harm.

In December 2011, in the face of mounting congressional pressure and criticism, Julie Williams finally provided a list of twenty-two servicer errors that the OCC felt could result in financial harm to borrowers in testimony before the Senate Banking Committee. However, Ms. Williams's testimony also made clear that the consultants would decide the amount and type of compensation that banks would have to pay. She indicated that the OCC was "considering guidance that will clarify expectations as to the amount and type of compensation recommended for certain categories of harm. Any such baseline expectations would not, however, override the independent judgment of the independent consultants."

The banks have now hired consultants to conduct the lookbacks. They are relying primarily on a mass direct-mail campaign to identify harmed borrowers. The onus will be on borrowers to come forward to file claims with consultants, who are being paid by the banks and have long-standing consulting relationships with the industry. The whole effort is a ruse and a waste of time and money, in my view. My guess is that the consultants will make big profits while ultimately finding that very few borrowers, if any, were financially harmed. But I know that many of the borrowers could have made payments if they had been given the modifications for which they qualified. Will they be compensated? I would like to be proven wrong, but my guess is that the consultants are going to make a lot more money out of this than the borrowers are.

Bank consultants can play an important, valuable role in providing confidential technical advice to banks on regulatory compliance matters, similar to the way you might hire an accountant or tax lawyer to make sure you comply with the tax rules. But even the best of them will be hopelessly conflicted in trying to judge whether a harmed borrower should receive compensation from the same bank that pays their consulting bills. Even if they can rise above the very real conflicts the process presents, the perception of bias will remain. It has put both the banks and the consultants into a hopeless position.

And what happened to the global settlement talks from which we were excluded? In November 2011, four months after I left office, I received a call from Shaun Donovan, asking me if I would be interested in serving as the monitor for the global settlement—the person who would be responsible for making sure the banks complied with the settlement once it was reached. I wanted to help Shaun, but I had a number of preexisting contractual commitments, including one to write this book. Of all the senior officials in the Obama administration, next to the president, I think he cared the most about trying to resolve the foreclosure mess in a way that would help borrowers and be fair to all parties. But my sense is that he never got the support he needed from Tim and the OCC. If they had put pressure on the big banks to reach a settlement, the banks would have been more willing to agree to meaningful reforms and financial redress. But without a clear signal from their two chief protectors, Geithner and Walsh, they were reluctant to give much.

On February 9, 2012, the administration finally announced a $25 billion settlement. The banks didn't give much, but neither did the state AGs. Though the banks received relief from state AG suits related to mortgage-processing errors, they still face substantial litigation risk from borrowers and mortgage-backed investors, as well as state AG suits based on fraud and illegal discrimination. But the big banks had to pay only $5 billion in cash, some of which will support the operations of budget-constrained state AG offices. The other $20 billion will be devoted to principal write-downs and refinancings. The banks were likely to do that much principal reduction anyway, and it is a drop in the bucket given that home owners in the aggregate owe about $700 billion more than their homes are worth. Like most of this administration's initiatives, the settlement will help on the margin, but litigation and troubled mortgages will continue to drag down the economic recovery.

And as the banks escaped forceful government action to correct and remediate servicing errors, many were also allowed to pay increased dividends. The Fed did consult with us when reviewing the dividend increase applications. It agreed with us and did not approve BofA's application to increase dividends (even though BofA's CEO had inexplicably stated publicly that it would be approved) and kept Citi's dividend to a token penny. We acquiesced in its decision to approve the healthier banks' applications, though we objected to some of its decisions to allow weaker regional banks to increase shareholder payouts. As further losses from the troubled housing market and litigation still loom large on all the major banks' balance sheets, I wish that the Fed had held off on any dividend increases, but at least it worked with us and said no to BofA and Citi. In contrast, the OCC made some efforts to consult us but ignored our objections by letting Citibank pay a whopping $3 billion to its holding company. The Fed did not let the holding company pay the money to shareholders, but nonetheless, it is no longer available to protect Citigroup's bank (and the FDIC).

CHAPTER 22

The Return to Basel

Europe was to pay dearly for its ill-advised implementation of Basel II and failure to impose a leverage ratio. Its thinly capitalized banks had little capability to absorb losses when the 2008 crisis hit and government bailouts were required of a number of insolvent or near-insolvent major European financial institutions. What's more, European banks had invested heavily in higher yielding debt issued by weak sovereign nations such as Greece, Portugal, Spain, and Italy because Basel II treated those investments as having zero risk. This helped give rise to a new problem—the sovereign debt crisis—which continues to plague Europe and is now spilling over into the broader global economy.

European taxpayers were outraged, and the European central bank heads, as well as the banking regulators, were feeling even more heat than we were in the United States to crack down on large financial institutions. And as the political climate changed, so did the willingness of the Basel Committee to achieve more meaningful reform. Basel Committee Chairman Nout Welling and Stefan Walter, who led the Basel Committee's technical staff, seized the opportunity by pushing a new Basel III framework. Throughout 2009 and 2010, under their leadership, we worked diligently on coming up with new, stronger capital standards. The work was reinforced when, in September 2009, the finance ministers of all the G20 countries issued a directive to regulators and central bank heads to develop a comprehensive set of financial reforms, including stronger capital requirements, by the end of 2010.

Basel III had many components, but its most important work focused on raising both the quality and quantity of capital held by large, internationally active banks. To my great satisfaction, an international leverage ratio was on the table and garnering increasing support among committee members. In addition, there was strong consensus to raise the amount of high-quality capital banks had to hold. During the crisis, we discovered that the only type of capital that the market had confidence in was the traditional kind: that raised through issuance of common stock or built up through retained earnings, also known as tangible common equity (TCE). Market analysts essentially ignored trust-preferred securities and other types of hybrid debt instruments when determining whether a bank was solvent. But under Basel II, banks were required to keep that kind of TCE at only a paltry 2 percent of assets.

The main challenge of the Basel Committee leadership was to raise the amount of TCE held by banks. But what should be the new requirement? Two percent was laughably low. Nout and Stefan were also proposing to have an additional amount above the new minimum, called a "capital conservation buffer," that banks could draw from during periods of economic distress. The idea behind the buffer was to act like a rainy-day fund for banks during economic downturns. When the economy entered a down cycle, regulators would let banks dip into the extra capital to support their lending activities, just as families dip into their savings when they face a job loss or pay reduction. However, once the banks dipped into their buffers, they would have to restrict dividends and bonus payments to conserve capital. During the crisis, regulators were caught flat-footed as even the weakest banks kept paying dividends and big executive bonuses, when they should have been retaining earnings to conserve capital and support lending. With the new capital buffer, the Basel Committee leadership wanted to create automatic restraints on dividends and bonuses for any bank once its capital level fell below the buffer.

The buffer was a clever idea, the product of research conducted by the Dutch Central Bank and refined by Nout and the Basel Committee staff. There was general consensus around the framework but wide disagreement over what the new capital minimums and buffers should be. Even though the Treasury Department was not a member of the Basel Committee (it is made up of only bank regulators and central bank heads), in the spring of 2010, Tim began calling us all to meetings at the Treasury to formulate the U.S. position. Ben and Dan Tarullo, the Fed's point person on bank supervision, dutifully attended the meetings, as did I, Bill Dudley, John Dugan, and later John Walsh.

I could tell that Ben and Dan were uncomfortable with the meetings. The Fed, not the Treasury, headed the U.S. delegation to the Basel Committee and had the statutory authority to set bank holding company capital standards, in consultation with us and the OCC. Moreover, it wasn't clear whether Tim was trying to build consensus among the U.S. regulators or trying to stir the pot. At each meeting, he would try to elicit our views on what the new standards should be, but he was very cagey when it came to expressing his own views. In his public pronouncements, he had been talking a very good game, calling for significantly higher capital standards (without specifying a number) and even endorsing our proposal for an international leverage ratio.

Ideally, bank capital should be high enough to keep the banks solvent and lending even during a downturn. The Fed staff produced a good analysis showing that a bank's tangible-common-equity ratio needed to be in the 8 to 10 percent range to achieve that objective, based on historical loss rates from the 2008 and previous crises. The Basel Committee staff conducted a similar analysis showing the range to be 7 to 11 percent. Never bashful, we opened by suggesting that the new TCE requirement (including the buffer) be at least 10 percent. George French of our staff presented an analysis showing that the big banks, in aggregate, could achieve a 10 percent tangible-common-equity standard over a period of five years simply by retaining half their earnings, meaning that they would have to cut back on dividends. For the two weakest banks, Citi and BofA, the time horizon was longer, and they would have to retain most of their earnings. But even they were capable of achieving 10 percent with a long enough transition period.

As usual, we were out there with the highest number. The Fed came back suggesting that 8 percent would be sufficient but that in addition the Basel Committee should impose some type of surcharge on the very largest banks. After further discussions, we agreed to 8 percent as the baseline, with the understanding that the United States would be united in pushing for a surcharge on the largest institutions—so-called systemically important financial institutions, or SIFIs—to bring their requirement up to 10 percent, the FDIC's preferred number. As we were meeting with Treasury, we were having parallel discussions with Nout and Stefan, who were in a major battle with the industry. For reasons I never fully understood, the Basel Committee routinely met privately with international bankers to solicit their feedback on ideas for reform. That was frequently done through the auspices of the Institute of International Finance, headed by Charles Dallara. I did not object to getting technical input from the bankers—that was essential—but I wondered why the public comment process was not sufficient for that purpose.

In any event, Nout agreed to hold one of those industry meetings in Frankfurt on June 1, in conjunction with a Basel Committee staff meeting taking place at the same time. I sent my deputy, Jason Cave. He reported back that the industry was pretty much opposing everything we were trying to do. Nout had refused to give ground, saying only that there would be an ample transition period for the banks to raise capital. He had also strongly defended the leverage ratio and was pushing back hard on the idea that the stronger standards would hurt the economic recovery. The IIF had already circulated a draft report, which it made public the following week, shamelessly suggesting that constraining big banks' leverage would reduce global output by more than 3 percent. More responsible studies released later by the Basel Committee staff, as well as a number of academics, show that the costs to economic output from higher capital standards are negligible and more than outweighed by the benefits of a more stable financial system.

Nout and Stefan were also struggling with the French, Germans, and Japanese. Throughout all of the postcrisis Basel discussions, it seemed that the lineup was the same. The United States, the United Kingdom, Canada, Switzerland, the Netherlands, Sweden, and most other Basel Committee members advocated, or at least were willing to support, higher standards; Germany, France, and Japan would resist.

Why did the votes break along these lines? Different people have different theories. Capital regulation has always been a more central part of bank supervision in the United States (thanks to the FDIC), Canada, and the United Kingdom than in Europe. The French, German, and Japanese governments have closer ties to their banks than even we do (if you can believe that) and are not so averse to backing them if they get into trouble. Their regulators are also closer to their politicians, in contrast to the United States, Canada, and other countries, where the laws try to insulate regulators from political influence. In addition, smaller European countries, such as Switzerland and the Netherlands, do not have large enough economies or budgets to bail out all of their megabanks, even if they wanted to. In Switzerland, for instance, total Swiss bank assets are six times as large as that country's GDP. So too-big-to-fail policies actually give a competitive advantage to banks domiciled in the larger economies, whose governments can credibly back them, if necessary. (The calculus has changed somewhat with the European sovereign debt crisis, as that crisis has called into question even France's ability to bail out its banks, given their high degrees of leverage and large holdings of distressed sovereign debt.)

Nout had hoped to have all the issues resolved at the Basel Committee's July meeting. The process he followed was to have the staff representatives of Basel Committee members meet first and hash out the technical recommendations. Those would then be presented to the agency heads, or principals, who met under the acronym GHOS, which stood for Governors [of central banks] and Heads of Supervision. Nout chaired the Basel Committee discussion, and Jean-Claude Trichet, the head of the European Central Bank (ECB), chaired the GHOS, with Nout as his cochair. After GHOS members approved the recommendations, they went to the G20 finance ministers for ratification. The G20 process was somewhat pro forma. The finance ministers deferred to the GHOS once that body achieved consensus. Nout had encouraged G20 ratification as a way to "lock in" the work of the Basel Committee and GHOS. The finance ministers had requested that the Basel Committee complete its work on capital in time for their next meeting, to take place in South Korea in November. That was his deadline for getting all of the reforms wrapped up.

The Basel Committee and GHOS meetings were held in a modern-looking, circular structure whose architecture was a metaphor for the roundabout way in which decisions were made. Throughout five years of attending Basel Committee and GHOS meetings, I found many of them to be as productive as watching fresh paint dry on a wall. Being voluntary organizations, the Basel Committee and GHOS chose to decide by consensus, not majority vote. That meant that meetings were typically dominated by those who opposed reforms. Reform opponents would typically filibuster—that is, talk endlessly to wear other members down—and the best at this, by far, were the Germans, led by Franz-Christoph Zeitler, a senior official at Germany's central bank, the Bundesbank, and Jochen Sanio, Germany's top banking regulator. Franz and Jochen could drone on for hours, and if we tried to accommodate them with some type of compromise, they would raise the ante and drone on some more. Sanio was more reasonable than Zeitler, but they were both pretty difficult. Their tactics were reminiscent of those used by segregationists on the Senate floor to try to block civil rights legislation. The Senate had responded by instituting a cloture rule, which meant that with 60 votes, the Senate could end debate and bring a bill to a vote. Unfortunately, the Basel Committee and GHOS had no cloture rule.

My deputy, Jason Cave, was our staff representative to the Basel Committee. He worked with Pat Parkinson, who represented the Fed, and Kevin Bailey from the OCC. The Fed representative was supposed to be the head of the U.S. delegation, but Pat hardly ever spoke up. He talked a good game when he met with us, but when it came to engaging the French and Germans during the Basel Committee discussions, he was reticent. Pat's a smart guy and articulate when he needs to be, so it made me wonder how committed he was to capital reform. That was frustrating to Jason, as protocol dictated that the Fed spoke for the U.S. delegation. Jason still jumped into the discussions when he felt he needed to, but Pat's silence weakened the force of his arguments.

I had a similar problem at the GHOS meetings. Ben hardly ever said anything. I think one issue was that of stature. As the head of the world's largest central bank, he didn't want to get down into the fray, which I understood. But he also had Bill Dudley and Dan Tarullo with him, who spoke with frustrating rarity. I didn't know if they were just intimidated by mixing it up with the French and Germans or whether I was being gamed and they didn't really want reform. We would meet among ourselves, ostensibly to work out a unified U.S. position, and the Fed would make concessions to us for higher standards to reach agreement. But it rarely wanted to commit the position to writing in a letter circulated to other Basel Committee members, as was a common practice with other countries. And when we got into the Basel Committee and GHOS meetings, they wouldn't vigorously defend the positions we had so painstakingly negotiated.

Fortunately, others were speaking up, even when the Fed remained silent.

I certainly wasn't afraid to vocalize my views. By 2010, though I can't say I was popular with the other GHOS members, they respected what we had accomplished at the FDIC during the crisis and feared the influence I had with the media. Moreover, Nout and Stefan welcomed my advocacy. As the chairman and staff director, they were supposed to play the role of moderator and consensus builder. If the capital hawks on the GHOS didn't speak up to counter the French and Germans, it made their job of getting agreement on strong reforms all the more difficult.

More important, other influential GHOS members were now weighing in, and by far the most forceful and eloquent was Mervyn King, the head of the Bank of England. Mervyn was a cherub-faced, frumpily dressed economist who had spent most of his career at the Bank of England. He prided himself on being a public servant and had no patience with rich, ostentatious bankers. He was as unmaterialistic as one could get. He was notorious for wearing clothes until they were threadbare. I remember once running into him at the Blue Mosque in Istanbul while we were there attending a G30 meeting. Visitors to the mosque were required to take their shoes off before entering, and I really tried hard not to stare at a huge hole in Mervyn's left sock, out of which his big toe protruded prominently. Mervyn had a razor-sharp intellect and wit to match. No one had a better command of the English language or ability to shape arguments using that language to punch opponents squarely between the eyes. Adair Turner, Mervyn's colleague who headed financial services regulation at the Bank of England, was also quite articulate. Together they were quite a "dynamic duo" in advocating for higher capital requirements.

Another strong champion of tougher capital standards on the GHOS was Philipp Hildebrand, a career banker who headed the Swiss National Bank. Hildebrand—impeccably dressed and movie-star handsome—was a contrasting bookend to King. He was just as forceful and effective in advocating for stronger capital requirements, but unlike Mervyn's, his position came as much from necessity as principle. If one of the giant Swiss banks went down, it would likely take the entire Swiss government with it. Phil knew that his Swiss banks needed more capital and was already raising their requirements unilaterally. But that could put Swiss banks at a disadvantage to their French and German competitors. It was essential to the interests of his banks and his government that there be an international agreement forcing all banks to raise more capital. Hildebrand's colleague Daniel Zuberbühler, Switzerland's top bank regulator, was also quite strong on capital and an authoritative voice during the meetings on the need for tougher standards.

To increase the ranks of pro-reform advocates, Nout did something very clever: just prior to the July 2010 meeting, he opened up the Basel Committee/GHOS membership to all G20 countries, which raised our membership to twenty-seven nations. That meant that the leaders of major developing countries, including China and India, were now at the table. Those officials, with their nascent banking systems, tended to be cautious and conservative when it came to capital. Their banks typically held significantly higher levels of capital than the overleveraged European banks, and they tended to use simpler, more concrete measures of capital adequacy than the easy-to-game Basel II standards. Virtually all of the new members supported Nout's and Stefan's reform agenda. That meant that the French, Germans, and Japanese would be in a much smaller minority if they continued their resistance to reform.

The GHOS meetings were conducted in a cavernous, windowless fluorescent-lit room, with each nation's representatives sitting around a huge oval-shaped conference table. The room was completely soundproof, as insulated from the outside world as the decisions the GHOS made. Perhaps to put me in my place, the seating order for the U.S. delegation always had me at the end, next to the representative from the OCC. I really didn't mind, because being at the end of the U.S. lineup seated me next to the U.K.

delegation, led by Mervyn, who was just as strong, if not stronger, on capital than I was. We would sometimes whisper and pass notes and almost always reinforce each other's policy positions. Between the U.K. and Swiss delegations, most of the arguments that needed to be said were said. I just wish more of them had come from the U.S. delegation.

Fortunately, the longer Dan Tarullo served on the GHOS, the more confident he became in speaking up. As I came to know and work with Dan, I became convinced that he really did want meaningful reform of capital regulation, even if he had to take on the big banks to do it. He was known for having a bit of an ego, and I think he didn't like hearing me take an active role in some of the discussions. In truth, I wanted him and Ben to speak up, as the arguments would mean more coming from the Fed than the FDIC. I started playing a little game to give Dan an extra prod. In front of each of our seats was a small button to press to turn on our microphone when we wanted to speak. It illuminated a red light that signaled we wanted to talk. Whenever I heard the French or Germans making an outrageous argument, I would make a noticeable gesture of moving my hand slowly toward my button. Dan would catch me out of the corner of his eye and almost always jump in first.

During the July 2010 meetings of the Basel Committee and GHOS, after a year and a half of work, we made significant decisions on several important issues. They included issues related to how much capital banks have to hold against the risk that their trading partners might default on their obligations and how much cash and other highly liquid assets they must hold to withstand creditor runs. Most important from the FDIC's perspective, we reached agreement to eliminate the use of hybrid debt as capital. Many countries allowed debtlike instruments to count as capital for banking organizations, even though they have no loss-absorbing capacity. The Collins Amendment had already taken care of most of this problem in the United States, but it was important to achieve agreement among all international regulators so that other countries followed suit. Indeed, I think the fact that the U.S. Congress had already ended the use of hybrid debt as capital put pressure on the GHOS to do the same. It showed that legislative bodies were ready to enact on needed reforms if the regulators and central bankers didn't act on their own.

At last we reached agreement on an international leverage ratio. It was an important victory, even if the standard was far lower than I wanted it to be.

The meeting that day was a far cry from the bruising I had taken in Mérida four years earlier. This time I had allies, including Mervyn and Phil, as well as irrefutable research on the value of a leverage ratio from the Basel Committee staff. The research showed that banks that reported strong risk-based ratios but weak leverage ratios were the most likely to get into trouble during a crisis. On the other hand, banks that reported strong leverage ratios were the least likely to get into trouble. It put the lie to the notion that regulators could rely solely on risk-based capital standards to ensure capital adequacy. Risk-based ratios were poor predictors of how healthy a bank was.

European banks were clearly gaming the Basel II framework to lower the risk weighting of their assets to ridiculous levels. Subsequent research by private financial analysts has borne this out. One research report showed that the majority of European banks were saying that their assets were getting safer even during the global recession, when delinquencies and defaults on loans and other assets were spiking up! As of the end of 2010, European banks risk weighted their assets at about half the level of U.S. banks.

Though the French and Germans eventually acquiesced in a leverage ratio, they successfully argued for a low number. We ended up with a paltry 3 percent, though we also agreed on a methodology to include some off-balance-sheet risks. Thus, even though the 3 percent is short of the 5 percent U.S. standard that we pushed for, it includes certain risks associated with derivatives and other off-balance-sheet items that are not captured by the U.S. rule. As I will discuss later, the leverage ratio, both in the U.S. and internationally, needs to be higher. But the 3 percent was an important start, and even at that level, the Basel Committee staff estimated that more than 40 percent of the world's largest banks (most of them in Europe) would have to raise capital to meet it.

The irony is that if the Europeans had agreed to a leverage ratio in 2006, when I first proposed it, they would not have run into many of the problems they now face with their sovereign debt crisis. The Basel II framework allowed banks to hold sovereign debt at a zero risk weight. That meant that the banks could load up on high-yielding distressed sovereign debt from Greece, Portugal, Spain, and Italy without holding any capital against those investments. So what did the European banks do? They amassed some $3 trillion worth of sovereign debt and are now stuck with it. The European banking systems' massive holdings have impeded efforts to restructure the debt to provide some fiscal relief to distressed countries. The banks, with their low levels of capitalization, don't have sufficient capital to absorb losses from a meaningful restructuring of the debt.

Though important agreements were finalized at the July meeting, the hotly contested question of the new risk-based capital ratio was punted until the next round of meetings in September. Nout and Stefan continued to wrestle with resistance from the French, Germans, and Japanese, and the industry kept up its relentless media campaign, with the self-serving argument that higher capital standards would hurt the economic recovery. In August, I published an op-ed in the *Financial Times* putting the lie to those arguments. "If we fail to follow through in strengthening bank capital," I argued, "we risk wasting the capital we already have and exposing the global economy to the onerous and indefensible costs of another financial crisis." We kept communicating with them and the Fed over the course of the next three months. At last they told us that they thought we could get agreement on a 7 percent standard as the baseline, with an additional surcharge on SIFIs.

The 7 percent was, again, disappointing but still a huge improvement over the laughable 2 percent standard already in place. Moreover, according to Nout and Stefan, we would either agree to the 7 percent or have no agreement, in which case the issue would be bucked to the G20 finance ministers. That was a group of politically appointed officials, not independent regulators and central bankers, and we feared that if the G20 finance ministers decided the ratio, it would be even lower than the 7 percent. Or worse, the finance ministers would not decide, leaving us with the status quo.

We and the Fed agreed that we would enter the September meeting strongly advocating for the 8 percent, but we were also prepared to fall back to 7 percent if that would get everyone on board, including the Germans, who had partially dissented from the decisions we had made in July. I told the Fed I could live with the 7 percent *only* if there were a firm, public, written commitment from the GHOS that we would also develop and impose a higher surcharge on the SIFIs. Ben and Dan were in complete agreement on that point. We also agreed to push for a shorter transition period. Again to appease the French, Germans, and Japanese, Nout was suggesting that banks would not have to comply with the new standard until 2020!

Our strategy set, we prepared to leave for Basel.

However, on Friday, September 10, two days before the GHOS meeting, I got a call from Tim strongly urging me to insist on an 8 percent requirement, even if it meant not achieving agreement at the GHOS meeting. He suggested that the impact of the higher 8 percent standard could be blunted by easing restrictions on dividends and bonuses once the buffer was breached. This sounded to me like having a meaningless standard; banks would have no incentive to maintain the buffer if there were no negative consequences in breaching it. I thanked him for the call but told him I had already committed to the Fed to support the 7 percent with the understanding that there would be a SIFI surcharge. I then called Ben and recounted the conversation. (He had received a similar communication from Tim.)

I was perplexed and not sure what Tim's true agenda was. In late July, he had seemed to be moving toward weaker standards. An FDIC staff member had attended one of his meetings for me on July 23. (I had been unable to attend the meeting because of preexisting commitments in New York.) Her report of the meeting had been alarming. She said that Geithner had been challenging the agencies on the 8 percent baseline standard, suggesting that it be lowered to 6 percent. According to her memo, Geithner received some support from John Dugan, who noted that "the impact is huge for some firms" (which I took to mean Citi and BofA), but the Fed had held firm at 8 percent.

Then, on August 6, I met with Tim privately in his office during one of our regular monthly meetings. It was a miserable meeting, probably the low point in our strained working relationship. He was agitated over Senator Dodd pushing me to head the new consumer agency. Without my knowledge or consent, Dodd had gone public, saying I was his preferred candidate and that he could get me confirmed in "two days." Tim ranted that "no one" could get confirmed; then he started pushing me on who should replace me at the FDIC, even though the end of my tenure was still a year away. I was so shaken by the meeting that I memorialized it in a memo to the file immediately afterward, writing that he had "lobbied me intensely on lower numbers for the Basel III calibration, knowing full well that our healthy banks will be just fine with a high numbers, but of course Citi and BofA will get killed. Why do we keep making banking policy to accommodate weak institutions? Keep hoping our relationship will improve, but this was a new low."

By pushing an 8 percent standard with a meaningless buffer, I don't think Tim was trying to strengthen the United States' position. I think his real agenda was to blow up the GHOS meeting, with the U.S. delegation being the spoiler. In that event, the question would be bucked up to the G20 finance ministers, who were scheduled to meet in Seoul in November. At that meeting, Tim, not the Fed or the FDIC, would be leading the United States.

The Fed stuck with the game plan. We went to the September 12 meeting in Basel, still knowing there would be a fight. Predictably, France was pushing for a 6 percent standard but Germany was moving our way, due to the good influence of Axel Weber, who headed the Bundesbank. On

September 8, Weber publicly refuted the industry's charges that the new capital standards would slow economic growth, saying that the new rules would "reduce the probability of individual banks failing and will represent a first line of defense against systemic crises." Weber was also a member of the ECB board and was in a running competition with Mario Draghi, the governor of the Bank of Italy, Italy's central bank, to replace Jean-Claude Trichet when Trichet's term expired in 2011. There was some speculation that Weber felt that supporting stronger capital requirements would enhance his prospects of replacing Trichet. Whatever his motivations (and I tend to think they were sincere) at the GHOS meeting, Weber played a positive role in reaching agreement, in stark contrast to his colleagues, the droners Zeitler and Sanio. The French proposal went nowhere. It was a long, intense meeting, but Jean-Claude held everyone's feet to the fire. As Nout and Stefan had predicted, we achieved agreement on 7 percent as the baseline and were able to shorten the phase-in to the end of 2018.

But the language in the Basel Committee/GHOS press release was squishy on the question of a surcharge to apply to the megabanks, the SIFIs. It simply stated, "Systemically important banks should have loss absorbing capacity beyond the standards announced today." I requested, and the Fed agreed, that the U.S. regulators would issue a separate press release strongly committing to even higher capital standards for the largest institutions. We all trooped upstairs to a suite of offices the BIS reserved for the Fed's use. Jason sat at a computer and typed while Tarullo, Dudley, Walsh, and I dictated the statement. For once, Tarullo, Dudley, and I were all on the same page with a clear statement on higher capital requirements for SIFIs, while Walsh kept trying to soften it.

In a bad development for the FDIC, the GHOS also decided to fold the issue of the SIFI surcharge into the work of a sister group called the Financial Stability Board (FSB). The FSB was working on a variety of issues associated with too big to fail. I viewed the FSB as an unwieldy bureaucracy, made up not only of bank regulators but also of securities, insurance, and futures regulators and finance minister representatives. It met interminably and achieved consensus only after endless meetings, and then the decisions were generally watered down to accommodate the group's diverse membership. Involving the FSB in the SIFI surcharge discussions was an unexpected setback for the FDIC. The Fed and Treasury were members of the FSB; we were not.

The FSB was headed by Mario Draghi, a smooth, articulate former managing director at Goldman Sachs. I had been trying to build a working relationship with him for several months. With the Fed's and Treasury's blessing, the FSB had taken over the work on developing international resolution mechanisms. The FDIC cochaired a Basel working group on cross-border resolutions along with the Swiss. However, since we are not members of the FSB, Draghi put the United Kingdom in charge of the FSB's work on resolutions. Our Basel group supported the FSB's work, but we were no longer in the driver's seat on resolution authority. That was unfortunate, because the FDIC clearly had the most experience in resolving failing banks. Indeed, in the wake of the crisis, most other countries were in the process of setting up resolution regimes similar to ours, and they were coming to us for technical help and training. In a twist of irony, a few years prior, Mervyn had asked me to detail FDIC staff to the Bank of England to help it set up its own resolution authority. Now it was running the process to develop standards for international resolutions, with us playing a secondary role.

Ever the gentleman, Mario reached out to me for counsel on addressing resolution issues and asked me to join an FSB steering committee meeting discussion of resolution issues on September 13. The timing was good because it would also give me an opportunity to weigh in on the SIFI surcharge. Mario seated me in between Dan Tarullo and Adair Turner. The meeting started with other agenda items, and I felt like a schoolkid, waiting to be called on for my turn to talk. When the agenda turned to resolution authority, I gave my presentation but then also took the opportunity to express my view (out of turn) that the SIFI surcharge should be high and made up of tangible common equity. I was delighted to hear Dan Tarullo say the same thing emphatically and unequivocally (unusual for the Fed).

The FSB discussions dragged on and on. A few months into 2011, I was watching the clock run out on my tenure as chairman. At the end of June, I would be stepping down. I was afraid that the SIFI surcharge would not be finalized before my departure. I called Stefan Walter, complaining that the FSB process was "a big mush" in contrast to the decisive actions taken by the Basel Committee and GHOS in 2010. Couldn't the Basel Committee recapture the process and drive the decision making? I openly confessed to him that once I was gone, I did not know how resolute the U.S. delegation would be on a high surcharge.

I had growing confidence in Dan Tarullo as a capital hawk, but I wasn't sure about Bill Dudley and some of the Fed staff, and I suspected that Tim was working behind the scenes to water down the surcharge. Those suspicions were confirmed when John Walsh, who had been keeping a very low profile, suddenly announced his view that the SIFI surcharge should be 1 percent maximum. That was a far cry from the 3 percent surcharge needed to reach the 10 percent TCE ratio we wanted to apply to the megabanks, as had been discussed in countless meetings at the Treasury.

Walsh refused to sign a letter drafted by the Fed endorsing the 3 percent that we had all previously agreed to. Tarullo and I had to send the letter without his signature. Dan asked him if at least he would refrain from sending a letter to the Basel Committee endorsing 1 percent as a maximum. He thumbed his nose at Dan and did just that. The Fed went ballistic, as did we. He was purposefully trying to undermine our negotiating position.

I suspected that Tim was behind it. It didn't make sense that Walsh would go so far out on a limb without some encouragement from Tim, his patron. My suspicions were heightened when a career Treasury staffer let it slip to a member of our FDIC Basel team that the Treasury Department's position on the FSB steering committee was to support a maximum surcharge of 1.5 percent. I forwarded the information to Dan Tarullo, who confirmed that that was the position the Treasury had been taking. I went ballistic. "Why weren't we in the loop?" I angrily asked. "There should have been a principals-level discussion. We insure these banks. I'm sick and tired of being kept out of key decisions after everything that we have been through."

Stefan and Nout were successful in wresting the SIFI surcharge issue away from the FSB and back to the domain of the Basel Committee/GHOS. I waited anxiously for word from them as to whether the decision would be made before I left the FDIC. A meeting was tentatively targeted for the end of June. My term was up on June 26, but I decided to delay leaving by a week to make sure I was still around for the final decision.

In the meantime Walsh went public with his outlier position on the SIFI surcharge. Walsh deservedly took a lot of heat in the media and in Congress for his very blatant attempt to protect the megabanks from higher capital requirements. Several influential Democratic senators called for his ouster, including Jack Reed of Rhode Island, Carl Levin of Michigan, Jeff Merkley of Oregon, and Sherrod Brown of Ohio. Walsh ignored them.

The industry was going on the offensive. Shortly after the Basel Committee's September 2010 announcement of the new 7 percent tangible common-equity baseline standard, Vikram Pandit—whose thinly capitalized Citigroup had received three government bailouts—had the chutzpah to complain to the press that the new rules would hurt lending. Other bankers, including JPMorgan Chase's Jamie Dimon, supported the 7 percent standard but balked at the SIFI surcharge. During a June 2011 Fed press conference, Dimon challenged Ben Bernanke on whether the regulators had conducted any kind of analysis of the impact of higher capital and other new regulations on economic recovery. Taken by surprise, Ben hesitated, but several days later, during congressional testimony, he delivered a ringing endorsement of higher capital requirements for megabanks. During an interview at the Council on Foreign Relations, *The New York Times'* Andrew Ross Sorkin asked me to respond to Dimon's question. With regard to higher capital requirements, I said, "full speed ahead." I also scoffed at the big banks' oft-repeated arguments that higher capital would hurt lending, observing that "Banks are not doing a lot of lending now and the ones who are doing a better job of lending are the smaller institutions that have the higher capital." Similarly, during numerous congressional appearances over my last several months in office, I strongly endorsed higher capital requirements for the nation's largest banks.

The GHOS meeting on the SIFI surcharge was finally scheduled for Saturday, June 25, a week before my scheduled resignation. I had committed to give a major farewell speech at the National Press Club on Friday, June 24, so I was forced to take an overnight flight out of Washington's Dulles International Airport, arriving in Zurich at 8 A.M. the day of the meeting. The BIS arranged for car service (a courtesy extended to all GHOS members) for the hour-long drive to Basel. I arrived at my hotel shortly after nine, took a quick shower, and barely made it in time for the 10 A.M. start of the meeting.

I took my usual seat between the OCC, now filled by John Walsh, and Mervyn King. The discussions had already begun, and Zeitler and Sanio were droning on. Axel Weber had unexpectedly resigned as the head of the Bundesbank in April to join the board of the Swiss banking giant UBS, taking himself out of contention to replace Trichet. In his absence, the German position was once again being led by those two, who were determined to lower the SIFI surcharge.

But Germany, at that point, was getting little support from the Japanese, and even the French seemed willing to compromise. I was horrified to hear Sanio openly embrace the OCC position. "My heart is with the OCC," I remember him saying. Trichet and Nout had corralled just about everyone else to support a top SIFI surcharge of 2.5 percent for the biggest banks, with a punitive 3.5 percent applying if they had any ideas about getting bigger. But Germany kept standing in the way, and Sanio was openly using the OCC for cover.

I whispered to Walsh that the Germans were using him to block any agreement. At that point it was him and the Germans against twenty-six other countries. I asked him if he would at least tell the group he could live with the 2.5 percent as a compromise. That would take the wind out of the Germans' sails. Otherwise, they were going to drag it out forever. Walsh looked thoughtful and nodded. He signaled that he wanted to speak and pressed his little mike button when Jean-Claude told him it was his turn to talk. Looking across the huge table at Sanio, Walsh smiled, got a laugh when he analogized the situation to Custer's last stand, and said basically that it was time to surrender. The OCC could live with the 2.5 percent, and he didn't want to get in the way of an agreement. Walsh never should have gone there with a paltry 1 percent, but at least he did the right thing in the end.

The Germans finally relented, and we all agreed on the 2.5 percent for the largest systemic banks. Added to the 7 percent baseline, we were at 9.5 percent, close to the 10 percent we had originally sought—good enough to declare victory. No one but Nout acknowledged my departure from public service, and that hurt. Nout again commended me for my work on the leverage ratio. His term as Basel Committee chairman was also coming to a close.

Nout's acknowledgment was really all the thanks that I needed. The Basel Committee had already agreed on a leverage ratio, and that 9.5 percent capital requirement was a good going-away present. We had won.

CHAPTER 23

Too Small to Save

My recitation of the financial crisis and its aftermath has focused primarily on the excess risk taking and abuses that led to the crisis, the ensuing bailouts, and the struggle for regulatory reforms that continues to this day. Throughout this period, the FDIC played a critical role in stabilizing the system and influencing the policy debates surrounding the housing market and financial reform that followed. But while the FDIC played a leadership role in these high-profile actions, there was also our day-to-day work of handling small-bank failures.

During my tenure we closed 365 smaller banks representing more than $650 billion in assets. Many of these banks were poorly managed and took excessive risks. Others were caught by the Great Recession, particularly those which served hard-hit, lower-income areas. Whatever the causes of their failures, they were subjected to the discipline of the market. Their shareholders were wiped out, their boards and senior management fired, but their FDIC-insured depositors were always fully and seamlessly protected.

Sometimes I think we made it look too easy. Indeed, the overwhelming majority of these closings went so smoothly that I'm having a hard time thinking of a way to describe our process to you that won't bore you to tears. It wasn't glamorous work, it was just hard work, meticulous and painstaking in its execution.

In the early chapters of this book, I described to you the serious morale problems that plagued the FDIC when I arrived in 2006. I've always found that the best way to improve morale is to get employees focused on and energized about their core mission. So one of the management reforms I implemented early on was to streamline and focus our annual corporate performance objectives, placing a heavy emphasis on the job we had to do to maintain system stability: we had not only to protect depositors but also to make sure they would have seamless access to their money.

A deposit insurance system is not really effective if the insurer cannot guarantee uninterrupted access to insured funds. How would you like to be denied access to your checking and savings accounts for several weeks or months? When bank depositors ran the United Kingdom's Northern Rock, it was not because they lacked confidence that the government would pay them; it was because they knew they might have to wait up to six months to get paid. No matter what else we did, we had to convince people that they would have uninterrupted access to their insured money. If they didn't have that confidence, they would pull their money out of the banks just like those Northern Rock depositors, and the consequences would be disastrous.

To reinforce the point, I instituted something called "stretch" objectives that gave all employees an extra 1 percent in their bonus pools if certain metrics were met. At the top of that list was making sure all insured depositors of failed banks had access to their money within one business day. We never missed that target.

Our corporate objectives also put a heavy emphasis on executing resolution strategies that maximized our recoveries while moving banking assets back into the private sector as quickly as possible. Those two goals were interrelated. Government operation of banks generally leads to a deterioration of franchise value. The longer the government remains in charge, the less the value of the franchise once it is finally sold. That is not to disparage those who run banks for the government; they can be very talented managers. But bank customers generally don't want to do business with failed banks under government control, given the uncertainty about who will own them next.

Early in the crisis, there were two schools of thought at the FDIC about how to handle failed banks. One school wanted to follow the model used by the FDIC during the savings and loan crisis, which had involved the FDIC taking over and running the thrifts for a time. The advantage of that approach was that it avoided the delicate task of trying to sell a bank before it was under government control. With the FDIC in charge, we had been free to openly market banks and auction them to the highest bidder.

The disadvantage of that approach was the immediate hit to franchise value, as large depositors and valuable business customers would leave the bank during its government stewardship. That is exactly the phenomenon we witnessed with the IndyMac failure (though IndyMac would have cost us dearly no matter what, given its large amount of toxic real estate loans and weak deposit numbers).

The other alternative—the strategy we ended up using—was to auction and sell the bank before it actually closed. The advantages of that approach were that it would achieve a better price for the bank and immediately return banking assets to the private sector. In addition, our administrative costs would be much lower because we wouldn't need the staff and contractor support required to manage hundreds of banks for several weeks, if not months, while we looked for buyers.

The problem, of course, was how to run an auction for the bank before it closed without signaling to the market that it was failing and precipitating an exodus of depositors and good-bank customers—exactly the kind of problem we were trying to avoid. In addition, potential purchasers of a failed bank would frequently want to have at least a few weeks to conduct a close inspection of the failing banks' loan portfolio before deciding how much they wanted to bid. Without sufficient time to conduct that type of due diligence, it was likely that interested buyers would come in with very low bids, given their uncertainty about the quality of the failed banks' loans.

That was a problem, but particularly after the IndyMac failure and our protracted struggle to find buyers for the bank, I did not want to be in the business of running troubled banks. Fortunately, Jim Wigand, our resolutions whiz kid, came up with a solution.

Usually, regulators can forecast months in advance when a bank is likely to fail. As previously discussed, bank failures are governed by something called "prompt corrective action." That means that once a bank's capital level falls below 2 percent, it has to be closed within ninety days unless it has some real prospect of raising capital. Based on the loss rates of a troubled bank's portfolio, examiners will generally have a good idea of when the bank's capital will dip below the 2 percent, triggering the ninety-day death watch.

So as a troubled bank's condition deteriorated, we would work closely with the other bank regulators to have the management actively hire a financial adviser and seek out investors, including other banks, to either buy the bank outright or invest additional capital in it. Because the bank management was soliciting the bidders, we avoided the signaling effect that would come from our involvement (though with some of the more difficult failures, we would have to get discreetly involved). Frequently, those efforts paid off and the bank was sold or recapitalized without failing. However, if the bank management was unsuccessful, its efforts to find new investors generally gave us a group of ready bidders who had already looked at the franchise and examined its loans. We would run our confidential auction a few days before the bank was closed and announce the acquirer on the day of the failure.

That seamless transfer of bank deposits and assets was no more disruptive than any other type of bank acquisition. Closings would typically occur on Friday, and on Saturday morning, the failed banks' customers could go to the same banking facilities and transact business as if nothing had happened. Indeed, from their standpoint, nothing had happened except a name change.

The other problem we had, particularly during the depths of the recession, was steeply discounted bids based on uncertainties about how bad the economy would be and for how long. Loan default rates are heavily influenced by economic conditions. Economic uncertainty continues to this day, but it was particularly acute in 2008 and 2009. Without knowing with any degree of confidence how high losses on a failed bank's loans could go, interested acquirers would give us very low bids. Again, through the good work of Jim Wigand and his marketing experts, we pulled a page out of the playbook Bill Seidman had used to move billions of dollars' worth of troubled real estate loans in the last phases of the S&L debacle cleanup. To get its price up, we offered to share some of the risk of loss on the failed bank's loans with the acquiring institution.

Those loss-share agreements were subject to a lot of public misunderstanding, but without them, our losses would have been $40 billion, or 50 percent, higher. We simply couldn't get decent bids on real estate loans— mortgages and commercial real estate. Because the outlook for these loans was so uncertain, buyers would assume a worst-case scenario and price the loans accordingly.

But by agreeing to share the losses with the acquirer, we were able to attract many more bidders and substantially increase the amount they were willing to pay for the failed banks. Most important, by reducing the acquirers' risk, we attracted other insured banks to bid on failed institutions. Healthy, well-run banks—the kind we wanted bidding—are generally a risk-averse bunch. They would not have otherwise wanted to assume future losses on loans originated by a failed bank, which, by definition, had been poorly managed. With loss share, they were willing to jump in.

Why did we want other insured banks bidding on those failed institutions? There again, we could maximize our recoveries. By selling the loans to another bank, the failed bank's deposits could finance the sale and provide funding to borrowers. Nonbank buyers would have to raise the cash to buy and fund the loans in the tough credit market. Selling one insured bank to another also preserved the continuity of banking services in the communities served by the failed bank. That is because other insured banks could acquire the whole bank, both deposits and loans.

A bank's most valuable customers are those who have multiple relationships with it, including both deposits and loans. Paying off the deposits and then separately selling off the loans to nonbank bidders would have destroyed those valuable relationships and made the franchise worth less. In addition, conveying the deposits together with the loans minimized the FDIC's cash needs. If we separated them, we would have to write a big check when the bank failed to pay off the depositors and then wait for the subsequent loan sale to close before receiving any cash from purchasers. Selling both the deposits and the loans together minimized the amount of cash both the FDIC and the acquirer had to put into the transaction.

Of course, by selling the whole bank, the acquirer would have to honor all of the insured deposit obligations. That wouldn't be a problem if the value of the loans exceeded the acquiring bank's obligations on the deposits; that is, in accounting parlance, if the assets exceeded the liabilities. But what if the loss rates on the loans were higher than the acquirer had anticipated? The loans would become much less valuable, but the acquirer would still be committed to honoring all of the insured deposits. That was the fear that dampened bid prices, and it was why we found it advantageous to provide loss sharing.

Even with loss sharing, at times the value of the failed bank's loans was so low that we would have to put cash into the deal to make sure all of the insured deposits were fully covered. In those instances, the press would make hay out of the fact that we were "giving" money to failed bank acquirers. They would consistently fail to point out that we were contributing the cash to make up for the shortfall between our obligations to insured depositors and the value of the failed banks' loans.

What if we hadn't been able to convince healthy, insured banks to buy failed banks from us? Who else would buy failed bank assets? Primarily speculative investment funds—hedge funds and private equity. Some of those funds specialize in distressed assets. They are called, somewhat unkindly, "bottom feeders," but their willingness to take risks in buying toxic assets plays an important role in economic recovery. Some of the funds saw the attractiveness in buying the whole bank from us, given the increased value in maintaining customer relationships as well as the reduced need for cash up front to buy the bank. So they started applying for bank charters and seeking approval to bid on failed banks.

Because they generally had ample money to capitalize a new bank charter and could provide competent management, the chartering agencies (the OCC, the OTS, and the states) gave many of them charters, and we approved some of them to bid. However, we started seeing problems. For instance, some of their bids reflected plans to flip their investment right away. Some also were owned by shell holding company structures located in offshore tax havens. The true owners of the bank were not transparent to us. I didn't want nameless sharpies buying banks from us just to make a quick buck. With an established insured bank, I knew who the owners were, I could see the management's track record, and I could know the bank's regulatory history. With the new banks created by hedge funds and venture capital firms, I didn't know any of those things.

As the number of failures escalated in 2009, we needed to find more qualified buyers to ensure a competitive auction process. Without multiple bidders, the prices we usually received on failed banks were very bad. So it wasn't as though we were in a position to be picky about bidders. On the other hand, I cared about the reputation of FDIC-insured banks, and, most important, I didn't want to see a failed bank coming back into our laps because the new management was more interested in turning a quick profit than responsibly providing banking services.

So in July 2009, I proposed to the FDIC board, and we approved for comment, a policy statement that put additional conditions on bidding by new banks backed by private equity. Perhaps the most important constraint: we proposed to require that the new banks maintain a 15 percent leverage ratio for the first three years—three times the 5 percent leverage requirement that applied to established banks. We also said that they had to keep their ownership interest for at least three years, to scare off flippers. Finally, we put very strict constraints on the ability of the bank to do business with any other entity owned by the same fund—so-called affiliate restrictions—and required that offshore owners make their books and records available to us as needed.

Some of the funds really went after us, including the Carlyle Group and WL Ross & Co. However, others, including Deryck Maughan at Kohlberg Kravis Roberts, came to our defense. And much to my surprise, we received support from the usually antiregulation *Wall Street Journal* editorial board. Saying that "the FDIC is right to drive a hard bargain for taxpayers," the newspaper's editors went on to conclude that "the FDIC is being roughed up—even by some in the Obama Treasury—for demanding capital and other standards from nonbank investors who won't have to meet current bank holding company rules. This is not the way to restore confidence in the banking system."

However, industry lobbying continued and the lobbyists made headway with some of my board members, notably John Dugan. To keep my board together, I fell back a bit on the higher capital requirement. We reduced it to 10 percent but required that the entire amount be filled with the highest-quality capital: tangible common equity. The private-equity funds still squawked, but they also kept bidding, and overall I think we struck the right balance.

Some of our sales to banks backed by private equity went through before the policy statement was finalized. The two most controversial of those was our sale of IndyMac to a consortium of investors, which included funds run by J.C. Flowers & Co. and John Paulson. The other was the sale of a Florida bank, BankUnited, to a new charter that was backed primarily by WL Ross & Co. and the Carlyle Group. Both of those deals made significant money for the acquirers, and both drew a lot of adverse press attention. However, both of the failed thrifts had a large volume of highly toxic mortgages in two of the most distressed housing markets in the nation. We beat the bushes for buyers and ran a competitive auction process, and those consortiums made the winning bids. The reality is that those who are brave enough to buy distressed companies in a down market—whether banks or any other type of company—expect to make a return commensurate with the risks they are taking. The FDIC, as seller, had no good options. Those sales gave us the best recoveries possible. Our total losses during my tenure were around $80 billion—all paid for by the industry. Though that number sounds high, it pales in comparison to the eye-popping numbers some industry analysts had been projecting. Even OMB had predicted significantly higher losses for the DIF than those we actually realized.

Notwithstanding the adverse media coverage of a few of the transactions, our strategy of selling whole banks with loss share proved to be enormously successful in minimizing our losses while providing seamless protection for insured depositors and continued services for all bank customers. It was also a highly efficient way to deal with the large number of bank failures that we experienced through 2010. We had only 3 failures in 2007, representing total assets of about $2.6 billion. The next year, we had 25, but they represented a whopping $373 billion in assets, with the failure of WaMu and other large thrifts. In 2009, the number ballooned to 140, representing $171 billion in assets, and it peaked at 157 in 2010, though those were smaller failures, with assets totaling $97 billion. The bank failure rate was tapering off as I left office. The number of failures in 2011 was "only" 92 banks, representing total assets of $36 billion.

That is not to say that all of the smaller bank failures were as smooth as silk. Some presented unique challenges. For instance, there was an $11 billion West Coast bank—United Commercial Bank (UCB)—that specialized in serving the Asian community. It had a subsidiary in China that was regulated by the Chinese Banking Regulatory Commission (CBRC) and branches in Hong Kong, which were regulated by the Hong Kong Monetary Authority (HKMA). In addition, one of its owners was a major Chinese bank, Minsheng. In November 2008, UCB's holding company had been approved for a TARP capital investment of about $300 million, amid the frenzy of stabilization measures and the rush to get TARP capital out to smaller institutions to support their lending. (Subsequent investigation found that UCB's managers had committed extensive fraud to conceal their troubled loans from bank examiners as well as their auditors and investors.)

Because of the complexities of cross-border resolutions, we notified both the CBRC and the HKMA months in advance of the bank's projected failure date to make sure they would provide the necessary regulatory approvals when it came time for us to sell the bank and its Asian operations. In discussions with CBRC, it came to light that Minsheng was interested in buying UCB. That would have been a great result from the standpoint of protecting the U.S. government against losses; it would have averted a failure and prevented losses to both the FDIC and the Treasury Department.

There was just one catch: the Fed would not let foreign banks acquire U.S. institutions unless it found that they had high-quality regulation in their home country. The Fed had not yet made that determination for China, which frustrated me no end. I had always found the CBRC—then led by Chairman Liu Mingkang—to be a serious, conservative, and prudent regulator. Whatever other issues and disagreements the United States has with China, I really didn't see how allowing Minsheng to buy the bank would violate U.S. public policy goals. But I suspect that the Fed—already reeling from public criticism, particularly from the right—didn't want to take on the issue of whether a Chinese bank should be able to buy a U.S. bank. It seemed to me that the acquisition of that relatively small bank by a Chinese bank could have provided a good test case for the Fed, but the Fed did not feel that it had time to fully consider the Minsheng acquisition. (In May 2012, the Fed finally gave approval to Chinese banks to invest in U.S. depository institutions.) So UCB failed, and we sold it to another Asian-oriented U.S. institution, East West Bank, and the FDIC took a $2.5 billion loss on it. The Treasury lost its $300 million investment, and Minsheng, as a large shareholder, lost its $120 million investment. On the positive side, the sale went smoothly. The Asian operations were also sold to East West, with all required approvals from the Chinese regulators.

Another one of our more challenging tasks: fully 25 percent of the Puerto Rican banking system failed in April 2010. We had been planning for the failures for months. The Puerto Rican economy had been hurt badly in 2005, when Congress had revoked special tax benefits that had drawn a large number of manufacturers and pharmaceutical companies to the island. Its energetic, charismatic governor, Luis Fortuño, was working diligently to rebuild the economy, but his efforts were not enough to save the Puerto Rican banking industry. The island had suffered a double whammy with the 2005 tax change and then the 2008 recession. Three of its banks, R-G Premier Bank, Westernbank, and Eurobank, were slowly but surely heading for insolvency.

Because of the island's economic woes, we were not optimistic that we could attract the support of bidders apart from the banks that were already doing business in Puerto Rico. That created a unique problem, because none of the Puerto Rican banks was in very good shape. But if we didn't qualify any of the stronger local banks to bid, we would likely have to liquidate the failed banks, with enormous losses for us and enormous consequences for the Puerto Rican economy. For a while, we toyed with the idea of letting bidding banks contribute some of their own troubled loans into a loss-share pool. That would strengthen their balance sheets and put them into a better position to absorb the failing institutions. On the other hand, that came dangerously close to a bailout of the acquiring banks, which was prohibited by our statute and anathema to our culture. After batting the idea around for several weeks, we finally dropped it.

We ended up qualifying all but one of the local banks to bid. We concluded that they would be in a much stronger competitive position with consolidation. That conclusion was reinforced by the fact that the healthier local banks were able to raise almost $2 billion in new capital as investors anticipated that many of their competitors would fail. The island's banking industry was far too large for the needs of its struggling economy, but with consolidation, investors saw the potential for significant profits as the Puerto Rican economy continued to improve.

As it turned out, the bids were surprisingly strong, and our losses ended up being much lower than expected. Five bidders came forward; all but one already owned banking interests on the island. The one that did not, Santander, bid primarily because I had called its CEO, Emilio Botín, and asked him to. I don't think Santander's heart was in it, but just by being a part of the process, it kept the other bidders honest and helped us achieve better pricing. The island's largest bank, Banco Popular, acquired Westernbank. The tiny but very healthy Oriental Bank and Trust bought Eurobank; and Scotiabank, backed by the deep pockets of Canada's Bank of Nova Scotia, bought R-G Premier Bank. I hailed the strong bidding interest as an "inflection point" in our failed-bank resolution process. With an economy gaining some strength, even in Puerto Rico, more investors were starting to come in and commit substantial capital to failed-bank acquisitions. Indeed, after the Puerto Rico failures, our pricing improved, and we even started doing some sales without loss share.

Puerto Rico also presented a challenge because the Puerto Rican citizenry was not as familiar with the FDIC as were citizens on the mainland. Given the close-knit nature of the Puerto Rican banking industry and the scope of its problems, we were very concerned that Puerto Ricans would lose confidence and run all of the banks, not just the weak ones. So we worked closely with the Puerto Rican government on a public education campaign months in advance of the bank failures. In addition, I personally visited the island on April 30, 2010, the day of the three bank failures, to provide media interviews and participate in a press conference with local government officials. Accompanied by Bob Schoppe, a senior staff member of our resolutions division, I attended staff meetings in preparation for the Friday evening closings and observed first hand our closing of R-G Premier.

We held a press briefing following the bank closings, with Alfred Padilla, Puerto Rico's top banking regulator. The briefing was packed—six cameras and at least fifty reporters—but I was well briefed and able to assure the media that there was no cause for alarm. Banking services would continue uninterrupted. Our public-education efforts worked. The bank depositors of the three failed banks left their money in the banks. There were no runs and no disruptions in banking services. I went to a late dinner that night at a local restaurant with Bob and Andrew Gray after an exhausting day. I was startled when, after taking our orders, the waiter bent down and gave me a big hug. I thought he was being fresh, but as it turned out, he had seen me on TV and wanted to thank me and the FDIC for protecting him and other bank depositors.

Though for depositors the failures were a nonevent, attending bank closings provided me with a stark reminder of how painful and frightening bank closings are for bank employees. I generally have little sympathy for senior bank management and board members. They are usually the ones responsible for the mismanagement and mistakes that bring a bank down and deserve to lose their jobs. But many other employees, particularly the bank tellers and administrative staff, are not culpable. Frequently the acquiring bank will keep them on, but not always. In Puerto Rico, for instance, the banking sector was bloated and needed to be smaller, but that meant some employees would be laid off (fortunately, all of the acquiring banks agreed to keep employees on for a six-month transition period). Still, bank closings are an emotional, tear-laden experience for employees, many of whom have loyally served their banks for decades.

FDIC staff generally call an all-hands meeting the evening of a bank failure to explain to bank employees that the bank has failed and typically introduce the new owner. Bank employees are also instructed to preserve all of the bank's books and records. (Every bank failure is reviewed by the FDIC inspector general to determine the cause of the failure and whether fraud was involved.) I sat quietly in a large conference room as our FDIC staff talked to the employees of R-G Premier. I could hear quiet gasps and sobs from the back of the room. The Scotiabank representatives did a great job of bucking up the employees and letting them know they were valued, but still, R-G had served Puerto Rico for a quarter of a century. Now it was gone.

If Puerto Rico was one of the more difficult logistical challenges, surely ShoreBank, a Chicago-based lender established to serve the needs of Chicago's low-income communities, was one of the most politically challenging.

Actually, any bank failure in the Chicago area was politically charged, given the red-hot animosity between President Obama and members of the House GOP. No matter what we did in Chicago, it seemed that one side or the other would go after us. A prime example was Broadway Bank, the family bank of Alexi Giannoulias, the Illinois state treasurer and Obama's favored candidate to fill his Senate seat. Broadway had once been a well-run, profitable bank, but, like many other banks, it had gotten caught up in the real estate craze. In the 2000s, it had started making out-of-area construction loans in overheated markets such as Florida (where it had no expertise) and funded a lot of those loans with brokered deposits. We jointly regulated the bank with the state of Illinois. In January 2010, we issued a tough order against the bank, telling it to raise capital and take other remedial action. The *Chicago Sun-Times* immediately called our press office, demanding an interview with me. It wanted to know if this was "part of Sheila Bair's war with the Administration" (in reference to my disagreements with Geithner over Dodd-Frank) and also questioned the timing of the consent order just "one week before the Illinois state primary."

Four months later, the bank failed, and the Republicans came after me for not closing the bank fast enough! Mark Kirk, the Republican candidate who was ultimately elected to the seat, made a lot of hay out of the bank failure during the campaign, and many feel it was determinative in the race. His close friend Congressman Darrell Issa demanded that the FDIC IG investigate the timing of the failure. Of course, there was not a scintilla of evidence to suggest political influence, but Issa's well-publicized request kept the bank closing in the newspapers for a bit longer, which helped Kirk. But that is the way people do business in Washington. I just threw up my hands. (The FDIC IG did look at Issa's charges, as he requested, and found absolutely no evidence of political influence.)

In truth, neither I nor my board drove any of those decisions. As was always the case, the timing of the enforcement order, as well as the bank's failure, was determined by our career examiners working with the bank's primary regulator—here the Illinois bank superintendent. Those decisions were, in turn, based on the prompt corrective action process, which, as I've previously discussed, has fairly rigid timelines for closing a failing institution. I did not think political appointees should drive those decisions, so although the staff would report to me and the FDIC board on their enforcement actions and seek our approval to close banks, the decision making and timing were left to them. I can't think of one case when the board did not defer to the career staff on a bank closing. That is the way I wanted it. It was not our job to go into banks, look at their deteriorating loans, and independently decide whether they were hopeless and at what point they would fail. We trained and paid our examiners and resolutions staff to make those decisions. And they made them very well.

Nonetheless, I was batted around on bank closings a lot. Closing a bank is never a happy task, and there were always two sides: those who said we had waited too long and those who said we had prematurely closed the institution. But the political maneuvering and finger-pointing reached its apex with ShoreBank.

All of the bank closings were heart-rending in their own way, but Shore-Bank was a particular tragedy. It was a $2.2 billion state-chartered bank whose roots in the Chicago community went back to 1939. In 1973, it had been purchased by an organization devoted to community development and had refocused its mission on providing financing for low-income housing and business development in Chicago's poor neighborhoods. For the first few decades of its operations, its model was enormously successful; it proved that banks could lend responsibly to economically distressed areas and remain profitable. Its efforts were replicated throughout the country. Indeed, ShoreBank was the inspiration for the hundreds of FDIC-insured community development financial institutions (CDFIs) that exist throughout the country today. It also received a lot of support from larger banks that drew from its pioneering work in serving low-income communities. Frequently, ShoreBank's model products and services, once proven, were replicated by larger institutions.

But in the early 2000s, ShoreBank started going astray. It began relying too much on its cachet and glamorous reputation among liberal groups and did not focus enough on the basics of running a bank. It made poorly underwritten loans and forayed into trendy areas beyond its core mission. For instance, it started making microloans in remote developing economies. And, rightly or wrongly, it became viewed as a "Democratic" organization, with a number of high-profile Democrats serving on its board. But I have to say that I never thought of the bank as exclusively "Democratic." When I served at the Treasury Department in 2001–2002, the bank had a good reputation with the Bush appointees in office at the time, and the Bush administration supported many of its programs.

Many management mistakes were made at ShoreBank, but it also suffered from the disastrous economic conditions in Chicago's low-income neighborhoods, where the bulk of its loans were made. Recessions always hit low-income neighborhoods the hardest, and the Great Recession of 2008 was no exception. In July 2009, the bank's condition had deteriorated enough that our examination staff issued, jointly with the Illinois Department of Financial & Professional Regulation, an order requiring the bank to raise capital. Throughout the remainder of the year, ShoreBank's board, aided by Eugene Ludwig, the comptroller of the currency under President Clinton, tried to raise new capital to stabilize the bank.

At the same time, the Treasury Department had established a new TARP specifically designed to help CDFIs, many of which were experiencing the same problems as ShoreBank. The plummeting housing market and high unemployment rate in low-income areas were hurting the CDFI community badly. Though the usual prerequisite for TARP investments for the smaller institutions was viability, meaning that the bank applying for TARP capital had to prove that it was viable even without the TARP money, this program required the bank to demonstrate only that it would be viable after the TARP capital infusion as long as it had raised an equal amount of capital from the private sector. The Treasury Department also imposed a cap on the amount of capital an individual institution could receive, which in the case of ShoreBank was $72 million.

The FDIC and Illinois state examiners had determined that ShoreBank needed an additional $175 to $202 million to be well capitalized. Ludwig therefore needed to raise more than $100 million to qualify for the Treasury's program.

I was very worried about the cost of a ShoreBank failure. The problem was that, given its business model, the only institutions that were likely to be interested in buying it were other CDFIs. However, CDFIs in general were experiencing problems, and most of them were much smaller than ShoreBank, with assets of a few hundred million dollars, not a few billion. There just weren't any healthy CDFIs out there that were big enough to buy ShoreBank. I was also skeptical that any other bank would want to bid on the bank because of the politically charged nature of its operations and loan portfolio. Indeed, another Chicago institution that had been closed the year before—Park National Bank—had also been active with local community groups and had made significant loans and other contributions to them. A very good, well-run bank, U.S. Bancorp, had bought Park National and was trying to deal with its many troubled loans in a fair and balanced way. Nonetheless, U.S. Bancorp had been subjected to much public criticism from community groups and Democratic members of Congress for not doing enough. It was truly a case of no good deed going unpunished.

Given U.S. Bancorp's experience, why would any other bank want to buy ShoreBank and confront the difficult task of dealing with its many troubled loans? Under our loss-share agreements, we had very firm rules about restructuring loans to preserve economic value, but the reality was that some of ShoreBank's loans would have to go into foreclosure. Foreclosing in those distressed neighborhoods would be a public relations nightmare for an acquirer.

Not that the Republicans were making it any easier on the right. Many of them basically took the tack that ShoreBank was an "Obama bank" and anyone who tried to help it was doing so under political pressure from team Obama. So, even though many investors wanted to help ShoreBank because they believed in its mission, helping with the recapitalization would open them up to criticism that they were just kowtowing to the administration.

Every Monday morning, I held senior staff meetings to receive status reports from our senior managers and set our priorities for the week. During the meetings, Sandra Thompson would always volunteer an update on ShoreBank's capital raising. It wasn't going well. Given the heat coming from both sides of the political spectrum, Ludwig was having a hard time. So in early 2010, I instructed Jim Wigand and his team to start beating the bushes for possible buyers, as it looked as though ShoreBank would fail. They developed a list of more than two hundred target institutions and started working the phones. Unfortunately, no one was seriously interested in buying the bank.

Ludwig then contacted me directly and said he had about $70 million in capital investments, just short of what ShoreBank needed to apply for funds under the Treasury program. Most of the major banks were investing, with the exception of Goldman Sachs and a few others, which had refused. I hit the roof. Goldman had made generous use of our debt guarantee program as well as the Fed's lending facilities and Treasury's TARP capital investments. Goldman had one of the stronger balance sheets in the industry, and other strong banks, including JPMorgan Chase, Wells Fargo, U.S. Bancorp, and PNC, had stepped up, bid, and purchased failed institutions from us. I felt that Goldman was more interested in taking than giving back.

Around that same time, the SEC had announced a major enforcement action against Goldman Sachs, based on its failure to disclose important information to investors about the risks of certain complicated securities deals. A few days later, Warren Buffett was quoted as defending Goldman's actions. I didn't know anything about the merits of the SEC's suit, but I wasn't feeling too charitable toward Goldman, so, still in a snit, I called Buffett to question his defense of the institution. I was probably out of line, but I told him that I was frustrated with Goldman's complete lack of interest in helping us recapitalize failing institutions (as Buffett had done with it during the depths of the financial crisis). It had reaped a lot of benefits from having an insured bank and becoming a bank holding company but didn't seem interested in working with the government to help with the postcrisis cleanup.

I don't know what Buffett said or did, but literally, within an hour, Goldman CEO Lloyd Blankfein was calling me, asking if there was something he could do to help me. I recounted to him my disappointment that he had refused to participate in the ShoreBank recapitalization. I explained that the bank was close to raising the required amount, but if the bank didn't make it, it would be a very expensive failure for us as we had no bidders. To his credit, Blankfein agreed not only to contribute to the ShoreBank recap but also to help recruit other investment interest.

Of course, nothing having to do with ShoreBank ever stayed out of the press. Within a few days, there was an article in *The Wall Street Journal* describing Goldman's leadership role in ShoreBank's capital raising. Then the public flogging began. A Democratic member of Congress, Jan Schakowsky, lambasted Goldman and the other big banks, saying that they "have a moral and economic obligation to step up and make certain that Shore-Bank can continue serving Chicago's low-income communities." The folks on the right immediately accused Goldman of trying to curry favor with the Obama administration. The worst critic, by far, was Charles Gasparino at Fox Business Network. Gasparino was usually a supporter of the FDIC and its antibailout philosophy. But for whatever reason, in covering this story, he was over the top with unsubstantiated accusations that the White House was putting pressure on all those banks to pony up and even suggested that I—a lifelong Republican—was helping it.

In truth, I was trying to minimize losses to the Deposit Insurance Fund by reaching out to potential investors, as I had done several times before when bank management and staff efforts had been unsuccessful. Why was this institution having such a hard time finding investors? A big part of the problem was all of the politicization on the left and right. If it had been a bank in Minnesota, we would not have had those issues.

Blankfein committed Goldman to a $20 million investment and called a number of other CEOs, asking them to invest. But the tenuous condition of the bank, combined with the adverse press and political heat, made his job difficult. By mid-May, ShoreBank's ninety-day time frame to raise capital under our rules was expiring, and the bank still hadn't raised the capital that it needed. So Jim Wigand intensified his team's efforts to find bidders and, keeping his fingers crossed, started soliciting bids, all to no avail. At the end of the week, on Friday, May 14, Jim Wigand and Chris Spoth called me late in the afternoon to deliver the bad news.

They found me on my cell phone in the backseat of a car heading to the University of Massachusetts, where I was supposed to deliver the commencement speech the next morning. I had thought I was going to enjoy a relaxing weekend in Amherst, where we had lived for four years.

The bank hadn't raised enough capital, they told me, and we had no buyers. After a long silence, Wigand said, "You better start making some calls." I agreed.

I asked Chris for the list of bank CEOs who had committed to invest in a recapitalization and the list of CEOs whom Blankfein had called but who had not committed. Instead of visiting with friends in Amherst over the weekend, I spent it holed up in a hotel room, "dialing for dollars," as we called it. Chris Spoth, a smart strategist, had suggested that I explain to the investors that there were two possible approaches: they could help Shore-Bank raise enough capital to stay open and qualify for additional capital under the Treasury program, or they could form and capitalize a new bank to bid on ShoreBank in our resolution process (the same technique private-equity funds were using to bid on failed banks). I mentioned both options to the CEOs when I called them, but Option 1 was the least complicated alternative, as there were many steps involved in forming a new bank.

I also asked Jim Wigand to give me our loss estimates if we had to liquidate ShoreBank, as I wanted the CEOs to understand the severity of the situation: if we had no bidders, we would be forced to pay off the depositors and auction the loans separately. Again, because of the bad publicity and political controversy surrounding ShoreBank's operations, I didn't expect us to see many bidders for the loans. Losses were always steep in a liquidation, which is why we always tried to avoid them; in that case, they were likely to be catastrophic.

Jim's team estimated the cost of liquidation at $400 million or higher. Armed with that information, I started calling the CEOs. I scripted my remarks carefully to let them know I was not putting pressure on them, I just wanted them to have all the facts in making their investment decision. I told them that after months of trying we did not have any bidders and our liquidation costs would be north of $400 million. Since they all paid premiums to cover our losses, ultimately they would bear these costs. Indeed, some of the bigger depository institutions, such as BofA, accounted for 10 percent of our premium revenue, so if our loss was $400 million, BofA would cover $40 million of it. A capital investment of half that, $20 million, by BofA (which is what Blankfein had asked for) would actually save it money by averting a costly failure.

The calls worked. Blankfein followed up and nailed down commitments for $153 million of new capital for ShoreBank. So the bank filed an application for TARP money from the Treasury Department. Our examiners presented their analysis of the bank's condition to the interagency group that voted on TARP applications. They stated their view that the bank would be stable and viable with the $153 million in private capital, combined with the Treasury's $72 million, and thus it would pass Treasury's main test for approval. However, the other bank regulators disagreed and refused to support the application. Were our examiners wrong, or had the other agencies been scared off by the political heat associated with doing anything to help ShoreBank? I will never know. TARP applications were handled by career examiners. Neither the chairman nor the board was involved. It might have well been a disagreement among career staff on the bank's capital needs. But the political controversy tainted the whole process, in my view.

The denial decision was relayed back to Goldman and the investment group. Most of them ultimately decided to invest in a new bank charter to bid on ShoreBank when we auctioned it off. That was a good result for us. We tried one more time but couldn't get anyone else to bid. Fortunately, with at least one bidder, we were able to do our standard whole-bank-with-loss-share sale and saved $250 million over our projected losses in a liquidation.

The new owners renamed it the Urban Partnership Bank, and the new bank continues to provide banking services to Chicago's poor. I would like to state for the record that whatever else their sins might be, Goldman Sachs and the rest of the big banks that invested in ShoreBank did so for a nonpolitical reason: to support its traditional mission and model of serving low-income populations. They also saved themselves and the Deposit Insurance Fund a lot of money. I certainly never received any pressure from anyone in the administration to help ShoreBank, nor did any of those banks to my knowledge. Indeed, the FDIC inspector general went over all of it with a fine-toothed comb and found no evidence of political pressure.

Whole-bank-with-loss-share transactions were almost always the least costly way for us to resolved failed banks. But occasionally we would have to liquidate a bank because we could not find buyers—or, even if we could find a healthy bank to buy the failed one, the healthy bank would not want to take all of the loans, even with loss-share support. In those cases we would auction the loans separately, using an online process that was open to both banks and distressed-asset purchasers, typically hedge funds and the like. Before auctioning a loan, we would always give the borrower the option of buying it back from us at par. Sometimes it did, but more often it would try to negotiate to buy it back at some type of discount. Under our procedures, we did not negotiate side deals with borrowers. If they did not want to pay off at par, the loan was auctioned off and sold to the highest bidder.

In auctioning loans, we found that pooling them by type and collateral characteristics was more important than pooling by performance status—although if we had many loans of a certain type, we would do both. So, for instance, we might auction a pool of loans, half of which were delinquent and half still performing. That pool would be sold at some discount to their par value (the amount of the unpaid balance) because of the high number of delinquent loans. So for instance, our best bid on that kind of pool might be 65 cents on the dollar.

We always disclosed our bids publicly, and here is what would happen. A borrower would see that we had only received 65 cents on the pool, when he might have been willing to buy back his individual loan for 80 cents. So he would complain to his member of Congress that we had sold his loan at a lower price than he had offered, and I would get an irate call from the member of Congress demanding an explanation. Some members would hear us out and drop the matter once our procedures were explained to them. But others really wanted their constituents to get a deal from us, facts be damned. The pressure was bipartisan. Dealing with Congress was one of the more difficult parts of running the FDIC, though looking back, in light of the nature of the FDIC's work, it is amazing that we didn't have more confrontation. Because I used to work in the Senate, I had (and still have) great respect for Congress as an institution, though I am appalled, as are most Americans, at its members' current inability to work together and make decisions for the benefit of the country. I always took their calls, met with them when requested, and testified when asked (even when I didn't want to), and for the most part, the FDIC maintained good, solid, bipartisan relationships on the Hill. I think that individually, most members of Congress are reasonable, public-service-oriented people (notwithstanding their collective dysfunction in making decisions) who just want openness and answers when they hear of issues or concerns from their constituents. If you explain things to them rationally, they will usually leave you alone to do your job.

Minimizing losses was a high priority for us at the FDIC. Notwithstanding our innovative strategies, the country was in the worst financial crisis since the Great Depression, and we were taking severe losses. I was bound and determined that we would not turn to taxpayers to cover them. Paying for deposit insurance was the industry's responsibility. As discussed in earlier chapters, for years industry trade groups had lobbied Congress to prevent us from collecting premiums to build up the fund in good times. When we finally got that authority in 2006, the American Bankers Association blasted us, saying, "There is no requirement to boost the revenues of the fund—and no need to given the $50 billion in the fund already. The banking industry is in exceptional health, and there is no indication that large amounts of revenue are needed by the FDIC."

The FDIC board unanimously raised premiums anyway. I stated at the time that it was in the industry's interests for us to build up the fund when conditions were good, to avoid the need for steep premium increases in a downturn. Unfortunately, we did not have enough time to grow the fund significantly before the crisis hit. The $50 billion we had started with depleted rapidly.

Our statute required us to keep the Deposit Insurance Fund above a minimum of 1.15 percent of insured deposits. By the second quarter of 2008, we had already breached the minimum. Our statute further required that when the minimum was breached, we had to adopt a plan to restore our fund to 1.15 percent in five years. In October 2008, we approved such a plan that included a 7-basis-point increase in the premiums we charged (7 cents for every $100 in deposits). For most banks, that meant a doubling of their premiums, though the assessment was still significantly below the 23 basis points that had been assessed on them during the savings and loan crisis. High-risk banks would pay a premium as high as 50 cents for every $100 in deposits.

Our staff, at that point, was predicting losses totaling $40 billion through 2013. That projection quickly proved to be overly optimistic. By the end of 2008, the fund had dipped to $17.3 billion, representing .36 percent of insured deposits. However, our total reserves still stood at about $45 billion. (As earlier discussed, we projected our losses twelve months in advance and set aside enough to cover those estimates in a special fund called our contingent loss reserve. The fund held about $28 billion in funds committed to cover those losses.)

By early 2009, it became apparent that the fund was going to dip into negative territory, though total reserves would remain positive. However, I was concerned that, given the rapid deterioration of hundreds of banks throughout the country, our total reserves could become depleted and we could run out of cash. If we were going to avoid borrowing from taxpayers, we would have to raise assessments again—significantly.

I held numerous discussions with the senior staff on how to maintain adequate reserves without resorting to taxpayer borrowing. Public confidence in the FDIC meant everything to me. I did not want us to have the taint of a government bailout. I also thought it would be sending all of the wrong signals if we turned to the government for a handout. Industry lobbying had blocked or delayed efforts to tighten lending standards, and the industry had also delayed the congressional authority we had sought to build the fund in good times. It was true that the vast majority of community banks and many of the big banks had not contributed to the high-risk activity that had brought us the crisis. Yet, frankly, the more prudent banks had sat on the sidelines during our earlier fights with industry lobbyists over tightening lending standards and building the fund. It was their responsibility now, not the taxpayers'. In any event, perhaps I was naive, but I believed that most banks wanted to maintain the integrity of industry funding of the FDIC. They took pride in the fact that they, not taxpayers, funded the FDIC.

At the same time, a big assessment would stretch a lot of banks. John Bovenzi, our COO, and Art Murton were suggesting a 20-basis-point flat assessment on the industry, with the possibility of another 10 basis points toward the end of the year. That would have brought in more than $35 billion in much-needed funds. The banks had plenty of cash to give us. Because of confidence in the FDIC guarantee, they were awash in funds. Insured deposits had increased by a trillion dollars since the crisis had begun, while loan demand was down because of the weak economy. What they didn't have was earnings, meaning that the 20-basis-point assessment would eat into their capital.

I asked our staff if we could simply require that the banks prepay their assessments over the next several years, instead of whacking them with a huge assessment that would have to be deducted from their earnings immediately. If they prepaid their premiums, it would be more like a loan to us, but instead of repaying them, we would simply give them a credit for the premium they owed us each quarter until the prepaid amount was used up. In that way, they could deduct the assessment from their earnings over time, instead of having to recognize it as an expense all at once.

In February, Art sent a memo to me raising all sorts of legal and accounting issues about the prepayment idea. It seemed as though no one on the staff wanted to pursue it. I eventually acceded to my staff's recommendations, and on March 2, 2008, we proposed a 20-basis-point assessment. A firestorm of controversy ensued. I must acknowledge that Edward Yingling, who then headed the ABA, as well as Cam Fine, who headed the Independent Community Bankers of America, tried to explain and defend the special assessment to their members. But the uproar was deafening, and we immediately started getting inquiries and pressure from the Hill.

I was not sure I would be able to withstand the political momentum building against us. It was not only from the big banks but from thousands of community banks. We had reached too far, and I was very afraid that Congress would pass an amendment restricting our ability to assess premiums.

So I decided to take the lemon and make lemonade. During that same time period, we were trying to get our borrowing authority raised to $100 billion. We were insuring nearly $5.5 trillion in deposits, with only a $30 billion line of credit with the Treasury Department. The $30 billion limit had been in place since 1991, when insured deposits had been less than half that amount. We were also trying to get authority to assess large nonbank financial institutions that were using our debt guarantee program for any losses on that program. As discussed earlier, we were having difficulty on the Hill because Geithner was sending mixed signals about whether the administration wanted such legislation to pass.

If the banks wanted to lobby against the 20-basis-point assessment, I decided to give them something constructive to do instead. I publicly stated that if Congress raised our borrowing authority and gave us new assessment authority over the big financial institutions, I would reconsider the 20-basis-point assessment. My reasoning was that the new authorities would give us additional tools to access funds in the case of an emergency, so we could be a little less demanding of the industry. The nation's community banks got the message loud and clear and went to work with their members of Congress. On May 20, 2009, the president signed the bill into law, and on May 22, the FDIC adopted a final rule imposing a 5-, not 20-, basis-point assessment.

But we were not out of the woods yet. I was skeptical that the board's May actions would be sufficient to sustain our resources through the next few years. The bad economy was taking its toll. As we moved deeper into 2009, bank failures were being driven as much by economic conditions as by bad lending. Toward the end of the year, it became apparent that we would have to go back to the industry for another assessment or swallow hard and borrow from taxpayers.

I revisited the idea of a prepaid assessment with the staff. It seemed like a good third way—an alternative to hitting the industry with another assessment or a taxpayer bailout. I pushed them again on the perceived legal and accounting issues. Except that this time, I had added to my staff a markets expert and former Senate Banking Committee aide, Joe Jiampietro. I gave Joe the task of pushing the prepaid assessment idea, and he was able to cut through a lot of the issues with the staff. Ultimately, we did find a way to do it that was compatible with our legal authority and accepted accounting rules. People frequently assume that the heads of government agencies have unfettered power to work their will, but the truth is that you have to have staff acceptance and support of an initiative to get it done. Staff resistance can fell even the best of ideas. A prepaid assessment was something we had never done before, and, in retrospect, I think the fear of the unknown was causing discomfort. But we talked it through and built consensus that it was our best option among a lot of bad choices.

In late September 2009, the board proposed a three-year prepaid assessment for comment, and on November 12, we unanimously approved the measure. Requiring banks to prepay three years' worth of deposit insurance premiums brought in about $45 billion in cash. For the most part, the prepaid assessment was lauded as a creative way to handle a very difficult problem. But we took some ribbing in the press about "borrowing" from the industry. I remember speaking on a panel with President Bill Clinton and Jamie Dimon at a New York conference and wasn't sure how to take it when Dimon announced that he viewed the FDIC as "creditworthy" and would be happy to lend us money anytime.

As I predicted, the Deposit Insurance Fund was negative for several quarters, though our total reserves always stayed positive and we never had to borrow from taxpayers, nor did we have to impose additional assessments on the industry. The $45 billion was more than ample to cover our needs through the remainder of my tenure and beyond. I was very pleased that in my final months in office, the Deposit Insurance Fund moved into positive territory again, and our financial position has steadily improved since then.

CHAPTER 24

Squinting in the Public Spotlight

Former FDIC Chairman Bill Seidman warned me when I first became chairman of the FDIC that managing the media would be a big part of the job. He was absolutely right. There were a number of reasons why.

First, we could not be successful in our public mission if people did not have confidence in us. And to have that confidence, the public needed to know who was in charge. Faceless bureaucracies don't do much to engender trust. People needed to hear from the person responsible for running the FDIC that their hard-earned cash was safe. That had to come from the person at the top.

Second, because of the unique, cyclical nature of our work, there just wasn't a lot of public understanding of the FDIC and our process. Nearly two decades had passed since the last banking crisis, with only sporadic failures during that time period. Nearly three years had passed without any bank failures at all. To convince the public that we were capable of protecting it, we had to get out there publicly, tell how we funded ourselves, and explain the mechanics of our process in a bank failure. That was all the more important, given some of the frankly irresponsible media and analyst coverage that exaggerated the number of banks that were in trouble and unduly questioned the adequacy of our financial resources to protect depositors.

Finally, I personally attracted a lot of media attention for a variety of reasons. I was the only female agency head during the crisis, and regrettably, it is still rare for women to hold senior financial positions in either the government or the private sector. In addition, I had had some well-publicized disagreements with my colleagues at other agencies, and I wasn't afraid to publicly articulate my views when necessary. Moreover, for the most part, the members of the press liked me because I was open with them and tried to explain things in a way that was understandable to the broader public. People were scared, and someone needed to tell them what was going on and reassure them. I tried very hard to do that.

I think one of the smartest (and potentially riskiest) things we did from a media standpoint was to agree to a request from *60 Minutes* to let one of its news crews accompany us on a bank failure. It was risky because even though I had utmost confidence in our bank-closing staff, it's impossible to control for all variables. If there were any missteps in our handling of the failure, the *60 Minutes* crew would be right there to film it all. (Indeed, they ended up shooting more than a hundred hours of footage for an eleven-minute segment, providing ample opportunity to film something going wrong.) In addition, there were plenty of media critics out there saying that we weren't up to the job and that we didn't have enough money to handle all of the upcoming failures. What if *60 Minutes* decided to take that tack in covering our resolution process? In that case, instead of instilling confidence, the *60 Minutes* coverage would undermine it.

I discussed *60 Minutes*' request at length with Andrew Gray, the head of our press operation and public education program, as well as my chief of staff, Jesse Villarreal. In addition, Scott Pelley came down to Washington from New York to discuss the proposal with me. After the IndyMac experience, I was particularly concerned that we might have panicked depositors rushing to the bank after it closed to withdraw their money. I had no desire to once again see frightened people on TV, banging at the doors of their bank trying to get their cash. But we had quickly learned our lessons from IndyMac and had handled two dozen closings since then without incident.

At the end of the day, the decision came down to confidence—my confidence in our people, our process, our mission, and our financial resources to form a convincing case to *60 Minutes* and the American public that we could and would protect them. So I authorized the *60 Minutes* coverage. I will tell you, I've never been as proud of our people as I was when watching them on CBS News the night of March 8, 2009, as the show demonstrated how they had calmly, confidently, and professionally closed Heritage Community Bank in Illinois on February 27, and transferred ownership to MB Financial, another Illinois lender.

Our team was led by FDIC veterans Cheryl Bates and Arthur Cooke in a closing we code-named Operation Happy. (In the interest of guarding against inadvertent leaks of the names of banks scheduled to close, all of them were referred to by code names.) Heritage was a forty-year-old, locally run bank that had made disastrous speculative loans on real estate. It was a relatively small bank, with 12,000 deposit accounts and about $200 million in deposits. Pamela Farwig, Jim Wigand's right hand, who oversaw our (now weekly) auctions on failed banks, had been able to draw several bids on Heritage. The winner, MB Financial, was committed to serving that area and, for a time at least, would keep all of its branches and nonmanagement employees. We had also let the *60 Minutes* crew observe our auction team and interview its members about our bidding process. We wanted to demystify our operations as much as possible.

What about the panicked depositors I had been worried about? Well, a couple did show up, but they turned out to be a blessing in disguise. Early Saturday morning, as Heritage reopened under its new ownership, Jim Hess and his wife, Audrey, came to the bank with an empty suitcase, ready to withdraw all of their money. Another FDIC veteran, Rickey McCullough, had been stationed outside the front door at Heritage. His job was to greet bank customers and answer their questions. "Can I help you sir?" he asked Mr. Hess. "I just don't care anymore" was Mr. Hess's response as he hurried into the bank's lobby with his wife. Rickey was alarmed and followed them in. "Please, can I help explain things?" he asked of the clearly distressed couple.

As Rickey explained our deposit rules and the fact that they were fully protected, the Hesses started to relax and understand that the bank failure had no practical impact on them. They left the bank without withdrawing their money. The *60 Minutes* crew filmed them leaving the bank, with a still empty suitcase in hand and singing the praises of the FDIC.

Scenes like this were playing out each week throughout the country as hundreds of smaller banks failed. Frightened people were reassured by our competent and professional staff. We protected hundreds of billions of dollars' worth of insured deposits. No one lost a penny, and no one had to wait more than one business day to access his or her funds.

Transparency generally served us well in dealing with the media. I tried to accommodate all requests for interviews, and under my direction our press office tried to respond openly and in detail to requests for information. The only exception was requests that would violate our rules involving confidentiality of the supervisory process or employees' privacy. That had not been the culture when I arrived at the agency. Indeed, the past leadership of our public affairs office had had a somewhat antagonistic attitude toward the press. Just a few months into office, I was completely blindsided by a *San Diego Union-Tribune* editorial telling me to "take a break from writing children's books" and ask the FDIC media staff to "do their jobs." As it turned out, the *Union-Tribune* had been trying to get information on an old, 1993 transaction between a member of Congress and the FDIC during the savings and loan cleanup. For some reason, it had become an issue in his reelection campaign. The *Tribune* reporter was clearly out of line, but instead of trying to deal with him, our press office simply did not return the phone call.

Many government press offices follow the same policy: don't deal with hostile reporters. There were a few instances when the reporters we dealt with had such an overwhelming bias that I decided it was best not to talk with them. But for the most part, full engagement was our policy. Andrew, one of the first people I hired when I assumed the FDIC chairmanship, fully shared my philosophy. And if we felt that that a reporter was not presenting a balanced story, we were not afraid to escalate the issue to their editors or take them on publicly.

I gave reporters lots of access, but I also didn't hesitate to give them a piece of my mind when I thought they were being unfair to the agency. I will never forget a *Wall Street Journal* editorial that appeared on September 1, 2009, saying that we were running out of money and that we should give up the ghost and borrow from Treasury instead of assessing higher premiums from banks. It was Labor Day weekend, and I was in Amherst with my family, trying to spend a few quality days with them and enjoy some bike riding through western Massachusetts' scenic countryside. I called Andrew and asked him to schedule a phone conversation for me with Paul Gigot, the *Journal*'s legendary senior editor, who oversaw the Review & Outlook section, where all of the editors' columns appeared. Unfortunately, the only time Paul was available was right in the middle of a bike ride that I had committed to take with my husband. Scott and I arranged our ride so that we could stop at a used-book shop, Montague Bookmill, located in a 150-year-old grist mill on the Sawmill River, at the appointed time so that I could make my call. Sitting outside the bookstore at a rusty wrought-iron table canopied with a faded green vinyl umbrella, I called Paul on my cell. I wondered how seriously he would have taken the call if he had known I was wearing biking shorts and a sweat-stained T-shirt, having just biked twenty miles in the hilly Massachusetts countryside.

Gigot was congenial—as I always found him to be, notwithstanding the bite he could take out of your hide with a critical column. I sometimes disagree with the *Wall Street Journal* editorial board, but I always read its opinion pieces because if nothing else the arguments are cogent, forceful, and extremely well written. But here, I thought, *The Wall Street Journal* was way off base. As defenders of the free enterprise system, it should support our efforts to make sure that the industry funded the costs of bank failures. The banks, not the taxpayers, were responsible for funding the FDIC, and letting them off the hook would simply reward some of the behaviors that had fed the crisis. Our analysis showed that increased assessments would not unduly stress the industry. If we inflicted a little cost and pain, the banks and their trade groups might think more carefully the next time they were tempted to resist our efforts to crack down on bad lending practices or build up our reserves when the industry was healthy.

I started off slowly with those arguments, but I believed very strongly in our position and also that ours was the right position from a market-based perspective. As I kept talking, I picked up speed and volume, and when he tried to interject a question or comment, I batted him down and just kept going. It wasn't one of my prouder moments; we had good arguments, and I should have been a bit more dispassionate. I violated my own first commandment for women professionals: never get emotional. But fortunately for me, Gigot took it in good humor and agreed to talk with me if the *Journal* would be writing future columns on the FDIC to make sure it understood our perspective. True to his word, after that, the columnists would contact us when they were writing FDIC-oriented pieces. Sometimes we agreed with them, sometimes we didn't, but we enjoyed a good relationship with them after that conversation.

With Paul Gigot, I was dealing with a mature, seasoned columnist who was willing to listen to competing viewpoints. My "assertiveness," however, was not always so well received. A good example was when I vociferously complained about the column written by Andrew Ross Sorkin on the Public-Private Investment Program (PPIP), discussed in chapter 14, when he savaged the FDIC as an unsophisticated agency that should keep to the "simple job" of insuring deposits, while comparing me to the guy who had run AIG into the ground.

I probably paid a price for those complaints. A few years later, in his lengthy tome about the financial crisis, *Too Big to Fail,* Sorkin again painted me in a very unflattering and inaccurate way. Though he may be plugged in to Wall Street, he had no personal knowledge of any of the events at the FDIC about which he wrote. He accepted at face value the portrayals of his nameless sources, without even contacting the FDIC for our perspective. Among the more troubling statements portrayed as uncontested facts were that WaMu had disrupted the markets and that I had kept everyone up all night fighting with regulators over whether to close Wachovia. But the one that bothered me most was his suggestion that our debt guarantee program had all been designed and put in place by Paulson, Bernanke, and Geithner, and they had sold it to me by promising that I would get the credit for it. In truth, as detailed in earlier chapters, those gentlemen originally proposed that I stand up and say the FDIC was guaranteeing all unsecured liabilities of all the major financial institutions free of charge. My staff and I pushed back and developed a program that had us guaranteeing only newly issued debt below certain caps and for which we charged a fee. Paulson and Bernanke readily agreed to that; it was really Geithner who wanted the draconian giveaway contemplated in their first proposal. But the program we put into place came from me and the FDIC, not them.

Margaret Thatcher once said that if you want something said, ask a man; if you want something done, ask a woman. Women frequently are the doers—yet when it comes time to handing out the credit for successful initiatives and programs, we are all too often given a bit role. The debt guarantee program was one of the most successful and transparent and least controversial of the bailout programs. And unlike the Fed's lending programs, the program did not add to the money supply, so there was no risk of inflationary impact down the road. We would not have offered such a program except for the pressure from the Fed and Treasury. But in the face of their insistence, we designed and implemented the program that we thought was the most responsible way to address the problem at hand: the difficulties of large financial institutions in renewing their outstanding unsecured debt. I suppose I should take it as a compliment that apparently some of them wanted to take credit for the program in Sorkin's book.

I suspected that gender bias would frequently creep into media coverage of me, and frankly, it cut both ways. I have no doubt that my ability to garner press coverage was enhanced by the fact that a woman heading a major financial agency was rare and a woman so visibly and publicly asserting herself against male colleagues even rarer. A lot of people in the media and elsewhere were rooting for me because they agreed with my policy proposals. A lot were rooting for me because I was a woman standing up to the guys.

Indeed, I believe there was a lot of sympathy for me and my views because the press perceived that my male colleagues were excluding me from important decisions and discounting my views because I was a woman. I was frequently asked by reporters whether I felt that gender discrimination played a role in the disagreements we had with the other, male-led government agencies. In truth, I'm not sure. People have their biases. I was different from my male colleagues in other ways too: I was a midwesterner, and I was a product of public schools (and proud of it). With some people in Washington, being born west of the Mississippi or attending a state university instead of an Ivy League institution can be a real disadvantage. I think there was also some arrogance toward the FDIC as an agency. The other regulators looked at us as the agency that took care of the little banks and depositors with less than $100,000. They may have felt superior because they viewed their role as dealing with the "big institutions," while we were supposed to take care of the "little guys."

There's always something that people are going to use to judge you, and there's nothing you can do about it. So my philosophy has been to just keep at it, do your homework, make your arguments, and don't back down. When young women ask me how to navigate through male-dominated power structures, I tell them that they should first forget about whether they are being discriminated against, because they will never know and they will drive themselves crazy wondering about it. Instead, they should be prepared, hone their arguments, try to build alliances, and, above all, demand to be heard and recognized. I think the best thing that women can do for one another in male-dominated situations is to support one another's right to be heard and assign credit to a woman when she has sponsored an idea or argument that prevails. I cannot tell you how many times I have been at meetings where I, or another woman, have made a point or proffered an idea that is met with dead silence. Then, ten minutes later, some guy says exactly the same thing and all the other guys in the room nod their heads and voice agreement. As women, we do not, and should not, feel obliged to always agree with one another. But we should support one another's right to be heard and receive credit by saying in such situations, "Yes, Jane just made that point ten minutes ago."

Reporters' perception of gender bias against me did help foster sympathetic press coverage. On the other hand, I think some of the coverage tried to personalize my motives instead of focusing on my policy positions. I have observed that tendency in the coverage of other women officials as well. Instead of ascribing our assertiveness to our desire to achieve a policy result, it is said that we are "difficult" or "not a team player" or that we are power-crazed or divas crying for media attention. I saw that kind of personalization creep into a number of stories about my leadership of the FDIC. It was frustrating to me because there were important public policy issues at stake in my disagreements with my colleagues. They deserved to be vetted and aired, not trivialized as petty personality disputes.

Of course, some of my detractors tried to feed that line of attack. When the hard-liners went after me on loan mods toward the end of the Bush administration, they whispered that I was difficult and wanted my pro-

gram or no program at all. They didn't talk about the very real differences
in views about the damage wide-scale foreclosures would cause to our housing market and broader economy. Those were the same folks who were saying that foreclosures wouldn't create downward pressure on home prices. It
reminded me of the line of attack used against CFTC Chairman Brooksley
Born's attempts to regulate over-the-counter derivatives markets in the late
1990s. Her opponents undermined her not by challenging the validity of
her policy position but by suggesting that she was "difficult" and "not a team
player." Regrettably, some in the press lapped it up.

Good reporters would fall prey to this kind of press angle. I will never
forget a front-page *New York Times* story about the "feud" between me and
John Dugan. Important policy differences between us on regulatory reform,
bailouts, and my efforts to secure management changes at Citigroup were
all boiled down to personality disputes. Similarly, when Tim tried to derail
the FDIC's independent rule making regarding reforms to the securitization market, *The Wall Street Journal* ran a story focusing on the "infighting"
and openly wondering whether regulators could work well together. Missing from the story was any meaningful analysis of the policy dispute over
requiring securitizers to retain some stake in the performance of loans they
package and sell to investors, as well as the propriety of the Treasury secretary interfering with the rule making of an independent agency.

It might be easier and more salacious for the press to cover personalities
instead of policies (and some of that may be more attributable to editors
trying to sell newspapers than the reporters themselves). But the problem
with that kind of media bias is that it reinforces the already considerable
pressure on financial regulators to conform to groupthink and not make
waves. Groupthink is exactly what led us into the crisis. First we were all
under pressure to believe in the merits of self-correcting markets and light-
touch regulation. Then, when the housing market started going south, the
conformist view was that subprime was contained. Finally, when the system
started to crash around us, the party line was to save Citi and the other mismanaged banks. Fixing the root cause of the problem—the mortgages—was
just too hard. We could write big checks to help deadbeat financial institutions, but we shouldn't spend any real money on home owners. That was
too controversial.

Now that I've duly chastised the press corps for personalizing policy disputes, let me also admit that some of that coverage was pretty darn funny.
The most hilarious came from the *New York Post,* which loved to caricature

my fights with Geithner and his ally John Dugan. One story, recounting my attempts to replace Citi's management, portrayed Tim Geithner as the Joker and me as Batgirl. Another, referencing my disagreements with John Dugan over restricting private-equity investments in banks, slapped my face on a cartoon picture of the Incredible Hulk and showed me holding Dugan in a very sensitive part of his body.

Photographers can be the bane of a female public figure's existence. It was amazing to me how the photos or drawings accompanying a story could do more to help or damage my message and actions than the story itself. I do think people tend to judge women more on their physical appearance, though certainly men can also be subject to hurtful comments and scrutiny of their physiques. New Jersey Governor Chris Christie, for instance, has frequently spoken about the harshness—and irrelevance—of commentary about his weight.

In 2007, Joe Nocera at *The New York Times* wrote a column on my early advocacy of mortgage modifications. It was a good, thorough piece but had the absolutely worst picture of me ever taken—a floor angle focusing in on my middle-aged neck. I had a big frown on my face. I would say that of the feedback I received on that piece, 10 percent was about my housing program suggestions and 90 percent was about the awful picture! A few years later, the *Financial Times Magazine* did a story about our bank resolution process with me strongly condemning bailouts of big financial institutions. The photographer took a picture of me in our lobby in front of a large wall sculpture of the American Eagle. I didn't know it, but he had positioned me so that my body blocked the eagle's torso. Only the wings were visible behind me, appearing to sprout from my shoulders. The photo made me look like an avenging angel.

Every once in awhile, both the story and the picture were positive. Some of the best pictures—and stories—ever published of me appeared in Ann Moore's *Time* magazine. I had the amazing privilege of appearing in a cover story in *Time* along with Mary Schapiro and Elizabeth Warren, entitled "The New Sheriffs of Wall Street." I was somewhat amused by the title, because though Mary and Elizabeth were new Obama appointees, I had already been around for three years when the story ran and had the battle scars to prove it. Similarly, *Time*'s previous coverage of me, in a 2008 profile piece, as well as when it put me on its "*Time* 100" list in 2009, included very nice stories and pictures—no cheap shots. But my favorite profile was a piece published in *The New Yorker*, written by Ryan Lizza. Lizza took the time to dig down into my Kansas upbringing and Republican populist philosophy. I felt that Lizza "got me," and the picture, while not particularly flattering, captured, I thought, my determination to protect the "little guys."

Sometimes physical appearance prevailed over content. In late 2008, Andrew was contacted by *Vogue* magazine. The people there said they were planning a women's "power" issue and wanted to include me. *Vogue* is renowned for making it subjects look beautiful. It sends in a team that includes wardrobe, hair, and makeup artists. Everything is done for you. I should have known better—they wanted a big time commitment—but I couldn't resist saying yes. I had been working hard, so I figured I owed myself that one indulgence.

I spent a few hours the night before the scheduled shoot with *Vogue*'s beauty experts, trying on clothes, shoes, and jewelry. They settled on a grey silk Armani suit, by far the most expensive thing I have ever worn in my life. The next morning they arrived early and spent hours more doing my hair and makeup. Then the photo shoot began. I adored the photographer. He was a real classic, wearing a tailored sports jacket over designer jeans, his neck wrapped in an expensive silk ascot. During the whole shoot, he chomped on an unlit cigar. He shot me in my office in all sorts of contorted poses. Then we went out to the FDIC balcony in the freezing cold, where he shot me with the Washington Monument and White House as our backdrop. I was shivering uncontrollably, and I kept falling off the stiletto-heeled Bruno Magli pumps they had given me to wear. (My own shoe heels seldom go higher than two inches.) He was a perfectionist, and that went on for most of the morning until Andrew finally told him he had to stop.

Notwithstanding the pain and torture of the photo shoot, I was like a schoolgirl, giddy over my upcoming appearance in *Vogue*'s glossy pages, and I made the mistake of telling several friends about it and getting everyone's expectations up. I just couldn't imagine that *Vogue* would approach me and put me through all of that without following through. Then the call came to Andrew. They were bumping me in the "power" issue for Michelle Obama, and they didn't want to have more than one woman from Washington. Fine, Andrew said, we certainly could understand that, but the pictures would appear in a later issue, right? No, they said, they would never publish the pictures, but they offered to put them online if we wanted. After all of that, we politely declined. Could I at least get copies of the pictures they took? No, they said.

Later, it was leaked by one of the *Vogue* editors that *Vogue*'s leadership didn't think I was attractive enough to appear in *Vogue*. But at least one of the photos somehow made it into print. Oprah Winfrey's *O, the Oprah Magazine* published one as part of her "power" issue. I guess *O*'s editors have different criteria for an appearance in their magazine.

The *Vogue* and Sorkin experiences were hurtful, but the media is populated with people who, like all human beings, have their preconceptions and biases. Sometimes folks just take a disliking to you, and there is nothing you can do about it. Though I thought (and still think) that Sorkin's coverage of me and the FDIC was unfair, I tried to develop some semblance of a positive relationship with him. I made courtesy calls on him when I was in New York and gave him signed copies of my children's books for his newborn twins. We've since had some positive interactions. Most important, he has supported many of the same policies we have surrounding resolution authority and ending too big to fail.

Sometimes, adverse media attention can be a little more nefarious. Industry-backed operatives can purposefully try to stir up problems for government officials. Because reporters never divulge their sources, one never knows for sure. Certainly I found it curious that Citigroup hired a Washington "insider" known for his skills in spreading negative information about government officials to reporters just a few months before a so-called investigative online journalist ran a mud-slinging story about my family's finances, as recounted in chapter 18.

That whole episode was one of the most difficult of my FDIC tenure. It gave me chills to think that people were out there investigating me and my family. I had taken hits in the press before, but they had always been targeted at my policies and decisions or my personal style of leadership. They had never questioned my integrity and had never brought my family into it; that was the only instance when that happened. In reacting to the story, Chris Whalen, a well-known financial analyst and commentator, stated:

> This article suggests to me that there is a complete breakdown in the internal systems and controls at HPIF [Huffington Post Investigative Fund]. Were it not for the fact that Chairman Bair was a public official, in my view the HPIF would surely be facing a liable [*sic*] litigation for this malicious and unwarranted attack.

Under the First Amendment, public figures have to meet a very high standard of proof to prevail in a libel action against malicious, untrue reporting, which makes us vulnerable to reporters with weak journalistic standards. With the advent of the Internet, it has become much easier for journalists of all stripes to publish their stories, without the rigorous checks and screens carried out by more traditional publications. That is why I have taken such pains to recount the whole sorry episode. If we want good people to undertake public service, if we want them to stand up and exercise independence of judgment from the industry they regulate, if we want them to have the courage to defy the monied interests and risk antagonizing them by telling them "no," journalists need to view with a jaundiced eye the dirt and scuttlebutt brought to them by industry-paid "insiders." Though I realize that journalists view their sources as sacrosanct, when the impetus of a story is provided by a paid industry operative, I think that fact should be disclosed. I strongly suspect that that was the case here. But I will never know.

As challenging as it was to be in the public and media spotlight, public recognition also had its rewards. I was privileged to be the recipient of numerous awards honoring our early warnings about the coming subprime debacle and early advocacy for aggressive intervention to prevent unnecessary foreclosures. Probably the most prestigious of these was the John F. Kennedy Presidential Library's Profiles in Courage award granted in 2009 to me, Brooksley Born, and Leymah Gbowee, an activist fighting violence against women in Liberia's horrific civil war. The John F. Kennedy Presidential Library and Museum hosted a private viewing of the Kennedy family artifacts for the honorees and a black-tie dinner the evening before the awards ceremony. I took Colleen—then nine—with me. She had read a children's picture book about Caroline Kennedy and the pony she used to ride on the White House lawn during her father's presidential term. Colleen was surprised when I introduced her to Caroline—she had pictured the young girl in her book!

Caroline was gracious enough to take us around the museum and share personal reflections of her father. The Kennedy years were truly a magical time, and I was glad that my daughter had that wonderful chance to experience them through Caroline's eyes. The next morning we all trooped onto a stage in the library's auditorium to receive our awards from Caroline and provide brief remarks. It was a moving experience for me. I have never thought of myself as particularly courageous; I just act when I think something needs to be done. As I said when accepting the award:

> We weren't trying to be significant or to do something great or even courageous. We were just trying to do something that seemed like basic common sense. But seeing what was happening, we couldn't stand on the sidelines and be insignificant, by doing nothing.

There is a wonderful line in the movie *The Iron Lady* when a young woman approaches the very elderly Margaret Thatcher and thanks her for being such a great role model. Thatcher, played by Meryl Streep, smiles and tells her, "Back then it was about doing. Today it's about being."

It mystifies me why people take government jobs if they don't want to act for the common good. That's what taxpayers pay us for. Some government officials today, I think, just want to "be"—they want the title, the office, the trappings of power. But they don't "do," particularly if it risks their reelection prospects.

Our "doing" at the FDIC garnered many more awards and other recognitions. The Leadership Conference on Civil and Human Rights gave me its highest honor, the Hubert H. Humphrey Award. My old boss, Senator Dole, joined me on the stage when I received the award and delivered a moving tribute to my FDIC record. I could barely contain my emotion. More than two decades earlier, as a young staff aide, I had watched him receive the same award from the Leadership Conference for his courage in steering the Voting Rights Act extension through Congress.

Probably the most frequently cited accolade was my being named by *Forbes* magazine as the second most powerful woman in the world for two years running. I remember speaking to my daughter's elementary school. The principal mentioned the honor in his introduction of me. After I spoke to the girls about the basics of banking and deposit insurance, I opened the floor to questions. "Who is number one?" they eagerly asked. (Answer: Germany's Angela Merkel.) It is very hard to impress kids these days.

There were many others. I was the top "woman to watch" in *The Wall Street Journal* one year and was included in *SmartMoney*'s Power 30 for several years, as well as the *Time* 100 and *Fortune* magazine's "power list." I received awards from the Better Business Bureau, as well as numerous consumer groups, including the California Reinvestment Coalition, Operation Hope, and the biggest of all, the Consumer Federation of America. I was the only bank regulator ever to be given a consumer award by that group.

Some of the awards and honors were less high profile, but I treasured them all as proof that "doing," even if controversial, was appreciated by the American people. The awards also frequently brought me into contact with interesting personalities. For instance, on May 26, 2009, I was awarded the Burton Foundation's first annual Regulatory Innovation Award at the Library of Congress. I was sitting backstage in the greenroom, waiting for my turn to go onstage to receive the honor. A woman who looked just like Michelle Pfeiffer was sitting next to me as we watched the ceremony on a closed-circuit monitor. We made polite chitchat, and I almost commented on her striking resemblance to Michelle Pfeiffer until I realized she *was* Michelle Pfeiffer. Her husband, a screenwriter, was also getting an award.

At another big Washington dinner, I found myself sitting at a table with Scarlett Johansson. I watched in dismay as several dozen Washington "wheels" stood in line like schoolboys, waiting to ask her if she would pose for a picture with them as their friends' cell-phone cameras clicked away. (She was gracious and accommodated all of them.) At another event, sponsored by California First Lady Maria Shriver, I appeared on a panel with Governor Schwarzenegger and Virgin Air CEO Richard Branson. The female-dominated audience was giving me the lion's share of applause, prompting tongue-in-cheek complaints from Branson that I was unfairly benefiting from my gender.

My frequent television appearances made my face somewhat recognizable to the general public. It gave me a little sense of what movie stars and other well-known media figures must experience every time they venture from their homes. Celebrity is a little disquieting, though usually people are very polite and complimentary. It makes me feel great when someone comes up to me at the grocery store or in a restaurant and thanks me for the job I did at the FDIC.

Sometimes you aren't sure whether they are going to be friendly or hostile. In 2010, my husband and I were heading into the Capital Hilton in Washington for the annual black-tie dinner hosted by the White House correspondents. The dinner is a big deal in Washington. The president and first lady attend, and virtually all of the who's who in Washington are there. As we were approaching the hotel, I saw a large demonstration of activists from Codepink, an antiwar group made up mostly of women. They were shouting at a number of administration officials and members of Congress about bringing our troops home from Afghanistan. The group looked a bit cranky, so I squeezed Scott's hand and whispered, "Let's hurry." We were almost past them when a woman shouted, "Hey, there's Sheila Bair!" Uh-oh, I thought, are they going to go after me on the bailouts? I decided to stop. I turned and smiled. Whether they were friend or foe, that seemed like the right move. Then I heard a number of voices call out, "We love you, Sheila! Give it to 'em, Sheila!" I was one relieved banking regulator. I smiled again and waved as Scott and I strolled into the hotel.

CHAPTER 25

Farewell to the FDIC

O ur vice chairman, Marty Gruenberg, took the lead in organizing farewell festivities for my departure. I told him that I wanted one big celebration. I knew it was going to be an emotional departure, so I wanted all of our good-byes said at once. We decided to have the farewell program in a large conference facility located in our offices in northern Virginia on July 7, the day before my departure. I wanted all D.C.-area staff invited, even if we had to set up overflow rooms, and I also wanted the program webcast to our regional and field offices so they could watch it. Every person in the FDIC organization had made a contribution to getting us through one of the most challenging times in the FDIC's history, and I wanted as many of them with me as possible.

I had already completed a round of trips to our six regional offices for teary-eyed farewells to the staff in the field. At every office I was met by lines of staff wanting to say a few words of appreciation and have their picture taken with me. I was regaled with gifts: a Chicago Cubs jersey and a Chicago White Sox hat from our sports-team-conflicted Chicago office; a food basket of southern delights from our Dallas office, known for its robust eating habits, particularly among the resolutions staff (closing banks works up an appetite); a picture of me with a group of examiners I had once accompanied to a bank examination in Atlanta; and a crystal replica of the Empire State Building, the location of our New York offices, from our New York staff.

Looking back, I wish that I had spent more time in our regional offices. I always learned a lot about local economic and banking conditions when I visited our outstanding staff in the field. Though I did make several trips to our regional outposts, the intense demands of my job kept me tethered mostly to Washington. Not only did I learn a lot about local conditions during my trips, but I just enjoyed meeting the people. Once I met a woman who worked in our Kansas City office whose husband had been a blind student at the University of Kansas when I went to school there. As an undergraduate student, I'd had a job reading to him. Talk about a small world! Many of our employees were actively engaged in altruistic endeavors, volunteering on their own time, for instance, to teach financial education in the schools. We had a special award we gave out each year recognizing employees who donated their time to volunteer.

In addition to my farewells at the FDIC, I also had a final round of speeches to make to various industry groups. They included the American Bankers Association's annual Government Relations Conference in Washington and the Independent Community Bankers of America's annual meeting in San Diego. I had spoken at each of those conferences every year during my five-year tenure at the FDIC. I thought carefully about my remarks for each of the events. It would be my last opportunity to engage those industry groups as a public official.

My relationship with the ICBA was much more positive than my relationship with the ABA. Throughout my tenure at the FDIC, I had found that the ICBA was more constructive in its approach to regulation and dealings with regulators than the combative ABA. To be sure, we had had our disagreements with both groups. The ICBA thought our examiners were too harsh on commercial real estate loans, and they criticized our efforts to curb the imposition of overdraft fees, which can cost bank customers thousands of dollars a year. But the ICBA also embraced our quest to end too big to fail and our efforts to significantly raise the capital requirements of large banks. It also supported the changes we made to the way deposit insurance premiums are assessed to shift more of the burden to high-risk big banks. The ABA, on the other hand, seldom supported us on anything. What's more, it seemed more interested in protecting the interests of megabanks, with their far-flung securities and derivatives activities, than it did in advocating the interests of the traditional banker. It had replaced its director of many years, Ed Yingling, a well-regarded banking attorney, with Frank Keating, a professional Washington lobbyist known for his combative, antiregulation views. Under Keating, the ABA had become even more hostile to any regulator who dared to express views independent of the industry's.

Notwithstanding our differences with the ABA over the years, I had always received a warm reception from the bankers who attended its Government Relations Conference. (I usually found it easier to deal with the bankers directly, rather than with their hired Washington guns.) But I was dismayed at some of the hardball (and ineffective) tactics ABA representatives had used during the battles over Dodd-Frank. Now, as the regulators were trying to implement the law, they were also virulently opposing most of the new rules.

So, in consultation with my staff, I decided to challenge them a bit on their attitude toward regulation. Rich Brown, our chief economist, who was also a fantastic speechwriter, worked with me to craft an artful speech that politely but firmly told them that good regulation was in the interests of responsibly managed banks by protecting them from the lax practices of the risk takers. Many once well-run banks had ended up succumbing to bad mortgage-lending practices because of competitive pressure from the shadow sector. If regulators had stepped in earlier, many of the abuses could have been prevented. We wrote in the speech:

> We need to get past rhetoric that implies that, when it comes to financial services, the best regulation is always *less* regulation. We need to stand together on the principle that prudential standards are essential to protect the competitive position of responsible players from the excesses of the high-fliers. And I would very much like to hear from the industry a constructive regulatory agenda that would use the provisions of Dodd-Frank to fix the problems that led to the crisis and help to protect consumers and preserve financial stability in the years ahead.

Based on research showing that the general public had a very low view of bankers, the speech stated:

> I would like to propose to you a radical-sounding notion. And it is that increasing the size and profitability of the financial services industry is not—and should not be—the main goal of our national economic policy.
>
> . . . in policy terms, the success of the financial sector is not an end in itself, but a means to an end—which is to support the vitality of the real economy and the livelihood of the American people.

The speech concluded:

> Every one of your branches prominently displays the FDIC seal. It is a symbol of public confidence that assures the public that their money is safe if your institution should fail. But that seal also carries with it the expectation of your customers that they will be treated fairly and protected from unsuitable loan products and hidden service charges.
>
> That public trust is sacred, and it is the very foundation of the long-term success of your industry.

It was a good speech, honest and heartfelt, designed to appeal to the better instincts of the industry. I wasn't sure about the reaction I would get, but what I said in the speech needed to be said.

I was actually nervous when I arrived at the Washington hotel where the conference was being held. As I'd given scores of speeches throughout my tenure at the FDIC, the butterflies I'd used to have when speaking in public had long since passed. But that time, I knew I was taking a risk. I was hoping that the group would listen to me and carefully consider what I was saying. But some of the points in the speech would obviously make them feel uncomfortable. As I entered the conference room, CNBC's Larry Kudlow was just wrapping up his remarks. I like Larry. I've known him for years, and I have appeared on his show several times. But he is not a fan of regulation, and he was whipping up the audience with antigovernment sentiments. He would be a difficult act to follow.

As I approached the podium, I started to lose confidence. For a moment I thought about scrapping the speech and just talking off the cuff. But no, I said to myself, I was going to do this. I wiped my moist palms on the skirt of my suit and took a sip from the water glass that stood on the podium. The crowd became silent. I read the speech word for word.

The applause at the end of the speech was weak and scattered. Audience members were casting glances at one another. I began taking questions, and they were clearly hostile. I was disappointed that almost all of the questions focused on our efforts to curb the excessive fees that were being charged bank customers when they overdrew their accounts. Alarmed about the thousands of dollars some customers were paying each year on overdrafts, we had issued a policy stating that overdraft fees should not exceed six in a twelve-month period and that if a bank customer was overdrawing his or her account more often than that, the bank should offer a less costly alternative for overdraft protection, such as linking the account to a lower-cost line of credit. All too many banks were reaping fat fees by charging financially strapped customers $35 each time they overdrew their account, even if the overdraft was just a few dollars. We also told banks that they could not sequence overdraft checks to maximize fees. When a customer wrote several checks that came through the bank on a single day, some banks would purposefully clear the largest check first, to create a negative balance. Then they would charge an overdraft fee for each of the smaller checks that they paid after the largest one. The guidance said that that practice had to stop.

I had been hoping for a discussion about the broader role of banks in supporting the economy, the lessons of the crisis, how we could work together for commonsense rules that would give all of us a more stable, productive financial system. Instead, I received a lot of heckling from bankers focused primarily on their narrow interests in maintaining fat overdraft fees. I later learned that the ABA leadership had whipped them up prior to the speech to confront me on the issue. It was disheartening. I had been expecting much better from the group.

CNBC filmed the combative heckling I received, and it went viral on the Web. Ironically, unpopular bankers bashing a regulator made me a hero. The speech received much more media play than it would have if I had received a civilized response.

The reception I had at the ICBA was completely different. My speech to the ICBA emphasized many of the same themes but also recognized the more constructive role the ICBA had played during the debates over Dodd-Frank as well as how it had tried to work with us in curbing overdraft fee abuses. In contrast to the ABA, which was run by a professional lobbyist, the ICBA was run by a community banker, Cam Fine. Cam is one of the most reputable, credible, and effective advocates for community banks in Washington. He is a big reason why so many of Dodd-Frank's new rules expressly exempt smaller institutions, as is appropriate. The ICBA also played a role in increasing the deposit insurance limits and shifting the premium burden more toward the megabanks. Fine did not have a conflicted membership, as did the ABA. Those were all provisions that clearly benefited smaller banks and will strengthen their competitive position over time.

The ICBA convention was held in a cavernous hall in the San Diego Convention Center. Thousands were in attendance. I was tired and jet-lagged, having arrived late the night before, but I was determined to give a good speech. The small banks, like so many others, had been the victims of the crisis, not its cause. They had struggled to serve communities ravaged by the Great Recession, even as they kept lending during the crisis. Though we had also had our disagreements, I wanted to pay them tribute for the remarkable courage and perseverance they had shown in weathering the terrible financial storm.

ICBA Chairman James MacPhee, the chief executive of Kalamazoo County State Bank in Schoolcraft, Michigan, gave me a very warm introduction, calling me a champion of community banks. I began my speech with a personal anecdote about growing up in a small town in southeast Kansas. When I was small, I used to love going to the local bank with my dad every Friday afternoon when he deposited checks from his medical practice. I was always fascinated with the large, steel vault that stood against the back wall of the bank lobby. One day, as we were waiting in the line for the teller, I saw that the vault door was open a crack, so I sneaked back to take a peek. Expecting to see mounds of cash, I instead saw rows of safety deposit boxes. I went running back to my dad, shouting, "There's no money in the bank!," which caused the bank president to hurry out of his office to assure everyone that their money was safe. "Ironic," I said, "that a six-year-old who nearly instigated a bank run that day would later become Chairman of the Federal Deposit Insurance Corporation."

The anecdote drew huge applause, and after that, it was a lovefest. My remarks were frequently interrupted by applause, and I received two standing ovations.

Feeling generous after the ICBA speech and not wanting to depart office on a sour note with anyone, I asked Jesse to reach out to Frank Keating's office to see if he would like to meet. Jesse contacted Wayne Abernathy, whom I knew well from his years as the staff director of the Senate Banking Committee. Working with Wayne, Jesse had tentatively arranged a meeting for Keating and me, but we decided to cancel it when Keating took public shots at me again in an interview with Barbara Rehm of *American Banker*. Rehm asked Keating whether he regretted the reception I had received at the ABA, contrasting it to the support I had received at the ICBA. His response, I kid you not:

> Quite truthfully I thought everyone handled themselves very well. . . . Nobody booed and nobody hissed. Sheila Bair came in and was, how do I say it diplomatically, aggressive to say the least in her prepared remarks, which rather puzzled me. These are regulated people who pay your salary. . . .
>
> No one gave her a standing ovation because no government official should ever be given a standing ovation, in my judgment. I feel very strongly about that. We are servants of the served.

Frightening, but that is how a lot of industry lobbyists see the role of regulators. We do not have our jobs to serve the public. The banks pay our salary, so we work for them—not the taxpayers, not the customers—the banks. And gosh forbid that anyone would ever thank us for the job we are doing.

I was also asked to speak to the National Press Club to provide farewell remarks to the media with which we had so closely worked over the years. I gave a speech about what I thought to be a core problem in today's American culture, not just our financial system but our political system as well. Again working with Rich, we crafted a wonderful speech on the theme of "short-termism," or the tendency to make decisions based on our immediate needs or desires without regard to the long-term consequences. Short-termism was rampant during the crisis, with loan originators, securitizers, ratings agencies, financial executives, and derivatives deal makers all being paid up front for loans and complex securities that had no hope of performing over the longer term. Today our government is also stuck in the vise of short-termism, with action (or more likely inaction) being based on short-term reelection prospects instead of the long-term needs of the nation's economy. As I stated:

> In a world obsessed with instant gratification and lightning-round debates, we are in dire need of leadership, both public and private, that will champion patience and sacrifice now in return for a brighter and more stable future for us and our progeny.

I followed the speech with an op-ed in *The Washington Post,* and I frequently warn against short-termism in my public speeches. It really is the common theme that impedes the proper functioning of both our financial and our political systems. Many of the reforms regulators are now trying to put into place will eat into the short-term profits—and share prices—of some large financial institutions, but they will provide a much more stable system over the long term. Yet short-term profit motives drive the relentless lobbying against commonsense measures such as higher capital standards. Similarly, we are borrowing trillions of dollars to finance increasingly generous public benefits and entitlement programs, while at the same time keeping our taxes at historically low levels. We can keep it up for a time, but eventually we will pay the price—or, more correctly, our kids will pay the price through reduced benefits, higher taxes, and the risk of uncontrollable inflation.

My final farewell party was everything I'd hoped for. Hank Paulson, now engaged in philanthropic work at Johns Hopkins University, reached out to me to wish me luck and offered to help me once I left the government. Notwithstanding our ups and downs, Hank and I had a good working relationship. It's easy to second-guess now, and to be sure, looking back, I wish we had done some things differently. The important point is that in the fall and winter of 2008, we had to do something, as the system was potentially "on the brink," as Hank says in his book. Hank showed leadership and took decisive action when the nation needed it. And I think history will treat his actions well.

I told him I wanted him, Ben, and Tim to attend my farewell party. Even though there were tensions among us, we were the four who had locked arms and gotten the nation through the crisis of 2008. I wanted one last reunion before I stepped down. He readily agreed and even persuaded Tim to come and speak at the ceremony. Ben also readily agreed. And in a surprise gesture, President Obama sent an emissary, his close friend and adviser Valerie Jarrett, who delivered a message from him.

We invited my old boss Senator Bob Dole and his wife, Elizabeth, as well as a number of other current and former members of Congress. I was very glad to see Senator Paul Sarbanes there, as well as several former FDIC chairmen, including Don Powell and William Isaac. We included all of the agency heads, past and present, including the ones I had butted heads with, such as John Dugan and John Walsh. And of course, hundreds of FDIC staff were there. We also invited several bankers and consumer group representatives who had worked with us over the years, including PNC's Jim Rohr.

Marty opened the program with touching remarks about our years together. He had been through the wars with me, and I was so pleased to see that President Obama would nominate him to succeed me as chairman. Next was Valerie, who jokingly referred to John Reich's famous email referring to the "audacity of that woman." Obama, she said, whose second book had been entitled *The Audacity of Hope: Thoughts on Reclaiming the American Dream,* had known immediately that he would like me. As dictated by protocol, Tim, as Treasury secretary, went next, drawing a good laugh when he told the crowd that notwithstanding what they might have heard, he had *not* been the author of that email. He downplayed our disagreements and paid tribute to the outstanding job the FDIC had done during the crisis. It was a smart, classy move on his part.

Ben, with his own droll sense of humor, went next. Noting that we had assumed our respective chairmanships in the same year, he said he appreciated my "creativity and courage" and joked that perhaps the NY Fed— which has published comic books for kids about financial matters—should publish a comic book about me, because I was "truly a woman of steel." He laughed about all of our midnight calls during the crisis and said he would miss my thoughtful insights, though with a twinkle in his eye, he commented that he was sure I would still be speaking out in my next position.

Finally Hank wrapped up, joking about the disagreements we had had over foreclosure prevention and telling people that I had felt so strongly about it, I had once tracked him down at Camp David and interrupted a meeting with the president to press him on approving a loan modification program. He acknowledged that we had frequently disagreed—sometimes vocally—but said he admired my sincerity, integrity, and intensity. He said that I "always came to play" and that I was the kind of person who would "not let a day go by without doing something to make a difference. That was Sheila."

I, of course, spoke last, with four very hard acts to follow. I drew a laugh when I said I was going to make it short because I didn't want to start crying and ruin my reputation as a toughie. I began with a tribute to my family and apologized for all of the things I had missed over the past five years. I recounted how I had attended my son's high school graduation dinner a few months earlier and had hardly known any of his teachers, his friends, or their parents. I reflected on how intense and insular the job had been and joked that when Preston had asked me what I thought of the Casey Anthony verdict, I'd asked, "Who's he?" I apologized to Colleen for missing almost all of the mother-daughter days at her school, as well as her choir and orchestra concerts (she plays the oboe). And I thanked my husband, Scott, for going to every one of them in my stead. I have said it many times, but I am married to a saint. Because he took the extra time to fill in with family duties, neither of our kids resents the five years I was missing in action from so many parental duties.

I also commented on the recent HBO movie *Too Big to Fail,* based roughly on Sorkin's book of the same title, as well as Hank's own memoir, *On the Brink: Inside the Race to Stop the Collapse of the Global Financial System.* I complimented my three amigos on the wonderful actors who had played them: Paul Giamatti, Ben; Billy Crudup, Tim; and William Hurt, Hank. "What woman of my age doesn't remember William Hurt in the movie *Altered States*?" I joked, referring to a 1980 movie in which Hurt had frequently appeared partly clad. Then I scratched my head and asked, "Who was that actress who played me during the ten seconds I was in the movie?" Then I added, "No matter, maybe they will make a real movie out of my book."

On a more serious note, I cautioned my fellow regulators about the need for writing clear, simple, easy-to-explain rules as part of financial reform, as well as engaging with the media to explain them publicly. I warned that the only way to counter industry lobbying against the rules was to make sure the public understood and supported them. "If the public does not support reforms, they will not succeed." I reflected on all of the mistakes that had been made during the years prior to the crisis and the need for common sense to prevail in regulating the markets.

Finally I paid tribute to the most important part of the audience, the FDIC staff, at which point the tears broke through, notwithstanding my resolve to contain them: "We've been through an incredible journey together. I've reached my port and I will be leaving you now, but I know you will carry on without me."

Following the program, scores of FDIC staff and other attendees lined up to shake my hand. Many asked me to sign their programs and have their pictures taken with them. After about twenty minutes of that, I caught out of the corner of my eye a towering African-American gentleman waiting patiently in line. It was Citi's Dick Parsons. I excused myself for a minute and walked back to the line to shake his hand and thank him for coming. I then returned to the head of the line and resumed the handshaking and picture taking.

After about an hour or so, the line started to thin, and three FDIC staffers—Pattie Lewis, Margaret Foster-Massey, and Mardie Amery— sheepishly approached me, asking if they could sing a song for me. Mardie had written the lyrics to the tune of "My Country, 'Tis of Thee." It is too precious not to quote in total here:

ODE TO SHEILA BAIR

Oh Sheila Bair, 'tis thee
Who saved the FDIC
For all these years
When banks were falling fast
She hoisted up the mast
Said we will not repeat the past
We will persevere

She made *Time* magazine
Forbes ranked her Power Queen
Of all the world
She warned of subprime loans
Listened to bankers' groans
Our financial Rosetta Stone
Her advice was sound

Now she'll have family time
Scott and the kids will find
She's lots of fun
No banks to make her sigh
With regs they won't comply
She's free just like a butterfly
Wander where she will

Thank you for all you've done
You were our number one
We're so grateful
No runs on banks we had
Your guidance was ironclad
We'll miss you but for you, we're glad
We wish you the best!

CHAPTER 26

How Main Street Can Tame Wall Street

Financial concepts are not that difficult if you have a little time to study them. The problems that drove the crisis—excess leverage, unbridled speculation, lack of basic consumer safeguards—are really not that hard to understand. Sometimes I think people in the financial sector don't want you to understand the issues. Of course, if Main Street voters are confused or don't feel they understand the problems, they are unlikely to exert political influence to correct those problems. That only serves the purposes of the bad actors, who do not want meaningful government protections against their risk taking.

Below is my list of reforms that I think are the most important to ensuring the stability of our financial system. I've divided them into three categories: things that will make our financial institutions work better; things that will make our regulators work better; and things that will make our entire financial system work better.

In making our financial institutions work better, I have long believed that the most successful regulations are those that create the right economic incentives and let market forces do the rest. That is why I like skin-in-the-game requirements—because they force market participants to put their own money at risk and suffer the consequences if their actions result in financial loss. Resolution authority, higher capital requirements, risk retention—all are examples of regulatory initiatives that are designed to create the certainty of financial loss if an institution's financial risk taking goes awry. Understanding that they—not taxpayers or consumers—will take losses resulting from their imprudent behavior, financial institutions and those who invest in them will have better incentives to curb their risk taking.

With resolution authority, Dodd-Frank was designed to make clear to stakeholders—the shareholders and creditors—that they will absorb the attendant losses if the institution they have invested in fails. It also makes clear to boards and management that they will lose their jobs and that those executives materially responsible for the failure will lose their last two years' worth of compensation. In that way, we created stronger economic incentives for investors as well as boards and executives to monitor and control excessive risk taking in their institutions.

Similarly, with higher capital requirements, the bank's owners—for whom the bank's board and executives work—are forced to put more of their own money at risk, which again will give them more incentives to monitor risk taking. In addition, risk retention requires securitizers to absorb some percentage of the loss each time a loan they have securitized goes bad. Knowing that they will be responsible for future losses, the securitizers will exercise more care in the quality of the loans they securitize.

Other types of regulations—those that seek to define the kinds of activities that are allowed and not allowed among market participants—are also important but less effective in my view. For instance, a lending standard for banks says that they must make sure the borrower can afford the higher payment when the interest rate goes up on an adjustable-rate mortgage. That is a way of restricting behavior among mortgage lenders.

However, there will inevitably be a degree of subjectivity in this standard. What is "affordable"? How big can mortgage payments be as a percentage of a borrower's income? Can the lender take into account likely future salary increases for the borrower in determining whether he or she will be able to afford the higher interest rate? The more regulators try to answer those questions, the more prescriptive the rules become, adding complexity, new opportunities for gaming, and unnecessary constraints on beneficial product innovation. But tell a mortgage lender that whatever lending standard it uses, it will be on the hook for 5 to 10 percent of the losses if the borrower can't afford his adjusted payments, the lender will have economic incentives to resolve those issues on his own in a way that reduces the likelihood that the borrower will default.

THINGS THAT WILL MAKE OUR FINANCIAL INSTITUTIONS WORK BETTER

Raise Capital Requirements

It is essential that regulators throughout the world fully implement the new Basel III agreements, as well as impose the additional SIFI surcharges for extra capital on the world's largest banks. If anything, the new Basel standards should be tougher, not weaker. Yet there is relentless industry pressure throughout the globe to dial them back. Main Street needs to weigh in with counterpressure.

I have spent a lot of time discussing capital requirements in this book. Among responsible people—conservative and liberal, Republican and Democrat—there is widespread recognition that reducing leverage is the best way to stabilize the financial system and lower the risk of failures. From Alan Greenspan to Paul Krugman, from the *Wall Street Journal* editorial board to the Huffington Post, you will find general agreement that excess leverage fueled the current crisis and higher capital requirements are the key to system stability.

Industry advocates argue primarily that higher capital standards will unduly constrict credit. They try to scare people by telling them that the rates on their mortgages or credit cards will go up if capital levels are raised. Or they say that higher capital requirements will hurt job creation by impeding the ability of businesses to borrow at reasonable rates.

Don't you believe any of it.

Healthy, well-capitalized banks will always do a better job of lending than weak, overleveraged ones. And when we have the inevitable economic downturns, banks with fat capital cushions will keep lending, while the overleveraged ones will cease lending and pull credit lines. I believe that that is why, when the crisis hit, the smaller banks as a group did a much better job of lending than did the more leveraged large banks. While the smallest banks increased their lending during the crisis, the biggest ones pulled trillions of dollars' worth of credit lines, and their loan balances declined by more than 10 percent. How many consumers' credit card lines were pulled? How many corporations and nonprofits couldn't find financing to buy new office space or expand operations? How many creditworthy entrepreneurs couldn't obtain credit to start a new business? The credit contraction that brought us the Great Recession was caused by large, overleveraged financial institutions pulling in their horns and going back to their stalls to lick their wounds. The better-capitalized smaller banks stayed in the arena, healthy enough to keep fighting.

If Congress does revisit financial reform, I hope they will look at strengthening, not weakening, Dodd-Frank on capital standards. With the exception of the Collins Amendment, Dodd-Frank did not strengthen capital requirements but rather deferred to the regulators to set the new standards. It is essential that we maintain the Collins Amendment, which prohibits regulators from letting big banks take on more leverage than is permitted for smaller institutions. The Collins Amendment also requires that bank holding companies—the organizations that own insured banks—have capital levels at least as high as their insured bank. That is the only way to ensure that the safety net provided by deposit insurance is supported by well-capitalized parents that can serve as a source of strength, not weakness, for the FDIC-insured bank you do business with.

Right now, the regulators are mostly unified on the need to raise capital requirements. However, looking back at the battles I fought before the crisis, when it seemed as though everyone except the FDIC wanted to lower capital requirements, I'm wary that this regulatory resolve will hold. As a consequence, I would like to see Congress impose a simple, hard-and-fast leverage ratio of 8 percent on any financial institution with assets of more than $50 billion. The requirement would apply not only to banks and bank holding companies but also to hedge funds, property insurance companies such as AIG, securities firms such as Lehman Brothers, commercial lenders such as CIT, and private-equity funds. An 8 percent leverage requirement would be consistent with the amount of capital healthy banks maintained up to and during the crisis. It is a simple, easy-to-enforce requirement that would bind the regulators and make all of the United States' largest financial institutions significantly safer.

Maintain the Ban on Bailouts

The FDIC has made great strides in educating the public about the mechanics of resolution authority and how it really will end bailouts for failing institutions. Yet some still try to portray this important part of Dodd-Frank as perpetuating bailouts.

Nothing could be further from the truth.

Dodd-Frank expressly prohibits the regulators from bailing out a failing institution. It requires that such institutions be placed into either bankruptcy or the FDIC's bankruptcy-like resolution process. It mandates that shareholders and creditors absorb losses, that boards and directors lose their jobs, and that institutions be broken up and sold off. About the only way a bailout of a failing institution could occur in the future is if Congress itself authorizes it, and I seriously doubt that will happen.

Those who argue that Dodd-Frank authorizes bailouts frequently point to the provisions that allow the Fed and FDIC to provide systemwide support to healthy institutions in the event of a systemic crisis. I supported those provisions as potentially necessary to keep healthy institutions open and operational when circumstances beyond their control undermine public confidence in the entire system. For instance, a terrorist attack on our financial system or the collapse of the European banking system could cause uninsured depositors or other creditors to temporarily lose confidence in all U.S. financial institutions and withdraw their funds. But recognizing that such programs could be abused as "cover" to help a sick, politically connected institution such as Citi, we pressed for tight controls on the Fed and FDIC providing this type of generally available assistance.

Ironically, big-bank advocates argue that Dodd-Frank does too much to tie the hands of government regulators. Indeed, if anything, the rules on the Fed should be tightened. My deepest fear is that in true Orwellian fashion, industry lobbyists and their congressional allies will try to repeal resolution authority in the name of opposing bailouts, when in reality they will be restoring the precrisis bailout status quo. Here again, Main Street needs to educate itself and oppose efforts to repeal resolution authority. Repeal would simply restore too-big-to-fail policies and reaffirm the competitive advantage large financial institutions have enjoyed over smaller banks, all at the expense of the American taxpayer.

Some also argue that resolution authority can't work in practice. They argue that some institutions are too big for the FDIC to resolve. MIT's Simon Johnson, a coauthor of *13 Bankers: The Wall Street Takeover and the Next Financial Meltdown,* has been of that school. He believes that the megainstitutions should be broken up by Congress now. Though I am sympathetic to that viewpoint, I do not believe Congress has the political will to take that step, and its legal authority to do so would no doubt be challenged if it tried. The Fed and FDIC do have the authority to restructure and downsize big institutions that cannot demonstrate that they will be resolvable in bankruptcy. As I discuss below, they should be prepared to take that step.

The FDIC staff has produced detailed analyses of how a megainstitution could be seized and broken up in an orderly fashion, essentially by taking control of its holding company. They have presented lengthy briefings to the FDIC's Systemic Resolution Advisory Committee on the strategies the FDIC would employ to resolve a megabank. All of that information is available on the FDIC's website. As a result of those briefings, even Simon Johnson acknowledged that "in a complex financial system with powerful special interests and myriad global risks . . . the F.D.I.C. is moving closer to a clear statement of the problem and, at a very granular level, what needs to be done. This is progress."

The markets also provide tangible proof of progress. The ratings agencies have reduced large banks' credit ratings, acknowledging that Dodd-Frank has made it much less likely that they will be bailed out in the future. In addition, large banks' funding costs have increased since Dodd-Frank's enactment, narrowing the cost advantages they enjoy over smaller institutions. That is a sign that bond investors and others who extend credit to big financial institutions are asking for a higher return. They are starting to understand that Dodd-Frank means what it says: no more bailouts; invest at your own risk. Congress must not roll back the clock.

Break Up the Megainstitutions

There have many proposals to break up the largest financial institutions. Some proposals would cap megabanks on the basis of size. Others would restore Glass-Steagall, the Depression-era law repealed by Congress in 1999, that required the complete separation of securities activities from traditional commercial banking. Still others would allow commercial banks to conduct some securities activities such as investment banking, but not brokerage or market making, in a kind of Glass-Steagall-light. As of this writing, at least, none of these proposals has any chance of passing Congress.

My own view is that the problem of too big to fail is really about complexity, not size, and thus "break-up" proposals should focus on simplifying the megabanks so that they can be easily resolved in bankruptcy or the FDIC's resolution process without resort to taxpayer support. For instance, even though Wells Fargo has assets of $1.3 trillion, I do not worry about the government's ability to resolve it because it follows a basic business model of taking deposits and making loans, and its operations are almost exclusively in the United States. If Wells did get into trouble (which I don't expect), it would not be a huge challenge to place its bad loans into a receivership, where losses would be absorbed by its shareholders and unsecured creditors, and transfer its deposits and healthy loans into a "good bank" that could be sold off or recapitalized with new private-sector investment.

The problem is the complexity that comes with banking organizations trying to be involved in areas as varied as lending, payment processing, asset management, investment banking, brokerage, securities and derivatives market-making, and insurance. Since the repeal of Glass-Steagall, banking organizations have been allowed to enter a wide range of activities that are more volatile, risky, and complex than traditional banking. In addition, as megabanks have grown, both internationally and domestically, they have created thousands of different legal entities, frequently to evade regulatory or tax requirements. This confusing tangle of legal entities operates as a kind of "poison pill" to breaking them up, even though these behemoths could operate more efficiently and safely if they were divided into their component parts. Derivatives activities are a particular problem; the megabanks do not conduct their derivatives activities in a single entity but rather scatter them throughout their organizations. That makes it difficult to know exactly how much money they have at risk in their derivatives transactions and even more difficult to unwind those transactions in the event of a failure. Similarly, international operations can be conducted through the auspices of numerous legal entities, which can be difficult to map to the activities in each country

Dodd-Frank gave the FDIC and Fed joint authority to order large financial organizations to restructure themselves if they are unable to show that their nonbank operations can be resolved in a bankruptcy without systemic disruptions. In addition, bank regulators have broad authority to require banks and their holding companies to operate in a safe and sound manner. The Fed and FDIC should use these powers to require the largest institutions to restructure themselves into a manageable number of distinct operating subsidiaries, each with their own boards and specialized executive management teams. Their commercial banking operations should be housed in their FDIC-insured banks and their securities, derivatives, and insurance functions should be housed in separate, stand-alone affiliates for each business line. Insured deposits should only be used to support traditional banking operations: lending, payment processing, and trustee functions. Securities, derivatives, and insurance business lines should be walled of and conducted without support from insured deposits.

Megabanks and others who oppose pushing nontraditional activities outside of insured banks argue that lending can be high risk too if done imprudently. That is true, but there is a longstanding public policy in support of allowing banks to use deposits to support lending, as providing credit to businesses and households is a social good that justifies a government subsidy. Moreover, risks associated with lending are much better understood by bank managers, investors, and examiners. And unlike securities and derivatives, loans are assets held by banks for the long term and thus not subject to short-term, sudden market losses. While there may also be a social economic benefit in more complex derivatives and securities trading (though with many derivatives, I doubt it), there is no consensus that government-backed insured deposits should support them. Thus, financial institutions should be required to attract funding to support these activities from the private investors who will no doubt charge a higher premium than an insured depositor to assume the risks associated with these activities.

Megabanks' international operations should also be simplified and subsidiarized so that major operations in each foreign country are housed in separate legal entities organized under the laws of that country. Some megabanks, notably Spain's Santander and Britain's HSBC, organize their operations in this way. It has not hurt their profitability and makes them much more resolvable.

Creating a manageable number of distinct, stand-alone subsidiaries within the broader banking organization would make it much easier to break up and resolve the behemoths if they get into trouble. Requiring separate boards and management would also improve the quality of management as executives would have a smaller, more specialized entity to oversee. Finally, separate boards and managers would reduce the opportunity for conflicts of interest, particularly between megabanks' securities activities and commercial banking operations. The megainstitutions, with their far-flung operations and diverse businesses, are simply too complex to manage centrally. Of course, a lot of people would prefer that the big banks be completely broken up, and that is an attractive option. However, I do not think the Fed and FDIC's legal authority extends that far, and as previously indicated, I do not believe there is sufficient support in Congress for passing legislation to break them up. In any event, much the same result can be achieved through restructuring their different business lines into discrete, separately managed legal entities. This approach also preserves benefits associated with diversification and keeps the entire organization under government supervision. A disadvantage of some break-up proposals is that they would push non-traditional financial activities back into the "shadow system" where there is very little regulatory oversight. This is exactly the problem we had precrisis, with shadow banks like AIG, Bear Sterns, Lehman Bros, and others feeding the subprime crisis.

Ironically, such a restructuring would not only help ensure that those institutions can be resolved in an orderly way if they get into trouble; it would also likely improve performance for shareholders. The megabanks have always performed more poorly than well-managed commercial banks that have stuck to the basic business of taking deposits and making loans.

Even during the go-go years before the crisis, bread-and-butter commercial banks such as Wells Fargo and U.S. Bancorp consistently delivered better returns than Citi, Bank of America, and even JPMorgan Chase. Since the crisis, the megabanks' share valuations have lagged the average performance of regional banks. Indeed, based on share prices at the beginning of 2012, the megabanks' shares in relation to their tangible book value traded significantly lower than that of regional commercial banks. Management efficiency would be improved by creating legal entities that focused on specific business lines. It would also make it easier for shareholders themselves to break up the megabanks if they concluded better value could be realized through such a step.

Megabanks argue that making them reorganize into smaller stand-alone units would impair their ability to meet the financial needs of big multinational corporations. But it's not clear that multinationals find it advantageous to do business with a huge, complex financial titan. Dealing with smaller, focused entities would give them specialized expertise and less risk of conflicts. Conversely, even the megabanks don't want to take all the risks of big deals for multinationals, which is why those deals are typically syndicated among multiple banks. If there was really that much value in megabanks' services, presumably it would show up in shareholder returns. But it doesn't.

Megabanks also argue that their economies of scale can lower costs for customers, and that they will lose those economies if they have to manage each business line as a separate, stand-alone unit. Studies show that some economies of scale exist, but they are limited by management difficulties in overseeing many different business lines. So although average overhead costs go down, average revenues go down even more. In short, there are no clear market or shareholder benefits from having complex, multitrillion-dollar institutions and many disadvantages from a public policy standpoint. If the FDIC had to resolve one of the megabanks now, it could do so by seizing control of its holding company. However, it would take months if not years to untangle its complex legal structures, split them up, and return them to private-sector ownership. That means the resolution would be costlier than it needed to be for the shareholders and unsecured creditors who, under Dodd-Frank, must absorb the losses. Taking steps now to restructure the behemoths into a limited number of smaller specialized, stand-alone subsidiaries would be in the public interest and in the enlightened interest of their shareholders as well.

Require Securitizers to Retain Risk

My book has spent a lot of time explaining the mechanics and structure of the securitization market and the skewed economic incentives it created. Those skewed incentives not only led to the origination of millions of unaffordable mortgages but also created incentives for servicers and certain classes of investors to choose foreclosures over loan modifications. I firmly believe that the only way to correct those incentives is to align the interests of securitizers with those of investors as a whole. The best way to do that is with a simple rule that says that every time an investor takes a dollar of loss on his investment, the securitizer must absorb at least 5 cents of it, as provided by Dodd-Frank. If I had it my way, we would make it 10 cents.

When I served as FDIC chairman, my home fax number somehow landed on a spam fax list used by a mortgage brokerage to advertise its mortgages. Each month I would get a fax advertising "adjustable fixed-rate loans," prominently noting that I could qualify even if I had no income documentation and a bad credit score and had filed for bankruptcy! This sleazy ad used the confusing oxymoron of "adjustable fixed-rate" to describe the loans because the rate on them was "fixed" during a brief introductory period, with a steep payment reset once the introductory period expired. I received those faxes all through 2007 and a good part of 2008. Each month, the only thing that would change on the ad was the phone number. I took the ads into the office and asked the staff to try to track the firm down, but they were unable to do so. It moved around too quickly.

Risk retention would put firms like those out of business. Why? Because they do not have a budget or financial resources to retain any of the financial risk. If securitizers have to retain 5 or 10 percent of the losses on securitized loans that go bad, they will want to have recourse against the broker who sold them the loans. If a broker cannot demonstrate the financial capability to make the securitizer whole, the securitizer will not buy loans from it. That would be a good result. A mortgage is by far the biggest financial obligation you and your family will ever undertake. We don't want lightly regulated fly-by-nights originating your mortgage. We want an established, reputable firm originating it, one that has some financial interest in making sure it is affordable to you.

Yet, as I write this, risk retention for securitizations is under assault in the Congress, and I regret to say that both Republicans and Democrats are succumbing to industry pressure. Unfortunately, some community groups are aligning with mortgage industry advocates. Here again, Washington needs a good dose of common sense from Main Street. If we are to keep the securitization-fed subprime debacle from happening again, it is essential that those who securitize mortgages keep some meaningful skin in the game.

Require an Insurable Interest for Credit Default Swaps

Congress made a huge mistake when it enacted legislation in 2000 that essentially insulated most financial derivatives from any regulation by state or federal regulators. Into that regulatory void, the credit default swaps (CDS) market exploded. By the end of 2007, the CDS market had grown to $62 trillion, nearly twice the size of the mortgage market, U.S. stock market, and government securities market combined.

As discussed in earlier chapters, CDSs are essentially a form of insurance protection that investors can buy to protect themselves against losses on debt securities they hold. Many investors in complex mortgage-backed securities—the CDOs discussed in chapter 5—bought CDS protection against losses on those securities. The company that sold a major part of that protection was AIG. Because of the 2000 legislation, AIG's CDS business was left unregulated. The standard tenets of insurance regulation—that insurance companies must charge premiums and hold capital and reserves that are adequate to cover losses on the risks they are insuring—did not apply to AIG's CDS business. During the go-go years before the subprime crisis hit, AIG made a lot of money selling large volumes of CDS protection at relatively low prices. As a consequence, its financial resources to pay out on CDS claims were woefully inadequate when mortgage losses spiked in 2007 and 2008. The government ended up investing a whopping $180 billion in AIG. As of March, 2012, about $45 billion of the government's investment had not been paid back.

Dodd-Frank fixed some of that by giving both the SEC and the CFTC authority to regulate the derivatives market. Among other things, the legislation mandated that the SEC and CFTC, working with the banking regulators, set standards for the amount of capital and margin that sellers of CDSs must hold. But Dodd-Frank continues to insulate the CDS market from traditional insurance regulation. Importantly, the new law does not require that purchasers of CDSs have an insurable interest.

When you go to an insurance company to buy fire protection on your house, it will want proof that you own the house. It does not want you buying insurance protection on your neighbor's house. That would give you an incentive to burn your neighbor's house down. For centuries, a central tenet of insurance has been to insure only against losses that the insured may actually sustain. Without such a requirement, insurance simply becomes a means to gamble on other people's losses, creating economic incentives to inflict harm on others to reap the insurance payout.

Without an insurable interest requirement, the CDS market has become primarily a speculators' game. The market is heavily subject to manipulation, given the lack of regulation and the ability of speculators to influence prices. Moreover, it has been able to grow to such an astronomical size because speculators are free to bet against default on a wide range of securities without actually owning any of them. Just as there is no limit on the amount of money that can be wagered on who wins the Super Bowl, there is no limit on the number of speculators who can bet on whether the Italian government will default on its bonds or, as was commonly the case in 2007, whether investors would suffer losses on mortgage-backed securities and the infamous CDOs.

Some of the early resistance to our loan modification initiatives came from hedge fund managers, who would make money if mortgage defaults went up. This was because they had purchased CDS protection against losses on mortgage-backed securities they did not own. If they had been required to hold mortgage investments that exceeded the dollar amount of their CDS protection, they would not have had an incentive to oppose loan modifications. Similarly, it used to be that when an investor bought the debt of a company and that company got into trouble, the investor would work with the company to restructure its debt to help the company avoid a costly bankruptcy. Now, with investors being able to buy CDS protection that far exceeds any underlying bondholdings, if anything, they have an incentive for the company to go bankrupt.

Opponents of an insurable interest requirement argue that CDS can be used to protect against losses on other investments that are related, but not identical, to losses covered by the CDS contract. For instance, a bank that has made a lot of loans to borrowers in Spain might be worried about the Spanish government defaulting on its debt and the adverse impact that could have on the Spanish economy. So the bank buys CDS protection on Spanish bonds, even though it does not own Spanish bonds.

I think there are probably more direct ways to hedge against an economic downturn in Spain—for instance, by curbing new lending activity and requiring more collateral from Spanish borrowers. Alternatively, the principle of insurable interest could apply by requiring the purchaser of CDSs to demonstrate that it has a financial risk that is correlated to Spanish debt and requiring that the purchaser document financial loss before being able to recover on the CDS claim. You have to prove you have suffered economic loss before collecting on an insurance claim. Why shouldn't they?

An insurable interest requirement for purchasers of credit default protection is yet another example of commonsense regulation that is needed. We do not want Wall Street speculators having incentives to drive our housing market or major corporations into trouble so they can collect on their CDS bets. Requiring CDS users to have some skin in the game aligns their economic incentives with the broader public interest.

Impose an Assessment or Tax on Large Financial Institutions

My deepest disappointment in the Dodd-Frank battles was over Congress's failure to give the FDIC authority to charge an assessment on the nation's largest financial institutions. With that authority, the FDIC could have imposed assessments based on all of the risk factors that fed the crisis, such as heavy reliance on short-term funding, high-risk lending, and trading in complex, illiquid securities. The assessment would have made the large financial institutions internalize the risks they pose to society and helped level the playing field between small banks and financial behemoths. Funds raised through the assessment would have insulated taxpayers from supporting the liquidation of big financial institutions, even temporarily.

Secretary Geithner worked hard to defeat the assessment in the Dodd-Frank bill. He has also traveled to Europe to work against European officials who are considering a transaction tax on large financial institutions. The U.S. administration has made token proposals to impose temporary taxes on financial institutions based on TARP expenditures, proposals that everyone understands will go nowhere. Perhaps with a new administration economic team in 2013, there will be more serious efforts to impose an assessment or tax on financial risk taking.

The FDIC assessment is not a tax, as the revenue collected would be held in a special fund and used only as working capital for FDIC resolutions. A tax, on the other hand, would go to general revenues and support government operations. (Both, however, would help reduce the budget deficit under government accounting rules.) I prefer the FDIC assessment because it provides the government with more flexibility to adjust the assessment based on new risks and avoid gaming, whereas a tax would be written by Congress and thus be harder to change once enacted.

However, either option would make it more expensive for financial institutions to engage in short-term transactions. That would have a stabilizing influence on our markets. For instance, if a financial institution had to pay an assessment or tax each time it borrowed money, it would become much more expensive to continually fund operations with repeated short-term borrowings. In contrast, institutions that funded themselves primarily with long-term debt would have to pay the tax only every few years, when the debt was renewed. Similarly, those who invested long term would seldom pay the tax, but those who actively traded to make short-term profits would be paying very high amounts.

Both the FDIC assessment and a financial transaction tax would provide incentives and rewards for long-term market behavior, as well as produce revenues to reduce the budget deficit and help restore the damage to our public finances caused by the financial crisis and ensuing recession. Main Street should strongly support either option.

THINGS THAT WILL MAKE OUR REGULATORS WORK BETTER

Keep the Consumer Agency

I don't know how anyone can say that we have done a good job of protecting consumers in financial services. Payment shock mortgages with abusive prepayment penalties, fee-laden credit cards, excessive overdraft fees—these are three examples of the types of products where disclosures have been inadequate and the products too complex for consumers to understand what they were getting themselves into. Moreover, the situation is worse with regard to nonbank financial providers, for example, payday lenders and money remitters, who charge fees and interest equivalent to several hundred percent. Similarly, the most abusive subprime loans were typically made by nonbank mortgage originators.

Pre-Dodd-Frank, the Federal Reserve Board had the job of writing the consumer rules for financial products, and its efforts were woefully inadequate. The core problem, I believe, was that the Fed's responsibilities for monetary policy and safety and soundness supervision always came first. Insufficient attention was given to what was happening to consumers. What's more, when the Fed did write consumer rules, they were generally lengthy and highly complex, making it difficult for consumers to understand their rights. The complexity and cost of complying with the rules also forced many community banks out of the business of consumer lending.

It is a very good thing that Congress has now created an agency devoted exclusively to consumer protection. I have high hopes that this new agency will work hard to simplify and strengthen consumer protections, while bringing much-needed enforcement of consumer rules to the nonbank sector. People of goodwill can differ on the structure of the new agency. I prefer that a regulatory agency have a board instead of a single director. A board brings a diversity of viewpoints that can help guard against regulatory capture, which is one of the reasons why I believe the OCC—if we keep it—should also be headed by a board. But the continuing debate about the structure of the consumer agency should not impede its ability to carry out its important functions. The agency deserves to have a Senate-confirmed head to lead it.

Restructure the Financial Stability Oversight Council

I credit Senator Chris Dodd with his effort to improve our financial regulatory structure to promote better quality, more independent decision making by the regulatory agencies. He was really the only member of Congress willing to tackle the issue head on. However, I believe strongly that vesting all power in a single agency would make it more prone to capture by the industry. Having a diversity of views and the ability of one agency to look over the shoulder of another is a good check against regulators becoming too close to the entities they regulate.

At the same time, the United States has gone too far in creating a plethora of regulators with responsibility for various pieces of the financial system. We do not have an efficient decision-making structure for them to collectively address systemwide problems. Each agency tends to focus on protecting its own turf, instead of stepping back and taking a broad view of regulatory measures that will protect the stability of the system as a whole.

My original proposal for a systemic risk council was to have it headed by a presidentially appointed individual with a fixed term whose sole responsibility would be to monitor and address risks in the financial system. The council head would have his or her own staff and be empowered to write rules for the financial system. The heads of each of the major regulatory agencies would serve on the council and would vote on the rules, but the rules would be approved by a simple majority. The individual agencies would retain responsibility for enforcing the rules against the institutions they regulated. They could also write their own rules for those institutions but only if they were tougher than the rules promulgated by the council. Allowing the individual agencies to write tougher rules would help change the captive mind-set of some of these agencies and also serve as a check on the council itself being too lax.

Unfortunately, the Financial Stability Oversight Council created by Dodd-Frank is chaired by the secretary of the Treasury, not an independent chairman. In addition, it has very little authority to write systemwide rules. Rather, those rules are now written as part of a painstaking negotiated process among rival agencies, producing rules that are hundreds of pages long, mind-numbingly complex, and sometimes riddled with special exceptions and exclusions, all too often to accommodate the interests of the individual agencies and the industries they regulate.

The ability of the council to function is also compromised by the fact that it is headed by an administration cabinet member.

As a member of the president's cabinet, the Treasury secretary's job is to serve the president and his political objectives. That sets up an inherent conflict with his FSOC responsibilities to promote a safe, stable financial system, even if it conflicts with administration policies or rubs powerful political constituencies the wrong way. We need an independent body with the ability and will to take away the punch bowl when the economy becomes overheated through excess leverage and risk taking. In the early and mid-2000s, it was obvious that investment banks were taking on too much leverage and mortgage-lending standards were out of control. It was obvious that the CDS market was getting out of hand. Yet in the face of massive industry resistance, the regulators did not act, and when Armageddon hit, each was able to say—with some justification—that it lacked the power to deal effectively with the problem because of its jurisdictional limits.

The council and its members need to have sole and complete ownership of system stability. They need to be led by an individual whose only job is to prevent another financial system meltdown. More than three years have passed since the crisis. Yet obviously needed reforms to raise capital requirements, reform the securitization market, and regulate the over-the-counter derivatives markets have yet to be completed and are bogged down in protracted interagency negotiations. The FSOC has played no role in cleaning up the robo-signing mess, which promises to be a huge drag on the financial system and our housing recovery. What's more, the council has failed to take a forceful stand on probably the biggest long-term threat to financial system stability: the inability of Congress and the administration to deal with our structural budget deficit.

We need an FSOC that will look beyond the parochial interests of individual regulators. We need an FSOC that will be insulated from the reelection prospects of elected officials or the political fund-raising influence of financial institutions. We need an FSOC that will stand up to protect the interests of Main Street. This will happen only if it is independent and empowered to write the necessary rules.

Abolish the OCC

When I assumed the leadership of the FDIC, I did not have an ax to grind with the OCC. On the contrary, I had positive working relationships with John Dugan and his predecessors at the agency. Though I was deeply disappointed in its decision to preempt state consumer laws, I still had an overall favorable impression of the OCC as a regulator. In fact, I wrote an academic paper when I was at the University of Massachusetts suggesting the OCC as a possible model for federal insurance regulation.

However, after five years of dealing with the OCC as FDIC chairman, I question whether culturally or structurally it is capable of adequately supervising the nation's largest banks. Let me hasten to say that there are many good people at the OCC, just as there were many good people at the Office of Thrift Supervision. Indeed, I found that John Bowman, who served on the FDIC board in his capacity as acting director of OTS, was much more supportive of regulatory initiatives than were John Dugan and John Walsh.

But let's face it, the OCC has failed miserably in its mandate of ensuring the safety and soundness of the national banks it regulates. Citigroup and Wachovia, two of its largest charters, would have failed had it not been for government interventions and, in the case of Citigroup, massive amounts of taxpayer aid. Citigroup is a textbook example of how not to run a bank. The OCC allowed the bank we insured, Citibank N.A., to essentially become a dumping ground for high-risk assets. There was little, if any, effort by the OCC to protect the bank and make sure it was protected from risk taking by other Citigroup affiliates. The supervision of Wachovia was similarly weak. Wachovia had held a huge volume of toxic pick-a-pay loans on the troubled West Coast, it had gotten itself into trouble with complex auction-rate securities, and it had done a poor job of originating and managing a sizable commercial real estate portfolio.

Widespread problems with mortgage foreclosures must also rest on the OCC's doorstep. The OCC has consistently thrown roadblocks in front of effective loan modification efforts. Beginning with its dissemination of grossly misleading redefault data in 2007 to its current efforts to gloss over widespread illegalities in foreclosure processes, it has consistently focused on protecting the interests of the large banks it regulates over the public interest. Years ago, the OCC should have been requiring the big national banks to hire the staff and resources necessary to restructure the avalanche of delinquent loans we could then see coming. Years ago, it should have made certain that the banks had the appropriate documentation and controls in place to ensure full compliance with state and local foreclosure requirements. Even now, it has failed to require that national banks spend the additional money necessary to service mortgage loans effectively. Our housing market cannot heal unless big-bank services are up to the task of dealing with the millions of delinquent loans still outstanding and the millions of properties now sitting vacant in communities throughout the country, hurting the home values of innocent neighbors. But so long as its regulator views its job as protecting the banks, not us, the situation will continue.

On other issues, the OCC has consistently argued for applying weaker standards to large national banks. Time and again, it pushed for lower capital requirements—during the stress tests, during the TARP repayment discussions, and finally during the Basel III discussions. It alone fought us on requiring servicing standards in the risk retention rules. But I think the most troubling of all my experiences over my five years in office was John Dugan's statement to me in 2008 that it was unnecessary to lower Citi's supervisory rating because the government was keeping it out of trouble with massive financial support. In other words, the OCC did not need to do its job as a regulator because taxpayers were bailing out the bank. Main Street deserves better from a regulator.

The FDIC is not perfect, but it has repeatedly proven itself to be significantly more independent of the big banks than the OCC. One reason for this is that unlike the OCC, the FDIC faces huge financial losses if big banks get into trouble. In addition, it does not have to rely on fees from the nation's biggest banks to fund itself, as does the OCC. The FDIC's operations are supported through mandatory premiums charged to all insured banks.

Indeed, the best model for banking supervision would be to let the FDIC supervise all of the banks that it insures, while the Fed should supervise all bank holding companies and nonbank systemic institutions. My experience is that the Fed is a more independent regulator than the OCC because of its financial exposure as a lender of last resort and its ability to fund its operations through its lending and trading operations, without having to rely on big-bank fees. To be sure, the Fed had many failings as a supervisor prior to the crisis. However, many of those failings were the responsibility of the New York Federal Reserve Bank, not the Fed board. Since the crisis, the board has moved to exercise greater management control over the supervisory activities of its regional banks.

Moving all bank supervision to the FDIC and all holding company supervision to the Fed would also allow for better specialization between the bank regulators. The FDIC could focus on traditional commercial banking inside the insured banks, while the Fed could focus on financial activities outside traditional banking, such as securities, derivatives market making, and insurance. Each agency could have backup authority against each other (as the FDIC now has for all banks and holding companies) to guard against regulatory laxity.

My friend and former colleague on the FDIC board Tom Curry was confirmed by the Senate to head the OCC in the spring of 2012. I very much hope that Tom can change the regulatory culture of the OCC and refocus it on protecting the public interest, not the banks. However, he will be fighting an uphill battle, as the OCC's decline as a regulator has been ongoing for many years. I wish him luck.

Merge the SEC and the CFTC

The securities and derivatives markets are heavily interrelated. Yet we continue to regulate them through separate and distinct regulatory agencies, the Securities and Exchange Commission for the securities markets and the Commodity Futures Trading Commission for most derivatives. The United States is the only developed nation that maintains separate regulators for those two markets. The agencies would be much stronger if they merged their respective staffs and pooled their areas of expertise. The combined agency would also have a broader perspective with a more diverse group of institutions to regulate, reducing the likelihood of regulatory capture.

Most experts on regulatory structure agree that the SEC and CFTC should be merged. So why hasn't it happened? Primarily because agricultural users of the futures markets fear that their interests would be ignored if the CFTC were folded into the much larger SEC. Though I am sympathetic to their concern, I believe it could be adequately addressed by creating a special office within the merged agency, dedicated to making sure that the futures markets serve the needs of the nation's farmers. Moreover, the Senate and House Agriculture Committees could retain oversight over the new agency, jointly with the Senate Banking Committee and House Financial Services Committee. That would help ensure that the new agency was attentive to agricultural users of the futures markets.

GIVE THE SEC AND CFTC INDEPENDENT FUNDING

Most financial regulatory agencies are "self-funded"—that is, they support their operations through fees that they assess on the industry. This gives them a great deal of freedom to plan their budgets and staff resources to carry out their mission independently of political interference. However, both the SEC and CFTC must rely on the congressional appropriations process for their funding. This means that each year they go hat in hand to the appropriations committees of the House and Senate to seek approval for money to continue to operate. (Both agencies collect registration and other fees as part of their work, but this money is turned over to the Treasury Department and then a portion of it is doled back to them as part of the appropriations process. The SEC in particular collects fees that are far in excess of the budget it is given by Congress.)

Regrettably, industry lobbyists have found that the best way to harass the SEC and CFTC and block efforts at financial reform is through convincing appropriations committees to restrict how these agencies can use their money. For instance, in the House, there have been attempts to prohibit the CFTC from using its funds to implement rules forcing more derivatives onto public trading facilities, and other measures. Such facilities would disclose pricing information to market participants before they decide whether to buy or sell a derivative (similar to the way you can obtain the current price of a stock before you decide whether you want to buy or sell it). This is an important reform that would help combat price manipulation in the derivatives market. The fact that the House Appropriations Committee would want to thwart it is even more troubling given the widening scandal over reports of major derivatives dealers manipulating a key interest rate index called the London Interbank Offer Rate (Libor) which impacts the price of hundreds of trillions of dollars worth of derivatives.

To be sure, this issue is about turf. The House and Senate Appropriations Committees do not want to give up their leverage over the SEC and CFTC. They argue that subjecting the SEC and CFTC to the appropriations process increases each agency's accountability to the public. But the Senate Banking Committee and House Financial Services Committee have plenty of power to conduct oversight of the SEC and CFTC, and those committees have considerably greater expertise on financial matters than do the appropriations committees. I regret to say that I cannot think of one instance where the SEC or CFTC appropriations process was used to promote reforms to protect the public. On the other hand, the process is routinely used by industry lobbyists to create trouble for these two regulators. To be sure, both the SEC and CFTC have made mistakes, but their effectiveness will not be improved if their senior staff and chairmen have to spend time and resources on the Hill constantly battling industry lobbyists for enough money to operate. If we want vigorous supervision of securities and derivatives markets, both regulators need to have a process in place that gives them certainty that they will have adequate funds to discharge their responsibilities over the long term.

End the Revolving Door

When things go wrong, it's usually the presidentially appointed heads of the agencies who take the heat. But in reality, the vigor with which rules are interpreted and enforced relies heavily on career staff. I have always been an advocate and supporter of career staff. While other agencies hired legions of advisers from the industry during the crisis, I pretty much relied on the FDIC's career staff to carry out the FDIC's vital mission.

If we want good people in government, we need to treat them with respect and let them know we value their work. If we signal through our hiring policies that we value industry professionals more than those who have chosen government as a career, we hurt morale and make it less likely that examiners and others will assert themselves against the industry when necessary. That is not to say that all career staff are perfect. I have seen many instances when career staff have been too deferential to industry wishes. At the FDIC, I did not want our examiners to be combative with the banks. But I did want them to exercise independent judgment and to understand that their job was to protect the public interest, not the banks.

It's not just the examiners who can fall captive to industry viewpoints. The lawyers and economists who work at agencies can also be far too accommodating, if not gullible, when it comes to industry arguments. Lawyers in particular can become too focused on maintaining an agency's jurisdiction, its "turf," at the expense of good regulatory policy. For instance, for years, the SEC and CFTC fought over which of them should regulate over-the-counter derivatives. With the agencies divided, the industry went to Congress and secured legislation banning both of them from regulating the industry.

I would like to see financial regulators, particularly examiners, develop a stronger esprit de corps. I would like to see financial regulation be viewed as a lifelong career choice—similar to the Foreign Service—rather than a revolving door to a better-paying job in the private sector. There should be a lifetime ban on regulators working for financial institutions they have regulated. We should impose higher educational and professional experience requirements for examiners and other staff when they enter government service, but also stronger training programs, ongoing educational support, and better pay. To be sure, industry experience can be helpful to a financial regulator, but that should be provided through government-paid industry tours of duty instead of an endless stream of staff moving back and forth between regulatory agencies and financial firms.

One area where a revolving door does make sense would be a requirement that federal regulatory staff accept rotations to other agencies. The financial regulators are not the only agencies where squabbling and infighting impede effective performance. We experienced tragic intelligence failures prior to the 9/11 terrorist attacks because of a lack of coordination and information sharing among law enforcement agencies. To promote better cooperation, the intelligence community has undertaken a mandatory rotation program for senior staff. This "joint duty" program requires all senior intelligence officials, as a condition of promotion, to undertake a duty rotation at another intelligence agency. Senators Joseph Lieberman, Susan Collins, and Daniel Akaka have introduced legislation to expand this program to include more agencies, and the Partnership for Public Service has recommended a similar program for the entire civil service. Just as it is doing for the intelligence community, requiring rotations of senior staff among the various financial regulators could help guard against regulatory capture and improve coordination and collaboration among the various financial agencies.

At the end of the day, we can pass all the laws and write all the rules that we want, but if we don't have good-quality people interpreting and enforcing them, our efforts at reform are destined to fail. Too often, media scrutiny and public interest are focused on the legislative battles and high-profile rule writings and not enough on the nuts and bolts of enforcing the rules. We have a number of good people in government, and we need to recruit more. Better policies to promote independence of judgment and breadth of perspective among career staff are essential if financial reform efforts are to succeed.

Reform the Senate Confirmation Process

By statute, the heads of all of the major financial regulatory agencies are appointed by the president and confirmed by the Senate. When the president and Senate are unable to agree on a nominee to head an agency, an acting head is named. As I write this in mid-2012, three of the seven major financial agencies do not have Senate-confirmed heads: the FDIC, the FHFA (the GSE regulator), and the CFPB. In addition, the Office of Financial Research—which was created by Dodd-Frank for the important task of centrally collecting and analyzing financial data to identify systemic issues before they become problems—does not have a Senate-confirmed head.

Responsibility for this rests with both the president and the Senate. Amazingly, notwithstanding the role of the GSEs in contributing to the financial crisis, it was not until late 2010 that President Obama submitted to the Senate a nominee to head FHFA. Similarly, notwithstanding the importance of ensuring effective supervision of the nation's big national banks, it was not until 2011 that he submitted his own nominee to take charge of the OCC.

But the Senate has not behaved well either. It inexplicably blocked a Nobel laureate to serve on the Federal Reserve Board and a well-regarded state bank supervisor to head the FHFA. Well-qualified nominees to head the FDIC and OCC and to serve on the FDIC and Federal Reserve boards have had their confirmations held up for months. It is very difficult for the leadership of those agencies to function with Senate confirmations hanging over their heads. Every decision, of course, ends up being weighed against whether it will antagonize anyone in the Senate. Under Senate rules, a single senator can hold up a nomination for months.

Financial regulators are not the only ones who have been held hostage to the Senate's confirmation processes. Virtually all other agencies of government have had their leadership held up at one time or another because of the vagaries of Senate rules. Judicial vacancies can languish for months or years as senators wrangle over whether to confirm nominees. Typically, the delay has nothing to do with the candidate. Rather, senators use nominations as leverage. For instance, when I was nominated to serve in the Bush Treasury Department in 2001, my nomination was quickly confirmed by the Senate, but the nominations of several of my Treasury colleagues were held up for months by a member of President Bush's own party, Republican Senator Jesse Helms of North Carolina. Helms had no objections to any of the nominees; rather, he wanted the Treasury Department to change one of its trade policies related to textile imports.

Regardless of which party is in control of the Senate, nominations are frequently held up to extract concessions from the administration. Indeed, the current Senate leadership has been known to call them "high-value targets." The unpredictable nature of the Senate confirmation process deters good people from entering government service. We want administrations to draw from Main Street talent throughout the country in recruiting people to accept senior government jobs. Yet what person in his or her right mind would willingly submit to a highly public and unpredictable Senate confirmation process, with no certainty about when he or she will be able to start the new jobs? Moving to Washington is a huge undertaking for the average Main Street American. You have to sell or rent your house, find a new house, find new schools for your kids, and if your spouse works outside of the home, he or she will want to find a new job. To undertake a career opportunity that risks being held up for months or longer is a burden many qualified individuals and their families are unable to accept.

Nominees should be guaranteed an up-or-down vote on their confirmations once the Senate committee with jurisdiction has approved their nomination. Senate committees have functioned pretty well in processing nominations; the holdups have really occurred on the Senate floor. The occasional unqualified candidate can be screened out in the committee. But once the committee has acted, the nominee should have an up-or-down vote within thirty days. If we want high-quality people of integrity to serve in government, we need to treat them with courtesy and respect, not as potential hostages in a high-stakes game of political cat and mouse. The Senate needs to reform the confirmation process. Otherwise, the only people left willing to take those jobs will be politically connected Washington lobbyists.

THINGS THAT WILL MAKE THE ENTIRE FINANCIAL SYSTEM WORK BETTER

Abolish the GSEs

One of the most intense controversies of the 2008 financial crisis surrounds the role of Fannie Mae and Freddie Mac, otherwise known as the government-sponsored enterprises (GSEs). Defenders of Wall Street try to put the bulk of the blame on them, suggesting that they caused the crisis in an effort to fulfill government mandates to back mortgages to lower-income families. Critics of Wall Street and GSE supporters argue that the lion's share of the toxic loans was originated and funded through Wall Street securitizations and that the GSEs consistently maintained higher lending standards for their securitizations than Wall Street did.

As is the case with most controversies, the truth lies in the middle. Wall Street did fund most of the toxic mortgages, and the GSEs did maintain higher lending standards for the mortgages they securitized and backed. Nonetheless, the GSEs did contribute to the crisis, and here's how: since bond investors viewed Fannie Mae and Freddie Mac as implicitly government-backed, the GSEs were able to raise money by issuing debt at very cheap rates. They would then take the cheap money and buy much-higher-yielding Wall Street mortgage-backed securities, that is, securities that were backed by all of those toxic subprime and nontraditional loans. In that way, the GSEs operated like huge hedge funds, reaping substantial profits for their executives and shareholders based on the spread between the interest they paid on their debt and the much higher returns they received on Wall Street securitizations. Of course, if the mortgages backing those securities went bad, the onus would be on the taxpayer. That is what happened. When the housing market started to deteriorate, Fannie and Freddie lost money quickly. Since they had very low capital requirements, they had little capacity to absorb losses on those Wall Street securities.

The debate over Fannie and Freddie ignores the symbiotic relationship between the financial sector and the GSEs. It is not a case of one being culpable and the other innocent. Both are to blame. Since Fannie and Freddie were taken over by the government in 2008, taxpayers have plowed $180 billion into them to keep them operational. The $180 billion is another indirect bailout of the financial sector. Fannie and Freddie acquire loans from banks, securitize them, and then sell the securities to investors. Importantly, the GSEs guarantee investors against any losses. The biggest sellers of loans to the GSEs are, of course, the big banks.

The GSEs perform a very valuable service for them and other banks, particularly since there is no longer a private securitization market. Most banks do not want to keep low-interest-rate thirty-year mortgages on their books, and many are still worried about default risk, given the continued weakness of the housing market and economy. Fannie and Freddie take both the interest rate risk and the credit risk on these mortgages off the banks' hands. To be sure, their support makes it easier for households to obtain mortgages at reduced cost. But Fannie and Freddie are not charging banks enough money to cover their costs. That is why, quarter after quarter, taxpayers have had to infuse more money into them. By not charging the banks high enough fees to cover their costs, Fannie and Freddie are providing yet another indirect taxpayer bailout.

In the short term, Fannie and Freddie should immediately increase the fees they charge banks to end the need for continued taxpayer subsidies.

Ultimately, both institutions need to be liquidated. My personal view is that we do too much to subsidize the housing market already. We should let the private markets decide how much capital to allocate to mortgages. The generous government guarantees and tax subsidies we give to housing finance have skewed needed public and private investment away from other sectors such as manufacturing, technology, and physical infrastructure.

But if we decide to maintain a government role in buying and guaranteeing mortgages from banks and other mortgage lenders, let's at least do it honestly, through a government agency such as the FDIC. The costs of the guarantees should be accounted for in the federal budget, and the agency should charge sufficient premiums to cover projected losses in advance, as does the FDIC. The hybrid nature of Fannie and Freddie led to disastrous consequences. Taxpayers implicitly backed them, while executives and shareholders reaped huge private benefits. Those too-big-to-fail institutions took excessive risks on high-flying Wall Street investments, and bondholders lent them money to do it, relying on government bailouts if things went bad. And because their bet proved to be right, all their instincts would be to do it again.

Stop Subsidizing Leverage Through the Tax Code

When most people think about the causes of the financial crisis, they think of greed and regulatory failures. Though those were certainly driving factors, the tax code also played a role.

For instance, under current law, interest paid on debt is fully deductible, while dividends paid to shareholders are not. This is one of the reasons why it is cheaper for a financial institution to fund itself with debt than equity. Prior to the crisis, financial institutions lobbied regulators relentlessly to let them finance more of their operations with borrowed money and treat tax-deductible hybrid instruments as capital. Unfortunately, the Fed and SEC succumbed to some of those pressures, with the result that many large financial institutions had too little real-equity capital to absorb losses when the crisis hit.

The tax code also gives home owners every incentive to borrow to the hilt. A dirty little secret of the crisis is that the majority of toxic mortgages were not made to expand home ownership; they were refinancings aggressively marketed to home owners as a tax-advantaged way to pull cash out of their homes. (The biggest tragedy is that many long-standing home owners with safe thirty-year fixed-rate mortgages refinanced into toxic mortgages and ended up losing their homes.) For most home owners, interest on their mortgage is fully tax deductible, while interest on a credit card or other consumer loan is not. So they treated their house like a credit card. With an overheated housing market providing artificial gains in home prices, home owners could pull that cash out tax free and deduct the interest on their new, bigger mortgage to boot.

Hopefully, after the presidential elections, Congress and the administration will tackle meaningful tax reform. In doing so, they should end these subsidies, which encourage excessive, destabilizing leverage. For instance, we could homogenize the treatment of debt and equity in a way that would be revenue neutral by allowing corporations, including banks, to deduct some portion of both interest and dividends.

We should also recognize that there is a difference between promoting home ownership and promoting home finance. Canada has no mortgage interest deduction, yet it has a comparable rate of home ownership and fewer leveraged home owners. My first preference would be to get rid of the mortgage interest deduction and use the $100 billion in savings to reduce tax rates and pay down the national debt, while providing some transition time in fairness to those who bought their home in reliance on the deduction. A simpler tax code with lower rates would spur economic growth and additional tax revenue. But *if* we want to use the tax code to promote home ownership instead of subsidizing interest on debt, perhaps we should give home owners a tax credit based on how much of their original mortgage principal they pay down each year. The credit could also be extended to a down payment up to a certain cap, say $5,000. Such a credit could stimulate housing demand while providing incentives for home owners to build equity in their homes.

It used to be that the American dream of owning a home was a means to wealth accumulation, with families building substantial equity through regular payments on their mortgages over a period of years. Building that equity was a source of pride. The equity was used to support home owners in their retirement years, when empty nesters sold their homes for smaller living quarters. Or they passed their mortgage-free houses on to their kids after they died. That old-fashioned model of home ownership worked for decades. Any tax code incentives should be geared toward equity accumulation, not wealth-stripping serial refinancings.

Tax Earned Income and Investment Income at the Same Rate

One of the reasons Wall Street firms found it so easy to find gullible investors to buy their toxic mortgage-backed securities was that there were just too many investment dollars searching for returns. That was in part due to the Federal Reserve Board's years of easy monetary policy. But the tax code also provides incentives to seek income through investment instead of work.

Under our tax code, if you work for a living, your tax rate goes as high as 35 percent, but if your earnings come from capital gains or dividends, you have to give up only 15 percent to Uncle Sam. The rationale for this $90-billion-a-year tax benefit is that it spurs job-producing investments, though there is little credible economic evidence that this is the case. Equally likely is that it contributes to a glut of investment dollars searching for return, with too few opportunities for productive use in the "real" economy. So we create incentives for financial institutions to come up with an endless array of complex, structured financial products to meet investors' insatiable demand for return. Just how many jobs did all of those CDO-squared's give us anyway?

And for those (like me) who bemoan the fact that too many of our best and brightest are drawn to the financial services sector, what kind of message does the tax code send? Go get a job and find the cure for cancer, we will tax you at 35 percent. But go manage a hedge fund, and you will have to pay us only 15 percent.

We should tax labor and investment income at the same rate. As Warren Buffett has pointed out, if there is a profit to be made, investors will come. Whether they are taxed at 35 percent or 15 percent, they will still make a profit. I do not like the administration's proposed "millionaires' tax" because it adds to the complexity of the tax code and casts the issue as rich versus poor. The issue really to me is labor versus investment. We value both and should tax both at the same rate. Here again, the savings could be used to reduce everyone's rates and pay down the national debt.

Reduce the National Debt

The 2008 financial crisis began on Wall Street, where misguided bets on risky mortgages resulted in enormous damage to both our financial system and our economy. However, I fear that the next financial crisis, if we have one, will start not in New York but in Washington.

The annual federal deficit has grown from $161 billion in 2007 to $1.3 trillion in 2011. Each year, this deficit is paid for through increased Treasury borrowing. Our national debt has nearly doubled since 2007 and currently exceeds $15 trillion, or about $50,000 for every man, woman, and child in the United States. This explosive growth in federal borrowing was heavily driven by the financial crisis and the deep recession it caused. Tax revenues plummeted while the Obama administration and Congress authorized trillions of dollars in stimulus spending to try to counteract the economic damage. Unfortunately, much of the stimulus spending was designed to create short-term increases in consumer spending, without any long-term benefit.

The deficits are also attributable to the government's continued unwillingness to make the hard choices necessary to rein in our long-term structural deficits. Our two biggest entitlement programs, Social Security and Medicare, are both on a path to insolvency. Medicare will exhaust its reserves by 2024, and Social Security will run out its reserves by 2033. The politically popular, though fiscally foolish, payroll tax cuts cost the already wobbly Social Security system $105 billion in 2011 alone. Those retiring today will see their benefits cut short. For our kids and grandkids, there will be nothing.

Unsustainable budget deficits will not only create shortfalls in promised federal benefit programs but will also provide the catalyst for a financial crisis of the same if not greater magnitude than the one we saw in 2008. Our political system has repeatedly demonstrated an inability to deal with our fiscal problems. The country has already suffered the embarrassment of losing its triple-A credit rating. Those who discount the importance of the burgeoning national debt point to the fact that the U.S. Treasury can still borrow money at very low rates. This is true, but the Fed is printing money to buy a large percentage of the debt. In February 2012, the Fed held more than $1.6 trillion in U.S. Treasury bonds, triple its holdings of a year before. Another artificial factor stimulating investors' demand for U.S. debt is the lack of alternatives. Because of Europe's problems, investors there are limited in their choices of finding safe government-backed securities. In other words, interest rates on U.S. debt remain low because we are the best-looking horse in the glue factory.

Eventually Europe will solve its problems, or another country's debt may unexpectedly emerge as a more attractive investment than U.S. Treasury obligations. Understanding that our budget deficits and national debt are on an unsustainable path, bond investors will put their money elsewhere. The fundamentals of our fiscal health do not support the low interest rates bond investors are now paying. Just as the poor credit quality of securitized mortgages did not support the high values assigned to mortgage-backed securities before the crisis, the poor credit quality of our overleveraged government does not support low U.S. bond yields.

When investors do eventually turn to safer alternatives, interest rates will skyrocket, with devastating consequences for our financial system and our economy. Just about every interest rate on every financial credit product offered in the U.S. is influenced by the rate the U.S. Treasury pays on its debt. Banks and other financial institutions will have to start paying higher interest rates on their deposits and other borrowings to fund themselves, even though the loans they have on their balance sheets are paying lower rates. In making new loans, they will have to charge sharply steeper rates to try to stem their losses, which will hurt the ability of consumers and businesses to access affordable credit. The result will be more bank failures and another economic contraction. That is exactly the scenario being played out in Greece and to a lesser extent in Spain and Italy. It is a glimpse of our future if we do not get our fiscal situation under control.

The problem is made worse by the fact that the U.S. Treasury Department has suffered from its own case of short-termism. It has heavily relied on short-term debt issuances to finance operations. This means that $7 trillion will have to be refinanced over the next five years. The CBO has estimated that an interest rate increase of just 1 percent could add $1.3 trillion to the national debt over the next decade.

At the first closed meeting of the FSOC on October 1, 2010, I brought up our fiscal problems as a source of systemic risk. At my last FSOC meeting on March 17, 2011, I brought it up again. Tim and others expressed uncertainty about the FSOC weighing in, worried that it would look as though we were interfering with fiscal policy. Ultimately, however, we convinced our fellow FSOC members to include language in the FSOC's 2011 *Annual Report* linking fiscal responsibility to financial system stability.

In late 2010, the National Commission on Fiscal Responsibility and Reform came forward with meaningful, credible proposals to reduce our ballooning national debt through a combination of measures. They included reductions and caps on discretionary spending, comprehensive tax reform, and reforms to the Social Security system and Medicare program, including increasing the retirement age and revising cost-of-living increases. Though President Obama appointed the bipartisan commission, led by Erskine Bowles and Alan Simpson, he inexplicably turned his back on the commission's recommendations. Republicans have done no better in addressing the tough issues that the commission tackled in its report.

It seems that the only time Congress and the administration can work together in a bipartisan fashion is when they are shoveling money out the door through benefit increases or tax cuts. It took nearly a year for the Bowles-Simpson commission to develop its bipartisan recommendations to reduce our national debt by $4 trillion over ten years. Shortly after the report was issued, Congress added another $800 billion over ten years to our national debt. In a devil's deal, Republicans got an extension of the Bush tax cuts, while the Obama administration secured a cut in Social Security payroll taxes and an extension of unemployment benefits. Neither side made a serious effort to pay for any of it.

The irony is that I think Main Street recognizes the dangers in our government's excessive borrowing and would be willing to make sacrifices if they are fair and shared equally by all. The problem is that too many well-organized advocacy groups are vested in protecting every tax break or entitlement, whether it is hedge funds fighting for the lower tax rate on capital gains or the AARP opposing any adjustments to future Social Security benefits. Main Street needs to tell its elected representatives that they need a dose of common sense in managing the nation's finances. They need to ignore the special interests and get our national budget in order.

CHAPTER 27

It Could Have Been Different

A s you can tell from reading this book, I had a lot of strong objections and concerns about some of the "financial stabilization measures" (aka bailouts) that we undertook to deal with the financial crisis. Subtlety has never been my strength. Some people have asked me why I didn't just quit. Throughout 2008, I didn't feel that resigning was an option for the chairman of the FDIC. When public confidence in the nation's banking system hung by a thread, my departure would itself have been destabilizing. In 2009, as we moved from the crisis into the cleanup phase, I seriously considered stepping down, particularly as it became clear that that the new administration was going to pursue and expand the same bailout policies. But I decided to stay for two reasons.

First, the FDIC itself had a big job ahead of it with bank failures, which were not expected to peak until 2010. We had done so much to improve morale and our operational capabilities. Given the delicate and challenging task of closing so many banks, I did not feel I could abandon ship. It would have been unfair to the FDIC staff, all of whom were working around the clock.

Second, by sticking with it, I thought I could make a difference.

We forced stabilizing sales of WaMu and Wachovia with no government support of shareholders or creditors, instead of providing the expensive government bailouts that Geithner and others were pressing us to do. We limited our 2008 temporary debt guarantee program to newly issued debt and charged a fee, instead of guaranteeing all of the big financial institutions' debt free of charge, as we had originally been asked to do. We forced management changes at Citi. We refused to bail out CIT. We forced banks to raise significantly more capital than the other regulators would have required. We tirelessly advocated for loan restructuring for distressed home owners. And even though the government's loan modification efforts fell far short, hundreds of thousands of home owners were able to stay in their homes because of our efforts.

We fended off implementation of Basel II for FDIC-insured banks, and we successfully pressed the Basel Committee to adopt a leverage ratio and impose a 9.5 percent capital requirement on the world's largest banks, nearly five times as high as the Basel II standard. If I had not served on the U.S. delegation to the Basel Committee, I'm not sure what would have happened, particularly given Geithner's and Walsh's efforts to weaken the standards. And I seriously doubt whether Dodd-Frank would have contained the strong antibailout provisions and new FDIC resolution authority in the final legislation if not for my relentless efforts to include them.

Looking back, one of the saddest things about the financial crisis is that it could have been so easily avoided with a few commonsense measures. If we had raised capital requirements during the good times, we would have averted many failures, particularly among the investment banks. Instead, the leverage of investment banks and European institutions grew dramatically, and the FDIC had to fight a lonely battle to prevent the same thing from happening with the banks we insured. If the Fed had imposed lending standards for bank and nonbank lenders, so much of the mortgage lunacy could have been averted. And if Congress had not tied the hands of the CFTC, SEC, and state insurance regulators to impose some basic, commonsense regulatory controls on credit default swaps, the trillions of dollars of trading losses would have been much reduced.

This is not to excuse the conduct of the industry and place all the blame on the regulators. It was because of industry pressure that capital standards were lowered, mortgage-lending standards were blocked, and regulators were barred from overseeing the derivatives markets. It makes me very angry when I hear industry representatives try to blame the crisis on the government. Executives and traders at financial services firms are very well compensated for the jobs they perform. It is their responsibility, not that of regulators, to run their operations sensibly, in a way that delivers sustainable profits for shareholders. Yet far too few industry wrongdoers have owned up to their mistakes; far fewer have been held accountable by law enforcement officials. As I heard from the securitization group I spoke to in late fall of 2007, they felt they had a right to make fat profits by any means, and because the regulators hadn't stopped them, it was all the government's fault.

That is why I have written this book. I wanted you to see the crisis through my eyes and experience the obstacles that stood in my way as I tried to push for reform measures that were so obviously needed. Unless

Main Street fights back against the nonstop pressure from financial industry lobbyists to eviscerate needed reforms, we are going to be right back in
the soup again. Already amnesia has set in to the Washington political landscape. Industry lobbyists are fighting hard against meaningful measures to
raise bank capital requirements and reform the securitization market. In
the next Congress, I have no doubt that these lobbyists will wage an all-out
assault on Dodd-Frank reforms, including the provisions that ban bailouts
of failing institutions. Some of those efforts will be visible. Some will be
behind the scenes. Some may be supported by public interest groups that
should know better. Still others may be led by captive regulators themselves,
as we saw with the OCC leadership's fighting higher capital standards.

   Not everyone in the industry is bad, and not all members of the industry
will be supporting efforts to roll back reform. After two and a half decades in
Washington, I have learned that those who are most active in lobbying the
government are generally those with the weakest business practices, as they
have the most to lose from regulation. Unfortunately, the good industry
players usually remain silent but not always. For instance, Ed Clark, CEO of
TD Bank Group, has courageously spoken out in favor of the new Basel III
capital standards and a return to traditional banking. But precrisis, most
responsible banks stood idly by as we fought off Basel II and tried to tighten
lending standards. That was the appeal I tried, unsuccessfully, to make to
the American Bankers Association: that better-managed banks—like Main
Street voters—need to stand up and be counted when regulators take measures to constrain bad practices that risk tainting the entire industry.

   Unfortunately, there has been very little discussion of financial reform
in the 2012 elections. Jon Huntsman was really the only candidate to try
to engage in a meaningful debate over ways to make our financial system
more stable. There has been some hyperbole on the political right about
repealing Dodd-Frank, using the old industry saw that it is stifling credit
availability. To be sure, Dodd-Frank is not a perfect law, but we are much
better off having it than not having it. I suspect that the threats to repeal it
in total are more campaign hype designed to elicit campaign contributions
from financial firms than serious threats to completely undo this important
law. But here again, Main Street needs to be engaged lest Congress throws
the baby out with the bathwater and repeals the reforms that are essential to
financial stability.

   Regrettably, Dodd-Frank is a very lengthy, complex law, and too many of
the rules being written by regulators are only adding to its length and complexity. That is why I have tried to explain and simplify the reform measures

that I think are absolutely essential to keep and why I have suggested that a single council be empowered to write all systemwide rules.

The thing I hate hearing most when people talk about the crisis is that the bailouts "saved the system" or ended up "making money." Participating in bailout measures was the most distasteful thing I have ever had to do, and those ex post facto rationalizations make my skin crawl. What system were we trying to save, anyway? A system in which well-connected big financial institutions get government handouts while smaller institutions and home owners are left to fend for themselves? A system that allows government agencies unfettered discretion to pick winners and losers with taxpayer money? A system that has created cynicism and despair among honest, average working people who take responsibility for their own actions and would never in a million years ask for a government bailout? A system that has spawned two angry political movements on the left and the right that are united in their desire to end the crony capitalism characterized by too-big-to-fail policies? That is not a system I want to save.

With the millions of lost jobs and lost homes and the trillions of dollars of lost tax revenue, how can anyone try to rationalize what happened by saying that the bailouts "made money"? In point of fact, they did not make money.

When the Treasury Department states that the bailouts "made money," they are referring to the dollar amounts that were invested in the financial sector offset by the amounts that were paid back. Thus, the department does not count as a "cost" the very generous subsidies taxpayers provided financial institutions. As one distinguished group of academic experts has pointed out, this cash flow method of measuring bailout costs is inconsistent with government accounting rules:

> During the height of the crisis, few institutions were willing to commit funds in large amounts even on overnight terms. Acting on behalf of taxpayers, government agencies created new FDIC guarantees, TARP funding, and Federal Reserve lending and guarantee programs. Those programs supported extremely large amounts of financing at below-market terms for substantial periods of time. If those funds and guarantees had been priced at or near their true market value, taxpayers would have been entitled to substantially higher rates of return.

Even though on a cash-flow basis the TARP investments so far have made a profit, the government is not yet off the hook. It still has $45 billion at risk in AIG, another $27 billion in GM, and $147 billion and counting plowed into the GSEs, money that again supports the financial sector. In addition, the Treasury Department gave Citi, AIG, and GM special tax breaks to help them back to profitability. Those tax subsidies are worth tens of billions of dollars. And what about the less tangible but equally real costs of the moral hazard we created when we gave a helping hand to highflyers and bone-headed risk takers? I'm sure that with a wink and a nod, they would love to restart the party, figuring that the government will step in once more if things get too far out of hand. Hey, the bailouts made money, so what's the big deal? Let's do it again!

The bailouts, while stabilizing the financial system in the short term, have created a long-term drag on our economy. Because we propped up the mismanaged institutions, our financial sector remains bloated. The well-managed institutions have to compete with the boneheads. We did not force financial institutions to shed their bad assets and recognize their losses. Lingering uncertainty about the true extent of those losses made previously profligate management more risk averse when prudent risk taking and lending were most needed, particularly by small businesses. Only in 2012 are we finally seeing some meaningful pickup in lending by the big financial institutions. Economic growth is sluggish, unemployment remains high. The housing market still struggles. I hope that our economy continues to improve. But it will do so despite the bailouts, not because of them.

In my farewell remarks to the FDIC, I expressed amazement at the conduct we tolerated in the years leading up to the crisis. I said:

> Looking back, how could we rationalize letting big firms take on leverage at 30 or 40 to 1, giving millions of people mortgages they couldn't afford, a mortgage finance system which divorced the decision to make the mortgage from the responsibility if the loan went sour, the trading of hundreds of trillions of dollars' worth of derivatives without any ability of the government to police it?

I also quoted a favorite passage of mine from Robert Frost's poem "The Black Cottage":

> Most of the change we think we see in life
> Is due to truths being in and out of favor.

The "truths" that form the bedrock of our democratic culture fell out of favor in the first decade of the twenty-first century. Personal accountability,

honest dealing, the right to reap the rewards of your hard work and entre-
preneurship, the obligation to suffer the consequences if you fail—those
were the kinds of ideals most of us grew up with, but they were forgotten in
the shortsighted avarice that consumed our financial markets. The role of
government in a free society—not to protect us from ourselves but to protect us from one another, as Ronald Reagan once described it—was lost as
Washington deluded itself into thinking that self-correcting markets could
somehow substitute for basic common sense. It would be hard to find anyone on Main Street who was not in one way or another hurt by the horrible
debacle. Government fundamentally failed in its role of protecting us.

Epilogue

Robert Frost once said, "In three words I can sum up everything I've learned about life: it goes on." Unfortunately, that succinct phrase could also describe the kind of greed, short-sightedness, and misbehavior that brought us the 2008 crisis. It goes on.

Over a year has passed since I left the FDIC. It's getting so I don't even want to open up the morning papers. Let me highlight just a few of the more egregious parade of horribles.

In October of 2011, MF Global, a $41 billion securities and futures broker, went bankrupt, taking about $1.6 billion of misappropriated customer money with it. Still-weak capital and accounting rules allowed it to take on leverage of 40 to 1, and use the same kind of book-keeping gimmicks Lehman Brothers used to hide its bad assets. Eight months later, another big futures broker, Peregrine Financial, failed, taking about $200 million in misappropriated customer money with it. With both failures, the firms flagrantly violated the most sacrosanct of CFTC rules, those requiring futures firms to segregate and protect their customers' money.

In May, JPMorgan Chase was profoundly embarrassed by a projected $2 billion trading loss on risky credit default swaps, trades which Jamie Dimon himself characterized as "stupid." By the end of June, those losses had climbed to nearly $6 billion and counting. Though Chase's balance sheet is more than strong enough to absorb these losses and still produce a profit, they underscore the impossibility of managing complex mega-banks from the top, even at an ostensibly well-run institution like Chase. Indeed, both Chase's management, and its regulators, failed to grasp the risk of the outsized derivatives bets even after they were exposed several weeks earlier in the *Wall Street Journal*. Chase has at least announced that they will fire the traders and supervisors responsible for the losses and claw back up to two years' worth of compensation from them. Chase's regulators, on the other hand, have done nothing so far but hand-wringing.

Chase's trading debacle pales in comparison to the problems at another megabank, Barclay's, a multi-trillion-dollar institution based in the United Kingdom with significant trading operations in the United States. Barclays has admitted to U.S. and U.K. regulators that its traders tried to rig a key interest rate, the London interbank offer rate, or Libor, from mid-2005 to early 2009. Libor is used to determine interest rates on over $350 trillion of financial products used by businesses, households, and state and local governments. These include interest rates swaps, mortgages, credit cards, and variable rate notes and bonds. Nothing is more vital to the integrity of the banking system than the process by which interest rates are set. Yet, according to the government's enforcement actions, Barclays routinely and blatantly sought to manipulate this key rate and colluded with other banks to do the same. One Barclay's email shows two traders talking about breaking open a bottle of champagne to celebrate their rate fixing. It appears that most of the misconduct occurred at Barclay's New York trading desk, which was subject to the jurisdiction of the NY Fed, led by Tim Geithner. Other major U.S. banks may also be implicated. Secretary Geithner has defended himself by pointing out that he had suggested reforms to the U.K. authorities in 2008 when reports of abuse in setting Libor came to his attention. But the reforms he suggested did not fix the fundamental problems with Libor, and it appears that the NY Fed never sought to investigate reports of illegal behavior. The government's enforcement action was the result of an investigation conducted jointly by the CFTC, U.K. authorities, and the Justice Department, and did not involve Barclay's primary U.S. regulator, the NY Fed.

What does all of this say about our financial system and our regulators? It says that a culture of greed and shortsightedness continues to permeate our financial system, a culture that has infected even the best managed institutions and goes undetected by their executives and boards as well as their regulators. It is a culture that reflects a craven desire for personal profit that overrides any understanding or care about harm to others. Indeed, it is a culture that celebrates exploitation of an unwitting public for the sake of a fast buck. It is a culture that could not care less about preserving a bank's name and reputation or maintaining long-term customer relationships. But should we be surprised? In 2008 and 2009, we bailed out the risk takers, coddled their managers and boards, heck we even made sure that the high flyers who brought AIG to its knees got their year-end bonuses. Enforcement actions, to the extent they have occurred, have been paid mostly by banks and their shareholders, not the individuals responsible. Small wonder that no one on Wall Street has learned a lesson given the hand slaps they received for the subprime mess

I have been very candid and open about the policy disputes I had with my regulatory colleagues during the crisis and the years that followed. Let me hasten to say that notwithstanding our disagreements, I believe that they were trying to do what they felt was best for the country, and that they still are. The problem is that the financial regulatory system is so insular; regulators start to confuse what is best for large financial institutions with what is best for the broader public. They are not the same. It is true that we want financial institutions to be healthy and profitable in order to prevent failures and ensure their capacity to lend to the real economy. But their profitability is not an end unto itself; it is a means to an end. An institution that is profitable is not necessarily one that is safe and sound or one that is serving the public interest. All of the large financial institutions were profitable in the years leading up to the crisis, but they were making big profits by taking big risks that ultimately exploded in their—and our—faces.

When regulators confuse their regulatory mandate with maintaining bank profitability, the inevitable outcome is the system we have now— timid regulators fearful of being too tough on financial institutions because of the negative impact on their bottom lines. Members of Congress, fed by generous campaign contributions, as well as prospects of employment for themselves and their staffs when they leave office, can also be a part of the problem. They too have an interest in promoting the profitability of large financial institutions that fund the campaigns that help them stay in office and represent a potential source of lucrative jobs and consulting contracts once they leave. I wish I could say that Congress serves as a disciplining influence on the regulatory process, but throughout my career I have observed just the opposite. Whether it is deregulating the OTC derivatives market or using the appropriations process to stop necessary rule makings, Congress, more often than not, has been part of the problem, not part of the solution. Congressional pressure reinforces the tendency of regulators to be timid when dealing with the powerful financial interests that they regulate. If they antagonize the industry too much, they may find Congress withholding funds that they need to operate or stripping them of authority. This is exactly what happened to Brooksley Born when she tried to rein in derivatives trading.

So how does this get fixed? It has to start with you. Anger with our dysfunctional financial system and regulatory process cannot be confined to polarized advocacy groups on the left and right. Main Street—the heart and center of American democracy—needs to weigh in. It is not hard to fix these problems. We simply lack the political will and fortitude to get the job done. The reforms I have outlined in this book would not be difficult to implement, notwithstanding what financial industry lobbyists would have you believe. The tragedy of the crisis is that so much of it could have been avoided with a few simple measures. The Libor scandal is another example where the fix was straightforward and obvious. Banks should have been required to base rates on actual, bona fide transactions. But regulators let them use their "judgment," leaving the door open to sustained abuse.

The president needs to appoint—and the Senate needs to confirm—strong, independent people to regulate financial institutions and markets, people who understand that their regulatory obligation is to protect the public, not the large financial institutions. When Tim Geithner testified before Congress shortly after becoming treasury secretary, a congressman asked him about the effectiveness of regulation, and he proudly responded, "I have never been a regulator, for better or worse." He did not even understand that part of his job as president of the NY Fed was to regulate some of the nation's largest financial institutions. Indeed, he seemed offended that the congressman asking the question thought that he was a regulator.

Let your elected representatives know that you are tired of the continuing scandals, and that financial reform matters to you. Demand that the presidential candidates explain in detail how they propose to fix these continuing problems. Financial reform needs to be an issue as central to American electoral politics as the economy and jobs. Indeed, we will not get our economy on a sustainable path until we redirect our major financial institutions out of the gambling parlors that our derivatives and securities markets have become and back into the business of supporting the credit needs of the real economy. Tell the politicians that you support much tougher capital requirements for big financial institutions, assessments on their risk taking, and that you want your FDIC insured deposits to support lending, not their high risk securities and derivatives trading. Tell them that you want an end to speculation in the credit derivatives markets and that you want to abolish captive regulators like the OCC.

When you read about problems like the Libor scandal or the JPMorgan Chase trading losses, don't accept gobbledygook about regulators needing more information or needing more power—after Dodd-Frank, they have all the power they need. And don't let members of Congress off the hook by holding an oversight hearing or issuing a press release to tell everyone how shocked they are (while at the same time pressuring regulators behind the scenes not to be too tough).

Life goes on, as Robert Frost observed. But financial abuse and misconduct don't have to. Tell the powers in Washington that you want these problems fixed, you want them fixed now, and that you will hold all incumbents accountable until the job is done.

Sheila Bair
July 16, 2012

Notes

Chapter 1: The Golden Age of Banking

13 *For whatever reason:* Speculation at the time was that Diana's nomination had run into stiff opposition by members of the Banking Committee who had strong ties to the National Rifle Association. Diana was, and still is, the companion of New York City Mayor Michael Bloomberg, who had antagonized the NRA with tough gun regulation in the city.

16 *In June 2006:* 2001, 2002, and 2006 FDIC budget information is available at http://www.fdic.gov/about/strategic/report/index.html.

17 *That pervasive attitude:* In the 1980s and early 1990s, about 750 savings and loans failed from a combination of inadequate regulation, high-risk lending, and steep spikes in interest rates. The deposit insurer of those institutions, the Federal Savings and Loan Insurance Corporation, went bankrupt. The agency was abolished, and its insurance functions were transferred to the FDIC.

19 *John Bovenzi:* John was a valued adviser, but he was controversial with many FDIC employees because of his role in the staff cutbacks that took place before I arrived. He left about half-way into my tenure.

Chapter 2: Turning the *Titanic*

21 *Office of Thrift Supervision:* The 2010 Dodd-Frank financial reform law abolished the OTS and provided that the head of the new Consumer Financial Protection Bureau would serve on the FDIC board instead.

22 *CAMELS:* Bank examiners use a CAMELS system to evaluate the risk profile of banks. CAMELS consists of six components: Capital, Asset quality, Management, Earnings, Liquidity, and Sensitivity to market risk. Each component receives a score of 1 to 5, and based on these scores, the bank is given a composite rating of 1 to 5. Banks with CAMELS of 1 and 2 are generally viewed as safe. Banks rated 3 warrant additional examiner attention, and banks rated 4 or 5 are put on a special list of troubled banks kept by the FDIC and are viewed as being at risk of failure. However, historically, only about 20 percent of banks put on the troubled-bank list actually do fail.

23 *by the end of 2006:* FDIC, "Quarterly Banking Profile, Fourth Quarter 2006," www2.fdic.gov/qbp/2006dec/qbp.pdf, p. 1.

24 *"given the insignificant risks":* Steve Barlett to Sheila Bair, letter re deposit insurance assessments, October 7, 2006.

24 *"The banking industry"*: ABA press release, "New Deposit Insurance Premium Rates Far Too High, Says ABA," November 2, 2006. No longer available online.

Chapter 3: The Fight over Basel II

27 *Basel Committee:* In 2010, the Basel Committee membership was substantially expanded to encompass the G20 nations, bringing in China, India, and other developing nations.

29 *"loss-absorbing":* In addition to capital requirements, banks are also required to hold reserves against losses that are "estimable and probable" on loans and other assets. Under accounting rules, loan-loss reserves must be tied to expected losses, and bank managers must be able to provide specific information to support their analysis of expected loss, e.g., a large employer may close a plant in a community the bank serves. In contrast, there are no accounting limitations on the amount of capital a bank can hold. Thus it is available to absorb unexpected losses.

30 *the FDIC fought:* Though the FDIC was alone among regulators in opposing Basel II, we did receive support from some in the academic community, most notably Wharton's Richard Herring, one of the nation's foremost academic experts on bank regulation. See "The Rocky Road to Implementation of Basel II in the United States," *Atlantic Economic Journal,* November 2007, pp. 411–429. See also "Implementing Basel II: Is the Game Worth the Candle?" in *Basel II and the Future of Banking Regulation,* ed. Harold Benink, Jón Daníelsson, and Charles Goodhart, special issue of *Financial Markets, Institutions & Instruments,* vol. 14, no. 5, 2005.

31 *Even as Europe later plunged:* See, e.g., Barclays Capital Research, "Can You Trust Risk Weightings at European Banks?" April 6, 2011.

31 *one of the Fed's regional banks:* The Federal Reserve System is made up of a central governing body, the nine-member Federal Reserve Board, and twelve regional banks spread throughout the country. The regional banks are responsible for the supervision of banks and bank holding companies located in their regions. Thus the New York Fed was responsible for the oversight of the big New York bank holding companies, including Citigroup and JPMorgan Chase. As previously discussed, the FDIC-insured banks owned by these holding companies weres regulated by the OCC.

32 *I reluctantly agreed to issue:* FDIC, "Risk Based Capital Rules: Notice of Proposed Rulemaking on Modifications to the Risk-Based Capital Framework (Basel IA)," December 26, 2006, www.fdic.gov/news/news/financial/2006/fil06111.html.

33 *our staff analysis showed:* Jason Cave, email to Sheila Bair re, Basel II Strategy Bullets, May 16, 2007.

33 *Indeed, our studies showed:* FDIC, staff note to the Basel Committee, "Stocktaking on Supplementary Measure of Capital Adequacy," October 2006.

36 *a speech I gave:* FDIC, "Remarks of Sheila Bair, Chairman, Federal Deposit Insurance Corporation; Before the Basel Committee on Banking Supervision; Merida, Mexico, October 4, 2006," www.fdic.gov/news/news/speeches/archives/2006/chairman/spoct0406.html.

36 *That action by the SEC:* MIT's Andrew Lo has argued that the SEC's actions were not responsible for investment banks taking on additional leverage after 2004. See "Reading About the Financial Crisis: A 21-Book Review" (January 9, 2012), www.papers.ssrn.com/sol3/papers.cfm?abstract_id=1949908. He bases his argument on the fact that prior to the SEC's 2004 rulemaking, there were no capital requirements that

applied to an entire securities firm; thus there was nothing for the SEC to "lower." (Lo acknowledges that the SEC did have capital rules for the broker-dealer subsidiaries of these firms, which it also loosened.) Lo's views, which are based on statements made to him by SEC staff responsible for the agency's adoption of the Basel II rules, ignores the detrimental impact that bad regulations can have on market discipline. Indeed, when the SEC had no consolidated capital standards applying to securities firms, the market demanded higher capital levels of those firms. However, once the SEC created the illusion of government capital oversight, the market deferred to the weak government standards and tolerated higher levels of leverage at them. This is clearly an instance where no regulation would have been better than bad regulation. Lo also ignores the fact that the SEC's actions allowed these firms to escape tougher capital rules used by the Federal Reserve Board.

37 *"If anything goes wrong":* Kevin Drawbaugh, "US SEC Clears New Net-Capital Rules for Brokerages," April 28, 2004, http://securities.stanford.edu/news-archive/ 2004/20040428_Headline08_Drawbaugh.htm.

39 *had replaced Sue Bies:* Sue resigned from the Fed in March 2007.

Chapter 4: The Skunk at the Garden Party

42 *CRE loan balances had grown:* Mark Carlson and Gretchen C. Weinbach, "Profits and Balance Sheet Developments at U.S. Commercial Banks in 2006," http://www.federal reserve.gov/pubs/bulletin/2007/pdf/bankprofit07.pdf, July 2007, table on p.A40.

43 *the quality and performance:* CRE delinquency rates were highest among institutions with assets above $100 billion during the crisis, and lowest among those with less than $1 billion in assets. See email from Chris Newbury, FDIC, to Sheila Bair, re CRE Charts and Data (May 4, 2012).

44 *By the end of 2006:* Mortgage Bankers Association Press Release, "Delinquencies and Foreclosures Increase in Latest MBA Delinquency Survey (March 13, 2007), www .mortgagebankers.org/newsandmedia/presscenter/50974.htm Report.

47 *In the end, we compromised:* Board of Governors of the Federal Reserve System, "Federal Financial Regulatory Agencies Issue Final Statement on Subprime Mortgage Lending," June 29, 2007, www.federalreserve.gov/newsevents/press/ bcreg/20070629a.htm.

47 *Insured thrifts actually grew:* Office of Thrift Supervision, "Fourth Quarter 2007 Thrift Industry Report Graphs and Tables," February 20, 2008, www.ots.treas.gov/ _files/127400.pdf.

48 *"There was an explosion":* Financial Crisis Inquiry Commission, *The Financial Crisis Inquiry Report,* January 2011, http://fcic-static.law.stanford.edu/cdn_media/fcic -reports/fcic_final_report_full.pdf, p. xvii.

48 *a "careful review":* "Subprime and Predatory Mortgage Lending: New Regulatory Guidance, Current Market Conditions, and Effects on Regulated Financial Institutions: Hearing Before the Subcommittee on Financial Institutions and Consumer Credit of the Committee on Financial Services, U.S. House of Representatives," March 27, 2007, www.docstoc.com/docs/19817420/SUBPRIME-AND-PREDA TORY-LENDING-NEW-REGULATORY-GUIDANCE-CURRENT-MARKET -CONDITIONS-AND-EFFECTS-ON-REGULATED-FINANCIAL-I, p. 18.

48 *"The mind-set was":* Financial Crisis Inquiry Commission, *The Financial Crisis Inquiry Report,* p. 96.

Chapter 5: Subprime Is "Contained"

50 *However, the effort met:* See, e.g., B. Applebaum, "Do Homeowners Need Protection from Lenders?," *The Washington Post,* June 6, 2006.

50 *Bachus was forced:* Author's interview with Congressman Barney Frank, February 7, 2012.

50 *"field preemption":* Under the U.S. Constitution, federal laws may preempt contrary state laws. Typically, this occurs when a state law takes a contrary position on a specific matter lawfully addressed in a federal law. So-called field preemption is rarer and occurs when federal law addresses a broad category of matters and is said to "preempt the field" against any state laws that address that category. In bank regulation, the OTS and OCC have argued that federal standards on credit and underwriting standards preempt all state laws on those subjects.

52 *And prior to 2006:* Average ninety-day delinquency rate from 1979 to 2006. See C. Mayer, K. Pence, and S. Sherlund, "The Rise of Mortgage Defaults" (November 2008) www.federalreserve.gov/pubs/fed/2008/200859/200859pap.pdf.

54 *So far, the major banks:* Donal Griffin, "Bad Home Loans Top $72 Billion in 'Colossal Failure,'" February 8, 2012, www.bloomberg.com/news/2012-02-08/faulty-loans -top-72-billion-as-banks-seek-legal-deal-mortgages.html.

57 *They held more than $4 trillion:* FDIC 2006 Quarterly Banking Profile, Fourth Quarter, 2006, available at fdic.gov/qbp/2006dec/qbp.pdf.

57 *By mid-2007:* Board of Governors of the Federal Reserve System, "Speech: Chairman Ben S. Bernanke at the Federal Reserve Bank of Chicago's 43rd Annual Conference on Bank Structure and Competition, Chicago, Illinois," May 17, 2007, www.federal reserve.gov/newsevents/speech/bernanke20070517a.htm.

Chapter 6: Stepping over a Dollar to Pick Up a Nickel: Helping Home Owners, Round One

60 *Loan servicing has become:* The top five servicers are Bank of America, Wells Fargo, JPMorgan Chase, Citigroup, and GMAC.

63 *"The fact that a loan":* Nomura Fixed Income Research, "Modify This!—Policymakers Are Wrong to Push for Loan Modifications to Help Defaulted Borrowers," June 22, 2007, www.scribd.com/doc/19606927/Nomura-Modify-This-Policy-Makers-Are-Wrong -to-Push-for-Loan-Modifications-to-Help-Defaulted-Borrowers.

63 *"conflicts between different classes":* Nomura Fixed Income Research, "Sub-prime Mortgage Loan Servicing and Loss Mitigation," May 18, 2007, www.securitization .net/pdf/Nomura/SecRealEstate_18May07.pdf.

63 *bond investors took a beating:* See, e.g., Al Yoon, "Investors Sour on Subprime Bonds," *The Wall Street Journal,* January 7, 2012, http://online.wsj.com/article/SB100014240 52970204331304577144803354669424.html.

64 *Following our efforts:* United States Senate Committee on Banking, Housing, and Urban Affairs, "Dodd Unifies Industry Members, Consumer Representatives to Help Preserve American Dream of Home Ownership," May 2, 2007, http://banking.senate .gov/public/index.cfm?FuseAction=Newsroom.PressReleases&ContentRecord_id= e4507b48-341e-423b-8221-e994e25323ba&Region_id=&Issue_id=.

65 *issuing guidance:* Board of Governors of the Federal Reserve System, "Federal Regulators Encourage Institutions to Work with Mortgage Borrowers Who Are Unable

to Make Their Payments," April 17, 2007, www.federalreserve.gov/newsevents/press/bcreg/20070417a.htm.

65 *I do not think that the other regulators:* In May of 2012, OCC was cited by the Treasury Department's inspector general for numerous deficiencies in its examination of the big banks' mortgage-servicing operations. Specifically, the Treasury IG found that "OCC examination procedures during the period 2008 through 2010 were not sufficient in scope or application to identify significant weaknesses in national banks' foreclosure documentation and processing functions. During this time OCC did not consider foreclosure documentation and processing to be an area of significant risk and, as a result, did not focus examination resources on this function." See Office of the Inspector General, US Treasury Department Audit Report, OIG-12–054 Audit Report, "Safety and Soundness: OCC's Supervision of National Bank's Foreclosure Practices," May 31, 2012.

65 *"These guys will step over":* Another reported source of opposition to loan modifications was hedge fund managers and other investors who had "shorted" the housing markets. This means that they had placed large financial bets on something called the ABX index, which tracked defaults on subprime mortgages contained in a select number of securitization pools. The more such mortgages defaulted, the more profit for those who had shorted the index. To the extent that loan modifications reduced the number of defaults, ABX shorts would lose money. See, e.g., "Bear Stearns at Center of New Subprime Firestorm," June 7, 2007, www.housingwire.com/news/bear-stearns-center-new-subprime-firestorm.

66 *"Frankly, I'm frustrated":* FDIC, "Remarks by FDIC Chairman Sheila Bair at Clayton Holding Inc. Investor Conference—New York, NY," October 4, 2007, www.fdic.gov/news/news/speeches/archives/2007/chairman/spoct0407_2.html.

67 *"The mortgage crisis is growing":* Sheila C. Bair, "Fix Rates to Save Loans," op-ed, *The New York Times,* October 19, 2007, www.nytimes.com/2007/10/19/opinion/19bair.html.

67 *I received editorial endorsements:* "Moving Ahead on Mortgages," editorial, *The New York Times,* October 28, 2007, www.nytimes.com/2007/10/28/opinion/28sun1.html; "Mortgage Meltdown," editorial, *The Wall Street Journal,* October 24, 2007, http://online.wsj.com/article/SB119318185110369077.html.

67 *"there's been a realization":* Cheyenne Hopkins, "Modification: Tentative Steps Toward a Regulatory Consensus," *American Banker,* November 27, 2007, www.americanbanker.com/issues/172_231/-337575-1.html.

68 *Our efforts to convince:* Ibid.

69 *But the agreement:* Ibid. See also "Gov. Schwarzenegger Works with Lenders to Help Homeowners Avoid Foreclosure," November 20, 2007, www.highbeam.com/doc/1P3-1386790921.html.

Chapter 7: The Audacity of That Woman

74 *Citi and others were forced:* Shannon D. Harrington and Elizabeth Hester, "Citigroup to Consolidate Seven SIVs on Balance Sheet (Update3)," December 13, 2007, www.bloomberg.com/apps/news?pid=newsarchive&sid=aT0Ix2iDnZRk.

75 *There were thirteen such institutions:* The thirteen were Fremont Bank, Countrywide, IndyMac, Downey, WaMu, National City Corp., AmTrust Bank, Westernbank, Flagstar Bank, E*Trade, BankUnited, Merrill Lynch, and Colonial Bank. With the excep-

tion of E*Trade, all of these institutions have either failed or been acquired by other institutions.

77 *The local press in Seattle:* See, e.g., Bill Virgin, "Bank Depositors Stay Calm amid Turmoil," *Seattle Post-Intelligencer,* April 2, 2008, www.seattlepi.com/news/article/Bank-depositors-stay-calm-amid-turmoil-1269064.php.

77 *About 90 percent:* See, e.g., Offices of Inspector General, Department of the Treasury, Federal Deposit Insurance Corporation, "Evaluation of Federal Regulatory Oversight of Washington Mutual Bank," April 2010, http://fdicoig.gov/reports10%5C10-002EV.pdf.

78 *"This is something":* Sheila Bair, email to John Reich, April 3, 2008.

78 *analysts' commentary included:* Institutional Risk Analytics, "Is WaMu the Next Bear Stearns?," April 8, 2008, http://marketpipeline.blogspot.com/2008/04/is-wamu-next-bear-stearns.html.

85 *So they are the first:* Shareholders, of course, usually take a complete loss in an FDIC resolution. By the nature of their investment, they are stuck—that is, unlike debtholders, they have no right to be repaid at a certain point, which is why regulators say that equity capital has "loss-absorbing" capability. Similarly, long-term bondholders are stuck until their debt reaches its maturity date. That is another reason it is dangerous to delay a bank closing: The longer regulators wait, the more debt matures and is withdrawn, shifting the costs of failure onto the FDIC and uninsured depositors instead of bondholders.

89 *"glad to talk":* Sheila Bair to John Reich, email re W, August 6, 2011; John Reich, email to Sheila Bair re W, August 6, 2011; Sheila Bair, e-mail to Donald Kohn re W, August 6, 2011; Donald Kohn, email to Sheila Bair re W, August 6, 2011.

92 *"significant support":* Richard Kovacevich, letter to Sheila Bair, September 20, 2008.

Chapter 8: The Wachovia Blindside

98 *In Fed We Trust:* David Wessel, *In Fed We Trust: Ben Bernanke's War on the Great Panic* (New York: Crown, 2009), p. 222.

103 *"extraordinary actions":* Ben Bernanke, email to Sheila Bair, September 30, 2008.

Chapter 9: Bailing Out the Boneheads

108 *stood at $2.7 trillion:* FDIC Quarterly Banking Profile, Fourth Quarter 2008. www2.fdic.gov/qbp/2008dec/qbp.pdf.

111 *But the word I got back:* Email exchange among Sheila Bair, David Nason, and Keith Hennessey, October 1, 2008.

111 *"Do you want to discuss":* Email exchange between Jesse Villarreal and Christal West, October 8, 2008.

111 *"It is the policy":* Christal West, email to Sheila Bair, October 8, 2008.

112 *On the following Friday:* Sheila Bair, email to Henry Paulson, Ben Bernanke, and Timothy Geithner re Discussion Draft—systemic risk actions, October 10, 2008.

117 *"have also committed":* Board of Governors of the Federal Reserve System, "Joint Statement by Treasury, Federal Reserve, and FDIC," October 14, 2008, www.federalreserve.gov/newsevents/press/monetary/20081014a.htm; David Barr, email to Michele Davis re JOINT Statement 10-14-draft (October 13, 2008).

119 *"Our best available information"*: Sheila Bair, email to Henry Paulson and Ben Bernanke, October 9, 2008.

120 *the big banks still pulled back:* Loan balances at banking organizations with assets greater than $100 billion fell by 11.4 percent during the crisis, in comparison with banks with less than $1 billion in assets, whose balances grew by 3 percent. Smaller institutions also consistently maintained capital ratios 2 to 4 percent higher than the largest institutions. See following note.

120 *Throughout the crisis:* Christopher Newbury, email to Sheila Bair re Information on loan growth and capital, December 16, 2011.

Chapter 10: Doubling Down on Citi: Bailout Number Two

121 *Indeed, in 2007:* See, e.g., "Citigroup's Vanished Dividend," November 24, 2008, http://blogs.wsj.com/marketbeat/2008/11/24/citigroups-vanished-dividend/.

122 *A few months later:* David Enrich and Jenny Strasburg, "Citigroup to Close Hedge Fund; Blow to CEO," *The Wall Street Journal,* June 12, 2008, http://online.wsj.com/article/SB121323783398666999.html.

124 *"If they go down"*: Henry M. Paulson, Jr., *On the Brink: Inside the Race to Stop the Collapse of the Global Financial System* (New York: Business Plus, 2010), p. 409.

124 *Financial Crisis Inquiry Commission:* The FCIC was a special commission created by Congress to investigate the causes of the financial crisis. Its report, issued in January 2011, can be found at http://fcic-static.law.stanford.edu/cdn_media/fcic-reports/fcic_final_report_full.pdf.

126 *"Is that the standard now"*: Transcript of FDIC Board of Directors meeting, November 23, 2008, http://cybercemetery.unt.edu/archive/fcic/20110310194137/http://c0181567.cdn1.cloudfiles.rackspacecloud.com/2008-11-23%20Transcript%20of%20FDIC%20Board%20of%20Directors%20meeting,%20closed%20session.pdf, p. 21.

126 *"[W]hat is your supervisory strategy?"*: Ibid., pp. 22–23.

128 *"Why there's been"*: Damien Paletta, "FDIC Chief Raps Rescue for Helping Banks over Homeowners," *The Wall Street Journal,* October 16, 2008, http://online.wsj.com/article/SB122411533644338623.html.

128 *Ben Bernanke personally intervened:* Email exchange between Sheila Bair and Ben Bernanke re Interagency statement, November 9, 2008.

Chapter 11: Helping Home Owners, Round Two

131 *"use loan guarantees"*: Emergency Economic Stabilization Act of 2008, section 109, available at www.govtrack.us/congress/bills/110/hr1424.

131 *had initiated conversations:* Neel Kashkari, email to S. Bair re Insurance, October 7, 2008; Richard Brown, email to Neel Kashkari re Proposal-Guaranty Program to Encourage Loan Modifications, October 7, 2008.

134 *"Eliminating even all foreclosures"*: White House briefing paper, "Housing Policy Options," Principals meeting, October 27, 2008.

135 *According to RealtyTrac:* "Foreclosure Activity Increases 81 Percent in 2008," January 15, 2009, www.realtytrac.com/content/press-releases/foreclosure-activity-increases-81-percent-in-2008-4551.

135 *Home prices were already down:* Henry Blodget, "U.S. House Price Decline Could Be

Worse than Great Depression, Economist Shiller Says," September 4, 2008, http://finance.yahoo.com/tech-ticker/article/53094/U.S.-House-Price-Decline-Could-Be-Worse-than-Great-Depression?tickers=^gspc,fre,fnm.

137 *I communicated my concerns:* Sheila Bair, email to Henry Paulson re Questions on the Interest Share Proposal, October 30, 2008.

137 *We continued our discussions:* Sheila Bair, email to Henry Paulson re More on Loan Mods-plus our cost estimate, November 5, 2008.

137 *Even the American Bankers Association:* Edward Yingling, letter to Henry Paulson and Sheila Bair, December 11, 2008.

138 *The OCC press office:* In the first quarter of 2009, the OCC released a second report differentiating between loan mods that reduced payments and those that did not. To his credit, John Dugan acknowledged to me that "the evidence supports the premise that significantly reduced monthly payments have a much lower re-default rate" and that "less than half of the mods in 2008 reduced monthly payments." John Dugan, email to Sheila Bair, April 2, 2009.

138 *Duhigg had all:* Charles Duhigg, "Fighting Foreclosures, F.D.I.C. Chief Draws Fire," *The New York Times,* December 10, 2008, www.nytimes.com/2008/12/11/business/11bair.html?pagewanted=all.

138 *I liked Martin Feldstein's program:* Professor Feldstein's proposal took the same general approach as the HOP loans program we had proposed in early 2008 to provide lower interest, deferred payment loans to borrowers to pay down principal on unaffordable loans, with the government having priority for repayment from foreclosure sale proceeds if the borrower defaulted later on.

139 *Rather, it was being driven:* I think Hank truly wanted to launch a comprehensive loan modification program. He later told me that he had been caught between two administrations. Congress had given him only $350 billion of TARP money. He believed he needed the support of the Obama administration to get congressional support to release the second $350 billion installment of TARP. He felt he needed at least $350 billion for financial institution stabilization, so he was reluctant to commit substantial money to loan modifications unless it was combined with a takedown of the second $350 billion installment. However, the Obama team refused to work with the Bush team to take down the additional TARP funds (presumably because it wanted to offer its own program). Thus a decision on loan modifications stayed in limbo for several months. Ironically, when the Obama team did finally launch a program, it was the one that we had previously advised Paulson against because it was too operationally complex and the incentives were too weak to have an impact.

Chapter 12: Obama's Election: The More Things Change . . .

141 *He had been highly supportive:* John Podesta, email to Sheila Bair re Keynote Invitation, October 5, 2008.

141 *I offered my agency's help:* Sheila Bair, email to John Podesta re Congrats, November 7, 2008.

141 *also took the liberty:* Sheila Bair, email to John Podesta re My Vote for Volcker, November 10, 2008.

142 *would head the CFTC:* Unlike Geithner, Summers, and Rubin, Gensler very publicly

renounced his deregulatory views in the Rubin Treasury Department and has worked hard at the CFTC to provide better oversight of the derivatives markets.

142 *President Clinton himself said:* E. Harris, "Clinton: I Was Wrong to Listen to Wrong Advice Against Regulating Derivatives," ABC News.

143 *"Timothy Geithner":* Robert Schmidt, "Geithner Seeks to Push FDIC's Bair Out After Clashes (Update1)," December 4, 2008, www.bloomberg.com/apps/news?pid=wash ingtonstory&sid=aTFflUwD.Qbg.

145 *We gave Summers's people:* Email exchange between Michael Krimminger and Sarah Aronchick re FDIC Loss Sharing Proposal, November 28, 2008.

Chapter 13: Helping Home Owners, Round Three

152 *In the spring of 2011:* See, e.g., "Statement of Neil Barofsky, Special Inspector General, Troubled Asset Relief Program, Before the House Committee on Financial Services, Subcommittee on Insurance, Housing and Community Opportunity," March 2, 2011, http://financialservices.house.gov/media/pdf/030211barofsky.pdf.

152 *"scary redefault numbers":* "Executive Summary of Economic Policy Work," December 15, 2008, www.documentcloud.org/documents/285065-summers-12-15-08-memo .html#document/p1, p. 35.

Chapter 14: The $100 Billion Club

159 *The Dow Jones Industrial Average:* See, e.g., Eric Dash and Jack Healy, "Stocks Plunge as Geithner Announces New Bailout Plan," *The New York Times,* February 11, 2009, www.nytimes.com/2009/02/11/business/11markets.html?pagewanted=all.

159 *Ironically, Citi and other:* See, e.g., Colin Barr, "Bank Stress Tests Cause More Stress," February 18, 2009, http://money.cnn.com/2009/02/18/news/stress.test.fortune/.

159 *"[T]he capital needs":* Board of Governors of the Federal Reserve System, "Joint Statement by the Treasury, FDIC, OCC, OTS, and the Federal Reserve," February 23, 2009, www.federalreserve.gov/newsevents/press/bcreg/20090223a.htm.

159 *He was quoted:* Alan Rappeport, "Buffett Hits Out at Stress Tests," *Financial Times,* May 3, 2009, www.ft.com/cms/s/0/e7734cc8-3822-11de-9211-00144feabdc0.html #axzz1vHPV1iQV.

160 *In one situation:* Jason Cave, email to Sheila Bair re stress test update, April 5, 2009 (citing FDIC examiner analysis).

160 *The result:* John Corston, email to Jason Cave re Possible Concerns with potential below the line adjustments to the CAP stress testing, May 1, 2009; email exchanges among Daniel Frye, Robert Burns, Jason Cave, and Sheila Bair re Latest Stress Test Results, May 3, 2009.

161 *I issued a separate statement:* FDIC, "Statement by FDIC Chairman Sheila C. Bair on Stress Tests," May 7, 2009, www.fdic.gov/news/news/press/2009/pr09067.html.

161 *with Ben Bernanke's help:* Email exchanges among Sheila Bair, John Dugan, and Ben Bernanke re Capital Bogey, April 21, 2009.

162 *I was fearful:* Sheila Bair, email to Timothy Geithner re Monday, March 21, 2009.

162 *The column started snidely:* Andrew Ross Sorkin, "'No-Risk' Insurance at F.D.I.C.," *The New York Times,* April 6, 2009, www.nytimes.com/2009/04/07/business/07sorkin .html.

Chapter 15: The Care and Feeding of Citigroup: Bailout Number Three

165 *The institution continued:* Email exchange between Sheila Bair and Jason Cave re Citi Update, January 10, 2009.

166 *The ratings agencies:* Moody's press release, January 16, 2009 "Moody's Places Citigroup's ratings (snr at A2 and Prime-1) under review for possible downgrade," as corrected January 21, 2009, www.moody's.com/research/correction-to-text-jan-16 -2009-release-moody's-places-citigroup—PR_171191.

167 *We had also hoped:* Email exchange among Jason Cave, Lee Sachs, and Sheila Bair Re Press release, February 26, 2009.

167 *Treasury agreed to convert:* U.S. Department of the Treasury, "Treasury Announces Participation in Citigroup's Exchange Offering," February 27, 2009, www.treasury .gov/press-center/press-releases/Pages/tg41.aspx.

168 *included 305 banks:* FDIC, "Quarterly Banking Profile First Quarter 2009," www2 .fdic.gov/qbp/2009mar/qbp.pdf.

168 *Jason notified me:* Jason Cave, email to Sheila Bair re OCC-Citi, January 21, 2009.

169 *were actually raising capital:* Specifically, the holding company was issuing debt and then using the money to buy common stock from the bank. That made it look as if the bank's capital ratios were going up, but it was all coming from funds borrowed through our debt guarantee program.

169 *The following day:* Sheila Bair, email to Donald Kohn, John Dugan, and William Dudley re Citi, February 22, 2009.

170 *I would later read:* Ron Suskind, *Confidence Men: Wall Street, Washington, and the Education of a President* (New York: HarperCollins, 2011), p. 212.

170 *The next day:* Sheila Bair, email to Michael Krimminger and Jason Cave re Citibank, March 10, 2009.

171 *On May 26, 2009:* Sandra Thompson, letter to William Rhodes, May 26, 2009.

171 *William Rhodes:* Pandit was the CEO of Citigroup, the organization that included Citibank as a subsidiary. Rhodes served as the CEO of the bank. However, Rhodes had little real authority over the bank. That was one of the problems.

171 *Then, on June 5:* Damien Paletta and David Enrich, "FDIC Pushes Purge at Citi: Bair Wants to Shake Up Management, Sought to Cut Rating of Bank's Health," *The Wall Street Journal,* June 5, 2009, http://online.wsj.com/article/SB124417114172687983 .html#mod=todays_us_page_one.

172 *they were put to rest:* Bradley Keoun and Alison Vekshin, "Citigroup Gains Geithner Backing as Pandit Bucks Bair," June 8, 2009, www.bloomberg.com/apps/news?pid= newsarchive&sid=alp4yE9HJBtI.

172 *That was acknowledged:* Email exchanges between Sheila Bair and Mike Bradfield re Citigroup Disclaimer, June 7, 2009.

173 *Throughout the ensuing negotiations:* Email exchange between Sheila Bair and William Dudley re Citi, June 25, 26, and 28, July 14, 2009.

173 *to run the bank:* Regrettably, after my departure from the FDIC, both Grundhofer and McQuade announced they were leaving Citi, depriving it of much needed commercial banking expertise.

174 *At the end of July:* Rita Proctor, email to Sheila Bair re Parson's Request for a Meeting, July 31, 2009.

174 *When the "independent consultant" report:* Email exchange between Sheila Bair and Jason Cave re Meeting with EZI, October 8 and 9, 2009.

174 *until we found out about it and objected*: Email exchange between Sheila Bair and Mike Bradfield re Citi-EZI Engagement Letter, August 5 and 6, 2009.

Chapter 16: Finally Saying No

175 *The charge was*: SEC, "SEC Charges Steven Rattner in Pay-to-Play Scheme Involving New York State Pension Fund," November 18, 2010, www.sec.gov/news/press/2010/2010-224.htm.

176 *I had half jokingly told him*: Sheila Bair, email to Henry Paulson re GM, December 17, 2008.

176 *a "comfort letter"*: Timothy Geithner and Ben Bernanke, letter to Sheila Bair, March 19, 2009.

177 *On May 20, 2009*: GMAC, "GMAC Financial Services Announces Key Capital and Liquidity Actions," May 21, 2009, http://media.gmacfs.com/index.php?s=43&item=331.

178 *Then, in March*: Saskia Scholtes, Francesco Guerrera, and Joanna Chung, "Debt Wait for GMAC and CIT," *Financial Times,* March 31, 2009, www.ft.com/intl/cms/s/0/d44090e6-1d53-11de-9eb3-00144feabdc0.html#axzz1vHPV1iQV.

179 *I finally told Lee*: Sheila Bair, email to Lee Sachs re CIT, July 12, 2009.

Chapter 17: Never Again

181 *On Sunday*: Edmund L. Andrews and Peter Baker, "A.I.G. Planning Huge Bonuses After $170 Billion Bailout," *The New York Times,* March 14, 2009, www.nytimes.com/2009/03/15/business/15AIG.html.

183 *On March 19*: Opening Statement of Chairman Christopher J. Dodd, "Modernizing Bank Supervision and Regulation," Hearings Before the Senate Committee on Banking, Housing, and Urban Affairs (March 19, 2009) Hearing Transcript, Senate Banking Committee. See also email from Paul Nash to Sheila Bair Re Congress Daily Report on Today's Hearing (March 19, 2009, Congress Daily).

183 *They had already given*: Email exchange between Sheila Bair and Paul Nash re Draft Resolution Language, March 24, 2009.

183 *On March 25*: U.S. Department of the Treasury, "Treasury Proposes Legislation for Resolution Authority," March 25, 2009, www.treasury.gov/press-center/press-releases/Pages/tg70.aspx.

188 *"Everybody should have"*: FDIC, "Remarks by FDIC Chairman Sheila Bair to The Economic Club of New York; New York, New York," April 27, 2009, www.fdic.gov/news/news/speeches/archives/2009/spapr2709.html.

189 *But I also made*: Sheila Bair, email to Rahm Emanuel re Regulatory Reform, May 27, 2009.

189 *"I don't believe"*: Robert Schmidt and Rebecca Christie, "Geithner Signals Openness to Council of Regulators in Shift," June 9, 2009, www.bloomberg.com/apps/news?pid=newsarchive&sid=aSo.cw4af5l0.

190 *"UST [U.S. Treasury] would vest"*: Michael Krimminger, email to Sheila Bair re Treasury White Paper, June 21, 2009.

191 *"a comprehensive regulatory reform plan"*: "President Obama to Announce Comprehensive Plan for Regulatory Reform," White House press release, June 17, 2009, www

.whitehouse.gov/the_press_office/President-Obama-to-Announce-Comprehensive
-Plan-for-Regulatory-Reform.

191 *"codifying TARP"*: Paul Nash, email to Sheila Bair re Treasury White Paper, June 22, 2009.

192 *"For big banks"*: Darrell Delamaide, "Political Posturing Plays Increasing Role in Regulatory Reform Debate," November 6, 2009, www.finreg21.com/news/political-posturing-plays-increasing-role-regulatory-reform-debate?page=3.

192 *But the idea quickly ran:* See, e.g., Bill Swindell, "Congress Daily: Dodd's Plan for Single Bank Regulator Runs into Frank," September 23, 2009, www.financialservicesforum.org/index.php/forum-in-the-news/83-dodds-plan-for-single-bank-regulator-runs-into-frank-.html.

193 *However, earlier in the year:* FFIEC, "FFIEC Statement on Regulatory Conversions," July 1, 2009, www.ffiec.gov/pdf/pr070109_statement.pdf.

193 *As I wrote in an op-ed:* Sheila C. Bair, "The Case Against a Super-Regulator," op-ed, *The New York Times,* August 31, 2009, www.nytimes.com/2009/09/01/opinion/01bair.html.

194 *The company's assets:* See, e.g., Linda Sandler, "Lehman Enters Final Bankruptcy Phase as Judge Approves Plan," December 6, 2011, www.bloomberg.com/news/2011-12-07/lehman-enters-final-bankruptcy-phase-as-judge-approves-plan-2-.html; Anthony Bond, "Lehman Gets Permission to Exit Bankruptcy Three Years after Catastrophic Collapse," *Daily Mail,* December 7, 2011, www.dailymail.co.uk/news/article-2070992/Lehman-gets-permission-exit-bankruptcy-years-catastrophic-collapse.html.

194 *In 2011, the FDIC staff:* "The Orderly Liquidation of Lehman Brothers Holdings Inc. Under the Dodd-Frank Act," *FDIC Quarterly* 5, no. 2 (2011), www.fdic.gov/bank/analytical/quarterly/2011_vol5_2/lehman.pdf, p.18.

196 *"Congress should also":* "Statement of Sheila C. Bair, Chairman, Federal Deposit Insurance Corporation, on Systemic Regulation, Prudential Measures, Resolution Authority and Securitization before the Financial Services Committee, U.S. House of Representatives," October 29, 2009, www.house.gov/apps/list/hearing/financialsvcs_dem/bair.pdf, p. 7.

196 *"To be credible":* Ibid., pp. 8–9.

197 *Paul Nash immediately received:* Paul Nash, email to Sheila Bair re Ex Ante Fund, October 29, 2009.

197 *"gets enormous":* Phil, Mattingly and Benton Ives, "Frank Outlines Possible Adjustments to Financial Regulatory Package," CQ, November 3, 2009; Mike. Ferullo, "House Panel to Consider Systemic Risk Bill with Amendments on Size Limits, Funding," November 4, 2009.

197 *Subsequently, his staff:* Paul Nash, email to Sheila Bair re Summary of Resolution Bill, October 24, 2009.

197 *Chairman Dodd's staff was also:* Paul Nash, email to Sheila Bair re Dodd Meeting, November 4, 2009.

197 *But Frank was sticking:* Paul Nash, email to Sheila Bair re another quote, November 6, 2009.

199 *I received an irate call:* Sheila Bair, email to Paul Nash re No Go, December 7, 2009.

Chapter 18: It's All About the Compensation

207 *"interagency sharing of data"*: SIGTARP, "Exiting TARP: Repayments by the Largest Financial Institutions," September 29, 2011, www.sigtarp.gov/Audit%20Reports/ Exiting_TARP_Repayments_by_the_Largest_Financial_Institutions.pdf, n.p.

207 *"exclusion of such information"*: Ibid., p. 3.

207 *"There is nothing"*: Louise Story and Eric Dash, "Banks Prepare for Big Bonuses, and Public Wrath," *The New York Times,* January 9, 2010, www.nytimes.com/2010/01/10/ business/10pay.html.

208 *They were working on a story:* Keith Epstein and David Heath, "FDIC Chief Got Bank of America Loans While Working on Its Rescue," January 21, 2010, www.huffington post.com/2010/01/21/fdic-chief-got-bank-of-am_n_431316.html.

212 *"We saw no evidence"*: Office of Inspector General, FDIC, "Evaluation of Allegations Pertaining to the Chairman's Mortgage Loans with Bank of America," April 2010, www.fdicoig.gov/reports10/10-003EV.pdf.

Chapter 19: The Senate's Orwellian Debate

214 *13(3) authority:* 13(3) is an obscure provision in the Federal Reserve Act authorizing the Fed to lend to a broad range of entities, not just insured banks, in crisis situations. The Fed did not use 13(3) for seventy-eight years—even after the 9/11 terrorist attacks—fearing the kind of precedent it would set and the potential to create moral hazard. However, beginning with the 2008 crisis, the Fed started using 13(3) in unprecedented ways, providing trillions of dollars in loans to a wide variety of institutions.

214 *The term "financial market utility"*: Peter Nash, email to Sheila Bair re definition of utility, March 18, 2010. The definition was as follows: "The term financial market utility means any person that manages or operates a multilateral system for the purpose of transferring, clearing, or settling payments, securities, or other financial transactions among financial institutions or between financial institutions and the person."

215 *"If the Congress accomplishes"*: "Remarks by FDIC Chairman Sheila C. Bair to the Independent Community Bankers of America's 2010 National Convention and Techworld; Orlando, Florida," March 19, 2010, www.fdic.gov/news/news/speeches/chair man/spmar1910.html.

215 *That same day, Dodd announced:* See, e.g., Peter Mattingly, "Dodd to Cut 'Back-Door Bailout' from Financial Regulation," March 20, 2010, www.pressherald.com/busi ness/dodd-to-cutback-door-bailout-from-financial-regulation-plan_2010-03-19 .html.

216 *He wrote Tim on March 25:* Senator Richard Shelby, letter to The Honorable Tim Geithner, March 25, 2010.

216 *In a subsequent letter:* Senator Mitch McConnell, letter to Senator Harry Reid, April 16, 2010.

216 *On April 13:* Rebecca Christie, "Wolin Says Partisan Fights Shouldn't Weaken Financial Overhaul," April 13, 2010.

216 *"Obama administration officials"*: Associated Press, "White House Urges Change in U.S. Bank Bill," www.usatoday.com/news/washington/2010-04-16-obama-financial -reform_N.htm.

216 *I forwarded the story:* Email exchange between Rahm Emanuel and Sheila Bair, April 16, 2010.

217 *Polls showed:* Washington Post-ABC News Poll, April 26, 2010, www.washington post.com/wp-srv/politics/documents/postpoll_042810.html.

217 *Indeed, there were press reports:* On April 12, 2010, Fox News reported that Senator McConnell had met with several hedge fund managers and other Wall Street executives to discuss financial reform, On April 13, McConnell called for dropping the prepaid fund.

218 *"the prepay model":* Andrew Ross Sorkin, "To Prepay for a Crisis, or Not," May 25, 2010, http://dealbook.nytimes.com/2010/05/25/sorkin-to-prepay-for-a-crisis-or-not/.

218 *"The real question is":* Sheila C. Bair, "The Right Way to Close Down a Failed Bank," letter to the editor, *The Washington Post,* May 2, 2010, www.washingtonpost.com/wp-dyn/content/article/2010/05/01/AR2010050102809.html.

220 *Indeed, one actually had:* Sheila Bair, letter to Larry Uhlick, May 21, 2010.

221 *"Sen. Collins' amendment":* David Reilly, "Still a Hill to Climb on Bank Capital," *The Wall Street Journal,* May 20, 2010, http://online.wsj.com/article/SB100014240527487 03691804575254810469124620.html.

223 *The provision went further:* Sheila Bair, letter to Senator Christopher Dodd, May 11, 2010.

224 *an inflammatory analysis:* Edward Yingling, letter to Martin Gruenberg re Impact of the Collins Amendment (June 10, 2010).

224 *"You might hear a collective":* Damian Paletta, "Financial Overhaul Likely to Be More Restrictive on Banks' Capital Requirements," *The Wall Street Journal,* June 17, 2010, http://blogs.wsj.com/economics/2010/06/17/financial-overhaul-likely-to-be-more -restrictive-on-banks-capital-requirements/.

225 *at the time a top official:* Diamond was subsequently promoted to the position of Chairman and CEO of Barclays, only to resign on July 3, 2012, over a scandal involving Barclay's efforts to manipulate the London interbank offered rate (Libor) a widely used benchmark for setting interest rates on loans and derivatives contracts. See Ben Protess and Mark Scott, "Barclay's CEO Resigns as Bank Frames a Defense" *The New York Times,* July 4, 2012.

225 *"as much as $1.5 trillion":* Meena Thiruvengadam, "DJ Barclay's President: Collins Plan Could Cut Credit Availability by $1.5T," June 23, 2010, http://tools.morning star.co.uk/uk/stockreport/default.aspx?tab=3&vw=story&SecurityToken=0P0000 7NZP]3]0]E0GBR$$ALL&Id=0P00007NZP&ClientFund=0&CurrencyId=GBP& story=111443663944971.

225 *Numerous government and academic studies:* Samuel Hanson, Anil K. Kashyap, and Jeremy C. Stein, "A Macroprudential Approach to Financial Regulation," first draft, July 2010, http://web.williams.edu/Economics/seminars/steinJEP.pdf; Macroeconomic Assessment Group, "Interim Report: Assessing the Macroeconomic Impact of the Transition to Stronger Capital and Liquidity Requirements" (Basel, Switzerland: Bank for International Settlements, August 2010), www.bis.org/publ/othp10.pdf; David Miles, Jing Yang, and Gilberto Marcheggiano, "Optimal Bank Capital," Discussion Paper No. 31: revised and expanded version, Bank of England, April 2011, www .bankofengland.co.uk/publications/Documents/externalmpcpapers/extmpcpaper 0031.pdf.

227 *Specifically, Geithner agreed:* See, e.g., Alison Vekshin and Phil Mattingly, "Lawmak-

ers Reach Compromise on Financial Regulations," June 26, 2010, www.bloomberg
.com/news/2010-06-25/lawmakers-reach-compromise-on-financial-regulation.html.

228 *"And finally"*: "Remarks of the President at Signing of Dodd-Frank Wall Street
Reform and Consumer Protection Act," White House press release, July 21, 2010,
www.whitehouse.gov/the-press-office/remarks-president-signing-dodd-frank-wall
-street-reform-and-consumer-protection-act.

229 *Senator Dodd had spoken:* Author's interview with Christopher Dodd, February 14,
2012.

Chapter 20: Dodd-Frank Implementation: The Final Stretch (or So I Thought)

232 *I also instituted:* See, e.g., Tim Fernholz, "FDIC's Sheila Bair Embraces Transparency,"
The American Prospect, July 12, 2010, http://web01.prospect.org/article/fdics-sheila
-bair-embraces-transparency.

233 *The combined effect:* FDIC, "FDIC Board Proposes Implementation of Dodd-Frank
Assessment Changes and a Revised Assessment System for Large Institutions,"
November 9, 2010, www.fdic.gov/news/news/press/2010/pr10248.html; FDIC, "FDIC
Approves Final Rule of Assessments, Dividends, Assessment Base, and Large Bank
Pricing," February 7, 2011, www.fdic.gov/news/news/press/2011/pr11028.html.

234 *in May 2010, we proposed:* FDIC, "FDIC Board Approves NPR Regarding Safe Harbor
Protection for Securitizations," May 11, 2010, www.fdic.gov/news/news/press/2010/
pr10112.html.

235 *When I did finally:* Ben Bernanke, email to Sheila Bair re securitization rulemaking,
September 27, 2010.

236 *We also pushed:* Email exchange among Sheila Bair, John Walsh, and Daniel Tarullo,
January 10, 2010.

237 *Finally, after receiving letters:* Yves Smith, email to Sheila Bair re Citizens Call for
Tough Regulation of Residential Mortgage Servicers, January 4, 2011.

237 *"By mandating":* Floyd Norris, "A Flaw in New Rules for Mortgages," *The New York
Times,* March 31, 2011, www.nytimes.com/2011/04/01/business/01norris.html?page
wanted=all.

238 *We finalized it:* Board of Governors of the Federal Reserve System, "Agencies Adopt
a Final Rule to Establish a Risk-Based Capital Floor," June 14, 2011, www.federal
reserve.gov/newsevents/press/bcreg/20110614a.htm.

239 *In addition, I circulated:* Sheila Bair, email to Tim Geithner et al. re Interim Final
Regulation, September 17, 2010.

239 *Nevertheless, John Walsh argued:* Michael Krimminger, email to Sheila Bair re Consultation Requirement, September 24, 2010.

239 *we waited until October 12:* "FDIC Board Issues Proposed Rule on Claims Process,"
October 12, 2010.

240 *"Geithner feels that Treasury":* Michael Krimminger, email to Sheila Bair re Heads-up
Important, January 12, 2011.

240 *On March 21:* Sheila Bair, letter to Timothy Geithner, March 21, 2011.

Chapter 21: Robo-Signing Erupts

243   *On September 20:* See, e.g., David Streitfeld, "GMAC Halts Foreclosures in 23 States for Review," *The New York Times,* September 20, 2010, www.nytimes.com/2010/09/21/business/21mortgage.html.

244   *The OCC and Fed:* Michael Krimminger, email to Sheila Bair re SBC Meeting on "robo-signing" issue, October 18, 2010.

244   *HUD and the Treasury Department:* Michael Krimminger, email to Sheila Bair re Draft Joint Statement for Wednesday Inter-agency Meeting, October 19, 2010.

246   *"Given the continued":* Sheila Bair, letter to Ben Bernanke, November 5, 2010.

246   *I sent a similar letter:* Sheila Bair, letter to John Walsh, November 5, 2010.

247   *The disagreements came to a head:* "Statement of Sheila C. Bair, Chairman, Federal Deposit Insurance Corporation, on Problems in Mortgage Servicing from Modification to Foreclosure, Part II, Committee on Banking, Housing, and Urban Affairs," December 1, 2010, http://banking.senate.gov/public/index.cfm?FuseAction=Files.View&FileStore_id=318beba2-a775-4a7b-98b8-14aff84c07ab.

247   *"While quite preliminary":* Statement by Daniel K. Tarullo, Member, Board of Governors of the Federal Reserve System, before the Committee on Banking, Housing and Urban Affairs, United States Senate, Washington, D.C.," December 1, 2010, www.federalreserve.gov/newsevents/testimony/tarullo20101201a.pdf, pp. 4–5.

248   *The day after the hearing:* Sheila Bair, email to Daniel Tarullo re OCC, December 2, 2010.

248   *"This will give us":* Sheila Bair, email to John Walsh re Foreclosure Examinations, December 17, 2010.

248   *Walsh responded:* Email exchange between Sheila Bair and John Walsh re Foreclosure Examinations, December 19, 2010.

249   *which I had advocated:* Opening Address by FDIC Chairman Sheila C. Bair, Summit on Residential Mortgage Servicing for the 21st Century, sponsored by the Mortgage Bankers Association, Washington, D.C., Wednesday, January 19, 2011, http://fdic.gov/news/news/speeches/archives/2011/spjan1911.html.

249   *As numerous studies have documented:* See, e.g., Fitch Ratings, "Global Rating Criteria for Structured Finance Servicers," New York, August 2010, pp. 1, 2, 7; Barclays Capital, "Evolution of Loan Modification Performance," New York, June 2010, pp. 1, 3, 5; Standard & Poor's,. "Servicer Evaluation: Quantum Servicing Corp," New York, December 2007, p. 10; Moody's Investors Service. *Rating Methodology and Housing Research.* Moody's Housing Finance, New York, September 2007, p. 86.

249   *"If we are":* "Opening Address by FDIC Chairman Sheila Bair, Summit on Residential Mortgage Servicing for the 21st Century, Sponsored by the Mortgage Bankers Association; Washington, D.C.," January 19, 2011, www.fdic.gov/news/news/speeches/chairman/spjan1911.html.

249   *"this would be":* Ibid.

250   *A number of influential members:* Senator Jack Reed, letter to Timothy Geithner, January 5, 2011.

250   *On February 7:* The five biggest servicers are BofA, JPMorgan Chase, Wells Fargo, Citigroup, and GMAC. See Sheila Bair, email to Timothy Geithner re FSOC Statement, February 7, 2011.

253   *one of the servicers:* J. Cave, email to Sheila Bair re Foreclosure Exams, January 25, 2010.

254 *I issued a separate statement:* "FDIC Statement on Enforcement Orders Against Large Servicers Related to Foreclosure Practices," April 13, 2011, www.fdic.gov/news/news/press/2011/pr11069.html.

254 *In early June:* Sheila Bair, email to John Walsh, Daniel Tarullo, and John Bowman re Look-Back Reviews, June 6, 2011.

254 *At the end of June:* Office of the Comptroller of the Treasury, To: Chief Executive Officers of All National Banks, Department and Division Heads, and All Examining Personnel, Description: Supervisory Guidance, Subject: Foreclosure Management, OCC 2011-29, June 30, 2011, www.occ.treas.gov/news-issuances/bulletins/2011/bulletin-2011-29.html.

255 *"considering guidance":* "Testimony of Julie Williams, First Senior Deputy and Comptroller and Chief Counsel, Office of the Comptroller of the Currency, Before the Subcommittee on Housing, Transportation, and Community Development of the Committee on Banking, Housing, and Urban Affairs, United States Senate," December 13, 2011, http://banking.senate.gov/public/index.cfm?FuseAction=Files.View&FileStore_id=58a4114b-0e86-4cbf-ad4b-70852d55253d.

256 *The Fed did not let:* Jason Cave, email to Sheila Bair re CBNA Dividend, December 1, 2010.

Chapter 22: The Return to Basel

257 *The work was reinforced:* "Leaders' Statement, The Pittsburgh Summit, Leaders Statement, September 24–25, 2009," www.g20ys.org/docs/Pittsburgh 0.pdf.

259 *In his public pronouncements:* U.S. Department of the Treasury, "Principles for Reforming the U.S. and International Regulatory Capital Framework for Banking Firms," September 3, 2009, www.treasury.gov/press-center/press-releases/Documents/capital-statement_090309.pdf.

259 *He reported back:* J. Cave, email to Sheila Bair re Basel Mtg, June 1, 2010.

260 *The IIF had already circulated:* IIF June 2010 Interim Report on the Cumulative Impact on the Global Economy of Proposed Changes in the Banking Regulatory Framework, available at http://www.iif.com/press/press+151.php.

263 *Philipp Hildebrand:* Hildebrand resigned in January of 2012 amid a controversy surrounding his wife's currency trading.

265 *One research report showed:* Barclays Capital Research, "Can You Trust Risk Weightings at European Banks?" April 6, 2011.

266 *"If we fail":* Sheila Bair, "Road to Safer Banks Runs Through Basel," August 23, 2010, www.ft.com/cms/s/0/a1dfbd02-aee8-11df-8e45-00144feabdc0.html#axzz1vYHHAxtv.

267 *Her report of the meeting:* George French, email to Sheila Bair Re Treasury Meeting Summary, July 23, 2010.

267 *Then, on August 6:* As secretary of the Treasury, Tim was responsible for recommending candidates for all major financial regulatory positions, including the new consumer agency. Many CFPB proponents, including Dodd, had urged the administration to fill the job quickly with a bipartisan candidate, fearing that any delay would play into the hands of opponents of the new agency. Tim failed to recommend a candidate, and in fact, a nominee was not submitted to the Senate until the summer of 2011. In the interim, Republicans have become entrenched in their opposition and there is no prospect that the agency will have a confirmed head before the 2012 presidential elections.

267 *"lobbied me intensely"*: Sheila Bair, memo to the file re TF MTG-new low, August 6, 2010.

268 *"reduce the probability"*: Christian Vits and Gabi Thesing, "ECB's Weber Says Raising Banks' Capital Ratios Won't Slow Economic Growth," September 8, 2010, www bloomberg.com/news/2010-09-08/ecb-s-weber-says-tougher-bank-capital-rules -won-t-harm-economic-growth.html.

268 *a separate press release*: Board of Governors of the Federal Reserve System, "U.S. Banking Agencies Express Support for Basel Agreement," September 12, 2010, www .federalreserve.gov/newsevents/press/bcreg/20100912a.htm.

270 *My suspicions were heightened*: Jason Cave, email to Sheila Bair Re Treasury Cap Surcharge Position, June 16, 2011.

270 *"Why weren't we in the loop?"*: Sheila Bair, email to Daniel Tarullo Re Treasury Cap Surcharge Position, June 16, 2011.

270 *In the meantime Walsh*: Donna Borak, "OCC's Walsh Signals Discord Among U.S. Regulators on SIFI Surcharge," *American Banker*, June 20, 2011, www.american banker.com/issues/176_118/occ-john-walsh-signals-discord-regulators-1039160-1 .html.

270 *Several influential Democratic senators*: See, e.g., Ronald D. Orol, "Bank Regulator Draws Ire of Democrats," June 23, 2011, http://articles.marketwatch.com/2011-06 -23/economy/30738324_1_capital-requirements-large-national-banks-bank-capital.

270 *Vikram Pandit*: Heather Landy, "Pandit Says Basel III Looks Backward, Will Hurt Lending," *American Banker*, October 25, 2010, www.americanbanker.com/ issues/175_205/pandit-says-basel-III-looks-backward-1027574-1.html.

271 *Similarly, during numerous*: See., e.g., Donna Borak and Joe Adler, "Bernanke, Bair Defend the 'Balance' in Regulators' Plans for a Capital Surcharge," *American Banker*, June 22, 2011, www.americanbanker.com/issues/176_120/bair-bernanke-capital -surcharge-1039289-1.html; Nin-Hai Tseng, "Sheila Bair Steps into the Dimon-Bernanke Rumble," June 9, 2011, http://finance.fortune.cnn.com/2011/06/09/sheila -bair-steps-into-the-dimon-bernanke-rumble/.

Chapter 23: Too Small to Save

278 *So in July 2009*: FDIC, "FDIC Board Approves Proposed Policy Statement on Qualifications for Failed Bank Acquisitions," July 2, 2009, www.fdic.gov/news/news/ press/2009/pr09112.html.

278 *"the FDIC is right"*: Andy Stern, "Private Equity and the Banks," *The Wall Street Journal*, August 25, 2009, http://online.wsj.com/article/SB10001424052970203706604574370581617614424.html.

279 *We reduced it*: FDIC, "FDIC Board Approves Final Statement on the Acquisition of Failed Depository Institutions," August 26, 2009, www.fdic.gov/news/news/ press/2009/pr09152.html.

279 *Though that number sounds high*: See, e.g., David Evans, "FDIC May Need $150 Billion Bailout as More Banks Fail (Update3)," September 25, 2008, www.bloomberg .com/apps/news?pid=newsarchive&sid=amZxIbcjZISU. OMB projected losses of about $112 billion.

280 *There was just one catch*: See, e.g., "China Minsheng Bank recognises $120 mln US bank loss," Reuters (November 10, 2009), http://www.reuters.com/article/2009/11/10/ china-minsheng-idUSBJD00320720091110; "East West Bank, Pasadena, California

Assumes All the Deposits of United Commercial Bank, San Francisco, California," November 6, 2009, www.fdic.gov/news/news/press/2009/pr09201.html.

283 *It wanted to know:* Greg Hernandez, email to Andrew Gray re Chairman Interview Request, January 27, 2010.

284 *The FDIC IG did look:* Office of Inspector General, FDIC, "Evaluation of the Timeliness and Factors Considered in Closing Broadway Bank, Chicago, Illinois," August 2010, www.fdicoig.gov/reports10/10-004EV.pdf.

287 *A few days later:* Bianna Golodryga, "Warren Buffett: Nothing Improper in Goldman Transaction," May 3, 2010, http://abcnews.go.com/GMA/buffett-improper-goldman-transaction/story?id=10535378#.T7rdBWX8t8E.

288 *Within a few days:* John D. McKinnon and Elizabeth Williamson, "Goldman Joins Race to Save Chicago Bank," *The Wall Street Journal,* May 13, 2010, http://online.wsj.com/article/SB10001424052748703950804575242772016889464.html?mod=rss_whats_news_us_business.

288 *"have a moral":* Elizabeth Williamson, "Wall Street Scrambles for ShoreBank's Survival," May 17, 2010, http://online.wsj.com/article/SB10001424052748704614204575246760809392200.html.

290 *Indeed, the FDIC inspector general:* Office of Inspector General, FDIC, "Recapitalization and Resolution Efforts Associated with ShoreBank, Chicago, Illinois," March 2011, www.fdicoig.gov/reports11/11-001EV.pdf.

291 *"There is no requirement":* American Bankers Association, "New Deposit Insurance Premium Rates Far Too High, Says ABA," November 2, 2006.

291 *The FDIC board unanimously raised:* Alison Vekshin, "FDIC Sets Premium Rates Above Level US Banks Had Suggested," November 2, 2006.

292 *In October 2008, we approved:* FDIC, "FDIC Board Adopts Restoration Plan— Proposes Higher Assessments on Insured Banks," October 7, 2008, www.fdic.gov/news/news/press/2008/pr08094.html.

293 *That would have brought in:* FDIC, "Deposit Insurance Assessments: Final Rule on Assessments; Amended FDIC Restoration Plan; Interim Rule on Emergency Special Assessment," March 2, 2009, www.fdic.gov/news/news/financial/2009/fil09012.html.

294 *on May 22, the FDIC adopted:* FDIC, "Special Assessment: Final Rule," May 22, 2009, www.fdic.gov/news/news/financial/2009/fil09023.html.

295 *on November 12, we unanimously:* FDIC, "Prepaid Assessments: Final Rule," November 12, 2009, www.fdic.gov/news/news/financial/2009/fil09063.html.

295 *Dimon announced that he viewed:* "CGI Annual Meeting 2009," September 25, 2009, www.clintonglobalinitiative.org/ourmeetings/2009/default.asp.

Chapter 24: Squinting in the Public Spotlight

299 *"take a break":* "Snafu or Scandal?," *San Diego Union-Tribune,* October 11, 2006, www.utsandiego.com/uniontrib/20061011/news_lz1ed11top.html.

300 *a* Wall Street Journal *editorial:* "The Coming Deposit Insurance Bailout," *The Wall Street Journal,* September 1, 2009, http://online.wsj.com/article/SB100014240529702047318045743850721646196400.html.

304 *a front-page* New York Times *story:* Stephen Laboton and Edmund L. Andrews, "As U.S. Overhauls the Banking System, 2 Top Regulators Feud," *The New York Times,* June 13, 2009, www.nytimes.com/2009/06/14/us/politics/14power.html?pagewanted=all.

304 *"infighting":* Damian Paletta, "Infighting Besets Financial-Oversight Council," *The*

Wall Street Journal, September 29, 2010, http://online.wsj.com/article/SB100014240 52748703431604575522330414286778.html.

305 *One story:* Mark DeCambre, "Bair Baits Geithner," *New York Post,* June 10, 2009, www.nypost.com/p/news/business/item_sxvPNaDKoBA3nmFUxsZmqK;jsessionid =6112EBBF97E933469EEE2562ADF6A519.

305 *In 2007, Joe Nocera:* Joe Nocera, "In a Mess, Yes, but She's Got a Plan," *The New York Times,* December 15, 2007, www.nytimes.com/2007/12/15/business/15nocera .html?pagewanted=all.

305 *I had the amazing privilege:* Michael Scherer, "The New Sheriffs of Wall Street," *Time,* May 13, 2010, www.time.com/time/magazine/article/0,9171,1989144,00.html.

305 *But my favorite profile:* Ryan Lizza, "The Contrarian: Sheila Bair and the White House Financial Debate," *The New Yorker,* July 6, 2009, www.newyorker.com/ reporting/2009/07/06/090706fa_fact_lizza.

306 *Later, it was leaked:* The leak was first reported on the website Jezebel and later picked up by a number of blogs. See Jenna Sauers, "The Real Reason Women's Magazines Suck," July 28, 2009, http://jezebel.com/5324718/the-real-reason-womens-magazines -suck.

307 *published one:* "31 Ways of Looking at Power," *O, the Oprah Magazine,* September 2009.

307 *"This article suggests":* Chris Whalen, "Article on Sheila Bair by HuffPo Investigative Fund," January 22, 2010, www.ritholtz.com/blog/2010/01/article-on-sheila-bair-by -the-huffington-post-investigative-fund/.

308 *"We weren't trying":* FDIC, "Remarks by Sheila Bair, Chairman, Federal Deposit Insurance Corporation at the John F. Kennedy Presidential Library Foundation 2009 Profile in Courage Award Ceremony; John F. Kennedy Presidential Library and Museum; Boston, MA," May 18, 2009, www.fdic.gov/news/news/speeches/ archives/2009/spmay1809.html.

Chapter 25: Farewell to the FDIC

313 *"We need to get past":* FDIC, "Remarks by FDIC Chairman Sheila C. Bair to the ABA Government Relations Summit, Washington, DC," March 16, 2011, www.fdic.gov/ news/news/speeches/chairman/spmar1611.html.

315 *I began my speech:* FDIC, "Remarks by FDIC Chairman Sheila Bair to the ICBA National Convention, San Diego, CA," March 22, 2011, www.fdic.gov/news/news/ speeches/chairman/spmar2211.html.

316 *"Quite truthfully":* Barbara A. Rehm, "How Frank Keating Got to the ABA and Where He Aims to Take It," *American Banker,* May 25, 2011, www.americanbanker.com/ issues/176_101/frank-keating-aba-1037984-1.html?zkPrintable=true.

317 *"In a world":* "Remarks by FDIC Chairman Sheila Bair to the National Press Club, Washington, D.C.," June 24, 2011, www.fdic.gov/news/news/speeches/chairman/ spjun2411.html.

Chapter 26: How Main Street Can Tame Wall Street

326 *Dodd-Frank expressly prohibits:* See sections 204, 206, 210, and 214 of the Dodd-Frank Act.

327 *Ironically, big-bank advocates:* Rich Miller, "Dodd-Frank Law May Hinder Cri-

sis Response by U.S. Policy Makers," November 22, 2011, www.bloomberg.com/
news/2011-11-22/dodd-frank-may-hamper-policy-makers-shielding-banking-system
-in-a-crisis.html#, quoting John Dugan.

327 *"in a complex"*: Simon Johnson, "Progress on Letting Big Banks Fail," February 2, 2012,
http://economix.blogs.nytimes.com/2012/02/02/progress-on-letting-big-banks
-fail/.

328 *a kind of Glass-Steagall-light*: For instance, Senator Sherrod Brown (D-OH) has sponsored the SAFE Banking Act, which would place size limits on the megabanks. Senators John McCain (R-AZ) and Maria Cantwell (D-WA) have sponsored legislation
to reinstate Glass-Steagall. Tom Hoenig, currently an FDIC director has proposed
banning broker-dealer operations by commercial banking organizations but would
permit certain other types of securities activities.

333 *Congress made a huge mistake*: Commodity Futures Modernization Act of 2000,
http://thomas.loc.gov/cgi-bin/bdquery/z?d106:H.R.5660.

333 *By the end of 2007*: "ISDA Market Survey; Notional Amounts Outstanding at Year-
End, All Surveyed Contracts, 1987-Present," 2010, www.isda.org/statistics/pdf/
ISDA-Market-Survey-annual-data.pdf.

344 *Partnership for Public Service*: Max Stier, President and CEO, Partnership for Public
Service, letter to The Honorable Joe Lieberman et al., September 15, 2011.

347 *Since Fannie and Freddie*: "FHFA Strategic Plan for Enterprise Conservatorships,"
February 21, 2012 http://www.fhfa.gov/webfiles/23344/StrategicPlanConservator
shipsFINAL.pdf.

351 *As Warren Buffett has pointed out*: Warren E. Buffett, "Stop Coddling the Super-
Rich," *The New York Times*, August 14, 2011, www.nytimes.com/2011/08/15/opin-
ion/stop-coddling-the-super-rich.html?_r=1&gwh=5CE5728BB33F99D502CEFBC
E8736B466.

351 *Unsustainable budget deficits*: Sheila C. Bair, "Will the Next Crisis Start in Washington?," *The Washington Post*, November 26, 2010, www.washingtonpost.com/wp-dyn/
content/article/2010/11/25/AR2010112502215.html.

352 *In February 2012*: "Aggregate Reserves of Depository Institutions and the Monetary
Base," Federal Reserve Statistical Release, February 16, 2012, www.federalreserve
.gov/releases/h3/20120216/h3.htm.

353 *The CBO has estimated*: Congressional Budget Office, *The Budget and Economic Outlook: Fiscal Years 2011 to 2021*, January 2011, http://www.cbo.gov/sites/default/files/
cbofiles/ftpdocs/120xx/doc12039/01-26_fy2011outlook.pdf.

353 *FSOC's 2011 Annual Report*: FSOC, *2011 Annual Report*, July 2011, www.treasury
.gov/initiatives/fsoc/Documents/FSOCAR2011.pdf, pp. 4, 10, 32–35, 133, 134. The
FDIC also pressed hard for language emphasizing the need to end too big to fail and
effectively address mortgage-servicing issues as essential to long-term financial system stability. Though language to that effect was also included, the FSOC has failed
to prioritize those issues.

Chapter 27: It Could Have Been Different

357 *has spoken out in favor*: Remarks of Ed Clark, Group President and CEO, TD Bank
Group, "Building a Better Banking System for America," before the Chief Executives
Club, Boston College, April 26, 2012.

358 *"During the height of the crisis"*: Statement of the Shadow Financial Regulatory Com-

mittee on Treasury Mismeasurement of the Costs of Federal Financial Stability Programs, May 7, 2012, www.aei.org/files/2012/05/07/-treasury-mismeasurement -of-the-costs-of-federal-financial-stability-programs_13022735.

358 *$147 billion and counting:* As of the first quarter of 2012, the U.S. Treasury Department had invested $187 billion in Fannie Mae and Freddie Mac but had received $40 billion in dividend payments for a net outlay of $147 billion. See, FHFA First Quarter 2012 Conservator's Report, www.fhfa.gov/webfiles/24016/ Conservator'sReport1Q2012061512_FINAL.pdf.

Epilogue

364 *Indeed, he seemed offended:* "Addressing the Need for Comprehensive Regulatory Reform," Hearing Before the Committee on Financial Services, United States House of Representatives, March 26, 2009, p. 36.

Acknowledgments

Many thanks to the numerous FDIC staff who sacrificed their time in helping me reconstruct various events, chronologies, and bank and economic data. In particular, I would like to thank Mike Krimminger, Michele Heller, Andrew Gray, Jason Cave, Rich Brown, Chris Newbury, Paul Nash, Jim Wigand, and Jesse Villarreal. Thanks also to Evan Fitzpatrick for his top-notch research and data gathering, and Will Kryder for his help with the photos.

I would also like to thank my representatives at the William Morris Agency, Jennifer Rudolph Walsh and Eric Lupfer, my editor at Free Press, Dominick Anfuso, and the entire Free Press team, ably led by Martha Levin. Thanks to you all: Sydney Tanigawa, Suzanne Donahue, Larry Hughes, Carisa Hays, Nicole Judge, Phil Metcalf, Erich Hobbing, Eric Fuentecilla, and Leah Miller.

Finally, thanks to my family for all of their patience, support, and tolerance for the reams of file folders and binders scattered throughout the house during the eight months it took me to write this. Particular thanks to my husband, Scott, for serving as my in-residence senior editor, to Preston for his excellent copy editing, and to Colleen for her moral support and the healthy meals she cooked for us when I was busy writing.

INDEX

About the Author

Sheila C. Bair served as the Chairman of the Federal Deposit Insurance Corporation from June 2006 through June 2011, during one of the most tumultuous periods in the history of the U.S. financial system. Called "the little guy's protector in chief" by *Time* magazine, Bair wielded a steady hand in protecting bank depositors while handling hundreds of bank failures, including some of the nation's largest financial institutions. Long before the 2008 financial crisis, Bair was an early and consistent advocate for tougher regulation of large financial institutions, tighter mortgage lending, strong consumer protection standards, and aggressive foreclosure prevention measures. In recognition of her tireless advocacy of Main Street interests, she was the recipient of numerous awards, including the John F. Kennedy Profile in Courage Award and the Hubert H. Humphrey Award. She was twice named the second most powerful woman in the world by *Forbes* magazine, behind Germany's Angela Merkel, and was also recognized by the *Washington Post* and Harvard University as one of seven of America's Top Leaders.

A lifelong Republican and Kansas native, Bair has spent most of her career in public service, including stints as a senior advisor to Senate Majority Leader Robert Dole and a top Treasury Department Official in the Bush Administration. She holds an undergraduate and law degree, and honorary doctorate, from the University of Kansas, as well as honorary doctorates from Amherst College and Drexel University.

Bair currently resides in Chevy Chase, Maryland, with her husband, Scott Cooper, and two children, Colleen and Preston. She continues to work on financial policy issues at the Pew Charitable Trusts and writes a regular column for *Fortune* magazine. She also chairs the Systemic Risk Council, a private sector group dedicated to effective reform of the financial system, whose members include former Federal Reserve Board Chairman Paul Volcker and former Treasury Secretary Paul O'Neill.